ARK
OF THE
SUN

the improbable
voyage of life

Graeme Donald Snooks

I G D S

Institute of Global Dynamic Systems Books
Canberra

First published 2015
by **IGDS Books**
Canberra

© Graeme Donald Snooks

Printed in the United States of America by CreateSpace

National Library of Australia cataloguing-in-publication data
Snooks, G.D. (Graeme Donald)
Ark of the Sun
Bibliography
Index
    1. Theory of life and society
    2. Laws of history
    3. Biological and Technological transformation
    4. Climate mitigation
    5. Strategic *logos*
    6. Future Solar Revolution

ISBN: 978-0-9808394-3-2

Eternal Journey of Re the Great Sun God in His Barque—Ark of the Sun

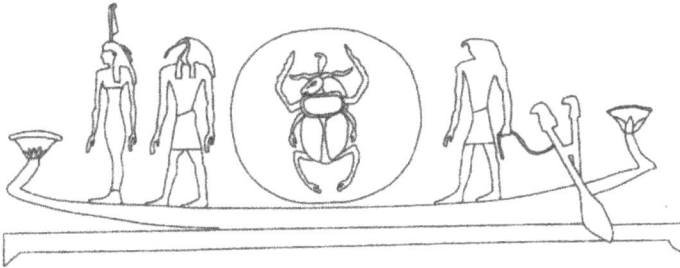

Hail Re in your rising …
You proceed, you set in the Evening Barque,
Your heart elated [after battle] in the Morning Barque.
You traverse the sky in peace, all your enemies are felled.
The Unwearing stars rejoice for you,
The Indestructible stars adore you.
You set in the horizon of the Horizon Mountain,
Perfect as Re every full day,
Living and stable as my lord,
Re the true of voice.

" Hymn" C, Annual Theban festival **(Quirke 2001: 68)**

Contents

Preface   ix
Prologue: Solar Journey Ventured   xiii
Overview: A New Vision of Life and Human Society   xv

1. **Improbable Voyage**   **1**
   The cosmos and the *logos*   1
   Odyssey of the *logos*   6

2. **Unfinished Odyssey**   **21**
   Diversity of life   22
   First forms of life on Earth   25
   Prokaryotic Revolution   26
   Eukaryotic Revolution   30
   Endothermic Revolution   36
   Where is it all heading?   62

3. **Patterns of the Past**   **63**
   Pathway of life   63
   Life's dynamic mechanism   67
   Continuing odyssey   79

4. **Engine of Life**   **80**
   Dynamic-strategy theory—a brief outline   80
   A self-creating engine of life   98

5. **Strategic *Logos* — the Ark of the Sun**   **99**
   Vehicle of life   100
   Defining the strategic *logos*   104
   Working model of the strategic *logos*   106
   Historical reality and ultimate reality   112
   Meaning of life   113

6. **Laws of the *Logos***   **114**
   New method of law-making—existential historicism   115
   Primary laws   118
   Secondary laws   123
   Tertiary laws   127
   Laws and their uses   129

7. **Citadel of the *Logos* — the Ephemeral Civilisation**   **131**
   Case study in institutional change—England, 1000–2015   131

A strategic model of institutional change   136
General model of cultural change   152

8. **Ideology of the *Logos* — from Religion to Scientism**   **157**
The hidden life-system and its myths   157
Mankind's existential anxiety   158
Emergence and transformation of the gods   161
God maker and god breaker   169
The rise of science—a new explanation   172
Scientism—a new strategic ideology   175

9. **Strategic Awareness of the *Logos* — the Selfcreating Mind**   **181**
Unravelling the mysteries of the mind   181
The strategic brain   183
Consciousness—the metropolis of the mind   200
A general theory of strategic awareness   206
The endangered self   211

10. **Restoring Damaged Consciousness — A Strategic Psychology**   **215**
Strategic dualism   215
Mental disorders   218
Strategic malfunction   227
A new psychology and psychiatry   236

11. **Understanding the Modern *Logos* — Societal Dynamics**   **237**
Limitations of orthodox economics   237
A new realist dynamics for the modern world   247
A more scientific policy-making   258

12. **The *Logos* at Large — Global Strategic Transition**   **259**
Economic development redefined   259
The "global strategic transition" (GST) model   264
The new "strategy function"   270
Policy for GST   276
The way ahead   282

13. **Choice of Futures for the *Logos***   **283**
The Solar Revolution   283
Orthodox economics fails to foresee the Solar Revolution   292
Dynamic versus static costs of climate mitigation   299
Mitigation as agent of collapse   306
What's to be done?   307

Epilogue: Solar Journey Challenged   314
Notes   317
References   331
About the author   341
About IGDS Books   343

Figures and Illustrations

Frontispiece:
    Solar Barque from Tomb of Panehsy, Iunu (Egyptian 26th Dynasty).
    With permission: Wolfram Grajetzki.   iii
2.1   Family Numbers for Marine and Land Organisms—Past 800 myrs
    (a) Marine Organisms;   22
    (b) Land Organisms   23
2.2   The Rise and Fall of Major Land Plants—410 myrs   24
2.3   Predator-Prey Systems of Land Vertebrates—Past 300 myrs   38
2.4   Ascending the Intellectual Staircase—Past 5 myrs   54
3.1   The Logological Constant—Past 4,000 myrs   65
3.2   The Great Waves of Life—Past 4,000 myrs   66
3.3   The Great Steps of Life—Past 4,000 myrs   68
3.4   The Great Steps of Life—Past 80 myrs   68
3.5   The Great Steps of Human Progress—Past and Future   69
3.6   The Great Wheel of Life   74
4.1   The Concentric Sphere's Model of Behaviour   97
5.1   The Strategic *Logos*   108
7.1   The Great Waves of Economic Change—England/Britain, 1000–2000 132
7.2   A General Model of Cultural Change   153
9.1   Structure of the Human Brain   188
10.1 The Schizo-Spectrum   231
11.1 The Very Long-Run Growth-inflation Curve, Britain, 1370–1994   251
11.2 The Long-Run Growth-Inflation Curve, Britain, 1870–1994   252
11.3 The Short-Run Growth-Inflation Curve, OECD Countries,
    Weighted Averages for 1950–70 and 1983–94   252
12.1 The Strategy Function   274
13.1 World GDP Under Mitigation and Revolution Scenarios—2007 to
    2100 (a) Geometric Curve;   301
    (b) Arithmetic Curve   302
13.2 Carbon Dioxide Concentrations Under Mitigation and
    Revolution Scenarios—2007 to 2200.   304

Tables

2.1   Growth Rates of Hominid Brain Size—Past 18 myrs   53
6.1   The Laws of Life—A Checklist   117

7.1	Strategic Institutions—Past 100,000 years	140
7.2	Strategic Organisations—Past 100,000 years	141
10.1	A Strategic Classification of Mental Disorders	219
13.1	Projected Growth of World GDP (US $ billion), 2007–2100	302
13.2	Costs of Climate Mitigation—Dynamic versus Static—2025–2100	303

Boxes

Box 1.1	The *logos* Revealed	3
Box 1.2	The Solar Revolution Explained	13
Box 12.1	The Development Impact of Displaced Persons	269

Preface

Ark of the Sun is the culmination of my work on the dynamics of life and human society. While this work spans about three decades, the preparation required to undertake it stretches back some five decades. It has its origins in my realisation as an undergraduate in the early 1960s that the discipline of economics was concerned not with dynamics but with order and equilibrium. And, as a result, orthodox economics was unable to provide convincing answers to the big issues of the day, such as: why much of the world at that time languished in poverty; why even the most advanced societies experienced major economic downturns; how we might resolve the apparent conflict between the demands of the economy and of the environment; and whether capitalism would prevail over communism.

Right from the beginning of my academic career—analysing the dynamics of cyclical activity—I had a vague sense that an entirely new approach to economics was required if we were to resolve these big issues.[1] There was a need, I thought, to replace the metaphysical deductive approach of orthodox economics with a realist inductive approach. Later I became aware of a long history of dissatisfaction expressed by economic dissidents with the orthodox approach, intermingled with a failure ultimately to provide a convincing alternative. The dissidents were critics rather than innovators. While this failure was intimidating, it was also challenging. Much to my surprise, in meeting this challenge and providing a realist general dynamic theory, my work has undermined and replaced the Victorian giants—Marx, Darwin, and Freud.

When I began this odyssey, the conventional wisdom about the nature of human society and life sounded very unconvincing, even alien. The preoccupation of economists and policy-makers with order, balance, and equilibrium, was shared by other social scientists, particularly in relation to pre-modern society. While it was generally accepted—with a degree of reluctance that has always surprised me—that modern society is addicted to materialism and economic growth, most social scientists were convinced that pre-modern society was economically irrational and static. Indeed, it was the counter-intuitive claim made by medievalists that the tax assessments and manorial income recorded in Domesday Book were not generated by rational economic processes, that made me determined, in the late 1970s and early 1980s, to employ the remarkable data recorded in the Conqueror's great document to test these matters statistically.[2] It was not surprising to find that the statistical results from this study confirmed my understanding of human nature—that man is vitally concerned to maximise the probability of survival and prosperity. The materialistic nature of medieval man was, of course, a prerequisite for the existence of a dynamic medieval community.

Despite this, economic historians—who should have known better, but were seduced by the elegant stasis of orthodox economics—were convinced that economic growth was a modern invention that began with the Industrial Revolution and was dependent solely upon technological change. Once again this defied what I knew of the world. By employing data sources such as Domesday Book (1086) and the accounts of Gregory King (1688) as end points, I was able to show in the late 1980s that the materialism of medieval man did indeed lead to long periods of rapid economic growth (alternating with long periods of downturn) in England over the past 1,000 years.[3] Since this initial work some twenty years ago, I have further shown that all viable pre-modern societies are both materialistic and have experienced long periods of rapid economic growth, even without technological change.[4] In other words, not only was economic growth an ancient invention, but it was achieved on a sustained and systematic basis using strategies not of technological change but of conquest and commerce.

In the beginning, there was much opposition to these radical ideas, but gradually the "strange" notion that all societies in a competitive environment are materialistic and dynamic began to catch on. No doubt in the future, it will be difficult for the younger generation to believe that anyone ever thought differently. While an older generation of opponents remains, their focus has shifted from a denial that there was any long-term growth in pre-modern societies, to disputing that it occurred **rapidly** over long periods of time. They are able to hold these agnostic views because they lack a general dynamic theory. But their days are numbered.

Once able to show that human society is, and always has been, dynamic, it was necessary to develop a general dynamic theory to explain why and how this was the case.[5] All existing theories about the progress of human society— whether orthodox (from Malthus, Ricardo, and Adam Smith to new neoclassical growth theory and evolutionary institutionalism) or radical (Marx)—were found to be inadequate for the task. It was necessary, therefore, to provide a realist theory—a theory based on systematic observation—that could explain the dynamics of very different societies and civilisations across the divides of space and time. What was it that all these societies shared that made them dynamic? What did hunting societies (on all continents) have in common with conquest societies (Babylon, Macedonia, Rome, the Aztecs and Incas), commerce societies (Egypt, Phoenicia, Carthage, Greece, Venice, Holland, Britain), and technological societies (Western Europe, European settlements, and East Asia)? The "dynamic-strategy" theory—a demand-side theory—holds the answer to this and many other questions.

Crucially, the dynamic-strategy theory provides, for the first time, a convincing explanation of the general progress of human civilisation, together with the rise and fall of individual societies. It also shows that human institutions and cultures possess no dynamic of their own (in other words, that social evolution is a myth); that it is indeed possible to formulate universal laws of history; that religion has a materialist origin and role; that economic development is the outcome of an automatic global mechanism; and that strategic inflation is central to the dynamic success of all societies. And much more.

Having come this far, the challenge was to go even further. It became obvious that if one claims to have a general theory that can explain one species in life (humanity), then it must be able—or be generalised to be able—to explain all species in life. The fact that Darwin's theory of natural selection cannot explain the emergence and progress of human civilisation—a fact readily admitted by neo-Darwinists—should long-since have rung the warning bells for its supporters. Hence, the task became one of demonstrating that the dynamic-strategy theory is able to explain the dynamics not only of human society but also of life in general. In the process, I was able to show that Darwin's supply-side hypothesis of natural selection is not up to the task in either respect.[6] Needless to say, the resistance to this finding is huge, owing to the massive Darwinian establishment, which has much to lose from the collapse of Darwinism. But it will happen.

The next step was to demonstrate that the dynamic-strategy theory could also explain the most complex entities in the Universe: the human mind and human nature. With this theory I was able to show that these entities are the outcomes of an autogenous process, involving the interaction between "strategic demand" and "strategic selection"—the outcome of the "selfcreating mind".[7] This work led to a general theory of consciousness, termed the "theory of strategic awareness", which operates at various levels of existence, including those of the human mind and of the metropolis. (As will be shown, the metropolis is more than just a metaphor of the mind.) On the basis of this research, I was also able to develop a theory of mental disorders that operates at the individual and collective levels. A theory that exposes the fatal flaws of Freud's analysis.

While this book is an overview of all my work on the dynamics of living systems, its whole is greater than the sum of its parts. This work has seen the emergence of the "strategic *logos*"—or dynamic life-system—which is an entropy-defying, shock-deflecting system that has enabled both life and human society to prosper in a universe extremely hostile to biological forms. It was to understand and influence this hidden life-system that strategic "ideologies"— later fashioned into what we recognise as religions—first emerged and were developed over hundreds of thousands of years.[8] By understanding the strategic *logos,* we also understand the rise and fall of the gods and their eventual replacement with scientism.

A NOTE ON THE TEXT

This work is based on a long series of books and articles that I published between 1986 and 2011. The purpose of those works was to use the patterns of the past as a basis for developing a general dynamic theory of both human society and of life. Those patterns were based on the abundance of historical detail. What I focus on in this book is the general dynamic theory—the dynamic-strategy theory—which describes the *logos*, together with the underlying historical patterns, rather than the shifting factual detail. Accordingly, no attempt has been made to bring the historical detail "up-to-date"—something that is, strictly speaking, impossible, as the minor details of the past are constantly changing. Much of the historical detail, where referred to, remains as it was when my series of books and articles were written. Not only is this pertinent to the task undertaken over time, but factual revision is rendered unnecessary by the theoretical objective of this work. While theory must be able to explain facts, the eternal nature of the dynamic strategic *logos* embraces and transcends the ephemeral nature of static historical details.

ACKNOWLEDGEMENTS

I am grateful to Adrian Snooks for persuading me to revisit the typescript of *Ark of the Sun*, which I had relegated to a bottom drawer some six years earlier while pursuing other interests, and for insightful comments on the text. Also I wish to thank Huw Mckay and Anton Roux, for many discussions and helpful comments over the years on some of the ideas presented in this work. Their enthusiastic interest and support are greatly appreciated. Thanks also are due to my old friend and colleague Selwyn Cornish, who has always provided my unorthodox ideas with a sympathetic hearing. Additionally, I am grateful to Art Archives London for making available the photograph of Re's solar barque for the cover design, to Julie Hamilton for designing the cover and formatting the text, and to Wolfram Grajetzki for permission to use the line drawing in the frontispiece. As always, my greatest debt is to Loma Snooks, who has made the journey both possible and worthwhile.

GDS of Sevenoaks

Prologue: Solar Journey Ventured

The ancient Egyptians, like many other earlier societies, realised that the Sun was the giver of life. They expressed this not in scientific but in mythological terms. The great Sun god Re was the most important "Guardian" in their huge pantheon of gods: he was regarded as the king of all the gods.

The greatest possible disaster that could befall the world, according to Egyptian thinkers, would be the failure of the Sun to rise in the eastern sky some twelve hours after it had set in the West (the land of the dead). They viewed the critically important solar journey through both the day and night skies as being fraught with danger. The Egyptians believed that the solar journey was a continuous struggle between the forces of order and chaos personified by Maat (the goddess of order, truth and justice) and Apophis (the great chaos monster in the form of a serpent who repeatedly attacked the solar barque in the underworld).

While the Egyptians thought the Sun to be the source of all creative authority, it was not regarded as being responsible for the success of the solar journey. As Re was a passive life-giving god, he required the support of a number of proactive beings. These included a number of select deities together with a range of personified divine characteristics. The deities included Maat (identified by a feather in her hair), Shu and Tefnet (children of the Sun god who possessed creative powers and were associated with the eternal recurrence), Geb (god of Earth), Isis (mother of kings and protector of ships), Horus (lord of the sky and embodiment of kingship), Thoth (god of wisdom and secret knowledge), and Hathor (goddess of rebirth of both the dead and the cosmos). The personified attributes of the cosmic ruler included Heka ("creative force"), Hu ("sustenance"), and Sia ("forthrightness"). With the active participation of this divine crew, Re the giver of life was transported safely by solar barque through the firmament. While the solar journey had been successfully achieved throughout the past in Egypt, it was believed that there would come a day when the forces of chaos would finally triumph over those of order, and human society would return to the dark primeval waters of its origins.

The Egyptian solar journey was a fusion of the cosmic and the terrestrial—the divine and the secular. It was the purpose of Egyptian religion to ensure order in the secular world by manipulating divine control of the cosmos. Religion was, in a very real sense, a strategic ideology dedicated to the world of the living, not the world of the dead. Its objective was to maximise the probability of survival and prosperity here on Earth.

****

Like the ancient Egyptians, I am concerned with the journey of life on Earth—a journey involving a struggle between the forces of order (the strategists) and chaos (the antistrategists). My focus in this book is on the progression of the strategic *logos*, or universal life-system (explained below), through an untameable cosmos. The strategic *logos*—a system of measurable material forces—can be viewed metaphorically as the "ark of the Sun"—a vehicle carrying all the species of life as well as humanity through space-time; a vehicle braving the hostile forces of the universe, defying the thermodynamic challenge of increasing entropy, and deflecting the impact of natural shocks on planet Earth; a vehicle deriving all dynamic energy from the Sun. Yet, while life-giving, the Sun is an entirely passive entity, just as the ancient Egyptians realised. Biological life forms owe their existence and complex development to the proactive strategic *logos*, which is a self-starting and self-sustaining engine of life that transforms the energy of the Sun into biological and technological complexity.

The ark of the Sun—the strategic *logos*—has on board a crew consisting of individual life forms (including humanity); societal structures; ideas of a technological, philosophical, and artistic kind; together with ideologies both religious and secular, just as did the solar barque of the great Sun god Re. It is remarkable how closely the ancient Egyptians came to an intuitive understanding of the scientific reality of the universal life-system—closer than any other society in either the ancient or modern worlds. Yet, Re's solar barque remains a mystical attempt to understand and manipulate an engine of life that they felt must exist in order to explain the mysterious cyclical nature of life. In contrast, the strategic *logos*, which remained beyond their rational grasp, is a scientific, not a religious, entity. An entity that is explored empirically and rationally in this book. The strategic *logos* possesses a material, not an ethereal, existence.

Overview
A New Vision of Life and Human Society

The strategic logos is an entropy-defying, shock-deflecting life system

Ark of the Sun is a book about the dynamic life-system that has enabled the emergence and exponential development of life forms, including humanity, in a hostile universe. I discovered this life-system, called the "strategic *logos*", towards the end of my fifty-year exploration of the dynamics of life and human society. It is a hidden system consisting of interacting forces occurring between biological agents striving for survival and prosperity on the one hand and societal structures generated to facilitate this, on the other. The strategic *logos* is vital to the success of life and human society because it is an entropy-defying, shock-deflecting system. As a hidden system that can only be seen reflected in the actions and reactions of agents and organisations, it can be compared with the cosmos, which is a scientifically-recognised system of hidden physical forces.

Ark of the Sun shows how the strategic *logos* was discovered, how it operates, what it tells us about the entire past of life on Earth as well as the present, and what glimpses it provides of the immediate and distant future. To do this, it discusses:

- the role of the *logos* in the cosmos;
- the discovery of the *logos* during the final step in an inductive sequence that began with a comprehensive examination of the emergence of life and human society on Earth, followed by the isolation of the main patterns of the past, and then by the development of a general dynamic theory—the "dynamic-strategy" theory—to explain these patterns;
- how the strategic *logos* emerged from an examination of the operation of the dynamic-strategy theory;
- how the laws governing life and human history were also derived from the dynamic-strategy theory;
- the nature of the interaction between the mind and the metropolis as key actors in the *logos*;
- how religion and, more recently, scientism emerged in response to the *logos*;
- and finally, how the dynamic-strategy model can be used not only to explain the modern world, both developed and underdeveloped, but also to predict how it will respond to climate change and where it will be proceeding in the future.

It should be realised from the outset that *Ark of the Sun* is the overview of an original research program that challenges all earlier theories of societal change—including those by orthodox economists, institutionalists, Marx and Marxists, Darwin and neo-Darwinists, Freud and Freudians, evolutionary psychologists, self-organisation theorists, and complexity theorists. The dynamic-strategy theory is a demand-side theory, consisting of a core mechanism involving a demand-supply interaction. A successful society generates a "strategic demand" for a comprehensive range of supply variables, including productive resources, institutions, organisations, and ideas of all types (technical, intellectual, cultural). In this model demand creates its own supply.

In contrast, all earlier theories are supply-side theories, where developments emerge spontaneously from internal characteristics, such as genetics and "culture". In these models, supply creates its own demand ("build runways and the planes will come"!). As such, these theories fail the test of reality. Further, these supply-side theories are unintentionally racist, because they argue that the differences in performance between societies are due to cultural differences; and cultural differences, in a model without dynamic demand at its core, can be caused only by differences between peoples (i.e. race). Only a dynamic theory based on dynamic demand, like the dynamic-strategy theory, is free from racist interpretation.

The dynamic-strategy theory is also a theory that extends across traditional disciplinary boundaries, embracing the fields (if not the partial supply-side theories) of economics, history, politics, sociology, psychology, philosophy, biology, and social physics. The dynamics of life and human society cannot be compartmentalised in a set of discrete academic boxes.

The remainder of this section provides a brief overview of the arguments presented in the following thirteen chapters.

Chapter 1: "Improbable Voyage" outlines how life emerged on Earth and has been sustained in a cosmos extremely hostile to biological forms. This has always been a mystery to scientists who rely on the laws of physics, or who employ the flawed Darwinian theory of natural selection. The key discovery here is the strategic *logos*, complete with its own laws of dynamics that are discussed in chapter 6. It is the *logos* that enabled life and human society to negotiate a series of biological and technological paradigm shifts, which have transformed primitive life forms inhabiting the oceans of the world into sophisticated self-aware beings responsible for constructing advanced forms of civilisation.

Chapter 2: "Unfinished Odyssey" provides an outline of the evidence concerning the emergence of life over the past 4,000 million years (myrs) and of human society over the past 2 myrs. It shows that life forms from the most simple to the most complex are driven by an unceasing urge to survive and prosper, which I call "strategic desire", and that they attempt to achieve this unrelenting objective by the adoption of a given set of "dynamic strategies". In this way, life forms became more numerous and complex; they generated a number of biological and technological revolutions; and they transformed the *logos* into a complex system of life where the agents and social structures are visible, but the interacting forces between them are obscured from view (just like the invisible forces operating on physical bodies in physics). The end result was an acceleration in the pace of history, both in life and human society.

Chapter 3: "Patterns of the Past" outlines the main structural changes that have occurred in both life and human society since their beginnings. These quantitative "timescapes", which must be explained by any credible dynamic theory, map the great biological and technological paradigm shifts together with the great waves of change within each paradigm. It is through the internal energy generated by these great waves that each paradigm is exploited and, finally, exhausted, making way for the next paradigm shift. The acceleration of these structural changes traces out an exponential curve that can be measured by what I call the "logological constant", with a coefficient of transformation of 3.0. The logological constant is to the biological world, what the cosmological constant is to the physical world.

Chapter 4: "Engine of Life" outlines the general dynamic theory I have developed to explain the patterns of the past. This model is realist (based as it is on detailed empirical work), self-starting, self-sustaining, and has at its core a dynamic demand-supply response mechanism. Accordingly, it is able to do what no other model in the social, biological, and physical sciences can do—explain and predict the complex process of biological and technological transformation at both the micro and macro levels. Only a demand-side dynamic model is capable of this feat. And the dynamic-strategy theory is unique in a world of flawed supply-side models. This is why my dynamic-strategy theory displaces those of the great Georgian and Victorian thinkers such as Adam Smith, Marx, Darwin and Freud, together with modern theorists in the fields of neoclassical economics, institutionalism, evolutionary psychology, social physics, and complexity.

Chapter 5: "Strategic *Logos*—the Ark of the Sun" presents my discovery of the hidden vehicle of life and human society. It shows exactly how the strategic *logos* enabled life to emerge on Earth and to develop exponentially into large numbers of complex forms in a universe unfriendly to life. Because the *logos* consists of a set of invisible social forces (conceptually similar to the invisible forces driving the cosmos, or the electrical impulses in the human brain that give rise to the invisible self-conscious mind), its discovery had to wait until a viable realist general dynamic theory had been constructed—a general theory that exposes the nature and mode of interaction of these invisible forces. As will be demonstrated, the *logos* is the shaper of life and human society.

Chapter 6: "Laws of the *Logos*" provides a comprehensive set of general laws that can explain the origins and dynamics of the real social world. This is the first time a comprehensive set of **dynamic** laws has been identified for either the social sciences or the life sciences. While the social sciences possess a long-standing collection of ad hoc **static** microeconomic laws, there are few in macroeconomics, none in history, and those in the life sciences are deeply flawed. Without exception, these disciplines have been unable to develop a realist general dynamic theory which, I show, is a prerequisite for developing dynamic laws.

Chapter 7: "Citadel of the Logos—the Ephemeral Civilisation" argues that institutions provide the vehicle, not the engine of material progress as institutionalists both old and new believe. To demonstrate this argument, a new strategic model of institutional and cultural change is developed. This strategic model demonstrates that institutions owe their origin, development, and inevitable demise to changes in strategic demand emanating from the *logos*, rather than evolving according to Darwinian supply-side forces. Only a demand-side model, which shows how agents respond to the requirements of society, can overcome the fundamental flaws inherent in the conventional institutional and evolutionary models, which incorrectly treat inherent characteristics of individuals and groups as proactive rather than passive. The temporary entity known as society—the "ephemeral civilisation"—is the citadel of the *logos*. They rise and fall together.

Chapter 8: "Ideology of the *Logos* — from Religion to Scientism" presents the entirely new idea that the world's great myths and religions are the outcome of mankind's attempt to understand and manipulate the hidden forces of the strategic *logos*. Societies have always considered it essential to understand these hidden forces in order to survive and prosper. Strategic survival is a difficult art, as demonstrated by the widespread ruined remains of former species, societies and civilisations. Because mankind has never felt confident about mastering the art of survival and prosperity, we have reached out in a mystical way to "strategic guardians", or gods, to guide us. This chapter shows that the changing nature of myths and religions has been a response to the great technological paradigm shifts over the past 2 myrs, while the demise of religion ("the death of God") in advanced societies and the adoption of scientism as the core "strategic ideology" is a response to the Industrial Revolution.

Chapter 9: "Strategic Awareness of the Logos—the Selfcreating Mind", analyses the remarkable strategic instrument—the self-conscious mind—employed by our species to supervise the strategic pursuit. This chapter focuses on the emergence and role of "strategic awareness" (a generalised version of self-consciousness) in both mankind and the great metropolises of society. A central metaphor in this analysis of the mind is the metropolis, which functions in an analogous way to the human brain. As will be shown, the concept of the "metropolis of the mind" is more than metaphor: it is a fundamental characteristic of the strategic *logos* at both the micro and macro levels. The selfcreating mind, which is an entirely new theoretical construct based on a systematic study of the empirical evidence, challenges all existing supply-side theories (such as those of Freud or currently fashionable evolutionary psychology).

Chapter 10: "Restoring Damaged Consciousness—A Strategic Psychiatry" is concerned with the difficult problem of restoring strategic awareness in the *logos* by employing a new "strategic psychiatry". Essentially the argument is that psychological illness emerges in individuals who suffer malfunctions in those psychic mechanisms that enable them to participate in the strategic pursuit. Mental disorders, just like dysfunctional processes in the metropolis, are an outcome of the dynamics of life. They are, in effect, "strategic disorders", which can be alleviated through a reversal of the process of "strategic malfunction", and the reabsorption of affected individuals and societies back into the strategic pursuit. The core issue is "strategic failure" versus "strategic success".

Chapter 11: "Understanding the Modern Logos—Societal Dynamics" attempts to restate the general dynamic-strategy theory developed in earlier chapters into a more specific model (highlighting, for example, the "growth-inflation curve", the strategy function, dynamic cost-benefit analysis, etc.) for analysing the modern world. It is argued that owing to the limitations of orthodox economic theory (which is only able to handle small, short-run and static issues), it is essential to develop a realist dynamic model. This new dynamic model is critical to the analysis and resolution of fundamentally important economic issues of both a short-run (inflation, financial crises, and periodic economic downturns) and a long-run (economic development, climate mitigation, and technological transformation) nature.

Chapter 12: "The *Logos* at Large—Global Strategic Transition" employs the general dynamic-strategy theory developed in earlier chapters to analyse how lesser-developed countries are being steadily drawn into the global strategic core through the mechanism I call "global strategic transition" (GST). It is a theoretical account of the *logos* at large in the world. A key feature of this chapter is the "strategy function"—a new concept in economics—that displaces the more narrowly conceived (or more correctly, misconceived) production function, and provides a more general and realistic approach to underdevelopment. It views society as a flexible organic entity rather than a constrained factory writ large. Needless to say, this new model provides new policy principles concerning economic development.

Chapter 13: "Choice of Futures for the *Logos*" focuses on the critical issue facing human society in the twenty-first century: the controversial matter of climate change. For the sake of argument, I do not challenge the claim by most scientists that climate change is real or man-made, even though there are still some important unresolved issues. As I argue, the real problem is not whether climate change is real and man-made, but how the potential problem should be resolved.

By taking this position and employing the general dynamic-strategy theory, it becomes clear that there are two alternative futures facing humanity. The first is the future that would be generated by the strategic *logos* left free to ensure the survival and prosperity of life as it has always done. And the second is the future that is being inadvertently proposed by the "mitigation engineers", who insist the world adopts a radical and comprehensive climate-mitigation program that will badly distort, even derail, the strategic *logos*.

The first option, according to the dynamic-strategy theory, will lead to a new technological paradigm shift—the Solar Revolution—emerging in the middle decades of the twenty-first century. This technological paradigm shift will massively transform human society by a relative order of magnitude similar to that of the Industrial Revolution within the space of little more than a generation. The rapidity of this transformation is the outcome of history speeding up. The second option will lead to long-run economic stagnation, massive mitigation costs, the emergence of global military conflict, and possibly the collapse of our entire civilisation. Clearly, the first option wins hands down in any **rational** debate. The trick, however, will be to negotiate increasing climate-related problems without resorting to the global command economy required by the level of intervention being advocated by powerful international lobby groups and organisations. As always in human history, we need to follow the requirements of the strategic *logos*, not the commands of the radical interventionists, who are the new antistrategists.

Epilogue: finally, the future of the strategic *logos* is discussed more generally in terms of the struggle between "strategists" and "antistrategists": between the forces of both life and anti-life.

Chapter One
Improbable Voyage

The logos *makes the improbable possible.*

Life has embarked on an improbable voyage through space and time. A voyage that has an observable beginning and a predictable end. It's improbable because the universe through which we are travelling is extremely hostile to complexity of any kind, whether inorganic or organic. It is improbable because the window of opportunity for the emergence of complexity is a very rare event in the history of the Universe. And the opportunities for the emergence of intelligent life are so rare that this is the most improbable occurrence of all. In this book we will explore how and why this improbable voyage was embarked upon, and where and when it will be likely to end. While life in the infinitely long-term is journeying into darkness, for a relatively brief season it will blaze with brilliance, if without ultimate meaning. Our exploration of this remarkable voyage is based on the discovery of the strategic *logos*—the "ark of the Sun". The *logos* makes the improbable possible.

THE COSMOS AND THE *LOGOS*
When our voyage is over, life will have occupied an infinitesimally small fraction of the history of the Universe. Even the era of inorganic complexity in the Universe will have been remarkably brief. In summarising the history of the Universe, one physicist has written that it will involve "a finite post-Big Bang spurt of life, followed by an infinite stretch of lifeless equilibrium."[1] By expanding this succinct statement with a few mind-numbing statistics, we can conclude that the Big Bang occurred about 14 billion years ago—which can be expressed approximately as 10^{10}—and the appearance of lifeless equilibrium will take another trillion or so years—or 10^{13}. While these are big numbers, there are bigger ones to come.

What is the current scientific hypothesis about the future of the Universe? We are told that the Universe is expanding at an accelerating rate. This means that the future of the Universe is not one of eternal recurrence—of an endless sequence of Big Bangs followed by Big Crunches followed by Big Bangs as previously thought—but of final exhaustion, stagnation, and heat death. The evidence usually marshalled for this relatively new hypothesis comes from data on supernovas, the cosmic microwave background, gravitational lensing, and so on. And the explanation centres on the existence of "dark energy: a smooth persistent component of energy that is spread uniformly throughout space and imparts an undiluted impulse to expand."[2] As this mysterious dark energy is thought to be constant—accounting for the cosmological constant—there is no possibility of the Universe collapsing in on itself. Accordingly—we are told by theoretical physicists—the Universe:

> Will continue to expand, matter and radiation will die away, the cycles of stellar and galactic evolution will use up their fuel and give out, and we'll be left with a cold, empty cosmos. Every particle will be moving away from every other particle, and eventually these particles won't even be able to see each other. For all intents and purposes, motion will have ceased forever.[3]

Also in contrast to the previous conventional wisdom, there will come a time when even matter will cease to exist in the Universe. While the eminent physicist Freeman Dyson believed that matter would last for all eternity, current particle theory predicts that protons—the basic building blocks of matter—will decay into lesser particles in about 10^{34} years. Of course, this is a vast expanse of time. Even white dwarfs and neutron stars are expected to "erode away in about 10^{36} years, spluttering into wan energies and small sprays of electrons and positrons."[4] Hence, from 10^{34} to 10^{36} years following the Big Bang, which created complexity, ephemeral order will finally be replaced with eternal disorder.

This relatively brief transition from order to disorder in the Universe is the outcome of increasing entropy. As is well known, this process is described by the second law of thermodynamics, which states that "there is no thermodynamic process whose sole effect is to extract heat from a colder reservoir and to deliver it to a hotter reservoir."[5] In other words, heat cannot, of its own volition, move from a colder to a hotter object. This is one of the most important laws in physics. At the micro level it accounts for the impossibility of developing a perpetual motion device, and at the macro level for the Universe's long journey into eternal night.

Hence, at the Universe's beginning, not long after the Big Bang, entropy was very low; whereas at its end, entropy will be very high. But we can be more specific, as physicists have attempted to quantify these general statements. In the beginning, "when matter was smoothly distributed and there were no black holes, the corresponding entropy was about 10^{88}; in the present state of the Universe, with its supermassive black holes at the centre of galaxies, entropy is about 10^{100}; and "in a maximum-entropy configuration" toward the end of the Universe, entropy will be about 10^{120}.[6] As physicists remind us, although all of these are very large numbers, some are much larger than others. For example, when we subtract 10^{100} from 10^{120}, the result is still basically 10^{120}; just as when we subtract one from a million the result is basically one million.[7]

There are two active processes at work that have, are, and will continue to shape the history of the Universe. The first of these is the simple process of entropy that increases steadily throughout the history of the Universe, and the second is the more complex and interesting process of the rise and fall of complexity. For the briefest period of historical time, the state of the Universe is complex and interesting. As physicists tell us, during this brief period of time

There is ordinary matter and dark matter, and the ordinary matter comes in a bewildering variety of ions, atoms, and molecules in different forms and combinations. Matter is grouped into clouds, planets, and stars, grouped into galaxies of various sorts, which in turn belong to clusters and superclusters. Each star and planet is the scene of a great deal of intricate nuclear and chemical reactions, all the way up to the ultimate in complex reactions: organic life.[8]

This complexity developed steadily from the beginning of time, and it will reach a climax some billions of years in the future. Then it will ineluctably decline and cease to exist. The destination of our improbable voyage, therefore, is eternal night.

In this history of the Universe, life in general—and mankind in particular— has played an amazing role. Life forms have been able to take the development of complexity to a level that could not be predicted by god-like observers familiar only with the physical forces of the Universe. By inventing the dynamic life-system, which I call the strategic *logos*, organic life forms have, for a relatively brief time, been able to defy entropy and overcome a physical environment extremely hostile to life. *Life, in other words, is a result not of "cosmic self-organisation" as many physicists have argued,[9] but of the emergence of the strategic* logos *with its very special laws of life.* Physicists who have recourse to the flawed supply-side concept of "cosmic self-organisation" are really saying that they have no idea at all about the origin of life on Earth or anywhere else in the Universe.[10]

While the laws of physics can explain the physical history of the Universe, they cannot explain the history of life. To understand life we need to explore the laws of the *logos*. It is the *logos* that can defy entropy and create biological order and complexity without transgressing the laws of physics. The strategic *logos* is an open biological system able to convert energy from a body like the Sun into work—a less than efficient process that loses energy to the environment in the form of heat—even though it is part of a larger closed system called the Universe that is on a long but inevitable journey to heat death and chaos. But, as we have suggested, this can only occur during the relatively brief period prior to the decay of matter, even if the *logos* with which we are familiar is able to escape the exhaustion of its birth star.

Box 1.1: The *logos* revealed

The ancient Greek word *logos* has a long history. But not until Heraclitus (around 500 BC) was it employed in reference to a mysterious "system" that had a controlling influence over human society. For Heraclitus, the *logos* implied that our world has unity, coherence, and meaning, which is established through ever present change or flux. While Heraclitus was the ancient world's expert on the dynamics of life and human society, he was unable to provide a scientific explanation of this mysterious vehicle of life.

Through the ages this mystery of mysteries has been called by many names. To the ancient Egyptians it was *maat*; to the Persians, *Asha*; to the

Vedic Indians, *Rta*; to the Toltecs, *Nelli*; to the Sioux, *Wakan-Tanka* ("Great Mystery"). All these societies, together with those who had no name for the hidden system underlying life, were and are extremely concerned to sustain it together with all its life-giving powers. Without understanding the scientific concept of entropy, they all had a strong sense of the world running down. To avoid catastrophe it was essential, they believed, to employ appropriate ritual and to live according to the laws of their life-system. This was the real origin and purpose of religion. Even today, some people have similar mystical views, referring to the hidden life-system as *Gaia*.

But the *logos* needs to be approached scientifically rather than mystically. This can only be done by observing the patterns of historical reality and developing a realist general dynamic theory. It may help in grasping the realist concept of the strategic *logos* to think of two forms of reality. First there is "historical reality", which consists of objects and events that can be perceived through the senses over time. Second, there is "ultimate reality", or the strategic *logos*, that is the outcome of a complex set of invisible relationships between *forces*, such as strategic desire and strategic demand (Figure 5.1). Only the agents (strategists) and outcomes (institutions, organisations, infrastructure, and material wealth) generated by these invisible forces can be detected by the senses. The forces of life themselves can only be detected through theories about the material patterns in historical reality.

The relationship between invisible forces and visible objects in the social world is similar to that in the physical world explored by physicists. For example, we can observe the pattern of planetary motion, but not the invisible force of gravity that shapes them; and we can detect the patterns of atoms and molecules in matter, but not the invisible but powerfully controlling nuclear and electromagnetic forces. The laws governing these physical forces are derived not from the observation of objects directly, but from theories about the relationships between objects. Such theories penetrate the mysteries of our world. The discovery of the strategic *logos* is similar in nature to these discoveries in science. And by discovering the *logos* we can confidently step into the future.

My concept of the "strategic *logos*" emerged only towards the end of a research program spanning some three decades. Over that time, my "dynamic-strategy" program went through three main phases. First, I established the quantitative pattern of dynamics in both human society and life; second, I developed a realist general dynamic theory that could best explain this pattern; and third I employed this theory to provide a picture of the hidden underlying life-system. Only once this life-system had been discovered did I attempt to see what others had said about this "mystery of mysteries". Hence, while I call this life-system the "*logos*" in recognition of the first great inductivist, Heraclitus, I distinguish it from his essentially mystical concept by adding the adjective "strategic"—strategic *logos*.

While the ability of life forms to gain access to energy from the Sun (or from the molten core of the Earth in the ocean depths) is usually taken for granted, this is no easy task. It is necessary for life forms to develop either biological or technological methods to extract energy to do work and create order and complexity. This is a matter beyond the capability of individual organisms. It is something that can only be achieved by the emergence of a dynamic life-system or strategic *logos*. Biological and technological "ideas" do not just emerge spontaneously as do events in the physical world (such as the flow of heat from hot to cold bodies), but rather require the *deliberate* investment of time and resources in dynamic social structures—a process I call the "strategic pursuit", whereby materially motivated organisms attempt to maximise the probability of survival and prosperity through the adoption of dynamic strategies.

Energy is needed, therefore, to develop dynamic life-systems that in turn can protect and sustain the extremely difficult process of survival and prosperity in a hostile world that is continually running down. *And these protective life-systems, or strategic* logoi, *need to be dynamic because it is essential to continually reinvent ways of gaining access to sources of energy and other resources, because the biological and technological methods employed to survive and prosper are also continually running down, owing to strategic exhaustion.* Only the dynamic *logos* can provide life and society with continuity and sustainability. In other words, the emergence of complexity and order in life is not an automatic outcome of a predictable evolutionary pathway as most scholars believe, but rather a special and vulnerable process arising from a strategic exchange between biological organisms and their physical environment. The strategic *logos* is a time-travelling vehicle of life, battling the forces of an unwelcoming cosmos.

The laws of physics determine the conditions under which the strategic *logos* might emerge, but it is the internal laws of the *logos*—the laws of life and history—that determine the way in which life unfolds. These laws can only be understood through the systematic observation of the strategic *logos* in operation throughout life on Earth over the past 3,800 million years (myrs), and by the construction of a general dynamic theory that can explain what is observed. In turn, this general dynamic theory can be employed to construct a model of the strategic *logos*. This is what I have attempted to achieve over the past few decades and what I discuss in this overview volume.

While the strategic *logos* is a dynamic system consisting of hidden forces, all human societies are and have been aware of its shadowy presence. Pre-industrial societies sought to understand it through their mythologies and religions, while post-industrial societies have attempted to penetrate its mysteries through rational thought. Although unable to analyse it, economists such as Adam Smith (1723–1790) and Friedrich Hayek (1899–1992) were aware of the existence of a hidden economic system—which they referred to as the "invisible hand" or "spontaneous order"—that operated without conscious human control. Only with the completion of the dynamic-strategy project has it been possible to identify, expose, and explore the hidden dynamic life-system, and to employ it to explain the improbable voyage of life. The nature of the strategic *logos*—the ark of the Sun—is discussed in greater detail in chapter 5.

ODYSSEY OF THE *LOGOS*

Like the history of the cosmos, the odyssey of the *logos* has barely begun. By careful observation we can reveal the patterns of the past, which in turn can be used not only to explain the emergence and development of both life and humanity, but also to construct a general dynamic theory of human and nonhuman systems that provides a model of the strategic *logos*. While we can see where the *logos* has travelled in the past, its future pathways can only be chartered by using our general dynamic theory to make predictions. In this way we can see more clearly through the mists of uncertainty than others who use unrestrained guesswork, flawed algorithms, or simplistic extrapolations of recent trends (simple historicism).

Landscapes of the Past

The origin of life on Earth is a matter of much speculation. While some argue that the origin of life on Earth was the outcome of primitive migration in the Solar System, the majority favour an Earth-bound explanation. Yet in both cases the argument is unconvincing. As discussed in my 2005 *Advances in Space Research* article, orthodox astrobiologists lack a realist dynamic theory of life. Darwin's theory of natural selection predicated on the assumption of highly **scarce** resources is unable to cope with the specific conditions existing at the beginnings of life—namely the **abundance** of natural resources. There is, in other words, a mismatch between the requirements of Darwinian natural selection and the competitive conditions under which life first emerged some 3,800 myrs ago. Natural selection can only operate under high levels of sustained competition, and this did not emerge until the end of the Proterozoic era at about 550 myrs BP.

How then do we do we explain the development of life during the first 2–3 billion years—or, indeed, during those extended periods following global dynastic collapse? In my 2005 *ASR* article I propose a realist general dynamic theory—the "dynamic-strategy" theory discussed in chapter 4—to show how life can develop under all forms of competition, from low, through moderate, to high. Essentially, the success of life depends on the emergence of a strategic *logos* (or *logoi*) that provides both the necessary protection for life forms from a hostile physical environment, and the dynamic life-sustaining process of selfcreation. Until a successful *logos* establishes itself, providing the protective context for the strategic pursuit, life will emerge and disappear many times. This is why the debate over the source of life is a secondary matter. The emergence of life is not difficult—and, hence, the postulation of a source external to the

Earth is not necessary—what is difficult is sustaining the life that emerges. This requires the locally generated strategic *logos*.

As shown in chapter 3 the pathway of life over the past 3,800 myrs is dominated by three features. First, there is the rate of acceleration of life that I call the "logological constant", which was discovered when writing my 1996 book *The Dynamic Society*; second, there are the very long-run fluctuations by which this explosion of life has occurred, here called the "great waves of life"; and finally, there are the biological and technological paradigm shifts—or "great steps of life"—that are required to enable life's growing access to energy sources to generate ever-greater complexity.

The "logological constant", which is a measure of the accelerating pace of history, has a significance similar to the cosmological constant that measures the accelerating expansion of the Universe. It is also a measure of the effectiveness of the strategic *logos* in delivering a constant *geometric rate* of the growth of life in a world dominated by entropy and subject to random physical shocks, including climate change. What the logological constant shows is that each biological transformation during the history of life on Earth took only one-third the time taken by its predecessor. Biological change, in other words, is exponential in arithmetic terms and constant in geometric terms. What this means is that the strategic *logos* is an entropy-defying and shock-resisting life system that protects and sustains life. Without the *logos*, biological and technological transformation would be impossible and individual life forms, even had they managed to emerge, would have been swept away long ago by a hostile physical world.

The "great waves of life" describe the manner in which life at its greatest level has progressed over the past 3,800 myrs. This series of great waves consists of four massive surges in life reflective of an increasing intensity of activity measured by the logological constant: the first is about 2,000 myrs in duration; the second about 600myrs; the third about 180 myrs; and the fourth, which is by no means complete, about 60 myrs. Not only is there a geometric reduction in the time taken to complete each great wave—each is about one-third as long as the one preceding it—but there has been a proportional increase in global biomass. In chapter 4, it is argued that this systematic pattern is not coincidental but is driven by a powerful endogenous mechanism embedded in the strategic *logos*.

The "great steps of life" define the dynamic structure of existence. Structural change in life and human society is driven by a number of major genetic and technological revolutions. And because of the logological constant, these great steps have been changing exponentially in two dimensions: simultaneously increasing in height and diminishing in depth. In the past 3,800 myrs there have been three genetic paradigm shifts (the Prokaryote, Eukaryote, and Endothermic Revolutions) and three technological paradigm shifts (the Palaeolithic, Neolithic, and Industrial Revolutions); and during the coming century, according to the dynamic-strategy theory, there will be a fourth technological paradigm shift (the Solar Revolution). These great structural changes are examined in chapters 2 to 4.

The changing genetic and technological structure of life—which underlies the great steps of life—provides the *potential* for organisms, including mankind, to increase in both complexity and sheer quantity. The *actual* utilisation of this potential has been a gradual wave-like process driven by the "strategic desire" of life and man in their pursuit of the non-genetic and non-technological dynamic strategies of family multiplication, commerce (symbiosis), and conquest.

While the conventional wisdom maintains that the "evolution" of life and human society has been a fairly straight-forward, even inevitable, process, the truth is very different. There was nothing inevitable about the orderly procession of the observed series of genetic revolutions culminating in the Intelligence Revolution. The contrary contention is the outcome of deeply flawed supply-side Darwinian thinking that persists to this time. It is argued in chapter 2 that if we could repeatedly rerun the odyssey of life on Earth, the chances of intelligent life ever appearing again are very remote. The emergence of intelligent life on Earth was the outcome of a long sequence of highly improbable events that are unlikely ever to be replicated. Owing to the stringent strategic requirements for the emergence of intelligent life, we should regard the "great wheel of life"—or the "eternal recurrence"— rather than the Intellectual Revolution as the normal condition for life systems throughout the Universe.

The "great wheel of life" comes into operation in a mature life-system when the "genetic option" has been exhausted—when genetic instruments cannot be further developed to squeeze more life out of the physical world. This stage in the history of life appears to have been reached by the time the dinosaurs were at their peak, about 80 myrs ago. The dinosaur dynasty took the Endothermic Revolution, which had been initiated by the earlier protomammals and carried forward by the archosaurs, a further and final step. Modern mammals, whose mighty dynasty was not based on a genetic paradigm shift, did not advance beyond the dinosaurs in this key resource-accessing ability. In fact, prior to the extinction of the dinosaurs, existing mammals came close to early extinction themselves. In effect, in terms of global biomass, the dinosaurs were only marking time. Their dynasty was little more than a variation on earlier warm-blooded dynasties (protomammals and archosaurs), as the limits of the genetic option were being approached. Life had been caught in what could have been an endless turning of the "great wheel" mechanism to be discussed in chapter 3.

By the pursuit of finesse rather than force in the management of their dynamic strategies, which gave rise to the growth of brain size and complexity, the mammal dynasty was able to escape the eternal recurrence—but only just. Had the pace at which the mammalian brain developed been only marginally slower, the great dynasty of which we are a part would have gone extinct before being able to replace the exhausted genetic option with the "technology option".

As we shall see in chapter 2, the technology option was the outcome of blind chance. The carrier of the Intellectual Revolution was a small insignificant species of the hominids, which eventually gave rise to mankind.

From 18 myrs ago to the present, hominid brains increased in size from 167cc (Proconsul) to 1,350cc (modern man)—or by a factor of 8.1. This development began slowly, but increased exponentially between early apeman (4 myrs ago) and early man or *Homo habilis* (2 myrs ago), settled down to a relatively high constant rate from early man to modern man or *Homo sapiens sapiens* (150,000 years ago), and since then has fallen to zero. As I will argue in chapter 2, this Intelligence Revolution was the outcome of the decision of one small branch of hominids to pursue a more general version of the traditional family-multiplication strategy—namely meat eating—that allowed these creatures to break out of their formative jungle habitat and explore, first, the African savannah, and, later, all other global habitats. Meat-eaters, in contrast to specialised vegetarians, can survive in all habitats that support animal life. The need, initially to scavenge, and, later, to hunt for meat, required larger brains (and smaller guts) in order to develop a facilitating technology (fire, weapons, tools) and socioeconomic organisation. While *Australopithecus garhi* and *Homo habilis* around 2.4 to 2.5 myrs ago were scavengers, *Homo erectus/ergaster*—with a brain 37 percent larger than early man—were, around 2 myrs ago, hunters and pioneers of the Palaeolithic Revolution with its new technology and socioeconomic institutions. But once man's brain had the capacity to introduce the technology option and support the various technological revolutions of the past 1.6 myrs, it ceased to develop further. It ceased to be the strategic instrument of choice. That occurred about 150,000 years ago with the emergence of modern man.

Prior to 11,000 years ago, mankind exhibited some interesting characteristics—the use of stone tools and fire, together with religious rituals— but essentially its life-style was not radically different from that of other hunting and gathering species, just that our naturally defenceless species had replaced the biological weapons and tools of natural hunters with technological weapons and tools of *nouveau* hunters. Even Darwinists—who resile from analysing modern man—feel confident about using the natural selection hypothesis to explain the "evolution" of early man. But, as shown in my book *The Collapse of Darwinism* (2003), this confidence has no secure foundation in reality. What would have been totally unpredictable to a hypothetical paleolithic "Darwinist" was the completely unprecedented emergence of urban living based on an agricultural and industrial technology. This urban life style, which we know as "civilisation", generated a flourishing of institutional (societal rules), organisational (societal networks), artistic, religious, philosophical, and mathematical ideas. Not only would our hypothetical Palaeolithic Darwinism have been unable to predict the emergence of civilisation, it cannot even explain civilisation's development over the past 11,000 years or its likely pathway in the future. This contrasts with the dynamic-strategy theory presented and employed in this book.

Civilisation emerged relatively suddenly—owing to the neolithic technological paradigm shift—between 12,000 and 8,000 years ago, following the very gradual progress made during the previous 2 myrs. It began with the domestication of animals and the sowing of unusually large grass seeds at a time when much of the big game of Europe, Asia, and North Africa had been eliminated. This was particularly the case in the Fertile Crescent stretching from the Nile, along the east Mediterranean coast, and throughout Mesopotamia to the Persian Gulf. The first animals to be domesticated were the wolf in Europe (15,000 years ago), and goats and sheep in Iran (11,000 years ago); and the first systematic "gardening" (rather than farming) emerged in conjunction with the raising of goats and sheep (for their milk, wool, and meat) in the rift valley of Jordan about 10,600 years ago. The main crops included emmer wheat and barley, which through human agency had developed from the wild grasses of the region.

These animal and plant experiments became the economic basis for what is thought to be the world's first town at Jericho, which consisted of a tightly packed huddle of clay buildings for human and animal habitation, together with grain storage. A wall about 4 metres high surrounded these buildings. The town, with a population of 2,000 to 3,000 (today it is about 20,000) was first permanently settled between 10,000 and 9,000 BC, using a local spring to support irrigated agriculture. The world's first city—called Catal Huyuk—with a population of 5,000 to 6,000 people, was established around 6,800 BC in Anatolia (Turkey). This city, with its cluster of houses and artistically decorated shrines, gave birth to the first truly urban culture that included the manufacture of woven cloth and baskets, obsidian weapons, pottery, jewellery, domestic objects, food and drink; and which supported specialised sociopolitical groups engaged in commercial, industrial, religious, and military activities.

In the New World, the agricultural base of Mesoamerican civilisation began at least 7,000 years ago with the domestation of corn, turkey and dogs. And permanent agricultural villages appear in this region about 4,000 to 5,000 years ago. The sophistication of this urban civilisation was both a shock and delight to the rapacious Old World invaders in the sixteenth century AD.

This "neolithic", or agricultural, technological paradigm provided the economic basis for the ancient, medieval, and pre-modern worlds. I employ the term "neolithic" to encompass the entire agricultural paradigm that underpinned human progress for the 10,000 or so years between the Palaeolithic and the industrial technological paradigms, even though "neolithic" means "new" (or later) stone-age—the era that gave rise to this agricultural revolution. By the adoption of either the conquest or commerce strategies, ancient societies were able to temporarily transcend the material limits of the agricultural paradigm. By pursuing the strategies of conquest or commerce, ancient and medieval societies could leverage their incomes and wealth to new highs, and they were able to increase their populations, and hence their geo-political power, markedly. By the time of Christ, an agricultural society could support cities of between 30,000 and 50,000 people; but by pursuing the conquest strategy, a conquest society like Rome was able to increase its population to about one million in an empire of more than 50 million, at least until it exhausted its conquest strategy and was thereby forced to "downsize".

The dynamic strategies of conquest and commerce also generated the "great waves of civilisation". By exploiting and exhausting their dynamic strategies, commerce societies such as Egypt and Greece, and conquest societies such as Rome, experienced great waves of progress of approximately 300 years duration. Those societies able to recover from the exhaustion and collapse of a great wave often went on to experience a "strategic sequence". In the case of Egypt this involved three great waves of commerce separated by shorter periods of chaos; in the case of Rome, a series of conquest waves; and in the case of Greece, a mixture of strategies in the sequence conquest▶commerce▶conquest. Similarly, societies in the medieval and pre-modern period exploited and exhausted a sequence of dynamic strategies, usually conquest followed by commerce. And as they did so, the Neolithic Revolution spread around both the Old and New Worlds and, from the sixteenth century, the New World as well. Until, that is, by the mid-eighteenth century when the strategic potential of the "neolithic" paradigm had been exhausted and further global progress depended on the emergence of a new technological paradigm. This "emergence" proved to be a difficult birth.

The new technological paradigm was heralded by the Industrial Revolution, and it was pioneered by Great Britain, as the leading member of a transforming Western Europe, from the late eighteenth century. Great Britain's experience and role were unique. Just as the neolithic paradigm was exhausting itself in the mid-eighteenth century, Great Britain was exhausting its commerce strategy, which had been responsible for three centuries of growth and prosperity. Instead of following the Greek strategic sequence of conquest▶commerce▶conquest, Great Britain became the first society ever to pass through the sequence of conquest▶commerce▶technological change. It was all a matter of timing, and Britain's timing was perfect. Had Britain exhausted its commerce strategy a century earlier, prior to the exhaustion of the neolithic technological paradigm, this mighty world power would have embarked on a new global conquest strategy, thereby repeating the pattern of the past. Indeed there are signs (various wars with global reach) that this was happening during the second half of the eighteenth century prior to the emergence of the Industrial Revolution. Adam Smith the worldly philosopher was very concerned about this eventuality, and it motivated his interest in pioneering the economic analysis of the wealth of nations in an effort to find a peaceful alternative. Britain's commerce empire would have formed the launching pad for an even greater conquest empire. Fortunately for the world, following the exhaustion of the neolithic paradigm, investment in the new industrial technology was more profitable than investment in the infrastructure of conquest.

The industrial technological paradigm shift initiated by Britain in a highly competitive West European environment, overcame the emerging stagnation resulting from an exhausted agricultural technological paradigm and powered the growth and prosperity of the world for the following three centuries until the mid-twenty-first century. In these three centuries, the global "strategic core", which began with Britain, expanded to embrace Western Europe, the offshoots of Western Europe in North America and Australasia, Eastern Europe, Japan, and, later, Korea, China, and India. This is a dynamic process I call the "global strategic transition" (GST), and it is discussed in detail in chapter 12. By the middle decades of the twenty-first century the strategic core will also include much of Asia and the Middle East. Probably only sub-Saharan Africa will remain in the "strategic fringe". And history is likely to leave much of that continent even further behind, because before these countries can be fully integrated into the strategic core of the industrial paradigm, the next great economic revolution—the Solar Revolution—will be underway. The problem of climate change will propel us forward without them. And even China, which was left behind by the Industrial Revolution, could possibly miss the solar boat and be left in the wake of logosian transformation once more, if it fails to complete its industrial technological transformation before the Solar Revolution bursts forth.

Future Landscapes

There is no shortage of stories about the future of life on Earth, or in the Solar System and the Universe. But these stories are merely the products of fertile imaginations. Even the more serious accounts are a form of science fiction parading as science fact. The underlying reason for the unsatisfactory state of futurology is the failure of futurologists to construct and employ a realist general dynamic theory. At their most "scientific", futurologists employ flawed partial theories like Darwinian natural selection or naïve historicist models based on the assumption that technology will develop exponentially of its own accord; and at their least "scientific" they indulge in a purely fictional methodology. These stories of the future take on a bizarre quality, usually ending in the transformation of human beings into some version of the farcical disembodied universal mind. In contrast, this book employs a realist general dynamic theory—the dynamic-strategy theory—to make predictions about human society in the *foreseeable* future.

The dynamic-strategy theory has much to tell us about the "immediate future"—the twenty-first century—and even some basic things about the "deep future"—the next million years or so. Of course, if we are to make predictions about the deep future, we need to be confident we can successfully negotiate the problem of climate change that will dominate our attention in the immediate future. To resolve the problem of climate change means being able to determine what will happen to the strategic *logos* during the course of the twenty-first century.

The immediate future

Mitigation or revolution?

The strategic *logos* is the vehicle of life. It is, as we will see in chapters 5 and 6, a "selfcreating system" that possesses its own laws of development. By isolating, identifying, and analysing those laws, it is possible to predict the dynamic pathway of the *logos.* The *logos* is undergoing a major transformation in the twenty-first century. Because it is approaching the limits of the prevailing industrial technological paradigm, the *logos* is readying itself to forge the next great technological paradigm shift, in the form of the "Solar Revolution". In chapter 13, I explain that the increasing exhaustion of fossil fuels—oil and coal—suggest that the Solar Revolution will get underway during the middle decades of the twenty-first century. Provided only that there is no global attempt to lock human society into various alternative versions—wind and solar-panel power—of the exhausting industrial paradigm. To do so will be disastrous. As I argue in detail in *The Coming Eclipse* (2010a), not only will this uninformed action be incredibly costly—amounting to $28 quadrillion or 91 percent of GDP by 2100 according to my **dynamic** cost-benefit study— it could even lead to the crippling of the *logos,* which would result in global collapse on a massive scale.

Box 1.2: The Solar Revolution explained

The dynamic-strategy theory makes a powerful prediction: a major technological paradigm shift—or economic revolution—will begin in the middle decades of the twenty-first century and will be complete within a generation. I call it the Solar Revolution. This seismic upheaval will be on the scale of the Industrial Revolution that began in the last few decades of the eighteenth century. The Solar Revolution, which will emerge from the exhaustion of the existing industrial technological paradigm, will completely transform life as we know it.

What will the Solar Revolution involve? While the dynamic-strategy theory can predict the timing, pace, and general characteristics of the new technological paradigm, it remains silent on the technical details, which are a product of unpredictably changing relative factor costs. Something can be said, however, about new sources of energy. The rapidly approaching exhaustion of fossil fuels, such as coal, oil, and natural gas, will be replaced not with wind, wave, or nuclear power, or even banks of solar mirrors and panels (all part of the old technological paradigm), but with direct access to the energy of the Sun. This revolutionary access to energy could be achieved by a fleet of satellites orbiting the Sun and beaming energy continuously back to Earth. Such a revolutionary use of energy will be equivalent to the innovative use of fossil fuels during the Industrial Revolution. Alternative energy sources in the late eighteenth century—windmills and watermills—were part of the old "neolithic" technological paradigm, and had no place in the Industrial

---

Revolution, despite their "green" credentials. The forthcoming Solar Revolution will be a response to the changing requirements of the strategic *logos* in its attempts to transform an exhausting industrial technological paradigm in the face of climate change. The *logos* will also require equally revolutionary changes in the ecosociopolitical structure of human society.

Where will the Solar Revolution take place? It will occur in those innovative societies that are on the frontier of paradigmatic exhaustion. Just as was the case for Britain—and, later, Western Europe—in the second half of the eighteenth century. They will be the societies pushing the old paradigm to its limits, as well as investing in the infrastructure of radically new scientific and technological knowledge, rather than those societies that lock themselves into uneconomic alternative technologies of the old paradigm. There will be a few winners and many losers as the Solar Revolution radically transforms the existing geopolitical power structure. Everything will depend upon our readiness to respond to the *logos*.

If, however, the global community focuses on repairing the damage actually created by climate change—rather than anticipating damage that may or may not eventuate—investing in the basic infrastructure of knowledge (science, research, and technology), and removing barriers to the effective operation of the new economic revolution, the problem of climate change will be resolved by the *logos* itself. The problem with modern orthodox economics—the tool-kit employed by climate mitigationists—is that it has failed to develop a realist general dynamic theory that can predict future structural change. It is merely capable of dealing with small (marginal), short-run issues within a static theoretical framework. As the Cambridge economist Joan Robinson famously said, neoclassical economics is ideal for determining the price of a cup of tea, but is hopeless when it comes to examining the important issues of life.

Hence, when it addresses large (non-marginal), long-run issues of a real-world dynamic nature—such as the impact of climate change on economic growth over the next century—it is all at sea. Rather than admitting this problem and retiring from the field, economists have insisted on applying their totally inadequate theory to this critically important issue. The results—that the (static) costs of mitigation will be limited to 1 % of world GDP—would be laughable if they were not so serious. What is wrong with these results? Orthodox economists have completely ignored the **dynamic** costs of climate change mitigation, namely the derailment of the new technological paradigm. The totally confused mitigationists are encouraging governments to interfere massively in the dynamic mechanism of the strategic *logos*—an entity they neither recognise nor understand. The only way to introduce and maintain a comprehensive mitigation program of the magnitude envisaged by the IPCC will be by establishing a global command system, which would critically disrupt the working of the *logos* in the same way that the Soviet command system undermined the Russian strategic *logos*. In the extreme-case scenario, this could lead to a global mitigation-dictatorship, which would eventually provoke a major conflict as dissenting societies or regions attempted to break away.

It is probably more likely that once a comprehensive mitigation program runs into the massive costs involved in this antistrategic operation, it will eventually be dismantled. But not before the Solar Revolution is seriously delayed. Hence, huge costs will be incurred. While the world will lose valuable time and suffer a totally unnecessary loss of GDP, which will never be made up, it should eventually get back on track owing to the long-run resilience of the strategic *logos*. Those countries that are less willing to follow the radical mitigationists and who invest more in the strategic infrastructure of the future— the capacity to create knowledge—will be the leaders in the next economic revolution, just as Britain was in the last one. Those countries that are most susceptible to seduction by the mitigationists and which invest least in strategic, as opposed to mitigation, infrastructure, will be the losers. And it will take the losers generations to catch up with the leaders, if ever.

There are other issues concerning the immediate future about which the dynamic-strategy theory has something to say. These include the issues of population, world leadership, and religion. First, a sustainable population is an old favourite of the environmentalists, which has been pushed aside by the excitement over climate change. But it is never far from centre stage. In the 1960s through to the 1990s, population growth was the major concern of Green groups. They were convinced that unless population growth was stopped in its tracks immediately, and reversed, the global environment would collapse and civilisation would be doomed. Sound familiar? When I wrote *The Dynamic Society* in the early 1990s, radical environmentalists such as Paul Ehlich (1968; 1990), and the "limits-to-growth" people (1972; 1992) demonstrated that they were unable to understand four critical matters: first, that population is not running out of control, but is responding to logosian demand; second, that economic growth does not drive population growth; third, that as countries pass through the global strategic transition the strategic demand for population stabilises and may even decline; and fourth, that owing to technological change, population has not and will not outrun natural resources.

Further, I argued that, by attempting to eliminate growth-inducing technological change, radical environmentalists would actually create the problem—of overpopulation—that they sought to avoid.[11] Indeed, as I showed, it could even lead to military conflict between dissenting groups who attempted to break away from any global environmental consensus. At that stage I had yet to discover the strategic *logos,* but, now that I have, it is clear that the *logos* will determine the optimal level of population required to sustain the survival and prosperity of humanity through "strategic demand". What is fascinating is that although the limits-to-growth people have been proven wrong by subsequent events, just as I said they would be, they have merely moved on, without comment, to the next "antistrategic" campaign designed to derail the strategic *logos*—the climate mitigation campaign. Climate change is most likely real, but supply-side interventionists will only exacerbate this critical problem, because they are oblivious to the role and power of the strategic *logos*.

A clash of civilisations?

Many today are concerned that religion could be the catalyst for global conflict. Some have attempted to persuade us that the differences between Christian and Islamic societies will result in a "clash of civilisations". This claim is the outcome of an erroneous interpretation of the origin, nature, and role of religion. As I demonstrate in detail in *Dead God Rising* (2010b), and outline in chapter 8 below, what we now call religion had its origin in Palaeolithic society as "strategic ideology", which consisted of a set of myths to compensate for man's inability to comprehend the strategic *logos*—the mystery of mysteries that determined society's success in its pursuit of survival and prosperity—and to provide the confidence needed to approach and seek support from superhuman "strategic guardians". With the Neolithic Revolution, the increasingly sophisticated *logos* not only demanded a more complex strategic ideology, but generated a surplus that was used to support a professional clergy—the "priestly philosophers"— who turned the simple strategic guardians into gods.

The idea of a single creator God also emerged in the agricultural societies of the Fertile Crescent. Not among the successful superpowers of Egypt or Mesopotamia, but in those societies occupying the borderlands between the superpowers—in Palestine/Syria and Arabia. Monotheistic religion—Judaism, Christianity, and Islam—arose among societies suffering from millennia of "strategic failure". In order to ease the psychological suffering arising from "strategic frustration", the Judahites, the Galilean Jews, and the Red-Sea Arabs developed ideologies for alternative (or nonstrategic) communities within larger strategic societies dominated by imperialistic superpowers. This new nonstrategic ideology constituted the invention of religion as we now know it. The "religion" of downtrodden communities in the borderlands of civilisation needs to be contrasted with the more general "strategic ideologies" supporting the successful strategic superpowers. Ironically, after the exhaustion of the Roman dynamic strategy of conquest and the demonstrated impotence of the old gods of war, Christianity and Islam were adapted and adopted by ambitious societies as strategic ideologies. God was made to serve mammon.

The "death of God" was caused by the Industrial Revolution. With the industrial technological paradigm shift, "scientism" replaced religion as the strategic ideology of advanced societies. Why? Because the modern *logos* depended not on God for its strategic success, but on science. Accordingly, in 1882 Friedrich Nietzsche could say, somewhat belatedly but famously, that "God is dead". Yet, while religion was cast aside as strategic ideology, a declining proportion of individuals in industrialised countries still relied on a perceived relationship with God for personal support. Eventually, religious observance will become a very minor activity in advanced societies. Only in the Third World, yet to be absorbed into the strategic core, have religious adherents increased in number. The logical conclusion of this analysis is that Islam will also be rejected as a strategic ideology—a strategic ideology that contributed to the highly successful conquest strategy of the Arabs in the medieval period—as Islamic countries go through the global strategic transition, and later it will become a minor social activity.

The clear implication of this dynamic-strategy argument is that a "clash of civilisations"—a clash between "Christian" and Islamic societies—will not occur. As a careful study of history shows, societies only engage in large-scale military conflict for strategic (material) reasons, not religious (spiritual) reasons. In the West, Christianity has been replaced by scientism as the strategic ideology, and in the East, Islam has long-ceased to be a successful strategic ideology. The current global conflict—the "war against terrorism"—is not a war between strategic societies, but a struggle between Western **strategic** societies (with their scientist ideology) and **antistrategic** groups (with their terrorist ideology, falsely dressed up in Islamic garb) that wish to destroy the West. Terrorism is anti-life as it is intent on destroying the strategic *logos*. True Islamic societies, which reject this anti-life or "antistrategic" approach, are keen to make the transition to the industrial technological paradigm.

The deep future

While predictions about the deep future of human society do not carry the urgent concern of predictions about the twenty-first century, they are of considerable interest and are increasingly exercising the imaginations of futurologists. The problem faced by serious futurologists is that they have no realist general dynamic theory to provide a rational basis for the stories they tell. They either employ flawed partial theories such as Darwinian natural selection (discussed in chapter 4), or give free rein to their poetic imaginations. The dynamic-strategy theory, in contrast, provides a scientific basis for making a number of key predictions about the deep future.

A disembodied supermind?

A major conclusion of deep futurology is that at some distant time in the future—say in another million years—human existence will have "evolved" into some sort of disembodied superintellect or supermind. This is often thought of as involving some sort of virtual world in which some combination of biological and synthetic intelligence would operate. Some writers envisage this disembodied superintelligence being able to convert all matter and energy in the Universe into an ultimate computer that will make it possible to create new universes characterised by physical laws compatible with the re-emergence of life. So, although this Universe, left to its own devices will eventually run down and end in heat death and the destruction of matter, the imagined universal intelligence will be able to create new initiating Big Bangs that will recycle the experience of life in a range of new universes.

While this is bizarrely fascinating, it is just not possible. Why? Because it completely fails to take into account the need for a driving force in life. As I show in *The Selfcreating Mind* (2006), the mind is merely an instrument—albeit a deeply embedded one—employed by the strategic organism to achieve its objective of survival and prosperity. While the "strategic organism" has existed for 3,800 myrs, the brain, or "strategic cerebrum" emerged a mere 500 myrs ago. The driving force in life—"strategic desire", or the need to fuel the internal metabolic process—is embodied in the strategic organism, not the strategic cerebrum. Hence, the concept of a disembodied mind is impossible, as the mind would have abandoned the force that drives the life process. There can be no strategic *logos* without strategic desire. And without the *logos*, life in a hostile world could not exist. For similar reasons, the idea beloved of science fiction writers—and all science futurology is science fiction—about robots overtaking their human creators is unrealistic. Robots will never compete with humans as they will never embody strategic desire. The implication of this dynamic-strategy argument, therefore, is that if human life still exists in a million years time, it will consist, like now, of both body and mind, and body and mind in biological form.

But surely in a million years the human mind will have "evolved" into a supermind—at least in comparison with our present intellectual capabilities. This is a common misconception. Essentially, the human mind stopped developing about 150,000 years ago, when modern man emerged. Prior to that time, hominid brain size increased in response to logosian demand so that hominid society could negotiate the technological requirements of its strategic pursuit. Once our intellectual capacity was sufficient to negotiate the Palaeolithic, neolithic, and modern technological paradigm shifts, logosian demand for increases in brain size ceased. An even larger brain was not required by the strategic *logos.* With the development of computer technology, it became possible potentially to negotiate *all* future technological paradigm shifts by the growth of artificial rather than biological intelligence. Of course, with continuing scientific work on the human genome, it will be possible eventually to undertake significant experiments in genetic engineering. But owing to the incredible complexity of the brain, and the very real danger of failure, the potential cost of technologically enhancing biological intelligence will deter any attempt to effect major cerebral structural change. Both the cost and risk of developing artificial intelligence will be so much less.

We also need to consider the nature of the human brain. Primarily it is a strategic instrument, not a deductive biological computer. The human brain developed to supervise the strategic pursuit through a process of observation and generalisation, which I call "strategic thinking". Computers on the other hand are deductive "thinkers". Hence, we have a comparative advantage in strategic thinking and computers in deductive thinking. It makes no sense to attempt to transform the strategic-thinking human mind into a deductive-thinking biological computer, when we already have electronic computers. The most likely outcome for the deep future, therefore, is that the human brain will remain much the same as it is today, while the electronic computer will become a super-deductive machine forever at our disposal. In other words, there will be specialisation and division of labour between the biological-strategic mind of man and the electronic-deductive "mind" of the electronic computer.

The Methuselah syndrome

A fascinating issue is the possibility that science will significantly increase the life-span of humans. No doubt, with continued progress in human genetics, nanotechnology, and the fight against disease, it will be possible to increase the life-span of mankind. Some have envisaged people eventually living for hundreds, even thousands, of years. If this did prove to be possible, there would be a number of severe costs to cope with.

The least problematical of the costs of super longevity will be the implications for new human life. Obviously, if the entire population of Earth were able to live for hundreds of years, the flow of new life would slow to a trickle. This flow would be determined by the much-reduced death rate together with the technological change that allowed an overall increase in population density, or the colonisation beyond our planet, even beyond the Solar System. One can imagine the problems of deciding who would be allowed to have children and when they would be allowed to have them; together with the dreariness of life without children and grandchildren. Even more problematical will be the psychological adjustment required to be able to handle living for hundreds of years. Would we be able to bear it? Many people today have great difficulty coping with the conventional "three score years and ten", and are forced to resort to alcohol, drugs, and even suicide. I suspect suicide would become a major form of death in a world where the overwhelming objective in life is materialistic in nature. It is the prospect of a timely death that makes life both possible and bearable.

Do aliens exist?

Finally, in the deep future, will we make contact with intelligent alien life forms? The implication of the "great wheel of life" argument mentioned above, and examined in more detail in chapter 3, is that the emergence of intelligent life is an extremely rare and unlikely event. A much more likely outcome is that a dominant dynasty of life (on any life-friendly planet) will exploit and exhaust the entire strategic sequence—of genetic change ▶ family-multiplication/symbiosis ▶ conquest—without experiencing the necessary Intelligence Revolution required for the emergence of some form of civilisation and technological revolution. Because of this "eternal recurrence", intelligence is the scarcest resource in the Universe. It is extremely unlikely, therefore, that we will ever encounter intelligent alien life forms. And if we do, the likelihood is that they will be considerably less advanced than our own, owing to the fortuitous sequence of events that enabled humanity to break out of the great wheel of life.

If, for the sake of argument, we did manage to make contact with competing life forms, the dynamic-strategy theory suggests that there will be a struggle to the death, just as there was between modern man and his cousin Neanderthal man. Just in case alien life forms are more developed than our own, we would do well not to advertise our presence in the Universe! A warning that is already too late. In any event, the funds being spent on trying to discover and make contact with intelligent alien life would appear to be irresponsible. But no doubt they will continue to be spent by this powerful lobby group.

We can conclude, therefore, that the most probable outcome of this most improbable voyage of life is that we are, and will continue to be, making it on our own. But this does not mean that we will not embark on the exploration and colonisation of, first, the Solar System, and eventually, the Universe. This new adventure will be imperative if we wish to escape the inevitable death of the Sun—an event mankind has always feared. The deep future will be about the travels of the *logos* throughout the cosmos.

Chapter 2
Unfinished Odyssey

History is accelerating, not ending.

The story of life has been told ever since early humans gathered around their campfires at night. Constantly changing, this story has only recently gained any precision, because only recently have the storytellers been able to assemble the necessary fossil evidence. Yet even now that we have a better understanding of what has happened, we have little idea of what made it so. Why? Because our explanations are based on flights of fancy rather than on the growing body of fossil evidence. We either cling to badly flawed Darwinian explanations and reject the evidence, or we embrace the evidence and offer fanciful explanations concerning the patterns it displays in terms of exploding mountains, crashing asteroids, biblical-like floods, regular visitations from "Death Stars", climate-change catastrophes, and the end of history. The inhabitants of ancient Sumer—mankind's first great civilisation—would have felt perfectly comfortable with these stories of life. But, as we shall see, history is accelerating, not ending.

Any persuasive theory of life must be based on a sound foundation of evidence. Of the Darwinists only the paleontologists, through their detailed study of the fossil evidence, have taken the historical patterns of life seriously. Their misfortune is that, instead of developing a new dynamic model to explain these patterns, they have attempted to force them into a Darwinian straitjacket. The outcome is complete confusion. They could have succeeded only had they rejected Darwin's theory of natural selection and begun anew. While sympathetic to their historicist approach I cannot accept their *analytical* explanations—particularly the statistical pseudo-explanations of the biometricians—which possess the same kind of technical aridity as econometrics in the social sciences.[1]

The fossil evidence suggests that life on Earth has experienced four distinct long-term phases of development. These comprise the 2,000 myrs dominated by the single-celled bacteria known as blue-green algae (until about 900 myrs BP—before the present); the 600 myrs following the decline of bacteria, dominated by primitive plant and animal (including reptiles) life in the seas and on the land; the 180 myrs following the mass extinction of these primitive life forms at about 245 myrs BP, which was dominated by dinosaurs on the land and in the air; and finally the 60 myrs following recovery from the extinction of the dinosaurs, which has been dominated by birds, mammals and, finally, mankind. As suggested in the final chapter, this unfinished odyssey has a future that can be predicted using a realist general dynamic theory.

THE DIVERSITY OF LIFE

The best quantitative measure available to substantiate these main phases of life is the number of families of marine and land animals (metazoa) as shown in Figure 2.1. These timescapes are really pictures of the fluctuating diversity of life over the past 600 myrs (known as the Phanerozoic eon)—a vast expanse of time. Little diversity existed before that time owing to the dominance of blue-green algae. While this general pattern of diversity has been known since John Phillips first sketched its outlines in 1860, John Sepkoski did so with greater precision in the late 1970s and early 1980s.[2] When examining this figure it should be realised that, as the recovery rate of fossils increases the nearer we approach the present, it exaggerates the expansion of families over time. Also the apparent downturn in land families in the early and late Jurassic is largely a figment of the poor fossil record.[3] Finally we should not confuse fluctuations in families with changes in biomass, because there is a trade-off between size and quantity of individuals on the one hand and diversity on the other.

What these timescapes show is a succession of surges and retreats in the diversity of life. The initial radiation of marine and land animals between 570 and 245 myrs BP (the Paleozoic era) was terminated by a major extinction resulting in a sharp decline in the number of marine (by 52 percent) and land (by 49 percent) families; the renewed expansion between 245 myrs and 65 myrs BP (the Mesozoic era) was brought to an end by widespread extinction of marine (11 percent) and land (14 percent) families that was much worse in terms of species; and the very rapid increase in diversity since 65 myrs BP (the Cenozoic era) has recently been eroded by the activities of mankind.

Figure 2.1a. Family Numbers for Marine Organisms—Past 800 myrs

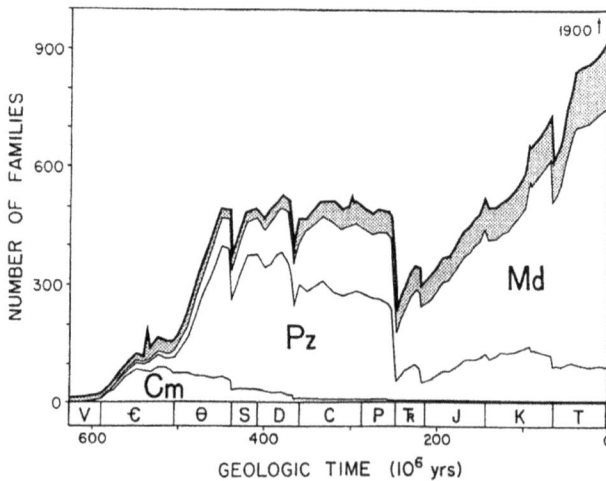

Source: Sepkoski 1984: 249 (with permission).

Figure 2.1b. Family Numbers for Land Organisms—Past 800 myrs

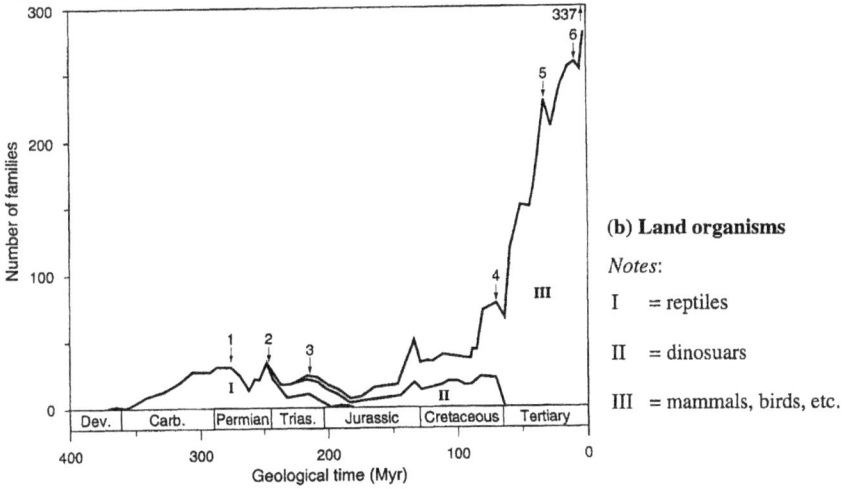

Source: Benton 1985: 811 (with permission).

It is important to realise that the timescapes presented in Figure 2.1 are a reflection of genetic diversity rather than total biological output. The general pattern is one of exponential growth in genetic diversity in the early history of any dynasty, followed by stagnation, or even slow decline, and later by collapse and extinction.[4] This should not be interpreted as indicating that total biological activity by any dynasty followed the same pattern. Quite the contrary, dynasty population continues to increase rapidly after genetic diversity stagnates and reaches a peak just prior to collapse and extinction. The pattern of genetic diversity reflected in Figure 2.1 is, it will be argued, the outcome of the pursuit of different dynamic strategies. The exponential growth of diversity is an outcome of the dynamic strategy of genetic change, while the long phase of stagnation in diversity (wrongly identified by Eldredge and Gould (1972) and Sepkoski as a state of "equilibrium"), is an outcome of the pursuit of the dynamic strategy of family multiplication (procreation and migration).

The timescapes in Figure 2.1 also show that these major radiations and extinctions comprise a number of overlapping developments in both marine and land fauna. Each new radiation of families and species was launched only after an earlier radiation was on the decline or had suffered major extinctions. What it means is that speciation—the formation of new species—has only taken place once competition has been eliminated. Why is this important? Because Darwin's theory of natural selection is irrevocably based on the assumption that evolution is the outcome of intense competition for scarce resources. The evidence suggests the very opposite: that speciation occurs only during periods of minimal competition and of resource abundance. Hence, natural selection is unable to explain the major phases of genetic change and speciation during the past 3,800 myrs—a major limitation for any macro theory.

23

Any survey of the fluctuations of life, no matter how brief, would be incomplete without mention of the world's flora. As can be seen from Figure 2.2, there have been three main stages in the development of Earth's land flora involving three very different plant types. As in the case of the fauna, with which a close association was formed, each new radiation occurred only after the decline of the previously dominant one.

Figure 2.2. The Rise and Fall of Major Land Plants—410 myrs

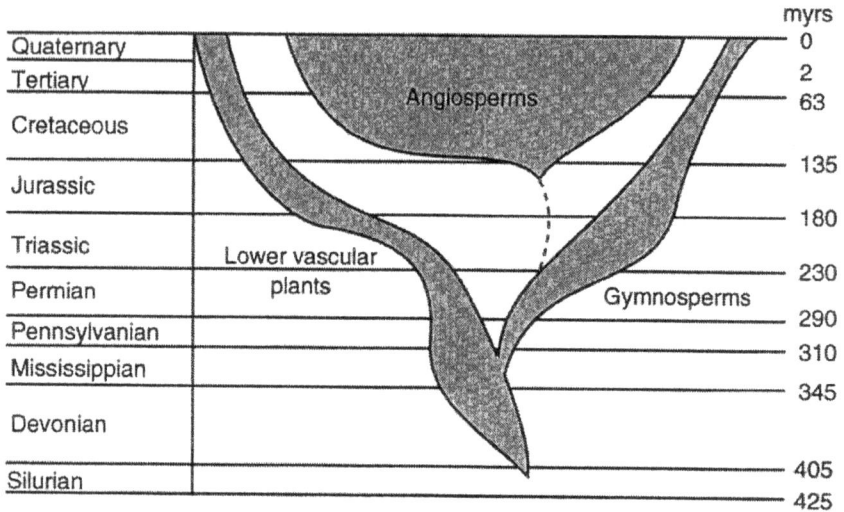

Source: Based on Newell 1978: 183.

The first stage of plant development on the land concerned the lower vascular plants—such as ferns, lycopods (club mosses), and horsetails—which expanded rapidly from about 405 myrs BP to reach a peak at about 290 myrs BP. This coincided with the invasion of the land by animals such as insects, amphibians, and reptiles. The second stage involved the gymnosperms (plants with naked seeds)—such as conifers, cycads, and ginkgos—which diversified from about 310 myrs BP to reach a peak at about 180 myrs BP. This was the period associated with reptiles, protomammals (therapsids), and protodinosaurs (thecodonts). Thereafter their number of genera declined and, like the lower vascular plants, they have continued to today by playing a more modest role. The last stage involved the great expansion of angiosperms (flowering plants), beginning at about 135 myrs BP and diversifying rapidly to the present. This incomparable radiation began during the age of the dinosaurs—with some arguing that it was made possible by changes in their feeding activities—and has reached its greatest expression during the era of birds and mammals.[5]

THE FIRST FORMS OF LIFE ON EARTH

Sometime before 3,850 myrs BP protocells emerged through the concentration of organic chemicals, possibly by evaporation, freezing, or one of a number of other suggested causes.[6] These protocells grew by absorbing simple organic substances from seawater, and they divided as they grew. As this occurred in a passive and accidental way in the beginning, these cells cannot be regarded as being "alive." While the dividing line between living and non-living protocells is rather unclear, the conventional wisdom tells us that "a protocell could have been called living as soon as protein formation, nucleic acid formation, and cell division became integrated and reliable".[7]

This is, however, a rather mechanical and passive definition of life. It reflects a widely held view in biology, indeed in the natural sciences generally, that organisms merely respond to a changing environment in a passive way. Most explanations of the history of life treat exogenous physical conditions as the driving force. Paleontologists do not even consider the possibility that the driving force might reside *within* the life forms themselves operating as part of the strategic *logos*. No one to my knowledge has successfully attempted to develop an endogenous dynamic theory of life. It would require a very different vision to that held by the Darwinists.

I want to suggest a more realistic definition of life that focuses on the origin of the driving force rather than on the mechanism of replication. The central thesis of the dynamic-strategy theory is that life contains a dynamic that drives it to grow and prosper. This dynamic, which can be observed operating throughout the history of life, had its origin in the emergence of biochemical processes in simple cells. In order to generate and sustain life, these simple cells had to be able to maintain an internal metabolic process. This involved the capture and fermentation of organic molecules (fuel) to produce the energy needed to sustain life. Once an individual metabolic system is established—there is still no agreement about how this occurred—the simple cell generates a "metabolic demand" (or hunger) for fuel to feed this chemical process. If this demand for fuel is not met, the cell begins to starve and its structure begins to break down. Starvation leads the cell to frantic efforts to find a new source of fuel. This need to meet metabolic demand was the beginning of what I call "strategic desire". And the different ways that organisms have attempted to meet this need I have called the dynamic strategies of life. This is the beginning of the strategic *logos*—the "ark of the Sun".

Life emerges, therefore, when a simple cell is able to develop a workable metabolic system. Without it life cannot be sustained. Replication, the core of the neo-Darwinian definition, is a secondary matter, because it is not essential in sustaining the life of the initial simple cell. In the beginning of life on Earth, new cells emerged without the ability to replicate. It was a situation that probably existed for a considerable period of time before the trick of systematic replication was learnt. In fact, replication—and the development of the tools of replication such as RNA, DNA, and protein formation—was a response to strategic desire. It was one—what I call, "family multiplication"—of the four dynamic strategies by which organisms have attempted to meet metabolic demand. Strategic desire, together with a primitive strategic *logos*, emerged before—long before—the need or ability to reproduce.

There is considerable controversy about how the first living cells obtained the energy they needed to meet their metabolic demand. The conventional wisdom is that the first forms of life were cells that absorbed fuel for their simple metabolic systems directly from seawater. This fuel, which is still employed by organisms today, was adenosine triphosphate (ATP), composed of three phosphates. By detaching one of these phosphates from ATP a living cell is able to create metabolic energy, which provides the fuel of life. Recent research, however, suggests that before the use of ATP, living cells probably absorbed pyrothermic energy from hot springs.

Whatever the first source of fuel, we know that supplies of freely available ATP were relatively quickly exhausted. This meant that existing cells had to develop a more complex fermentation process, known as heterotrophy, in order to extract energy from captured organic molecules and to convert adenosine diphosphate (ADP), consisting of two phosphates, into ATP. In effect living cells had to employ genetic change as a strategic instrument in the pursuit of the protostrategy of conquest. By chemically breaking down organic molecules captured in and absorbed from seawater, these first dynamic strategists were able to effectively fuel their internal energy systems.

This, then, is what the history of life is all about: devising more effective ways of obtaining fuel—what we call food—to fire up the internal metabolic system in order to survive and prosper. In this case the heterotroph pursued the protostrategy of conquest, which involved the capture and consumption of organic molecules. Only later did it pursue the protostrategy of family multiplication, which involves replication and migration. Right from the very beginning, life was devising dynamic strategies to achieve its objectives, and it did so within the protective embrace of a primitive strategic *logos*. Clearly, intelligence was not required to join in the "strategic pursuit".

THE PROKARYOTIC REVOLUTION

The Prokaryotic Revolution occurred some time before 3,500 myrs BP when the heterotrophic life form had exhausted the supply of freely floating organic molecules. It was created by what has been called "the world's first energy crisis".[8] The response to this crisis by heterotrophs was the development of a metabolic system based on photosynthesis, which involved the substitution of a "genetic strategy" for the earlier conquest and family multiplication protostrategies. This prokaryotic transformation constituted a genetic revolution, or a genetic paradigm shift, because it greatly increased the potential development of existing life forms by opening up their access to the Earth's natural resources.

The new autotrophic cells had constructed a metabolic system based on photosynthesis. As is well known, this process employs sunlight through the agency of chlorophylls together with carbon dioxide and hydrogen to fuel the ATP/ADP process. These autotrophic cells were also able to build up and store energy-rich molecules such as glucose that could be used to feed a fermentation process when sunlight was not available. The waste product from this revolutionary metabolic system was either sulphur or oxygen depending on the form in which hydrogen was employed.

The first and least efficient autotrophic process was employed by sulphur (or green and purple) bacteria, which broke down hydrogen sulphide (H_2S) releasing sulphur as a waste product. More efficient (by a factor of six) is the process employed by cyanobacteria (or blue-green algae) which break down water (H_2O) to gain access to hydrogen and release oxygen as a waste product. Water not only fuels a more efficient chemical process, it is one of the Earth's most abundant substances. But there is one unfortunate side effect: oxygen is highly toxic to life and must be handled with extreme care. It created acute problems for blue-green-algae when the oxygen levels in the seas rose to significant levels. This was the first case of a dominant life form on Earth polluting its own environment—the "oxygen holocaust"[9]—and it led to the transformation of biological systems to cope with it. Once this transformation had occurred, the rising levels of oxygen in the oceans and the atmosphere actually enabled the further expansion and development of other life forms.

Following the Prokaryotic Revolution, blue-green algae spread steadily in colonies in the shallow waters around continents and islands and probably in a thin floating layer across the ocean surface through the pursuit of the "family-multiplication strategy". Family multiplication usually follows genetic transformation as it enables organisms in the new species to exploit their capacity to access natural resources. The colonial approach became the most effective and enduring way to survive. Through simple cell division blue-green algae built new colonies called stromatolites consisting of layers of bacterial mat and sand cemented together with protective layers of slime secretions. These colonies also harbored uninvited guests that flourished by employing a "commerce (symbiosis) strategy". The top layer of the stromatolites consisted of blue-green algae, which operated as the powerhouse of the colony through its use of photosynthesis to produce organic matter that could be exploited by other life forms. The middle layer comprised green and purple bacteria, which used a less efficient form of photosynthesis and produced sulphur rather than oxygen as a waste product. And the bottom layer consisted of heterotrophs, which lived off the organic matter generated by the higher layers of life. Together they produced a colony that gave protection to them all, particularly from the worst effects of ultraviolet light and oxygen.

Fossil evidence for stromatolites can be traced back 3,500 myrs in the Warrawoona series in the north-west of Western Australia, and their living counterparts can be seen today in nearby Shark Bay. By 3,100 myrs BP the evidence shows that stromatolites had diversified into two different styles and by 2,800 myrs BP they had invaded salty lakes as well as coastal regions. Thereafter the expansion of this life form in these environments through the family-multiplication strategy was rapid, continuing for a further 2,000 myrs. During this later phase, at least, blue-green algae was the dominant form of life on Earth.

This is not to imply that the first great wave of life developed smoothly or without interruption. By generating oxygen as a waste product, the stromatolites polluted their own environment in two ways, both of which threatened their survival and caused a major interruption to their expansion. First, as oxygen is toxic to all forms of life, special methods have to be developed to cope with its presence. After initial setbacks before 2,500 myrs BP blue-green algae finally developed an antidote—an enzyme called superoxide dismutase—which saved them from the fate experienced by competitors that were less innovative. They also invented ways of employing oxygen in a new process called respiration, whereby the by-products of fermentation (lactic acid) are oxidised down to carbon dioxide (CO_2) and water, thereby releasing up to eighteen times more energy per sugar molecule than by simple fermentation. Once these "add-on" pieces of genetic technology were developed, the early reverses were left far behind, at least until overexpansion of blue-green algae took place around 1,000 myrs ago. This dominant life form, unlike all those to follow, had the time to develop new genetic technologies because they had no serious competitors until after they had resolved this problem and the rapid growth of oxygen levels enabled the emergence of dangerous new life forms (such as snails and other grazing animals).

The second problem facing blue-green algae owing to the increasing levels of oxygen was the growing iron deficiency in the oceans. In the early years of this life-form's development the oceans contained a high content of dissolved iron, which was essential for its success. The iron deficiency arose because the rising levels of oxygen in these water caused the dissolved iron to precipitate, laying down vast banded iron formations on the sea floor between 2500 myrs and 1800 myrs ago.[10] Today these rich iron deposits are to be found in the Hamersley Range in north-west Western Australia, Krivoi Rog in Russia, Labrador and Minnesota in North America, and Brazil in South America. Hence, a by-product of the Prokaryotic Revolution provided, some 2,000 myrs later, a major input for the Industrial Revolution. But this gift for a very distant ancestor threatened the very existence of blue-green algae.

Survival and renewal of expansion for blue-green algae depended on their ability to invent a further piece of add-on technology. Remarkably they were able to develop molecular "cages"—complex molecules called siderophores—

that, triggered by iron levels falling below a critical level, can pass through cell membranes in pursuit of iron atoms. Having captured its prey the siderophore re-enters the parent cell through a special valve. This remarkable exercise is repeated until the cell's iron level rises to the required level. A set of genes is responsible for switching this process on and off. As explained in Chapter 4 below, this is the role of what I have called the "strategic gene", a role which was later played by the "strategic cerebrum".

This genetic response occurred not in just one bacterium, but in several hundred bacteria, all generating different types of molecular "cages." In fact these bacteria employed their siderophores to compete with one another. Some produced "Trojan horses" that were close copies of the siderophores of their competitors which, when accepted by their neighbors as their own, poisoned their hapless victims, while others produced iron-absorbing siderophores to starve their competitors of iron. It is just possible that this ingenious solution to the general problem of iron deficiency arose from bacteria pursuing the conquest strategy against their neighbors—it arose, in other words, as a weapon rather than as an anti-pollution innovation. But it could be employed for both purposes.

While these various forms of add-on genetic technology could, and did, extend the reign of blue-green algae it could not enable this life form to remain forever dominant. It only enabled them to reach their full potential. A potential met by pursuing the family-multiplication strategy—a cloning process—until blue-green algae had fully exploited all available ecosystems throughout the accessible world. The role of this add-on technology, which was a response to strategic demand, was to facilitate the dominant dynamic strategies of family multiplication (replication and migration) and of conquest.

By about 1,000 myrs BP, blue-green algae appear to have completely exhausted the prokaryotic paradigm. Further pursuit of the family-multiplication strategy led to overcrowding, intense competition, and starvation due to pressure on nutrition. To survive, bacteria substituted the conquest strategy for the family-multiplication strategy, employing weapons (siderophores) developed earlier to devastating effect. Also in these overcrowded conditions it probably became increasingly difficult for bacteria of various types to cope with their own waste products of oxygen and sulphur. The outcome for this dominant life form was slow but irreversible decline, which released resources for the newly emerging eukaryotic life forms. Renewed expansion was impossible because blue-green algae had reached the ceiling imposed by their genetic paradigm, and even recovery from crises of increasing intensity was hampered by competition from new life forms (grazing animals) that were able to take full advantage of the growing oxygen levels and the associated ozone layer (providing necessary protection for organisms living outside protective colonies) that blue-green algae had created. It is not surprising that from 550 myrs BP stromatolite fossils are rare. This was the world's first strategic struggle between the "old strategists" (in this case the prokaryotes) and the "new strategists" (the eukaryotes). The subsequent decline of blue-green algae was the first great collapse, if not extinction (they live on only in small protected enclaves), of life on Earth. Hence, while self-contamination can be overcome by modest genetic change—which I have called add-on technology—paradigm exhaustion can only be resolved by an entirely new biological revolution or paradigm shift.

Before we pass on to the second genetic paradigm shift, we should briefly consider the long-running success of blue-green algae. There is, as we shall see, a critical problem here for the neo-Darwinist. Blue-green algae were remarkably successful in their pursuit of the universal objective of survival and prosperity, dominating the Earth for over 50 percent of the history of life. Despite this unparalleled achievement, which involved the solution of major problems resulting from their pollution of the environment, it is generally acknowledged that blue-green algae was not held on a tight "genetic leash", as E.O. Wilson, the father of sociobiology, insists that it was. We are told that

> the DNA content of prokaryotes is small, and they have only one copy of it. There is little room to store the complex "IF . . . THEN . . ." commands in the genetic program that would turn on one gene as opposed to another. Therefore, *genetic regulation is not well developed in prokaryotes.*[11]

Yet without well-developed genetic regulation, bacteria were able to successfully—very, very successfully—pursue a number of dynamic strategies including genetic change, family multiplication, commerce (or symbiosis), and conquest. These are the universal dynamic strategies that even the most sophisticated human societies still employ. And we have yet to demonstrate that as a species we can solve our own pollution problems as effectively, or last as long. So far we have been the dominant species (if we adopt a generous span of 1.6 myrs) for only 0.08 percent of the time that blue-green algae held sway. Further, if this life form with its limited genetic control could successfully pursue the full range of dynamic strategies, how is it that more complex life forms need to be held on a tight genetic leash as claimed by the sociobiologists?

THE EUKARYOTIC REVOLUTION

The second genetic paradigm shift—the Eukaryotic Revolution—was underway by 900 myrs BP. What was the genetic basis of this revolution? It was the emergence of a cell—the eukaryote cell—that could go beyond the construction of simple colonies of other identical cells and build complex, integrated biological structures or organisms. The first stage of this revolution was confined to cold-blooded, or ectothermic, life forms, because the emergence of warm-blooded, or endothermic life forms some 550 myrs later constituted a revolution in its self. This was achieved by a transformed strategic *logos*.

Eukaryote organisms were far more mobile than their prokaryote forebears and, as a result, were capable of exploiting natural resources that lay beyond the reach of blue-green algae. This is the hallmark of a paradigm shift, whether genetic or technological, that it enables a radical increase in potential access to energy and other natural resources. Eukaryote organisms were able to make this advance by gaining greater control over genetic change owing to the "invention" of sexual reproduction. While reproduction through cloning produces offspring with the same DNA as its sole parent, sexual reproduction, by combining the DNA of two individuals (half each) enables parents to exercise some discretion over the characteristics of their offspring through the choice of a mate. This is discussed more fully in Chapter 4.

When and how did the eukaryote cell emerge? Until recently the earliest known eukaryote fossil was dated at 1,400 myrs old, some 400 myrs before prokaryotic life went into decline. A more recent discovery in north-western Australia suggests, however, that this might have to be pushed back to 2,700 myrs.[12] Quite clearly eukaryotic life was not competitive with bacteria at this early stage. It would seem that, like mammals in the mesozoic period (245 myrs to 65 myrs BP), this new life form only emerged fully once the earlier dominant form had exhausted its paradigm and released nutrients for the use of other life forms.

Some speculate that the eukaryote cell first emerged through symbiosis. This is the so-called endosymbiotic hypothesis, which suggests that the components of the more complex eukaryote cell—including mitochondria, plastids, and flagella—were originally free-living bacteria that became so closely associated through their symbiotic relationship that they eventually formed an integrated cell. The implication of this hypothesis is that the eukaryotic transformation was merely a matter of chance association—an accident. While it may explain how the eukaryote cell emerged, it does not explain why. I want to suggest that it was an outcome of the "commerce strategy" (exploiting opportunities created through an exchange of resources) employed by a number of prokaryote cells to overcome regional exhaustion of the more usual "family-multiplication strategy". It was not until the entire prokaryotic paradigm was exhausted some 1,700 myrs later that this new form of life seized its chance and diversified rapidly.

What were the fundamental differences between prokaryote and eukaryote cells that made it possible to develop more complex forms of life, even if not more complex dynamic strategies? First, in a prokaryote cell the DNA floated freely, whereas in a eukaryote cell the DNA, which was much more abundant (by a factor of one thousand), was contained within a nucleus. This provided the more abundant DNA with the protection required to construct complex organisms. Second, unlike the prokaryote cell it was subdivided into organelles that specialised in different functions. This enabled a "division of labor" that generated greater efficiency of energy use. Third, the eukaryote cell was much larger, with a diameter and a volume greater by a factor of ten and a thousand respectively. Fourth, in contrast to the prokaryote cell it was able to expand its membrane to engulf other cells. Finally, and most significantly, while prokaryote cells reproduced by dividing themselves to create clones, most eukaryote cells reproduced sexually by combining their own DNA with that of another cell to create unique offspring.

It is thought that sexual reproduction emerged in eukaryote cells at least as early as 1,400 myrs ago. I argue that the significance of this development resides in the greater control over genetic change that it conferred on individual organisms. Through sexual reproduction an organism was able to manipulate the genetic structure of its offspring in two ways. First, it was able to influence the genetic makeup of its offspring by a judicious choice of sexual partner. "Selective sexual reproduction" is based on those perceived characteristics in other individuals that will improve the prospect of survival and prosperity of the selecting individual. If this perception turns out to be correct, those characteristics will also be passed on to the individual's offspring. As I show in Chapter 4, mate choice is an important technique for implementing all four dynamic strategies, not just that of genetic change.

Second, sexual reproduction increases the probability of genetic mutation. With each act of conception, life goes back to the very beginning. The DNA of both parents is split, reproduced, and recombined in an entirely new way. This process increases the frequency not only of copying errors—of mutation—but also of favourable mutations that can be exploited by the organisms involved. When required, the favourable mutations can be amplified through appropriate mate selection. Why sex? Because it is the way individuals can gain greater control over the genetic strategy.

Early Life in the Seas and on the Land

The Eukaryotic Revolution made possible the emergence of a remarkable variety of new and increasingly complex life forms. It provided the genetic technology for the second great wave of life that surged upwards, stagnated, and then collapsed between about 900 myrs and 245 myrs BP. It also enabled individual organisms to seek survival and prosperity through the application of the usual quartet of dynamic strategies. In the process, the eukaryotic paradigm was exploited until it was finally exhausted in the sense that no further access to natural resources could be attained with this "technology."

In the beginning the main dynamic strategy was genetic change. Eukaryotic life radiated out from simple beginnings to form increasingly complex and specialised species of plants and animals in the seas and on the land. What is most unsettling for the Darwinist is that all this remarkable genetic innovation and speciation occurred in the absence of serious competition and in the presence of an abundance of natural resources. What is more, this revolution occurred only once the earlier paradigm had been exhausted and the dominant bacterial form of life had collapsed. Of course, this decline was hastened, but definitely not caused, by the grazing activity of some eukaryotic life forms.

The Eukaryotic Revolution, therefore, was a response not to scarcity as the Darwinian model predicts, but to abundance. And the genetic strategy was pursued by eukaryote organisms to gain access to this abundance. They were like monopolists in pursuit of supernormal profits: the prospect of large returns and adequate time provide the incentive and the "funds" to innovate, whereas "normal (or subnormal) profits" under intense competition and shortrun time horizons are an incentive for conflict (the conquest strategy).

Once a new genetic technique for gaining access to natural resources had been developed, and a new species had been created, this technique—or genetic style—was exploited through the more efficient and quick-acting dynamic strategy of family multiplication. New species continued to emerge, however, until all possible genetic styles in the paradigm had been adopted. Once a new genetic style had been perfected by individuals in the new species, no further directional genetic change occurred. Eventually that style was exhausted and the species was extinguished. Sometimes add-on technology would be developed in response to the strategic demand generated by other dominant dynamic strategies. This was particularly so in the case of weapons of offence and defense required to facilitate the conquest strategy that emerged during the intense competition resulting from the exhaustion of a genetic style or genetic paradigm. Even the threat of final extinction for an entire dynasty—*extreme* Darwinian scarcity—was not sufficient to generate major genetic change as the master had predicted. This was because conquest was regarded as a more effective dynamic strategy when time and returns were of the essence.

Between 900 myrs and 245 myrs ago a remarkable variety of plant and animal life emerged in the seas and on the land. As the details are well known only the main developments will be sketched here. One of the earliest major life forms to exploit the eukaryotic paradigm was the protozoan (plankton), which appeared at about 800 myrs BP. Plankton emerged to gain access to food sources in the below-tide shallows around continents and islands—waters deeper than stromatolites could colonise. Then from about 700 myrs BP the metazoans—sponges, worms, and cnidarians—appeared in order to exploit food sources on the sea floors. And from about 600 myrs BP organisms with hard bodies (trilobites) and, later, skeletons (fish) developed to harvest the oceanic depths. During the following 100 myrs, as can be seen from Figure 2.1, there was a "spectacular burst of innovation" during which most existing body plans emerged.[13] By this time the once dominant stromatolites had become "quite rare".[14]

Paleontologists appear quite puzzled about the sudden appearance of organisms with hard bodies and skeletons. They are puzzled because Darwin's theory of natural selection is unable to explain these genetic innovations at a time of resource abundance. Paleontologists are forced, therefore, to seek non-Darwinian explanations while maintaining the fiction, to themselves as well as their readers, that their ideas are consistent with the concept of natural selection. The usual *ad hoc* suggestions—or flying buttresses to the cathedral of Darwinism—are that these innovations were the outcome of higher levels of oxygen in seawater that enabled the production of hard body parts for the first time through biochemical reactions, or of the need for defense against predators.

Neither argument is very persuasive as far as the development of skeletons is concerned. The dynamic-strategy argument, on the other hand, is more systematic and part of a larger explanation. Skeletons were needed by organisms to develop strong muscles in order to propel themselves more effectively through the seas or along the sea floors in search of new supplies of food. In other words, like all major genetic innovations, the development of skeletons was necessary to explore strategic opportunities in the constant pursuit of survival and prosperity. It was, therefore, a response to strategic demand—inputs required to exploit strategic opportunities—and was not driven by the abundance of resources itself. But, of course, it did exploit changing supply conditions. The dynamic-strategy theory is a single general demand-side theory rather than a series of *ad hoc* and partial supply-side hypotheses suggested, somewhat hopefully, by paleontologists.

The emergence of vertebrates with functioning jaws was essential for the great invasion of the land. It began about 500–400 myrs ago probably by millipedes and then by primitive fish (rhipidistians and lungfish) that gradually transformed their lower fins into limbs and certain internal organs into lungs, and became amphibians. While it is more efficient to extract oxygen from air than from water, this is not the reason these animals invaded the land. Once again it was the internally driven strategic pursuit of living organisms for access to more abundant resources both for food (there had been a prior explosion of land invertebrates, such as grubs, worms, and insects) and for shelter. Nor was it a result of Malthusian pressures, because, as the paleontologists tell us, "only *one* line of rhipidistians took this evolutionary path," and that "*aberrant* rhipidistians (or evolving amphibians) spent more and more time at and near the water's edge, sunning and basking, while *normal* rhipidistians remained creatures of open water".[15] Clearly those that remained were not all immediately extinguished.

Nevertheless these "aberrant" individuals were responding to the changing conditions in the seas and on the land as the second great wave of life gathered momentum. They were responding in an intuitive way to the material benefits and costs in their actual and potential environments. Between 500 myrs and 400 myrs BP (see Figure 2.1a) there was an exponential increase in the number of marine families—and, of course, in their species and populations—which would have increased the energy costs of access to resources. At the same time there was an explosion of plant and invertebrate life along coastal regions, thereby increasing the potential benefit for those "aberrant" vertebrates that could also make the transition from water to land. The important point, however, is that the exploitive response to these changing conditions—the driving force—was made by innovative individuals that some followed and others ignored.

Life possesses a strategic imperative that results in organisms actively seeking out an improvement in their living conditions. They are not just the playthings of external forces. In terms of my dynamic-strategy theory, the "aberrant" individuals are the strategic pioneers who "pursue" the genetic strategy to explore economic opportunities that consist of unused or underused resources for both food and shelter. This was not a matter of Darwinian survival of the fittest—because the "normal" individuals continued their old fishy way of life—but rather of the materialist pursuit of "supernormal profits" that accrue to those who can enter into the competitively restricted world of the innovating monopolist. In this context the Darwinian mantra sounds particularly hollow.

The Age of Reptiles

While the "aberrant" rhipidistians, or pioneering land strategists, had turned themselves into amphibians by at least 368 myrs BP, it was not until some of these had been transformed into reptiles by 350 myrs BP—a further attempt to improve access to natural resources—that the land invasion gathered momentum (see Figure 2.1b). This was the age of the reptiles and was the last phase in the exploitation of the eukaryotic paradigm by ectothermic life forms. In this period, from 350 myrs to 245 myrs BP, reptiles extended their dynasty to all those ecosystems—employed all those "genetic styles"—that were available to cold-blooded animals. The strategic *logos* became even more complex.

The reptile dynasty included species ranging from small herbivores such as *Trimerorhachis* (3 kg) to large herbivores such as *Ophiacodon* (150 kg), *Eryops* (175 kg), and *Diadectes* (250 kg), to predators such as *Sphenacodon* (60 kg) and the finned *Dimetrodon* (150 kg). Fins were employed by the latter to more effectively extract heat from a low sun at the extremities of the day and season.

So successful were the reptiles in gaining access to natural resources through these various genetic styles that by about 240 myrs BP they had exhausted the Eukaryotic/ectothermic Revolution. In other words this genetic paradigm could not be employed to extract any further energy and resources because it had, through the family-multiplication strategy, been taken around the accessible world. Any further resource-access by life forms would require a genetic paradigm shift. As for the reptiles, the exhaustion of their paradigm meant the stagnation of their dynasty and, ultimately, its extinction.

When a genetic paradigm approaches exhaustion, as reflected in a declining origination rate and a growing extinction rate, dynastic extinction normally follows. This is an outcome of the adoption of the conquest strategy which offers a short-term solution in these intensely competitive circumstances to the strongest individuals and species. Here we have the Darwinian scenario of intense competition, associated with the non-Darwinian response of conquest and anti-speciation. In the case of the reptiles, collapse occurred more suddenly than it might have done, harried as they were by a newly emergent and superior life form—the therapsids or protomammals. This is another example of the strategic struggle between the old and new dynamic strategists.

It is important to realise that the dynamics of life necessarily involves a process of rise and fall as genetic styles/paradigms are successively exploited and exhausted through the pursuit of a series of dynamic strategies. Physical catastrophes play only a marginal and non-systematic role in this dynamic process. While they might add their weight to a downturn that was going to happen anyway as a result of strategic exhaustion, they could never be responsible for *driving* a dynamic process of biological change. Hence, if the major volcanic eruptions in Siberia, roughly at the time of the collapse of the reptile dynasty, did have a short-term impact on life as some claim,[16] it was merely to reinforce the inevitable outcome of endogenous strategic forces. Life has its own dynamic and its own logosian laws that enables it to survive even radical changes in the physical environment.

THE ENDOTHERMIC REVOLUTION

The primitive reptiles lived and died at a pace that we would regard as unbearably slow and ponderous. They were slow-growing, slow-breeding, slow-moving, and slow-witted creatures possessing a slow metabolism. Their cold-blooded (ectothermic) biological system meant they were unable to colonise the Earth's colder regions towards the poles or on the higher slopes of low latitude regions. They were, in other words, unable to exploit the natural resources of all parts of the planet as warm-blooded animals can. Clearly there was still scope in the old "genetic option" (prior to the availability of the "technological option") for further development.

Cold-bloodedness, however, was not a disadvantage for as long as reptiles were the dominant form of life. But it would be an entirely new ball game if they ever had to face a competitor that could generate body heat internally. Such competitors would be unstoppable, because this new breed would be able to live and die at a furious pace. They would be fast-growing, fast-breeding, fast-moving, fast-digesting, fast-thinking creatures with a high metabolism. And as they could maintain a constant body temperature it was even possible that they might eventually be able to develop larger brains. They would also speciate more rapidly, would exhaust their genetic styles more quickly, and their carnivores would have the advantage of an early start and a late finish to their day and would not slow down during winter. They would also have greater speed and stamina. They would, in other words, be a "super race" of animals. As far as the reptiles were concerned it would be a complete mismatch. Yet this endothermic lifestyle has its costs as well as its benefits. It requires a higher input of food and it leads to a higher turnover of species and families.

The Protomammals

The Endothermic Revolution began with the emergence of the therapsids, or protomammals, at the end of the Permian period at about 245 myrs BP (see Figure 2.3). The first protomammals were "slender-limbed, wolf-sized predators," but they diversified rapidly by pursuing the genetic strategy and quickly sweeping aside the remaining cold-blooded reptiles that were struggling to cope with the collapse of their old paradigm. Within a few million years of the collapse of the age of reptiles—a period when there was no serious competition for resources—the protomammals "had taken over all the carnivorous roles—large, medium, and small—nearly all the herbivorous roles, and produced dozens of small insect-eating species as well".[17] This was the most rapid genetic diversification the world had yet seen, and it was an outcome of the Endothermic Revolution—of warm-bloodedness. Not only was their speed of emergence unprecedented, but the protomammals diversified to a greater degree—developed more genetic styles—than the old reptile dynasty. In the first few million years there were four families and eight to ten species of predators—including the anteosaurs (500 kg) and the gorgons (200 kg)—and five families with twenty or so species of herbivores—including the struthiocephalids (1,000 kg) and *Titanosuchus* (1,500 kg). But this faster pace of life, during which these genetic styles were exploited more rapidly, led to a high turnover of species and families. Protomammals, unlike the reptiles, actually generated three waves of rapid speciation and extinction between 250 myrs and their final disappearance by 200 myrs BP.

The dynamic-strategy model can explain how these waves of speciation and extinction occurred. The protomammals emerged only once the older paradigm had been exhausted and the reptilian species, which were going extinct owing to overpopulation of their ecosystems, were not being replaced by new species. In order to survive and prosper, the early protomammals adopted the conquest strategy to eliminate the remaining large reptiles in this great Permian strategic struggle. Owing to their greater speed, stamina, and logistical ability, the early protomammals quickly drove the remaining large reptiles to extinction.

Once this competition for resources had been eliminated—once they had created a non-Darwinian world—the protomammals, with time and resources on their hands, were able to diversify biologically by employing the dynamic strategy of genetic change to exploit food supplies in both warm and cold regions. Having created the optimum number of genetic systems, which gave access to all types of habitat, the protomammals switched to the family-multiplication strategy to exploit them to the full all around the globe. In this way they asserted their world dominance.

Once a species had spread around the world and exhausted its genetic style, the family-multiplication strategy led to overpopulation, degradation of their ecosystem, and to the adoption of an insidious form of the conquest strategy—civil war. Such conflict left a species vulnerable to a takeover by existing or

Figure 2.3. Predator-Prey Systems of Land Vertebrates—Past 300 myrs

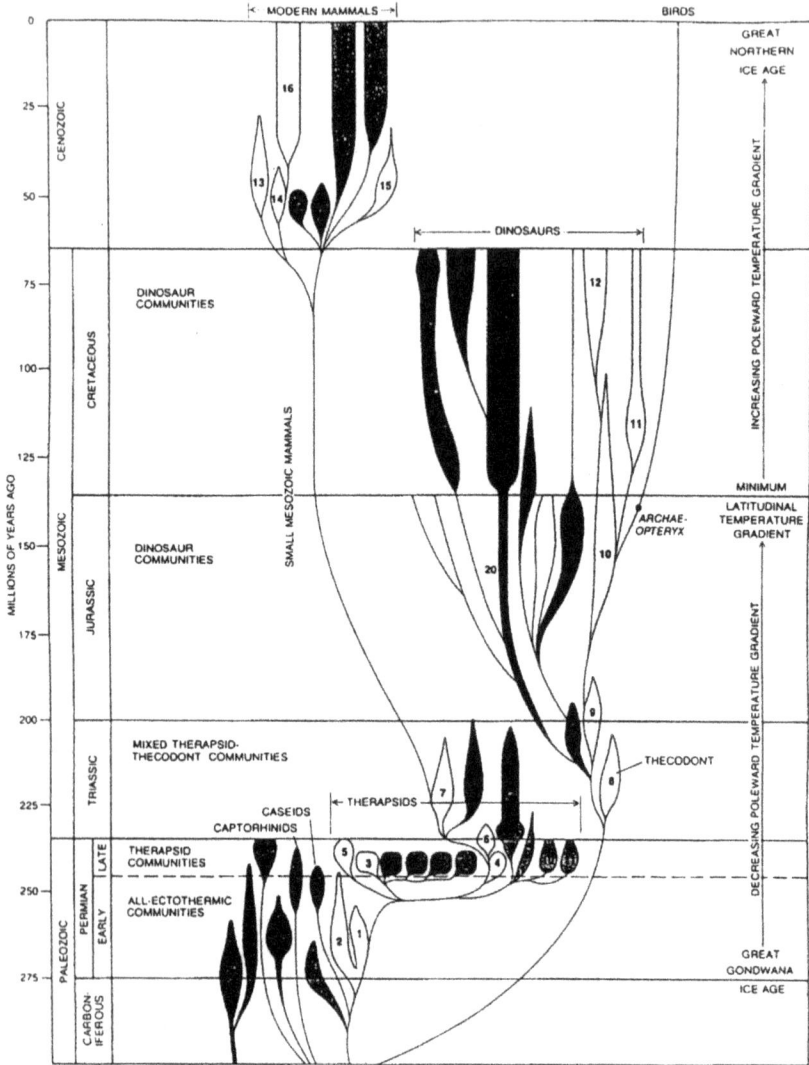

Source: Bakker 1978: 135 (with permission).

new species. When this genetic-style exhaustion was more general—when it took place in groups of species—the more usual conquest strategy was pursued, endangering entire orders and classes. This appears to have occurred on three occasions—at about 230 myrs, 225 myrs and finally 210 myrs BP—and may have occurred again but for the intervention of an opportunistic interloper, the archosaurs or "protodinosaurs."

It is interesting that once again intense competition—the Darwinian scenario—led not to genetic change and speciation but to conquest and extinction. When resources were scarce, life forms had no time to transform themselves biologically. In turn the resulting widespread extinction created a non-Darwinian world of minimal competition and abundance, which enabled diversification through genetic change. Once again natural selection is unable to explain the rise and fall of dynasties, families, or even species. There can be no doubt by now that Darwinism is as dead as these long extinct species. Essentially, Darwinists are "dead men walking".

The Age of the Dinosaurs

The age of the dinosaurs was built on the ruins of the first stage of the Endothermic Revolution. The protomammals had emerged rapidly and powerfully, and overwhelmed the remaining large reptiles, had flourished for a brief season (50 myrs!), had passed through a number of coordinated genetic styles, had embarked on a war with the upstart archosaurs, and had disappeared forever once they had exhausted their genetic paradigm. With one exception. The descendants of the carnivorous cynodont, which regressed in size from an 80 kg animal to a very small shrew-like nocturnal mammal about 10 cm long and 25 g in weight, departed from the therapsids before their demise to spend the following 160 myrs as very minor players on the margins of the main game.[18] To the archosaurs and the later dinosaurs the defeat of the protomammals appeared all but complete. This is one of the wonderful ironies of life.

The war between the protomammals and the archosaurs has been referred to as a "titanic ecological battle".[19] In fact it was the greatest and most destructive strategic struggle the world had ever witnessed, beginning at about 225 myrs ago during the Triassic period. Gradually the archosaurs—whose top predators included the erythrosuchid (300 kg) and coelophysid (200 kg) and the giant "crimson" (as its fossilised bones were stained red by the soil) crocodile that was terrestrial—advanced and the protomammals retreated, until by the late Triassic (about 215 myrs BP) the surviving protomammals had been reduced to a group of small to medium-small predators and herbivores.

Because the archosaurs won this great strategic struggle, it is usually concluded that the "protodinosaurs" had a biological edge over the protomammals. When viewed in terms of dynamic-strategy theory it is not clear that this is correct. The protomammals were unfortunate to encounter their determined adversary at a critical stage in their own development. They had, as we have seen, already passed through two earlier stages of expansion and extinction and appeared—as reflected in a declining "origination rate"[20]—to be facing the exhaustion of their entire dynastic paradigm. In this overpopulated and weakened state they were an easy target for the upstart archosaurs. But even so, the archosaurs could not have won this "world war" if they had not also shared the benefits of warm-bloodedness.[21]

With the demise of the protomammals, and the creation of a non-Darwinian world of minimal competition and of resource abundance, the triumphant new strategists—the archosaurs—quickly filled all accessible ecosystems with predators by the pursuit of the genetic strategy. By the late Triassic they had also branched out into heavily armed herbivores (aetosaurs). But, having won their great war against the protomammals and flourished briefly, they disappeared completely from the scene by about 210 myrs BP. Indeed, as can be seen from Figure 2.1b, by about 180 myrs the number of families of land animals was at an all-time low—lower than that achieved during the time of the most celebrated extinctions of 245 myrs and 65 myrs BP. Most paleontologists are at a complete loss to explain why.

The dynamic-strategy model, however, has the likely answer. Like all other endothermic dynasties, the archosaurs rapidly generated an optimum number of genetic styles through the genetic strategy and then even more rapidly exhausted them through the family-multiplication strategy, whereupon the resulting overpopulation and intense competition led to conquest and extinction. This process passed, as it did for the earlier protomammals, through a number of cycles until the entire dynastic paradigm for archosaurs had been exhausted. In the end a great "world war" broke out between carnivores and their prey, resulting in a deterioration of the environment and the extinction of the archosaurs. The extent of the environmental devastation accounts for the slowness with which the surviving true dinosaurs—which had branched off from the archosaurs in the mid-Triassic (about 225 myrs BP)—were able to diversify and expand. Indeed in the early Jurassic the fate of the dinosaurs appears to have hung in the balance.

Triumph of the dinosaurs

In the early Jurassic (200 myrs ago) the dinosaurs had the world before them. All their competitors—the protomammals and the archosaurs—were extinct and they were faced with an abundance of natural resources. After a shaky start they took up this non-Darwinian challenge, as all other dynasties did before and after that time, by adopting the dynamic strategy of genetic change. They had all the time and potential resources they needed to do so.

According to the most perceptive authority on dinosaurs, Robert Bakker, "a horde of new species" took advantage of these "ecological opportunities."[22] Hence, while "in the Late Triassic times the dinosaurs had been a minority group . . . in the Jurassic every single land predator and herbivore role was filled by their newly evolving species." He also argues that the speed with which this was achieved was only possible because dinosaurs were warm-blooded creatures. When first promulgated by Bakker this idea — together with convincing evidence — caused quite a stir because, in the main, his colleagues (together with popularisers such as Richard Attenborough) regarded dinosaurs as cold-blooded reptiles. But in fact they, together with the archosaurs and the protomammals (widely regarded as warm-blooded), were products of the Endothermic Revolution. It would be a remarkable backward step if the evidence had shown dinosaurs to be cold-blooded, because they and the archosaurs would have been no match for the warm-blooded protomammals. Other more direct evidence has recently emerged that confirms Bakker's hypothesis about the warm-blooded nature of dinosaurs.[23] A fossilised heart belonging to a *Thescelosaurus*—a four metre, two-legged herbivore found in Dakota in 1993 and acquired by the North Carolina Museum of Natural Sciences in Raleigh— was subjected to medical imaging techniques. The resulting three-dimensional images show that the heart was "highly advanced," being more like that of a mammal or bird than a reptile. Dinosaurs were certainly warm blooded.

The dinosaurs were able to take advantage of the strategic opportunities opened up to them once the devastating effects of the world war between the archosaurs had subsided. As is always the case in a non-Darwinian world of resource abundance, the dinosaurs energetically pursued the dynamic strategy of genetic change. The outcome was the generation of a diverse range of dinosaur genetic styles. The carnivores included, amongst others, the short-lived coelophysids (200 kg), the mighty allosaurs (3,000 kg), the small but vicious deinonychids (70 kg) and, later (about 100 myrs ago), the frightening *Tyrannosaurus* (2,000 kg). The more numerous herbivores included the early prosauropods (1,500 kg), the diplocids (17,000 kg), the camarasaurs (25,000 kg), the stegosaurs (3,000 kg), the brachiosaurs (40,000 kg), the ornithopods (2,000 kg), the ankylosaurs (2,000 kg), and the ceratopsians (2,000 kg). Of the herbivores the largest had gone extinct by the early Cretaceous (about 120 myrs ago) leaving their smaller, armed relations to struggle for survival against the fearsome tyrannosaurs. In addition to these land animals we should note the Pterosauria or flying dinosaurs that emerged in the Triassic period and, of course, *Archaeopteryx* (from the separate Theropoda line) that possessed feathers and is thought to have given rise to modern birds. Hence by the end of the Jurassic (145 myrs ago) the dinosaurs had effectively generated a sufficient number of genetic styles to fully exploit all ecosystems available to land and air-bound creatures in both warm and cold climates. No other dynasty had, until that time, been able to spread so widely throughout the world or to exploit so effectively the Earth's natural resources. It is interesting that the dinosaurs had no interest in returning to the seas, possibly because reptiles (sea and swan lizards) in the oceans did not suffer the same disadvantages of those on the land.

As with the protomammals, the dinosaurs generated a number of waves of species diversification and extinction. The species that emerged in the early Jurassic—particularly the early predators and the gigantic, long-necked herbivores—were extinct by the early Cretaceous. Paleontologists appear puzzled about the causes of these waves of extinction: Bakker for example, refers to it as "the *mysterious* hand of worldwide disaster."[24] Yet, as we have seen, they can be explained quite simply by the dynamic-strategy theory, which focuses on the exploitation and exhaustion of dynamic strategies. These earlier versions were replaced by the heavily armored, low-grazing herbivores and by the king of the carnivores, *Tyrannosaurus rex*.

Robert Bakker, in his usual innovative fashion, has argued that this changing of the guard had a profound effect upon the nature of the Earth's vegetation.[25] The replacement of high-browsing, long-necked brontosaurs by low-grazing, beaked herbivores conferred an advantage on plants that could grow quickly to heights above grazing level and that could distribute their seeds widely onto overgrazed areas to produce fast-growing plants that could extend out of reach before the low-grazers returned. The early angiosperms met both these requirements and thereby gained a competitive advantage over the longer-established gymnosperms that included conifers, cycads, and tree ferns (see Figure 2.2). Once they gained a foothold, the angiosperms employed the familiar dynamic strategies of genetic change, family multiplication, commerce, and even conquest (by invading the territories of other plants and plundering their sunlight, water, and other nutrients) to populate the Earth with a vast variety of species and individuals. Like animals, plants diversified in the absence of intense competition.

As with every pre-existing dynasty the dinosaurs substituted the family-multiplication strategy for the genetic strategy once a genetic style had been successfully created. In doing so members of that species spread gradually around the accessible world. Only once the genetic style had been exhausted and overpopulation had occurred did individuals switch from family multiplication to conquest. An interesting feature of the dinosaurs' conquest strategy was the demand it generated for weapons of offence and defense. While there were insufficient time and resources to employ genetic change for speciation it could, and was, employed to develop "add-on" technology. Add-on technology is easier, quicker, and cheaper than a strategy required for complete genetic transformation. What we have here, therefore, is genetic change designed to support the zero-sum game of conquest, rather than an independent strategy designed to give direct and revolutionary new access to natural resources.

The conquest strategy of the dinosaurs generated a strategic demand for either additional armor or more effective defensive weapons in herbivores, or sharper/larger teeth and claws or more powerful jaws in carnivores. There were a number of stages in the development of this "military technology." In the conquest strategy of the Jurassic, herbivores such as the stegosaurs developed war-club tails with spikes about a metre in length, together with sharp defensive triangular-shaped plates along their backbones, while those species without armor developed slashing claws and powerfully long lashing tails. The carnivores, such as the allosaurs, were as large as elephants, were fast and agile, had large powerful jaws, and possessed slashing claws on their hind legs.

In the period of Cretaceous conquest the herbivores were also able to deal out as good as they had to take. The nodosaurs were heavily armored with large shoulder spikes, the ankylosaurs were built like small tanks with war-club tails, the pachycephalosaurs had giant bony head domes that were used like flying projectiles, and the *Triceratops* were built like giant battering rams with monstrous heads and metre-long horns. With all this offensive and defensive armor, the top carnivore had to be a frightening creature. And it was. *Tyrannosaurus* stood six metres tall, was as heavy as a small elephant, yet was fast and nimble with huge, powerful jaws and, a major advantage, stereoscopic vision. Both sides in this conflict were equipped for Armageddon—a world war that ended the era of the dinosaurs.

The role of genetic change in the conquest strategy of the dinosaurs was just the same as the role of technological change in the Roman conquest strategy. It was a response to military demand. Conquest is a strategy to gain control over resources, not through new methods of gathering, hunting, or production, but through plunder that accrues to more effective techniques of waging war. It is fascinating how closely the offensive and defensive weapons developed genetically by the dinosaurs paralleled those developed technologically by the Roman (and other ancient) conquerors: tank-like structures, battering rams, flying projectiles, armored and armed foot soldiers, and armored cavalry with lances.

Extinction of the dinosaurs—a new explanation

This brings us to the relatively sudden extinction of all dinosaurs—with the sole exception of the line that developed into modern birds—around 65 myrs ago. Within the space of probably five hundred thousand years the mighty dynasty of dinosaurs that had flourished for more than 135 myrs was brought to a dramatic end that has fascinated the expert and layperson alike. As we have come to expect, natural scientists argue that large-scale extinctions are the result of exogenous physical events. It is curious that not one of them, even among those concerned with plants and animals, is prepared to grant living organisms the dignity and credit of being responsible for their own rise and fall. Also the list of external physical causes of extinction is rather long and there is little agreement on the subject. Everyone has his/her own pet hypothesis.

As Robert Bakker has said of his own colleagues:

> I keep a file of published "solutions" [to the problem of dinosaur extinction]. Among its contents, it is suggested the dinosaurs died out "because the weather got too hot;" "because the weather got too cold;" "because the weather got too dry;" "because the weather became too hot in the summer and too cold in the winter;" "because the land became too hilly;" "because new kinds of plants evolved which poisoned all the dinosaurs;" "because new kinds of insects evolved which spread deadly diseases;" "because new kinds of mammals evolved which competed for food;" "because new kinds of mammals ate the dinosaur eggs;" "because a giant meteor smashed into the earth;" "because a supernova exploded near the earth;" "because cosmic rays bombarded the earth;" or "because massive volcanoes exploded all round the earth."[26]

We could also add: "because a Death Star returns regularly every 26 myrs".[27]

Yet what has Bakker, after a long career devoted to reconstructing the lives of the dinosaurs in an interesting and exciting way, got to offer that differs from this natural scientists' wish-list? As it turns out, not a great deal. Bakker's conclusion that "some shift in the habitat must have doomed the dinosaurs" is a truly great disappointment.[28] Like all his colleagues in the natural sciences, Bakker fails to see, despite marshalling all the evidence that can be used as the basis for a radically new and realistic interpretation, that the answer lies *within* rather than *without* the dinosaurs themselves. These scientists all suffer from a form of myopia called Darwinism. They are all too busy building buttresses around the crumbling cathedral of Darwinism to see the obvious.

Bakker conveniently summarises the chief characteristics of the impact of major extinctions.[29] They:

1. kill on land and sea at the same time;
2. strike hardest at large, fast-evolving families on land;
3. hit small land animals less hard;
4. leave large cold-blooded animals untouched;
5. do not strike at freshwater swimmers—most of these creatures are cold blooded;
6. strike plant-eaters more severely than plants.

He also investigates the changing structure of families and species in the lead-up to all major extinctions, and finds that the universal pattern is one of initial faunal "evenness" (or diversity) followed by a decline in evenness ending in collapse.[30] This collapse took thousands to millions of years. While all this is good historicism it leads to the wrong conclusions because it is forced into a Darwinian straitjacket.

But at least these facts do eliminate the popular catastrophe stories about asteroid impacts[31] and massive volcanic eruptions,[32] because the timing is not right (would take only years or decades to deliver a death blow), and because too many species on the land and in the water survived. In any case there have been other catastrophes in the past and they have had no long-term impact on life; and most earlier extinctions were not associated with catastrophes. Of course, the suggestion that an unidentified "Death Star" returns every 26 myrs[33] to precipitate a deadly shower of comets (that conveniently leave little trace) is just out of this world! Some natural scientists clearly prefer to invoke metaphysical ideas rather than to empirically examine the dynamics of life forms on Earth.

Like Bakker, most paleontologists reject the catastrophe stories of the few, and opt for the idea of extinctions being induced by climatic change brought about by the physical dynamics of the Earth expressed through continental drift. In this vision, catastrophes are, at most, only the final blow to a system operating under stress from climate change. As Bakker, more than any other, is responsible for changing our perceptions of the lives of the dinosaurs, his hypothesis is outlined in more detail.

Bakker argues that, owing to a cooling of the planet around 65 myrs ago, the oceans fell, the shallow seas drained off the continents, separate continents were connected by land bridges or island chains, and the weakening of mountain-building forces reduced barriers to migration. This sequence of events led both to the extinction of shallow sea animals and to an exchange of land animals between the emerging modern continents, which in turn led to an outbreak of disease and to takeovers by certain species at the expense of others.

In the light of the richness of the information that Bakker has uncovered about dinosaurs, this extinction explanation is extremely disappointing, and not all that different from those on his ridicule list. And despite his closing rhetoric—"The grand rhythm of extinction and reflowering of species on land and in the sea must surely go to the earth's own pulse and its natural biogeographical consequences"—his hypothesis cannot be regarded as a general theory.[34] Like all other natural scientists, Bakker overlooks the grand *internal* rhythms of life. A close study of life—like his own study of the dinosaurs—shows that the physical environment merely establishes the rules by which the game of life must be played, and it is up to the players—the various life forms—as to if and how this game is to be played. This interaction between the physical rules of the game and the players is explored in detail in my book *The Dynamic Society* (1996).[35]

In the end, the explanation provided by Bakker—of the changing rules of the game of life—is no different in kind to those provided by other natural scientists about asteroids, volcanoes, and climatic change. The point is that none of these events is able to shape the *systematic* rise and fall of species or of dynasties. This rise and fall is, as argued throughout this book, the outcome of an endogenous dynamic in life, which is played out within the protective strategic *logos*. The ball is in the players' hands. It is this internal dynamic that explains the success of the dinosaurs as well as their ultimate extinction. What I am arguing is that the dinosaurs would have risen and fallen in the absence of any one or all of these external happenings, even if they actually happened. At the very most they might have acted, either individually or together, as a marginal influence, a final straw in the extinction of the dinosaurs. But they will never account for the dynamics of life of which the age of the dinosaurs was an interesting and important part.[36]

The dynamic-strategy theory provides an entirely new explanation for the fossil evidence, without resort to convenient catastrophes. It does so by focusing on the internal dynamics of life forms. We have already seen how individual dinosaur species or groups of species exhausted their genetic styles after about 5 to 6 myrs through the rapid pursuit—made possible by warm-bloodedness—of the family-multiplication strategy; and then how, through population pressure, the herbivores degraded their environment and terminally weakened their ability to survive, and how the carnivores overkilled their prey and suffered accordingly. Once the entire endothermic paradigm, of which the dinosaurs were the third great dynasty, approached exhaustion, unsustainable pressure was placed on available natural resources, and there was an increasing degradation of the global environment, a loss of ecological balance, and a widespread adoption of the conquest strategy. This led to a "world war" between the various species of the dinosaur dynasty. It was a struggle to the death. Not just of individuals but of entire species, families and, ultimately, of the dinosaur dynasty itself. This world war raged with varying degrees of regional intensity for hundreds of thousands, even millions, of years. And at its conclusion the global environment was devastated and not a single dinosaur was left standing. Only the ancestors of modern birds that had sought refuge in flight survived into the age of the mammals.

In the execution of this world war, the military technology of the dinosaurs, both herbivores and carnivores, was brought to deadly perfection. This was genetic change in support of the dynamic strategy of conquest—a response, in other words, to strategic demand. As food sources for the armored herbivores diminished under intense population pressure, they turned upon each other. One can imagine the clash between the giant *Triceratops* (5,000 kg) as they charged at each other with their huge heads (more than two metres in length) lowered and their metre-long double horns deployed to kill the intruder on their diminishing territory. No Darwinian nonsense here about the evolution of male weapons through "sexual selection" for access to the females. The prime *imperative* was survival, not sex. Also we can visualise the king of the carnivores, *Tyrannosaurus*—heavy as a small elephant but as agile as a prize-fighter—desperate to bring down its heavily armored prey with its massively powerful jaws. And as these prey declined in numbers to critical levels, *Tyrannosaurus* began to turn on its own kind as they battled over degraded territories.

Victory, no matter how glorious, was ultimately hollow as the great dynasty of dinosaurs continued its long and inevitable journey into eternal night. Much as Rome was to do, and for the same reasons, between AD180 and 476. In the process, much of the world's vegetation at one time or another was destroyed, some (such as the cycadeoids) permanently. Plants recovered fully only after the warring dinosaurs had fought each other to extinction.

Mammals and protobirds escaped the worst effects of the dinosaur wars. Like other small societies (such as Switzerland during the twentieth century) they were "neutral." Mammals lived in logs and burrows and fed on insects and worms that remained largely unaffected by the carnage. Any difficulties experienced were probably balanced by the declining attentions paid to them by their traditional dinosaur predators such as the turkey-sized *Stenonychosaurus*. Protobirds could use flight to escape the combatants and to seek protection in the larger trees or higher crags and to locate diminishing food supplies. Small reptiles were able to find refuge in logs, under rocks, or in the ground, while some of the larger reptiles retreated to the depths of inland waters or even put out to sea. While the survival of these animals is an embarrassment for the catastrophe and the climate-and-habitat-change theorists, it can be easily and consistently explained using dynamic-strategy theory.

Nor does the apparent coincidence of widespread extinctions in the seas as well as on the land present the stratologist with a problem. It should be realised that marine animals—particularly the long-bodied sea lizards and the long-necked swan lizards that we know experienced waves of expansion and extinction[37]—went through a similar dynamic process to land animals. That extinctions in the seas and on the land coincided at some point in a period that extended over millions of years should not surprise us. The endogenously generated decline would have been exacerbated for shallow-sea creatures that were unable to move into deeper oceanic waters—particularly plankton, sponges, and shellfish, but not the sea lizards—by the new "ice-house" period that emerged from about 68 myrs BP with its growing polar caps, falling ocean levels, and diminishing continental shelves. Yet while there may have been a marginal role for physical events for certain types of shallow-sea and continental-shelf creatures, they played no significant role in the fluctuating fortunes of ocean-going and land-based animals that could move as physical conditions changed. Even Darwin recognised this.[38] Life, it must be concluded, is driven by an internal dynamic rhythm. A dynamic rhythm presided over by the strategic *logos*.

The Age of the Mammals

The age of the mammals is the fourth and most recent cycle of biological expansion to take place within the endothermic paradigm. As we have seen the first three—those of the protomammals, the archosaurs, and the dinosaurs—flourished for a season, exhausted their versions of this genetic paradigm, collapsed and disappeared. Each cycle was more complete and impressive than its predecessor. Each cycle involved greater genetic finetuning of the same endothermic paradigm.

This process of biological baton-passing is central to the "great wheel of life"—discussed more formally in chapter 3—whereby a dynasty emerges to exploit a genetic paradigm, exhausts their version of it, collapses and is followed in the same way by a new dynasty operating within the *same* paradigm (Figure 3.5). The great wheel of life rotates without gaining traction, without being able to generate a new paradigm shift to replace the old exhausted paradigm. Without gaining more intensive access to the Earth's natural resources. This eternal recurrence, of dynasty replacing dynasty without generating further significant progress, is a sure sign that the "genetic option" which began with life some 3,850 myrs ago had finally been exhausted—that it was no longer possible to gain further access to natural resources through genetic change alone. When the age of the mammals dawned, following the collapse and extinction of the dinosaurs, this new endothermic dynasty promised to go the same way as the rest.

If life had relied only on the genetic option it would never have escaped the eternal recurrence. New dynasties would have emerged as old ones disappeared and would have gone through the same strategic process with only slight physiological variations. And the great wheel of life would have continued turning in space, until the Sun finally engulfed the Earth.

But, towards the end of the age of the mammals, something remarkable happened. Although there was no key innovation behind the radiation of the mammals, they carried with them, completely by accident, the potential for the greatest innovation of them all—intelligence. But even this did not lead to a new genetic paradigm shift as in the past, whereby the innovating species (in this case mankind) generates a large number of genetic styles. There is only one extant species of man. Rather the emergence of intelligence enabled the most intellectually advanced line of the mammals to replace the genetic option with the "technology option", which was to spawn a series of "technological paradigm shifts" (or economic revolutions) and, within each of these, a series of "technological styles". This process is discussed in detail in chapter 3.

Clearly the importance of the technology option was that it enabled one line of mammals to break free from the great wheel of life and to escape the fate of all previous dynasties of endotherms—the fate of extinction. If the dynasty of mammals had not discovered the technology option, there can be no doubt they would have collapsed and gone extinct once they had re-exhausted the endothermic paradigm. This would have provided some other species with its chance of escape, even if it were a very, very slim chance.

From the very beginning the mammals relied to a far greater degree than their predecessors on intelligence in the pursuit of their dynamic strategies. They depended on **finesse** rather than **force**. While mammalian strategies were the same as those pursued by other dynasties, they were undertaken more effectively because of this emphasis on finesse. The point is that finesse requires larger brains. But why did the mammals favour finesse? To answer this question we need to go back to the time of the dinosaurs. During their long exile throughout the age of the dinosaurs, the shrew-like mammals had to live by their wits as their main predator appears to have been the relatively large-brained—literally bird-brained (not a term of abuse in the dinosaur age)—*Stenonychosaurus*.[39] The interaction between these two adversaries probably led to the increase in brain size of both. But it was the smaller mammalian creature that was forced to specialise entirely in finesse in the pursuit of its dynamic strategies. The larger *Stenonychosaurus* only needed to use finesse when force failed, which was not often enough.

Once *Stenonychosaurus* was extinct, the mammals had no intellectual peer; and once the entire dynasty of dinosaurs had passed into oblivion the mammals could come out of hiding and use their intelligence to more effectively facilitate the usual sequence of dynamic strategies—genetic change, family multiplication, commerce and, when necessary, conquest. With their greater intellectual potential the expanding mammals were able to head off a short-lived challenge from large flightless birds and savage crocodiles, both survivors of the dinosaur age. But it remained to be seen whether mammals could employ this intelligence to discover the technology option before their version of the endothermic paradigm was exhausted. If not they would be extinguished and the great wheel of life would continue to turn slowly, silently, and unobserved.

The role of the Endothermic Revolution was critical to the eventual success of the mammals in this unwitting race between brain size and paradigmatic extinction. The fabric of advanced brains, as is well known, is sensitive to even modest changes in temperature. While it functions well at $37°C$, a drop of just $5°C$ of body heat causes higher cerebral activity to become erratic, while an increase in temperature by the same amount will damage brain tissue. Constant body temperature made possible by the Endothermic Revolution, therefore, was a prerequisite for the development of large and sophisticated brains. Yet while the precise control of body temperature was a necessary condition for the emergence of intelligence it was not a sufficient condition. And it was a passive rather than an active force. The prime role in this, as in all dynamic issues, is played by strategic demand generated by an unfolding dynamic strategy within the strategic *logos*.

Animals with small brains can pursue successful dynamic strategies, but animals with large brains can pursue them more flexibly, creatively, and effectively. Primitive mammals had, during the late Cretaceous, finally outwitted their dinosaur predators. And it would appear that this lesson was not lost on their Cenozoic or modern descendants. The greatest prizes in this new era went to those who had the most powerful brains. Strength, size, ferocity, and defensive and offensive weapons were all important, but intelligence was even more so in the strategic pursuit of the mammals. *It was the age of finesse rather than force.*

Intelligence was a response to strategic demand generated by those individuals who were pioneering the exploitation of strategic opportunities opened up by the demise of the dinosaurs. And as new species emerged from the pursuit of the genetic strategy they took with them a greater intellectual capability than the dinosaurs had ever bothered to do. Most of this brain development occurred in the centres of higher learning—in the cerebral lobes— which were responsible for improving the effectiveness of the strategic pursuit.

Enlargement of the brain appears to have occurred at speciation, that initial phase in which individuals pursued the genetic strategy in order to gain favourable access to natural resources. And the size of the mammalian brain increased from species to succeeding species. Hence, the modern jaguar has a brain twice the size of the saber-toothed cats of some 30 myrs ago; and, among the hominids, modern humans have a brain twice the size of that of *Homo habilis* about 2.4 myrs ago. The reason for this steady increase in brain size is that success in the strategic pursuit by a mammalian species depended not on the sheer size, strength, or effectiveness of its weapons, but on the more subtle ability to outwit one's opponent, both individually and in groups, **and** to pursue one's dynamic strategy with finesse. Sheer, crushing force was being replaced by degrees with a more subtle and skilful execution of the strategic pursuit. But, of course, when finesse failed, force was—and still is—employed.

This emphasis on finesse rather than force can be seen in the characteristics of the first wave of mammals that replaced the dinosaurs during the early Cenozoic. The ferocity of the predators, which included the creodonts (10–200 kg), the miacids (20 kg), and the mesonychids (100 kg), paled in comparison with the tyrannosaurs (2,000 kg) that were ten times larger than the largest of the early mammal carnivores and possessed offensive weapons that would have terrified and destroyed them. Even the later mammalian carnivores—the wild cats and dogs (10–200 kg)—would have been no match for their dinosaur counterparts. Similarly the mammalian herbivores were also small and relatively docile. Compare the early condylarths (1–100 kg), the coryphodontids (400 kg), the perrisodactyls (10–1,000 kg), or even the unitantheres and titanotheres (up to 5,000 kg) with the brachiosaurs (40,000 kg). It is significant that the larger early mammal herbivores, such as the titanotheres, did not survive the end of the Eocene (35 myrs BP), because they lacked the necessary finesse to adapt to changing environmental conditions. Even the more modern herbivores (such as elephants, hippos, and rhinoceroses) cannot compare with the size, ferocity, and armor of their dinosaur counterparts. True, there was a brief mammalian experiment with a megafauna consisting of giant herbivores (mammoths, rhinos, marsupials) and giant carnivores (saber-toothed tiger), but none of these relied on dinosaur-like weapons and all of them proved to be more vulnerable to large-brained hominids than their smaller counterparts. They were all driven to extinction by that master of finesse, *Homo sapiens*, between fifty and one thousand years ago. Once we get to the modern era, individuals in some 90 percent of all mammal species weigh less than 5 kg. In the mammalian world force is no match for finesse.

The Emergence of Man and Civilisation

We come now to those experts in finesse among the mammals, the primates. Early primates were small, tree-dwelling animals that hunted insects on narrow branches high in the canopies of trees. Even today most primates fit this description. Interestingly, primates are most closely related to tree shrews and bats, which are also tree-dwellers. It would appear that primates continued where premodern mammals left off—living obscurely by their wits in the forests far from the main action on the savanna, where the larger herbivores and, hence, carnivores roamed. Who could have imagined that these insignificant creatures would ever move to, let alone dominate, centre stage? The sight of an unarmed primate was enough to make even a hyena laugh. The emerging characteristics of the primates, from which the anthropoids—the higher primates including man—arose, are: a larger brain size than other mammals owing to the more rapid growth of brain relative to body at the foetus stage; the development of considerable dexterity in the use of hands and feet as they leapt from branch to branch; the use of hands (the "opposable thumb") to grasp rather than to lunge at their prey and risk injury from falling; the development of stereoscopic colour vision from the hunting of small insects; and the production of small numbers of offspring that develop slowly and live for a relatively long time, thereby enabling the creation and propagation of knowledge from generation to generation. All these characteristics were important in the employment of dynamic strategies that enabled anthropoids to cope effectively with their changing environment and, eventually, in discovering the technology option.

From early primates to modern man

The story of the origin and development of primates down to modern man changes significantly from decade to decade as new fossils are discovered. And it will continue to do so. This need only concern us if any new evidence contradicts the realist dynamic theory we are employing. Certainly, the continuous stream of additional fossil evidence that has emerged over the past three decades has not done that.

At the time of writing, it was generally thought that primates emerged in Africa during the Paleocene (65–56 myrs BP) and thereafter migrated to Asia and North America (where they died out). Recently (early 2009), a debate arose about whether *Darwinius massillae* (or "Ida"), which is a 47 myr-old fossil found in the Messel pit near Frankfurt in Germany, is the "missing link" between lemurs (prosimians) and our own evolutionary line of monkeys, apes, and humans (simians)—between humans and the rest of animal life. It has also been argued that North Africa—this time during the Eocene (56–35 myrs BP)—was the location of the origin and initial radiation of the anthropoids (monkeys and apes). Surviving anthropoids include Old World monkeys (cercopithecoids), New World monkeys (ceboids), and hominoids, which include gibbons, apes, and humans. The likely ancestor of Old World monkeys—and of *Proconsul* which led to the hominids—is *Aegyptopithecus* (the "Dawn Ape"), a small anthropoid, about 33 to 35 myrs old, discovered near Cairo. The primates that migrated to South America in Oligocene times (35–23 myrs BP) eventually gave rise to the New World monkeys but not to any ape-like species.

Living hominoids include the hylobatids (gibbons), pongids (only the orangutan, or Asian ape, survives), panids (African apes, gorillas, and chimpanzees), and hominids (only *Homo sapiens* survives). According to DNA evidence, hominoids split off from the Old World monkeys during the Oligocene at about 33 myrs BP, the gibbons departed at about 22 myrs, the orangutans at about 16 myrs, and the hominids somewhere between 10 myrs and 6 myrs BP. The sparse fossil evidence, particularly between 30 myrs and 18 myrs BP, suggests later dates for all these speciation events. Some argue that hominids and panids (chimps and gorillas) may have parted company as recently as 3.5–4 myrs ago.[40] Certainly we share anywhere between 94 and

99 percent of our DNA with the panids—which strongly supports my idea that human intellectual development has nothing to do with Darwinian supply-side arguments about genes, and everything to do with demand–side arguments about the central role of strategic demand generated by different dynamic strategies and different *logoi*.

Amongst the earliest apemen so far discovered are *Ardipithecus ramidus* and *Australopithecus anamensis*, who emerged in Ethiopis (4.3 to 4.4 myrs BP) and Kenya (4.2 myrs BP) respectively. They had brain capacities about the size of a modern chimpanzee. *Ardipithecus ramidus* was probably the more primitive of the two, living in the forest, while *A. anamensis* was almost certainly bipedal. Both were displaced by *A. afarensis* ("Lucy") around 3.7 myrs BP. In turn *A. afarensis* succumbed to the forces of extinction about 2.5 myrs ago and was succeeded by *A. africanus* in South Africa from about 2.8 myrs BP and by *A. garhi* in East Africa, who is known to have been a meat-eating scavenger employing crude stone tools at about 2.5 myrs BP.[41] Both species of apemen appear to have existed for about 1 myrs.

While there are particular difficulties with the fossil evidence at 3–2 myrs BP, it appears that at this time either *A. africanus* or *A. garhi* gave rise to the first true human, the large-brained *Homo habilis*, sometime before 2.4 myrs BP, followed by *H. ergaster* ("working" man) and *H. erectus* at about 2 myrs (or so) BP. They were the first humans to migrate out of Africa into Eurasia, possibly as early as 1.9 myrs BP.[42] In the Middle East and Europe these species gave rise to *H. sapiens* (archaic) about 300,000 years BP and *H. neanderthalensis* about 120,000 years BP; in China to Peking man about 500,000–300,000 years BP; and in Southeast Asia to Java man about 1,000,000–500,000 years BP.

Finally in this genealogy, *H. sapiens sapiens*, or modern man, emerged in South Africa about 150,000 years ago from *H. ergaster/erectus*, and possibly separately in Asia as well. We do know that modern humans moved out of Africa and encountered their distant relative, Neanderthal man, in the Middle East at about 100,000 years BP. The genetic difference between the two is about four times greater than we would expect between individuals in our own species. Then around 40,000 years BP, modern humans moved north into Europe and within 15,000 years Neanderthal man was extinct.[43] Indeed, each stage in the emergence of modern humans appears to have been accompanied by the elimination of earlier stages. Intelligence was employed as an offensive weapon in the line of primates called hominid.

A remarkable growth of brain power

The important issue here is not the precise timing of the emergence of new primate species—the story changes slightly with each new fossil find—but the tendency for each new genetic strategy to be characterised by larger brain capacity. By 18 myrs BP, for example, a small species of *Proconsul*, which is thought to have been the ancestor of the higher apes, had a body weight of only

9 kg but a baboon-sized brain of about 167 cc. It was a tree-climbing, fruit-eating animal that may have spent some time on the ground, and have been able to stand upright when required.[44] Once again this larger brain must have provided the flexibility to cope with the exchange of animals both northwards and southwards when Africarabia docked with Eurasia during the Miocene (23 myrs to 5 myrs BP). From the north came giraffes, advanced deer, and other ruminants (cattle, etc.), and from the south departed elephants and hominoids.

It is possible to provide a quantitative outline of the growth of intelligence over the past 18 myrs. Reflected in Table 2.1 and Figure 2.4 are a number of fascinating features regarding the change in hominoid brain size. The first of these is the transition from constant *rates* of brain growth between *Proconsul* and *Ardipithecus ramidus* (18 myrs to 4 myrs ago) to exponential *rates* between apeman and early man (4 myrs to 2 myrs ago), and back to constant rates between early man and modern man (2 myrs to 150,000 years). Certainly nothing had prepared the world for this sudden acceleration of growth *rates*, nor for the increase in brain complexity in these add-on parts, from the appearance of the first apemen to the first appearance of modern humans. The past 150,000 years is also interesting because, after the emergence of modern humans, the rate of brain growth, for the first time since the extinction of the dinosaur dynasty, actually fell to zero.

Table 2.1 Growth Rates of Hominid Brain Size—Past 18 myrs

Period	Brain size	Absolute increase in brain size per generation	Compound growth rate
(myrs BP)	(cc)	(cc)	(% per myrs)
18	167	—	—
4	400	.00042	6.4
3	450	.00125	12.5
2	650	.00500	44.4
1	925	.00688	42.3
0	1350	.01063	46.0
Entire period			12.3

Source: Figure 2.4 and text.

The second interesting characteristic is that, while sounding impressive, these growth rates are based on time units of one million years each. If we think about what this means in terms of increases in absolute brain power per generation the achievement appears much less impressive. By arbitrarily imposing our concept of a generation—of about twenty-five years—on the data, we can see from Table 2.1 that brain size increased by only 0.0004 cc per generation during the 14 myrs before the emergence of the first apeman. While this absolute increase for each generation is very small, the important point is that it continued to accumulate generation after generation for some 560,000 cycles. Yet even these marginal increases gave each generation of hominoids an edge over other mammals in their determination to survive and prosper. And of course the generational increase in brain size grew significantly during the four million years from apeman to modern man: a 25.3-fold increase from 0.0004 cc to 0.01 cc per generation. It is also suggested in Figure 2.4 that the increase in hominid brain size took place through a series of escalating steps as each new species replaced its progenitor.

The dynamic-strategy story

What accounted for this sudden increase in the size and complexity of hominid brains from about 3–2 myrs ago? And why did this growth rate level off at about 2 myrs ago and decline to zero from about 150,000 years BP? The acceleration in intelligence was due to the transformation of apemen's family-multiplication strategy. Until this time their existence both as individuals and as a species was precarious owing to their small and scattered populations. At about 3 myrs BP *Australopithecus* probably numbered no more than a few thousand individuals located in the rift valley of East Africa and in coastal South Africa. If they were to increase the probability of their survival as individuals and families, it was essential to be able to extend their territorial range, increase their populations, and improve their control over resources.

Figure 2.4. Ascending the Intellectual Staircase—Past 5 myrs

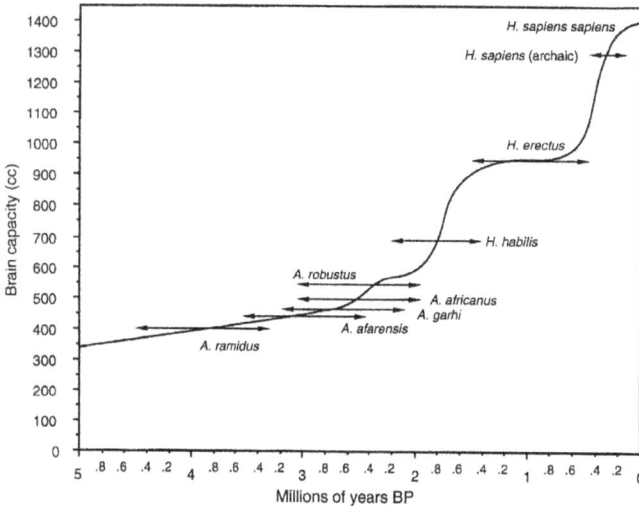

Source: Snooks 2003: 188.

To achieve this would require a revolution in their family-multiplication strategy. While hominoids had always attempted to improve their prospects through improved intelligence—the reason for the slow but steady increase in brain size—from about 3 myrs BP their intelligence level appears to have passed the threshold that enabled them to make major advances in implementing their dynamic strategy. In addition, greater strategic flexibility was required owing to the changing climate (cooler and drier) and vegetation (advancing savanna) caused by a new ice age at about 2.5 myrs BP.

The breakthrough in the family-multiplication strategy was achieved by transforming it from a highly specific to a very general instrument of survival and prosperity. The higher primates had become very specialised in their diet and habitat, living on fruit, leaves, and nuts in tropical forests. With the emergence of apemen there is evidence that this diet was supplemented with high protein foods such as crabs and crocodile eggs to be found around lake shores in those fairly wooded, well-watered regions. But even this extension of diet and habitat would have limited the range over which apemen could have safely migrated. Certainly there was no possibility of their migrating to the cooler, drier, grassland regions, which were later occupied by *Homo*.[45]

This existential fact changed forever when the decision was made by some families of apemen to take up meat eating. Meat-eaters were not limited by a specific diet and associated habitat, because they were able to consume those animals that were highly specialised consumers, wherever they might live. In other words, the family-multiplication strategy based on meat-eating is a far more general strategy than one based on the eating of specific nuts, fruit, and leaves. This revolution in diet liberated hominids from their birthplace and enabled them to spread rapidly throughout the world.

But it did even more than this. By revolutionising the basis of their family-multiplication strategy, some apemen were transformed into true men. What I am arguing is that the genetic change underlying the leap in intelligence was a response to the strategic demand generated by the family-multiplication strategy. The *raison d'être* for genetic change is always the attempt to gain greater access to natural resources, and it is pursued either as a strategy in its own right when resources are abundant following a mass extinction, or as an input—a "strategic instrument"—into another dynamic strategy, as in this case. This genetic change was required by apemen so that they could break out of their original primate environment and pursue their family-multiplication strategy in the rest of the world. In doing so they took their first great step in asserting their independence from the environmental constraints of life. Of liberating their strategic *logos* from its regional shackles.

The essential point here is that the sudden increase in brain size was a response to systematic changes in strategic demand and not to *ad hoc* changes in supply as suggested by some scholars.[46] It has been recently argued by other scholars that hominids were able to increase their brain size, without increasing overall energy intake, by releasing energy constraints through meat eating, either by reducing the size of the gut to allow a transfer of resources for brain-building or by enabling mothers to supply high-protein nourishment through the placenta before birth and through breastfeeding after birth.[47] In other words, meat eating, by reducing the constraints on brain size, was the driving force in the sudden increase in intelligence. Others prefer the idea that cooked tubers rather than meat "prompted the evolution of large brains".[48] Similar supply-side arguments have been advanced in earlier publications.[49]

As usual these *ad hoc* supply-side arguments are incapable of explaining the forces and timing behind any increase in the use of resources. The problem here is that supply-side forces are not treated as part of a general dynamic theory. These arguments are the biological equivalent of the catastrophe hypotheses of the physical scientists and paleontologists—involving *ad hoc* forces external to individual life forms. Ironically these supply-side arguments are also non-Darwinian and sound very Lamarckian to my ear—an increase in protein in mothers' milk allows an increase in brain size that can be passed on to future generations. Apart from the random reference to "evolution" or "natural selection" these scholars have in reality abandoned Darwin. Certainly they do not, indeed cannot, explain how mother's milk is related to natural selection.

In contrast, my argument about the adoption of a new diet by the apemen is part of the general dynamic-strategy theory that has been used to explain the fluctuating fortunes of life over the past 3,800 myrs. Strategic demand called into being larger brains and all other anatomical changes—a smaller gut and richer mothers' milk—required to facilitate it, together with the associated technological ideas (fire, weapons, tools) and socioeconomic organisation. Where there is a strategic demand there will always be a supply response, owing to the higher returns offered. Yet, while strategic demand creates its own supply, supply cannot create strategic demand.[50]

The importance of the decision of some apemen to generalise the family-multiplication strategy by meat-eating/high-intelligence/technological change can be seen more clearly against a backdrop of the majority of apemen—such as *A. robustus* (1.8–1.5 myrs BP)—that stuck to the old specialised family-multiplication strategy based on nut-eating/low-intelligence/technological-stagnation. The chewing power involved in grinding down hard nuts and tubers required small front teeth but massive molars, which in turn required a robust-shaped face with large jaws and a ridge on the top of the skull to anchor strong jaw muscles. Although *A. robustus* had a brain slightly larger than *A. africanus*, a contemporary, they did not require one as large as that developed by the meat-eating generalists. Hence, the different substrategies of family multiplication led to very different physical (including brain) changes. This is a very important conclusion because it shows how genetic change is an outcome of the strategic pursuit—of choices made by strategists. Unfortunately for *A. robustus* they made the wrong choice and disappeared from the fossil record around the time that the large-brained *H. habilis* appeared. The "big-brains" outsurvived the "big-jaws." Finesse triumphed once again over brute strength.

But exactly what path did this strategic revolution take? Essentially the decision to adopt meat eating in order to transform the family-multiplication strategy required greater organisation and technological abilities than formerly possessed by apemen. This transition took place in a number of stages. The first stage was based on the use of scavenging techniques. Scavenging required teamwork and primitive weapons, such as sharpened sticks and heavy clubs, to "persuade" carnivores to surrender a large carcass, and to keep other scavengers at bay. Also as apemen were not well equipped with the necessary teeth and claws to butcher a carcass, they needed to fashion sharp rocks for this purpose. They also required tools to extract marrow from bones, and they had to master fire to make meat eating easier and more palatable. There is clear evidence that scavenging was employed by *A. garhi* in East Africa at least 2.5 myrs ago.[51]

This substrategy finally bore fruit at least by 2.4 myrs BP when a large-brained hominid "suddenly" emerged. This was *Homo habilis*, possibly the first in our own line (*Nature* 2007), who possessed a brain 50 percent larger than *A. africanus*, but still only about half the size of that of modern mankind. The structure of the economy and society of early man bore a close resemblance to that of modern man before the emergence of civilisation (about 10,600 years ago) and of modern hunter–gatherer societies down to the present. They formed small kinship groups in which the males supplied meat through competition with other scavengers, and the females gathered fruit, nuts and roots and they bore and suckled the children.[52] These family groups foraged over increasingly longer distances searching for large carcasses that they brought back for butchering to central locations equipped with crude shelters protected by barriers made from thorn bushes.

Scavenging, however, is not a secure basis for globe-trotting. It is not always possible to find a freshly killed carcass just when required. To employ a viable generalised family-multiplication strategy it is necessary to be able to successfully hunt large animals on the open savanna. This placed significantly higher demands—strategic of course—on the intellectual capability of the African apemen. Hunting large and dangerous animals requires even more effective teamwork, particularly the abilities to plan and communicate clearly and precisely. No doubt this was the beginning of primitive but effective forms of language. Improvements were also needed in social structure—the emergence of leaders and greater specialisation and division of labor—and in tools and weaponry. All of these matters established a strategic demand for higher intelligence.

A major breakthrough occurred about 2 myrs ago with the appearance of *Homo ergaster/erectus*. It involved a significant increase in brain size of about 37 percent over *H. habilis* and, just as important, this occurred particularly in the regions of problem-solving and language.[53] This growing intellectual capability led to a shift in mankind's economic role from scavenger to hunter—a shift as revolutionary in our history as that from hunter to farmer some 10,600 years ago, and from farmer to industrial worker about 200 years ago. These transformations reflect more fundamental changes taking place in the strategic *logos* of humanity. For the first time in the entire history of life on Earth, a door had been forced open that might just lead to an escape from the eternal recurrence through the transcendence of the genetic option. The hunting (or paleolithic) revolution was the first technological paradigm shift in hominid—indeed life—history.

The new substrategy of hunting is reflected in the new stone tools (the Acheulean type) fashioned and employed by *H. erectus*. These included more sophisticated butchering, cutting, and scraping tools, together with deadly looking heavy axes and cleavers. It is thought that they also employed other hunting weapons fashioned from less durable materials, such as wood and bone, that have not survived.[54] And they used fire, both for cooking and, no doubt, for managing the savanna grasslands.[55]

Because of this strategic breakthrough—which called into being greater intelligence, technology, and a more effective economic and social organisation—*H. erectus* not only became the world's leading predator (displacing the saber-tooth tiger and eliminating other hominids) but also the first hominid to pursue the family-multiplication strategy outside Africa. This was the first "great dispersion" of mankind and it took *H. erectus* around much of the Old World, reaching the Middle East by 1.9 myrs BP, eastern Asia by at least 700,000 (possibly 1,800,000) years BP, and Europe sometime later. And *erectus* carried his strategic *logos* with him.

To take the great dispersion to its logical conclusion—crossing great rivers and lakes, small seas, large mountain chains, and surviving extreme climates—the dynamic strategy of family multiplication generated strategic demand for even higher levels of intelligence. Consequently, by about 500,000 to 300,000 years BP Peking man in China had a brain size of 1,100 cc, about 80 percent of that of our own species, and by about 150,000 to 120,000 years BP both Neanderthal man and modern man had brain sizes of up to 1,400 cc.[56] In early *H. sapiens sapiens* this greater intelligence can be seen reflected in the manufacture of more efficient stone tools (involving the Levallois technique by which long flints were extracted from within suitable rocks), a greater control over the animals they hunted, more effective management of their physical environment, improved methods of communication, and more sophisticated social, economic, and political organisations (groups) and institutions (rules).

The birthplace of modern humans

There is considerable controversy over whether modern man emerged only in South Africa and spread throughout the world, replacing the descendants of *H. erectus* in a second great dispersion, or whether our species emerged in various parts of the world—including Africa, the Middle East, China, and Southeast Asia—at about the same time. In contrast to the majority, I prefer the regional theory to the replacement theory because it is a natural outcome of the strategic story I am outlining in this book. My argument is that as human societies in different parts of the Old World—*H. erectus* did not get to the New World—struggled to extract the most from natural resources through family multiplication, they employed both genetic change and technological change as strategic instruments. There is no reason that this would have occurred only in South and East Africa. Neanderthal man, who had a slightly larger brain than modern man, demonstrates this. Also my theory suggests that Neanderthal man in Europe (and Denisovian man in Asia) was eliminated by our forebears owing not to their superior intellect but to a slightly more effective substrategy. While Neanderthal man in Europe hunted wild cattle and lived in fixed settlements, our forefathers lived a more nomadic life by hunting reindeer and salmon that required the development of a wider range of weapons and tools. The reasons that one succeeded and the other failed after some 12,000 thousand years of competition (prior to 25,000 BP) are no different to those that account for success and failure in competing civilised societies (such as ancient Rome and Carthage, Macedonia and Persia, or medieval Venice and Genoa). The issue here is strategic rather than genetic. The outcome depended on which society possessed the superior strategic *logos.*

Recent DNA analysis of the Neanderthal genome (*Science,* 2010) does not change this interpretation of the fate of Neanderthal man. My analysis is based on 2 myrs of historical evidence concerning the way individuals and groups have behaved, together with the application of an empirically derived realist **general** dynamic theory. In contrast, the interpretation of natural scientists and their intellectual groupies, is based on an ad hoc approach to individual pieces of fossil evidence (each new discovery is hailed as changing our view of evolution!), together with the use of partial and conflicting theories. Nevertheless, it is now generally accepted (subject to possible modern human DNA contamination) that 1 to 4 percent of the genome of modern Eurasian humans (but not of sub-Saharan Africans) is shared with our Neanderthal cousins. This is not a very large percentage, and it must owe something to our common ancestry. But, having said this, a degree of interbreeding is to be expected, as it is consistent with the interpretation of annihilation. History has shown repeatedly that hostile groups invading the territories of competitors usually kill all the males and children and take the females as booty. Assertions by popularisers that our ancestors made "love not war" is ludicrous.

The strategic dynamic that led independently to both Neanderthal man and "African" man could also have led in other parts of the Old World to the independent emergence from *H. erectus* of modern man who subsequently migrated to the New World. The reason that the out-of-Africa, or replacement, theory is preferred by most natural scientists is that it seems to fit modern Darwinist theories about peripheral isolates—that genetic change occurs in a geographically isolated population, which on later contact eliminates the larger parent population.[57] But, as I have shown in *The Collapse of Darwinism* (2003: pts I and II), the Darwinist theories cannot be sustained.

Why did the human brain stop growing and why doesn't it matter?
Before passing onto the next question, about the abrupt cessation of brain development about 150,000 years ago, we need to clarify the transitional

period over the previous 2 myrs when *both* the genetic *and* the technology options were involved in human development. This transition began with the emergence of *H. erectus* and it ended with the appearance of *H. sapiens sapiens*. During these 2 myrs mankind employed both genetic change and technological change as dual instruments in the application of the family-multiplication strategy. Although the hunting (or paleological) revolution had begun about 2 myrs ago with the emergence of *H. erectus*, it could not be taken to its logical conclusion—the maximum population that could be supported by a hunter–gatherer lifestyle—without further joint increases in both genetic and technological change. But after the emergence of *H. sapiens sapiens* about 150,000 years ago, the size and complexity of man's brain were sufficient not only to exhaust the paleolithic revolution but also to launch and follow through with the neolithic (or agricultural) revolution (10,600 BP) and the modern (or industrial) revolution (1780–1830).

The major question about hominoid genetic change is: why in the past million years did the *rate* of growth of brain size slow and actually come to a halt about 150,000 years ago? This is usually glossed over by Darwinists, because natural selection is not the answer. Those who do attempt an explanation do so in non-Darwinian terms, such as the physiological constraints on foetus head-size imposed by female pelvic dimensions. This is not very persuasive as female anatomy changed considerably between *A. afarensis*—when females were only half the size of males—and *H. sapiens*, and could have changed still further in 150,000 years if strategic demand had so required.

The real answer is strategic in nature. One line of modern mammals had by 150,000 BP finally achieved what the dinosaurs had been unable to do: to replace their exhausting genetic paradigm with a technological paradigm. By 150,000 years ago our hominoid line had reached the level of intelligence required to pursue the hunting paradigm to the ends of the Earth. In other words, the strategic demand for genetic change generated by the family-multiplication strategy dried up after the emergence of modern man. The reason is that, when the paleolithic technological paradigm was finally exhausted—when all accessible hunting lands in the Old and New Worlds were finally used to capacity about 10,600 and 7,000 years ago respectively—it was found that human intelligence was sufficient to generate a new economic revolution or technological paradigm shift without any further genetic change. This neolithic (or agricultural) revolution involved the domestication of wild grass seeds and certain wild animals. And again, when the neolithic technological paradigm had been exhausted in the late eighteenth century in Western Europe—when all accessible agricultural lands throughout the world had been used to capacity—it was found that human intelligence was sufficient to generate the industrial technological paradigm shift known as the Industrial Revolution. Accordingly there was no further strategic demand in either of these revolutions for increases in intelligence, only for increases in technological ideas.

As strategic demand creates its own supply in the longrun, technological ideas were forthcoming and genetic "ideas" remained static.

In each of these technological paradigm shifts (or economic revolutions) the human race, through its transformed strategic *logos*, was able to transcend the old exhausted paradigm so as to release the hidden potential of the Earth's natural resources. And it was able to do so without making any further strategic demand for increases in brain size or complexity. The reason is that, once the threshold brain size has been reached, the technological strategy is a more precise, predictable, and precipitous instrument than the old genetic strategy. It is a strategic instrument that can be used to totally transform the world within the span of one lifetime rather than the hundreds of thousands of generations necessary under the genetic strategy.

In all other respects both strategies are very similar. For example, the new technological strategy, like the old genetic strategy, was employed in its own right only once scarcity had been removed. Once the paradigmatic breakthrough had been made, the technological strategy (like the genetic strategy in earlier times) was employed to develop all the technological styles (comparable to genetic styles) required to exploit natural resources in different circumstances. In the neolithic revolution, for example, these included wheat/barley and cattle in the Middle East; corn, pigs, and dogs in Mesoamerica; and rice, poultry, and oxen in Southeast Asia. Once fully developed these technological styles (like the old genetic styles) were exploited through the familiar family-multiplication strategy until they were exhausted. Further progress for individual societies and for human civilisation in the pre-modern world depended on the successful pursuit of either the conquest or commerce strategies. This led to the "great wheel of civilisation" that rose and fell without gaining traction—without generating any long-term increase in prosperity (that is, more intensive access to natural resources, measured in terms of real GDP per capita), only the short-term increase in monopoly profits that occurs in this zero-sum game as great conquest (Assyria, Rome, Macedonia, Tenochtitlan) and commerce (Egypt, Phoenicia, Carthage, Greece, Venice) societies rise and fall as part of the human eternal recurrence.[58]

Just as mighty animal dynasties were doomed to the eternal recurrence until one dynasty was able to develop that rare commodity, intelligence, so the mighty human societies were doomed to the circular motion of the great wheel of civilisation until one society, Britain, was able to develop and adopt *industrial* technology. Throughout the past two centuries, the industrial technological paradigm has spread steadily around the world, at first in Western Europe and its colonial settlements in North America and Australasia, then in Eastern Europe, and now in eastern and southern Asia. Without the "Intelligence Revolution" the mammal dynasty would have collapsed by now and have become extinct just like the dinosaurs; and, without the Industrial Revolution, Western civilisation would have collapsed and become extinct just like the ancient Egyptian or Roman societies. And without the forthcoming Solar Revolution (see chapter 13), global civilisation will collapse under the weight of the massive intervention policies of the metaphysically oriented climate-mitigationists.

The patterns and dynamic explanations of both life and human society are very similar. Which is why any dynamic model that claims to be able to explain one part of life *must* be able to explain *all* parts of this great pageant. To be able to explain the collapse of the dinosaurs or the sudden increase in hominid brain size 3–2 myrs ago, it is necessary to employ a theory that can also explain the rise and fall of Rome, of Greek democracy, of any of the great religions, of the USSR, together with what the future may bring for our species and our society. These among many other matters, both great and small. On the other hand, how do Death Stars, sundry catastrophes, cooked tubers, gut reduction, mothers' milk or, indeed, natural selection, stand up to this challenge? Obviously not very well at all. It is essential to realise that human society is neither "artificial" nor special, as Darwinists claim in order to rationalise their obvious failure to explain its origins and development. Like it or not, human society is an integral part of the entire pattern of life on Earth.

One final point about the interaction between the genetic and the technological strategies is worth raising here. As we have seen, once mankind achieved the threshold level of intelligence necessary to substitute the technology option for the genetic option and, thereby, to break free from the eternal recurrence, we were unable to achieve any higher level of intelligence. We are only as intelligent as was necessary to invoke the technology option. And the basic reason is this, that life does not attempt to maximise its IQ only to maximise the probability of survival and prosperity of its individual organisms. Only in the future might it be possible to maximise both through genetic engineering. But even this possibility may never be fulfilled because of the huge risks involved in changing the structure of our brains. It will be less risky and more economical to continue to focus on technological or artificial intelligence (AI) rather than genetic intelligence. In this matter, like everything else, continued survival and prosperity will only be achieved if we respond to the requirements of the strategic *logos*, rather than the dictates of false prophets.

WHERE IS IT ALL HEADING?

It is clear from this survey of life's unfinished odyssey, that the pattern of the past is more complex than most scholars have recognised. Yet at the same time there is an endogenous regularity and predictability that can be chartered and persuasively modelled. But only if we abandon Darwinism in all its forms. Darwinism can be replaced using the inductive method employed here to develop a single dynamic theory to explain the history not only of life but also of human civilisation. It is a theory that can even be employed to make sensible predictions about the future of both. In chapter 3 the main patterns of the past are identified, and in chapter 4 they are used to develop a realist general theory of life. In turn this theory has led to the discovery of the strategic *logos,* which is modelled and discussed in chapter 5.

Chapter 3
Patterns of the Past

The greatest enemy of progress is the eternal recurrence.

Over the past 3,800 million years (myrs), carbon-based life forms have flourished on this planet, despite its difficult environment. In the course of this great odyssey, life has been transformed from very simple organic forms into highly complex and intelligent structures. While life as a whole has been extremely successful, individual species, populations, societies, and dynasties have emerged, flourished for a brief season, and then suddenly disappeared. Until recently we have been unable to explain the rise and fall of major life forms. This has generated in our species a profound anxiety about the future, which, I have argued, is responsible for the creation of mankind's many myths and religions, and for its massive interventions such as climate change mitigation. This chapter, which presents a diagrammatical sketch of the patterns of the past based on the story of life on Earth presented in chapter 2, provides the foundation for the theoretical chapters in this book. In contrast, deductive theorists (such as orthodox economists) base their theoretical structures on assumptions, hunches, and guesses.

THE PATHWAY OF LIFE

The pathway of life over the past 3,800 myrs possesses three sets of characteristics. First, there is the rate of acceleration of life, which I call the "logological constant"; second, there are the very long-run fluctuations by which this development occurs, called here the "great waves of life"; and finally, there are the biological and technological paradigm shifts—the "great steps of life"—which make the entire odyssey of life possible. It was by observing, recording, and analysing these pathway patterns that I was able to construct a general dynamic theory capable of explaining and predicting the fluctuating progress of life, which in turn led to the discovery of the strategic *logos*. As we shall see, the greatest enemy of progress is the eternal recurrence.

The Logological Constant

The most remarkable aspect of life is its ability to thrive in an extremely difficult physical world—a world dominated by entropy, or increasing disorder, and subject to random physical shocks. This has only been possible because of the entropy-defying, shock-resisting life system that I have called the strategic *logos*. It is the *logos*—a dynamic system of interaction between a community of organisms and their societal system—that protects and sustains life. Without the *logos*, biological/technological transformation would be impossible, and individual life forms, even if they managed to emerge, would be swept away by a hostile physical world.

Second only to the ability of life to thrive in a hostile physical world, is its capacity to develop at a constant exponential rate. My research in the early 1990s revealed that each major biological transformation during the history of life on Earth (see Figures 3.2 to 3.4) took only one-third of the time taken by its predecessor.[1] It was also discovered that the geometrically declining duration of these paradigmatic transformations was accompanied by an approximately proportional increase in biomass (species population multiplied by average weight).[2] This geometric increase in biomass is the outcome of greater access by organisms to the planet's natural resources made possible by either, or both, genetic change and technological change.

The relationship between global biomass and time was expressed in my book *The Dynamic Society* (1996) as:

$$y = a \ (3^{t-1})$$

where y is global biomass generated by genetic and technological change over the past 3,800 myrs and t is time. This has been called the Snooksian algorithm.[3] What this algorithm tells us is that the biomass generated by nature and human society is accelerating at a constant rate. In 1996, these results were also plotted on both arithmetic and logarithmic scales and are reproduced as Figure 3.1. While the growth of Earth's biomass over 3,800 myrs is exponential—thereby approaching the vertical on the right-hand side of the arithmetic curve—it is also log-linear—in this case an approximately 45° straight line in the logarithmic box.

What can be called the "coefficient of acceleration of life" is approximately 3.0. As mentioned earlier, this means that each great wave of biological/ technological progress—and its underlying technological paradigm shift— occurs in just one-third of the time take by its predecessor (Figures 3.3 to 3.5). In other words, while the dynamic process of life generates an increasingly larger quantity of global biomass per unit of time, its compound (or geometric) rate of growth is constant. This is true under both the "genetic option", which prevailed before 2 myrs BP (before present), and the "technology option", which prevailed thereafter (Figures 3.3 and 3.4).

This constant rate of biological transformation, as measured by the coefficient of acceleration, is what I have called the "logological constant". It is the great constant of life generated in a hostile physical world by the strategic *logos* (hence the name). This constant of nature is the outcome of what I have elsewhere called the Law of Cumulative Biological/Technological Change, which states that the relationship between a series of genetic/technological paradigm shifts is geometric owing to the cumulative effect generated when the "technological" (either genetic or industrial) output of one paradigm becomes the input of the next.[4] A parallel concept in the physical world is the "cosmological constant" governing the expansion of the Universe. But while the engine of change in the cosmos is vaguely ascribed to the presence of mysterious "dark energy", that driving life and society is analysed transparently here with a realist general dynamic theory.

Figure 3.1. The Logological Constant—Past 4,000 myrs

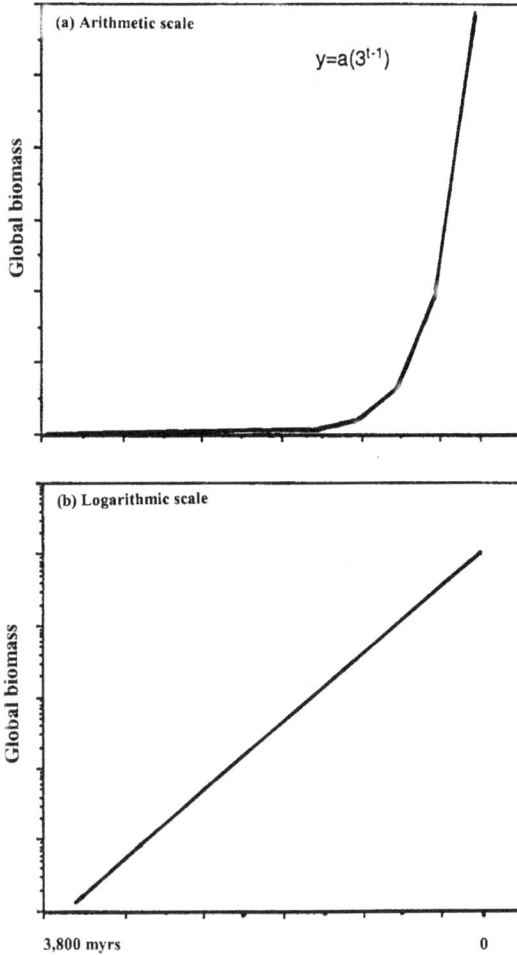

$$y=a(3^{t-1})$$

(a) Arithmetic scale

(b) Logarithmic scale

3,800 myrs   0

Sources: Snooks 1996: 80 & Snooks 2010b: 279–81.

The logological constant is a measure not only of biological/technological transformation, but also of the effectiveness of the strategic *logos* in generating the great odyssey of life. The strategic *logos*, which operates according to its own laws (see Chapter 6), is, therefore, able to provide life with a degree of independence from the laws of physics. Consequently, the expansion of life can be understood not in terms of physical laws but only in terms of the laws of life and history. These laws have been isolated, presented, and discussed in my books *The Collapse of Darwinism* (2003) and *The Laws of History* (1998a).[5]

The Great Waves of Life

The great odyssey of life over the past 3,800 myrs has occurred in a fluctuating but systematic manner. Figure 3.2, which is based on the discoveries of paleontologists concerning the fluctuating diversity of the Earth's flora and fauna, shows that life has proceeded by what I have elsewhere called the "great waves of life". With the progression of time, those great waves have experienced a geometric reduction in duration and expansion in amplitude.

Figure 3.2. The Great Waves of Life—Past 4,000 myrs

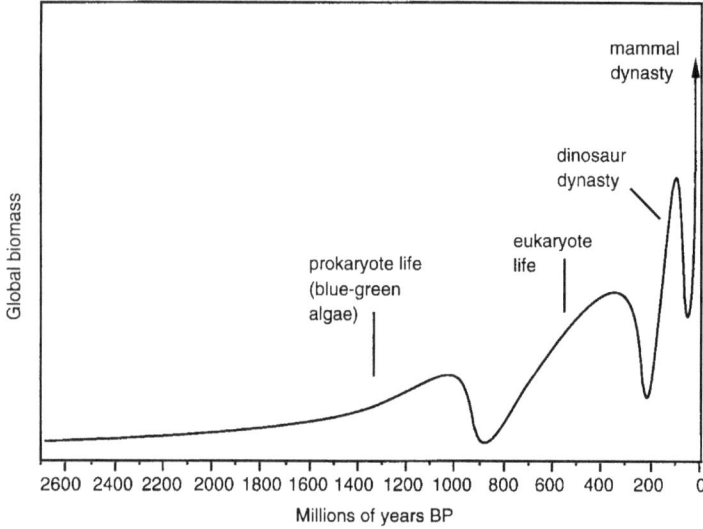

Source: Snooks 1996: 75.

The dynamic "timescape" presented in Figure 3.2 shows a series of four great waves of biological activity: the first is about 2,000 myrs in duration; the second about 600 myrs; the third about 180 myrs; and the fourth, which is by no means complete, about 60 myrs. While it is not possible to provide a precise vertical scale, the available evidence suggests that the reduction in duration—each great wave is about one-third as long as the one that preceded it—is matched by a proportional increase in global biomass. There can be little doubt, therefore, that the momentum of life on Earth is accelerating, owing to the increasing access to natural resources made possible initially by genetic change (the "genetic option") and more recently by technological change (the "technology option").

Either this systematic relationship between the great waves is purely coincidental or it is powerful evidence that it is endogenously determined, rather than being exogenously and randomly driven by natural catastrophes or fortuitous genetic occurrences. In *The Dynamic Society* (1996) I first argued that this systematic pattern is not coincidental but that it is driven by a powerful endogenous mechanism embedded in a dynamic life-system that I now call the strategic *logos*. The endogenous mechanism is discussed in Chapter 4, and the strategic *logos* in Chapter 5.

To understand the great waves, we need to identify the main turning points in life, when one major dynasty of life gave way to another. These transformations, as shown in chapter 2, include the shift from prokaryotic life (blue-green algae) to eukaryotic life (plant and animal organisms) at about 900 myrs BP; the shift from ectothermic life (cold-blooded reptiles) to endothermic life (warm-blooded protomammals) at about 245 myrs BP; and the replacement of dinosaurs with mammals at about 65 myrs BP. Other setbacks, such as the widespread extinctions around 435 myrs, 370 myrs and 215 myrs BP constitute major fluctuations within the great waves, just as more minor fluctuations can be detected within the major fluctuations, and so on. It is a system of waves within waves, all generated by an endogenous dynamic mechanism. Exogenous shocks were only responsible for minor distortions to this pattern. These biological transformations have been discussed at length in my book *The Collapse of Darwinism* (2003).

LIFE'S DYNAMIC MECHANISMS

There are two important dynamic mechanisms that help to explain the odyssey of life over the past 3,800 myrs. They are the "great steps of life"—the great genetic and technological paradigm shifts—and the "great wheel of life". One leads to biological and economic progress, and the other to the eternal recurrence. Both play a central role in life's dynamics.

The Great Steps of Life

The dynamic structure of life—reflected in Figures 3.3 to 3.5—is defined by a series of genetic and technological paradigm shifts, which I call the "great steps of life". These great steps, which outline the genetic/technological potential for biological/economic development, are driven by the major genetic/technological revolutions that I have examined in detail in *The Dynamic Society* and *The Collapse of Darwinism*. Owing to the logological constant discussed above, these great steps have been changing exponentially in two dimensions: increasing in height while reducing in depth. What this reflects is the accelerating dynamics of both life and human society over the past 3,800 myrs. Each great step, in other words, is not only greater, but is taken more quickly than its predecessor. In this sense, history is speeding up.

There have been three genetic paradigm shifts (Figure 3.3) and three technological paradigm shifts (Figure 3.4) since life began on Earth. And they are involved in a systematic geometric relationship. This pattern of change suggests that a new technological paradigm shift will occur soon—sometime in the middle decades of the twenty-first century—and that it will be completed rapidly, probably within a generation. I have called this forthcoming paradigm shift, the Solar Revolution; and its relative impact on the world will be even greater than that of the Industrial Revolution, owing to the exponential nature of the "logological constant". I first discussed the probability of this future development in *The Dynamic Society* (1996: ch. 13), and developed the evidence and argument in *The Coming Eclipse* (2010a).

Figure 3.3. The Great Steps of Life—Past 4,000 myrs

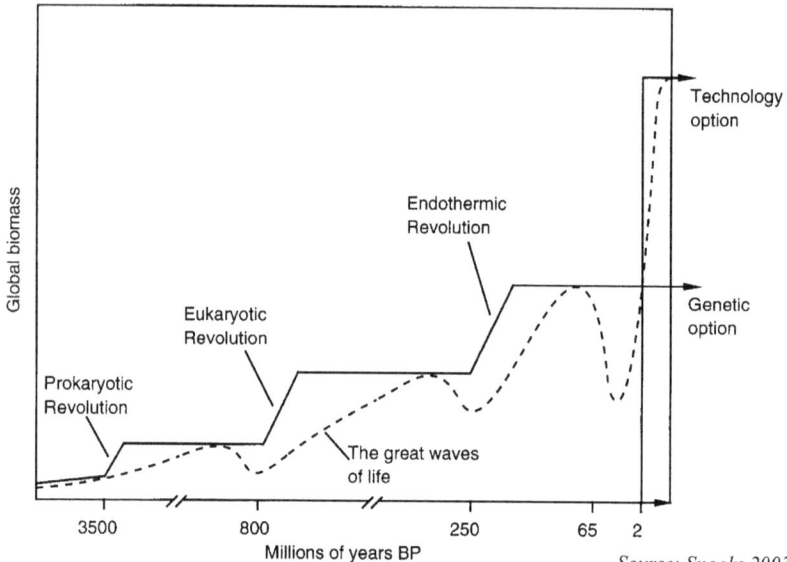

Source: Snooks 2003: 252

Figure 3.4. The Great Steps of Life—Past 80 myrs

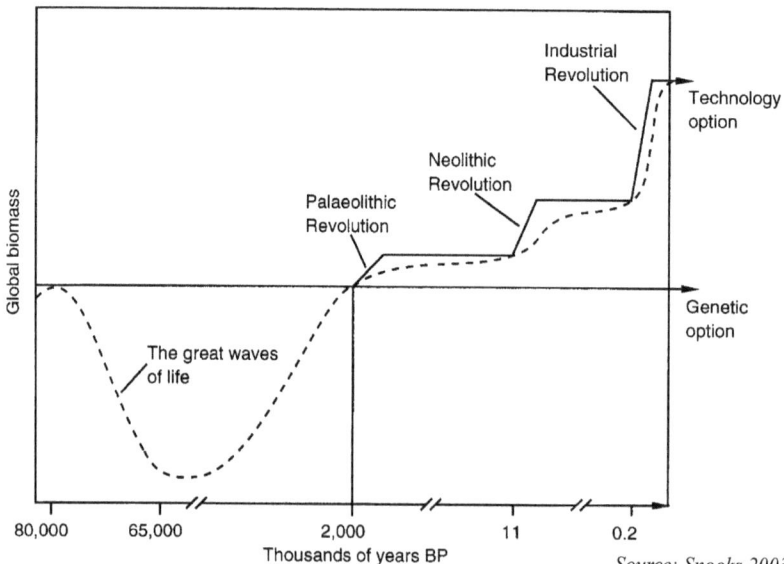

Source: Snooks 2003: 253

The genetic paradigm shifts are part of the "genetic option" and the technological paradigm shifts are part of the "technology option". Each "option" has dominated the progress of life on Earth. With each paradigm shift, the capacity of the genetic option was progressively exploited by life forms until it was finally exhausted around the time the dinosaurs were in their prime about 80 myrs ago. The technology option, however, only displaced the defunct genetic option when the intellectual capabilities of the hominids enabled them to employ the technological strategy, sometime before 2.4 myrs ago. During the almost 80 myrs between these major events, nature was dominated by the "great wheel of life" discussed below.

Figure 3.5. The Great Steps of Human Progress—Past and Future

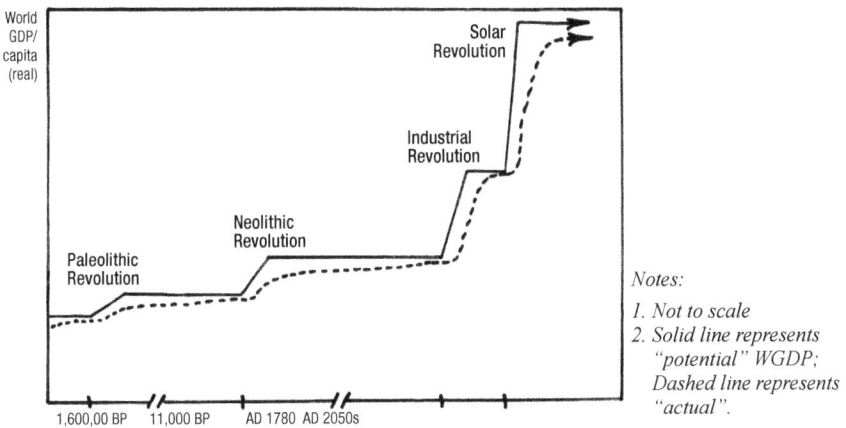

Sources: Snooks 1996: 403 & Snooks 2010b: 212.

As suggested earlier, the great paradigm shifts were generated by a series of genetic and, later, technological revolutions. The genetic revolutions can be summarised as follows:

- the Prokaryote Revolution—development of a metabolic system based on photosynthesis—by blue-green algae from 3,500 myrs BP;

- the Eukaryote Revolution—development of complex, integrated biological organisms—by plants and animals (beginning with cold-blooded types) from 900 myrs BP;

- the Endothermic Revolution—biological systems for the internal generation of body heat—by warm-blooded animals and associated plants from 250 myrs BP; and

- the Intelligence Revolution by the hominids from 2.4 myrs to 150,000 years BP.

The last of these genetic revolutions led not to a genetic paradigm shift but rather to a series of technological paradigm shifts. At this time, genetic change by itself was unable to provide more intense access to natural resources, only the ability to create and employ technology to do so instead. As shown earlier, these technological revolutions (Figures 3.3 to 3.5) include:

- the Paleolithic (hunting) Revolution from 2 myrs BP;

- the Neolithic (agricultural) Revolution from 10,600 years BP;

- the Modern (Industrial) Revolution from AD 1780; and

- the future revolution—the Solar Revolution—which can be expected from middle decades of the twenty-first century.

These technological paradigm shifts—as shown in my book *Dead God Rising* (2010b)—had a major impact on strategic ideology/religious ideas both through the new strategic demand they generated for ideological support and by the increases in surpluses available to fund ideological and religious institutions. The Neolithic Revolution was responsible for transforming simple views about supportive strategic guardians into elaborate theologies about creator gods; while the Modern Revolution replaced the old strategic gods with science and technology—of monotheism with scientism. As shown in chapter 4, the potential for material progress created by each technological paradigm shift was taken up gradually through the pursuit of one or other of the four dynamic strategies. Following the Paleolithic Revolution, this involved the family-multiplication strategy (of procreation and migration); following the Neolithic Revolution it involved the conquest and commerce strategies; and following the Industrial Revolution it involved the technological strategy. When, in Figure 3.5, the "actual" pressed against the "potential", there was great economic pressure for a new technological paradigm shift. The world is now approaching another critical phase of paradigmatic exhaustion and replacement—the forthcoming Solar Revolution (see chapter 13).

What the great steps of life represent is the step-like progress that has taken place in biological and economic activity throughout the history of life on Earth. Each giant step forward, which was facilitated by a genetic or technological revolution, made possible more intensive access to natural resources. In turn this enabled a higher level of biological/economic activity—or life "output"— to be achieved. In the pre-human era, this meant a growing number of more complex organisms that contributed to a higher level of global biomass. And in the human era, it resulted in not only a rapid increase in human and domesticated animal and plant populations, but also an exponential increase in human living standards, particularly concerning the consumption of services and nonperishable commodities. In brief there has been an exponential increase in the complexity of life on Earth. What of the future? For as long as we are confined to this planet, human progress will be measured in terms of increases in living standards rather than population. But, once we break out into the solar system and beyond, as we undoubtedly will, population expansion will become important again.

The reason for the step-like profile of global biomass/real GDP per capita is that with each genetic/technological revolution there was a quantum leap in *potential* access to natural resources owing to the occurrence of a major innovation or cluster of innovations. The *actual* utilisation of this potential, however, is a gradual and wave-like process driven by the "strategic desire" of materialist organisms (including man) in pursuit of their *non*-genetic or *non*-technological strategies. But in order to achieve this potential, it was usually necessary to develop add-on genetic/technological devices, such as those employed by blue-green algae to combat the adverse effects of their waste product oxygen, or newly conceived war machines to further Rome's conquest strategy. The relationship between potential and actual outcomes is represented diagrammatically in Figures 3.3 to 3.5.

In Figures 3.3 and 3.4, the *actual* curves (broken lines) represent the biological development path that I have called the great waves of life, measured in terms of global biomass; and in Figure 3.5 the *actual* curve (dotted line) represents the development path of global economic activity, measured by real GDP per capita. Once a particular genetic or technological paradigm has been exhausted (where the potential is fully realised), the *actual* curve presses persistently against the *potential* curve. Under the genetic option the resulting overpopulation leads to the collapse and extinction of the prevailing dynasty (such as the dinosaurs), due to the inevitable outbreak of "world war". Only once the intense competition for scarce resources has been eliminated—through dynastic collapse—is it possible to bring the slow-acting genetic strategy into play. In contrast, under the technology option, paradigmatic exhaustion leads to the adoption of a new technological revolution by the same, not a replacement, dynasty, owing to the much greater rapidity with which it can be introduced—a generation or less, compared with hundreds of thousands or even millions of years. Global conquest and collapse—possibly even extinction—could theoretically occur in human society if we were determined and able to eliminate growth-inducing technological change in the mistaken belief that this will save the environment or reverse climate change. This scenario was initially discussed in 1996 in my book *The Dynamic Society* (ch. 13) and developed further in relation to climate change both in *The Coming Eclipse* (2010a) and in chapter 13 of this book.

The interplay between genetic and technological change in the critical period between *Homo habilis* and *Homo sapiens*—between 2.4 myrs and 150,000 years BP—is fascinating, and a real test of any general dynamic theory. This period experienced what I call the "Intelligence Revolution". The strategic demand generated by the hominid family-multiplication strategy led to a *relatively* sudden increase in brain size in order to create and employ the *non*-biological tools that were required to change their diet from nuts and tubers to meat and marrow so as to enable the great global diaspora of mankind.

The Intelligence Revolution, therefore, led to a more intensive use of natural resources through the employment of better strategic instruments of a technological rather than a genetic nature. Genetic change was employed only until technology could take over, after which it was abandoned because technological instruments are more direct, precise, and quick-acting—in short, more economical. This, together with the much earlier exhaustion of the genetic option, is why the Intelligence Revolution led to a technological rather than a genetic paradigm shift.

As can be seen in Figure 3.4, the genetic paradigm profile continues as a horizontal line from the time the dinosaurs were at their peak, whereas the technological paradigm takes off vertically from about 2 myrs ago, thereafter tracing out the familiar step-like pattern, except that it occurs in a greatly accelerated fashion. Even in the future when genetic engineering will, no doubt, be undertaken on a large scale, it will lead to paradigm shifts not of a genetic but of a technological nature. Genetic engineering merely serves the dominant technological strategy. The technology option has permanently replaced the genetic option.

The Great Wheel of Life

The conventional wisdom is that the emergence of intelligence on Earth, once life had firmly established itself, was merely a function of "evolutionary" time. This wisdom is ill-founded. As I show in *The Collapse of Darwinism*, there was nothing inevitable about the rise of intelligent life on Earth, or anywhere else in the Universe. It was merely a matter of chance. Had we the ability to rerun the dynamics of life on Earth repeatedly, the chances that intelligent life would ever appear again are very remote. Or, to put it another way, even assuming that life is commonplace throughout the Universe, the probability that it would generate an intelligent species is very low. Why? Because the emergence of intelligent life was the outcome of a long chain of improbable and *unsought* happenings.

This is not to say, however, that the dynamics of life is unsystematic, just that it can take many different pathways. In fact, as I show in *The Collapse of Darwinism*, species and dynasties rise and fall in a predictable cycle, even though the detailed manner in which they do so cannot be known in advance. This suggests that there is a dynamic mechanism in life that could account for the regular rise and fall of dynasties without the emergence of intelligence, even until the solar system itself expired. Indeed, what I have argued is that such a dynamic mechanism should be regarded as the normal process for any mature system of life anywhere in the Universe. Intelligent life is the very rare exception, not the rule in our cosmos.

This dynamic mechanism, which drives the "great wheel of life", comes into operation in a mature life-system when the genetic option has been exhausted. That occurs when it is no longer possible to gain further access to natural resources through the use of genetic instruments—when all conceivable habitats or niches have been occupied as fully as possible through biological adaptation. At this stage, genetic change can no longer be employed to increase the global level of the biomass of life. This is not to say that minor variations in global "output" will not occur as the physical environment makes marginal adjustments (such as the rise or fall of sea levels), just that the available natural resources cannot be used any more intensively through genetic adjustment alone.

The exhaustion of the genetic option on Earth appears, as suggested earlier, to have occurred by the time the dinosaurs were at their peak about 80 myrs ago. Evidence for this comes from a comparison of the metabolic systems of the four great endothermic dynasties: the protomammals (therapsids), the archosaurs, the dinosaurs, and modern mammals. While advanced dinosaurs possessed more sophisticated metabolic systems—higher body temperatures, higher calorie intakes, faster reactions and speed—than the protomammals, they were similar to those of modern mammals.[6] What this implies is that the dinosaurs took the Endothermic Revolution, which had been initiated by the protomammals and carried forward by the archosaurs, a further and final step. Hence, they were able to employ the Earth's resources more intensively than all preceding dynasties. Modern mammals, whose great radiation was based not on any genetic innovation, do not appear to have advanced beyond the dinosaurs in this key resource-accessing ability. Indeed, while the dinosaurs existed on Earth, the mammals were only marginal players in life, unable to move to centre stage.

Some readers, who are aware that the mammals have been able to generate a greater range of species than were the dinosaurs, might claim this as a sign of greater effectiveness in accessing natural resources. This is not so. In life there exists a three-way trade-off between the number of species, the size of individuals, and the number of individuals that can exist at a particular time with a given supply of natural resources. If members of a dynasty "opt"—as a result of the "style" of their dynamic strategies—for large individual size and large numbers of individuals, then they will be limited to a lesser number of species. But if they opt for greater diversity—a larger number of species—together with a similar number of individuals, then the size of those individuals will be smaller. My argument in *The Collapse of Darwinism* is that the dinosaurs opted for size and numbers rather than diversity and numbers, whereas modern mammals did the reverse. The mammals were able to do so even though they were operating in the same genetic paradigm and at the same level of "genetic competence" as the dinosaurs.

We need to consider why and how the dinosaurs and mammals were able to opt for different degrees of diversity. This can best be done in terms of the "force versus finesse" argument developed in *The Collapse of Darwinism*[7] and outlined in chapter 2. Briefly, a dynasty, such as the dinosaurs, that favours force rather than finesse—because, for a successful species in the early stage of its development, force is more economical—will opt for size and numbers rather than diversity. Large size and numbers are essential for any dynasty that is accustomed to pursuing their dynamic strategies with brute strength. This was the case for all land dynasties before the era of modern mammals, and particularly for dinosaurs. Dinosaur herbivores reached sizes of 40,000 kg and carnivores attained sizes of 3,000 kg; whereas mammal herbivores (excluding the unsuccessful mega fauna) reached only 5,000 kg and their carnivores little more than 200 kg. Instead, mammals, which in the Mesozoic period (250–65 myrs BP) had been forced to live by their wits on the margins of life for 150 myrs by the aggressive dinosaurs, favoured finesse rather than force. Hence they opted for diversity rather than sheer size. And greater diversity, which requires more regular genetic innovation, needs greater intelligence to control the mechanism of "strategic selection" (to be discussed in Chapter 4). The need for greater finesse and greater diversity is why mammal brains were relatively larger than dinosaur brains, and why their brains continued to grow.

Figure 3.6. The Great Wheel of Life—The Rise and Fall of a Non-Innovating Dynasty

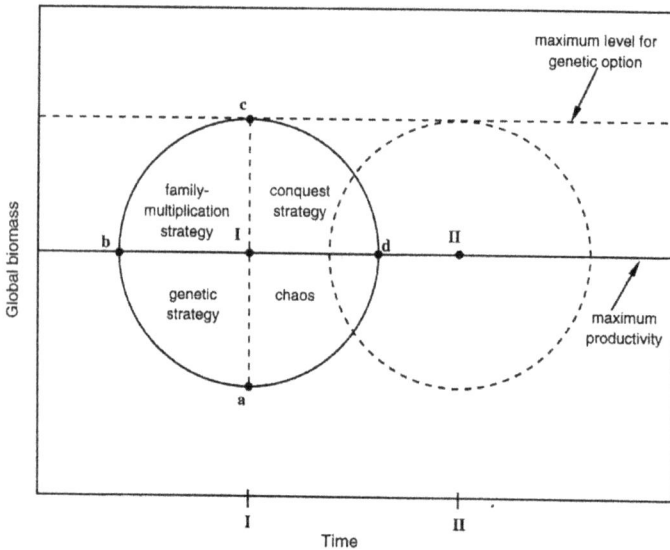

Source: Snooks 2003: 259

From the time that the genetic option was exhausted—somewhere between the times of the protomammals and the dinosaurs (275–65 myrs BP)—the "great wheel of life" displaced the great steps of life as the dominant dynamic mechanism underlying macrobiological activity. And while the great wheel rotated slowly in space-time no progress could be made in terms of intensity (or productivity) of resource use, or of increase in global biomass. Thereafter, new dynasties that were only able to resort to genetic (and not technological) change would merely replace old dynasties without gaining forward strategic traction. From this time, each great wave of life would be forced to peak at about the same level of biological activity as the early "endotherms". This is the "eternal recurrence" of life.

The great wheel of life is represented diagrammatically in Figure 3.6. When examining this diagram we should be aware of the different but related types of motion: the rotation of a point on the circumference of the wheel around its axis **I**; and the forward movement of the wheel from **I** to **II** over a very long period of time, say 100 myrs. Like any wheel traveling along a plane, the rotation leads to directional movement. In other words, the rotation of the wheel cannot lead to a reversal of time as would be implied by a fixed axis. Also, it should be noted that, as the genetic option has been exhausted, the plane along which the wheel travels through time is horizontal rather than upwardly inclined. This implies that there can be no "progress", in terms of biological outputs or productivity between this non-innovating dynasty and its predecessor.

The above argument can be cast in terms of the great-wheel diagram as follows:

- A new postgenetic-option dynasty begins its adventure in life at **a**, when competition is minimal and resources are abundant. Individuals are faced with the size/numbers/diversity issue, which they resolve unconsciously by pursuing the dynamic strategy of genetic change, with varying degrees of "preference" for force/finesse. This causes the great wheel to rotate upward in a clock-wise direction, thereby increasing biological output and moving forward in time (left to right) along a horizontal plane.

- Once they arrive at **b** the genetic strategy will be exhausted and the maximum level of "productivity" (or output per unit of input) in the use of energy and other resources will be achieved. Any further rotation of the wheel and, hence, forward movement through time will require the pursuit of the family-multiplication and commerce (symbiosis) strategies to drive their "genetic styles" (species) around the globe. As the wheel turns from **b** to **c**, global biomass (or biological output) will increase, but productivity remains the same, because the wheel is still traveling along the horizontal plane dictated by the exhausted genetic option.

- When the great wheel reaches **c** the family-multiplication strategy and the genetic paradigm for the dynasty as whole will have been exhausted. The only option for individuals in this Darwinian world of intense competition and scarce resources is to pursue the non-Darwinian strategy of conquest (the Darwinian strategy is genetic change). While this leads to gains for winners, it is at the expense of a growing loss of life, a reduction in diversity (Darwin predicts an increase in diversity), a decline in global biomass, and a severe deterioration in the environment. Hence, the wheel rotates slowly but inevitably from **c** to **d**, at which point conquest gives way to terminal chaos.

- Between **d** and **a** the wheel accelerates downwards as the entire dynasty begins to collapse. By the time **a** is reached, the dynasty has gone extinct. During the time taken to complete one revolution of the wheel of life—say 100 myrs in the case of this postgenetic-option dynasty—its forward motion has been along the horizontal plane **I-II**. In other words, there has been little or no progress in terms of biological output or productivity beyond that achieved by the former dynasty (except for some minor fine-tuning). Progress would require traction along an upward-sloping plane of the type that existed prior to exhaustion of the genetic option.

- With dynastic extinction, the opportunity is presented to the surviving species, previously on the margins of life, to take over centre stage where competition is now minimal and resources are abundant. As they do so— slowly, as the global environment has been severely damaged by "world war"—the great wheel begins to rotate around the same horizontally constrained axis once more. Hence, the cast of characters in the vehicle of life will have changed, but the play and its ending remains the same for a dynasty (including protomammals, archosaurs, and dinosaurs) trapped by an exhausted genetic option. The great wheel of life, therefore, leads to the "eternal recurrence", which should be regarded as the normal condition of mature forms of life throughout the Universe. Only by adopting the technology option before the great wheel begins its inevitable downward descent is it possible for a new dynasty to gain more intensive access to resources once all possible habitats have been saturated through genetic change. Only technical ideas under the driving force of strategic demand are able to transcend these acute biological limitations. And technical ideas depend on the emergence of an Intelligence Revolution.

It is sobering to realise that the technology option is the outcome of blind chance. The central reason is that this option does not bestow any advantage on the *individual* decision maker—the "dynamic strategist"—only on the species as a whole. And species do *not* make strategic decisions. In reality it is only something that can be recognised and valued in retrospect. And, so far, only by our species and only in this work. Why is this so? Why doesn't the individual see the technology option as being in his best interest? The answer is that all individuals die, irrespective of whether one species (mankind) stumbles on the secret of perpetuating its own existence. This is what I call the "organism/species paradox". Even had the apemen—or the mammal species that gave rise to them—recognised the very long-run implications of adopting the technological strategy, would one of its members have traded even a day's supply of food for the remote possibility that the species replacing theirs would, some 2.4 myrs later, break out of the eternal recurrence? The answer, of course, is no. The dynamic strategist is concerned only with his own immediate survival and prosperity or, at most, that of close family members. Hence the technology option is merely the unintended consequence—and a highly unlikely one at that—of the individual struggle for a secure and better life. And as it is unintended and unsought, the Intelligence Revolution was a matter of blind chance. Only those who believe in some sort of divine purpose—such as the creationists and advocates of scientism like James Lovelock and James Gardner—could conclude otherwise. The organism/species paradox is a major reason that James Gardner's argument about the cosmic supermind creating offspring universes with which it cannot communicate, is flawed.

What then is required to enable the inadvertent substitution of the technology option for the exhausted genetic option? What is required to break out of the eternal recurrence? Here are a number of essential, but not necessarily exhaustive, conditions.

- Life forms need to develop central nervous systems. This eliminates all non-vertebrate life forms such as bacteria, viruses, soft-bodied marine organisms, as well as the extensive plant kingdom. Hence, the vast majority of life forms that have ever existed on Earth must be disqualified from the race. As far as the technology option is concerned, the development paths "chosen" by these life forms were all dead ends. Yet these highly successful life forms neither know nor care.

- For vertebrates to develop the large brains required to stumble on the technology option, they needed to develop endothermic (warm-blooded) systems, so as to control body temperature and keep it at a constant level. Just a slight change of body temperature in either direction renders large and complex brains inoperative. This requirement rules out all ectothermic (cold-blooded) animals such as fish, amphibians, reptiles and insects. The ability to generate the technology option now depends on a few eccentric dynasties: the protomammals (or therapsids) that emerged as recently as 240 myrs ago; the archosaurs from 225 myrs BP; and the dinosaurs from 190 myrs BP. But most species in these dynasties failed an additional test.

- It is also essential that warm-blooded vertebrates opt for finesse rather than force in their strategic pursuit. Without this vital ingredient there will be no pressure to increase brain size from the minimum required to effectively pursue the four-fold dynamic strategies (see Chapter 4). This eliminates the archosaurs and dinosaurs completely (actually they, with the exception of birds, eliminated themselves!) and all but one small and insignificant (at the time) branch of the protomammals.

- Having barely survived the "world war" of the dinosaurs, a small shrew-like descendent of the protomammals needed not only to engage in the strategic pursuit with finesse rather than force just to survive on the margins of the dinosaur world, but to do so at a pace that enabled the technology option to be stumbled upon *before* the family-multiplication strategy of their extensive mammal family was exhausted and the terminal conquest strategy embarked upon. But none of these "decision makers" knew that time was running out; and had they known they would not have given a damn, as they would have been long dead before this occurred.

- In retrospect it is clear that only one small branch of the extensive mammalian family that had generally employed finesse rather than force in the strategic pursuit had the necessary intellectual potential. This small and insignificant branch was occupied by the primates. And among the primates only the hominids seemed to be keeping to a feasible time schedule by breaking out of their ancestral home and, thereby, force-feeding their IQ development; and among the hominids only *Homo* looked like getting across the finishing line, provided they got a move on! Had we all taken the path chosen by the apeman *Australopithecus robustus*, who pursued the more specialised substrategy (of the family-multiplication strategy) of nut-and-tuber eating rather than meat-and-marrow eating (which enabled the great global diaspora), then this race of blind man's buff would have been lost. Larger brains were needed to pursue this global version of the family-multiplication strategy. (Greater detail can be found in my book *The Collapse of Darwinism*, 2003: ch. 12).

- And it was a race barely completed by man—who had no realisation of his victory—because there are signs that the family-multiplication strategy for the entire mammalian dynasty was approaching global exhaustion. Indeed, the heroic attempt made by mankind to generalise their version of this strategy and to break out of their restricted and highly specialised environment (that trapped the apemen) reflects an obviously exhausting strategy. Had they not succeeded against all the odds, or had a modest catastrophe wiped out their very small (not more than a few thousand individuals some 3–2 myrs ago) and concentrated (in a few restricted regions of one continent, Africa) numbers, the great wheel of life would have continued to turn unwittingly and relentlessly in endless time without gaining any upward traction. Life on Earth only broke out of the eternal recurrence through the agency of one small, insignificant, and deviant species from the vast numbers that had existed over the previous 3,800 myrs.

Owing to these extremely stringent requirements, we can reasonably conclude that the probability of the technology option ever being "discovered" was extremely, extremely low. It was merely the fortuitous outcome of a long chain of highly unlikely, unforeseen, and unsought events. The implication, therefore, is that intelligence is not only the scarcest resource on Earth but also its likelihood of occurring or existing anywhere else in the Universe is very, very low. Most likely we are alone in the Universe and that any life elsewhere—

which undoubtedly exists—is dominated by the "great wheel". This makes nonsense of scientism's argument that the entire purpose of the Universe is to give birth to a supermind. In the highly unlikely event that intelligent life does emerge elsewhere, the probability is that it will lag considerably behind that on Earth owing to the remarkably fortuitous causal chain that we have experienced.

A CONTINUING ODYSSEY

This chapter provides a schematic outline of life's great odyssey over the past 3,800 myrs. It shows that this journey has been characterised by exponential growth in biological/GDP output governed by the logological constant; by the great waves of life of growing intensity; by the great biological and technological paradigm shifts; and by the great wheel of life. It has been argued that the mammalian break-out from the eternal recurrence was a matter of blind chance and that, accordingly, intelligent life is the most scarce resource in the Universe. This puts paid to the current idea in scientism that a superintelligence or supermind is shaping the destiny of the cosmos. These then are the characteristics, or patterns, of life that require explanation. To do so, a general dynamic theory—a theory showing how the odyssey of life will continue for some time to come—is presented in the next chapter.

Chapter 4
Engine of life

Desires drive, ideas facilitate.

The key to understanding life on Earth—past, present, and future—is to be found in the underlying dynamic mechanism. What we need, therefore, is a workable dynamic theory of life. Owing to the fatal flaws in all existing theories, it has been necessary to develop an entirely new approach, namely the dynamic-strategy theory, first presented in my books *The Dynamic Society* (1996) and *The Collapse of Darwinism* (2003). The dynamic-strategy theory, which reconstructs the engine of life, has shown itself to be highly successful in explaining the dynamics of both nature and human society. It is a realist theory about the process of "selfcreation", in which desires drive and ideas facilitate; a realist theory that contrasts with metaphysical theories of self-organisation and complexity; a realist theory that constitutes the engine of life.

What are the characteristics of a truly dynamic theory of life? Unlike the Darwinian algorithm of natural selection—the only universally accepted scientific theory of life—a general dynamic theory must focus on *processes* or mechanisms, as well as *outcomes*. These processes will involve the interactions between individual organisms and their social and physical environments, the "dynamic strategies" they adopt to survive and prosper, the manner in which these strategies operate at the micro- and macro-biological levels, as well as the impacts these strategies have upon the physical and social worlds.

An endogenous, or self-contained, dynamic theory will be self-starting and self-sustaining—in a word, "selfcreating"—subject only to *passive* inputs (sunlight and various chemical substances) from the physical world. And the dynamic life-system, or strategic *logos,* will respond positively and creatively, rather than passively and reactively, to external shocks. Exogenous shocks are likely to be of two main types: those emanating from the physical world, including shifting tectonic plates, changing climates, and changing sea levels; and those generated by other life forms, such as disease and invasion. Such a theory must be relevant to both the natural and human worlds because, as I show in Chapter 2, both share the same dynamic characteristics.

THE DYNAMIC-STRATEGY THEORY — A BRIEF OUTLINE
The dynamic-strategy theory consists of four interrelated endogenous (internal) variables and one set of random exogenous (external) forces, as outlined below:

1. The competitive driving force of individual organisms to survive and prosper—the concept of "strategic desire"—provides the theory with its self-starting and self-sustaining nature.

2. The dynamic strategies—including genetic/technological change, family multiplication, commerce (symbiosis), and conquest—are employed by individual organisms through the process of "strategic selection", to achieve their objectives.

3. The "strategic struggle" is the main "political" instrument by which established individuals/species (old strategists) attempt to maintain their control over the sources of their prosperity, and by which emerging individuals/species (new strategists) attempt to usurp such control.

4. The constraining force operating on the dynamics of a species/dynasty is the eventual exhaustion of the dominant dynamic strategy/paradigm pursued by its members, which leads to the emergence of internal/external conflict and to collapse.

5. Exogenous shocks, both physical (continental drift, volcanic action, weather events, asteroid impact) and biological (disease and invasion), impact randomly, distortingly, but marginally, on this internally driven dynamic system.

In the dynamic-strategy theory, therefore, the very long-run driving force arises from the universal motivation of all living organisms—to survive and prosper at any cost. And the wave-like process of biological/economic activity by which this is achieved is generated by the creative exploitation and exhaustion of the dynamic strategies aimed at accessing natural resources. The ultimate constraints on life, therefore, arise from the very sources of its expansion and growth. Both are internal to the theory, and they are strategic not physical. Exogenous, or external, forces, on the other hand, in the form of physical and organic shocks, do *not* drive or systematically shape the dynamic process of life, but they do occasionally distort the systematic pattern in a largely random manner. Importantly, the internal dynamic always rapidly asserts itself following any such shock, which, at most, temporarily impacts upon the endogenous dynamic pathway. The reason for this, as shown in Chapter 5, is the robust nature of the strategic *logos*.

The dynamic-strategy theory is a theory about "selfcreation". And the essence of selfcreation is found in the creative exchange between purposeful agents and their society's unfolding dynamic strategy. It is this "strategic exchange" that lies at the very heart of the self-sustaining dynamics of living systems. Social agents are self-motivated and self-driven, and they generate complexity and order in a *creative* response to a continuously changing "strategic demand" as the strategic *logos* is transformed. It is this *creative exchange* between the demand and supply sides of a dynamic life-system (or strategic *logos*) that generates changing genetic structures, technologies, ideas of all types, institutions and organisations. By attempting to meet this constantly changing strategic demand, both the agents and their society are transformed in the long run. The creative process of exchange by which this takes place constitutes the "life-system" for the group of social agents in whom we are interested. Living systems, therefore, are "autogenous"—or "selfcreating"—systems.[1]

The Driving Force

The endogenous force in life is the "strategic desire" of all individual organisms to survive and prosper. Basically, this is the need for living organisms, no matter how simple or how complex, to obtain sufficient fuel to feed their metabolic processes. Without fuel, the constituent cells in a living organism begin to break down and die. A systematic examination of the history of life and human society—presented in my books *The Dynamic Society* (1996), *The Ephemeral Civilization* (1997), *Laws of History* (1998) and *The Collapse of Darwinism* (2003)—shows that organisms attempt at all costs to survive *and*, having survived, to prosper. Prosperity is insurance for survival in an uncertain future. This motivation can be characterised as the "materialist organism" and "materialist man". It is the essence (and definition) of life, which has shaped our genetic and technological structure from the very beginning. Organisms that fail to embody strategic desire strongly, overwhelmingly, are eliminated from the gene pool.

To achieve life's fundamental objective, organisms adopt the particular dynamic strategy that is expected to maximise their probability of survival and prosperity. This trial-and-error procedure (*not* a cost-benefit calculation) is strongly influenced by the prevailing degree of external competition. In *The Collapse of Darwinism* (2003) I show that, contrary to Darwinian convention, intense competition leads to the adoption of the conquest strategy and to death and extinction; whereas minimal competition leads to the genetic strategy and to prolific speciation; and more "normal" competition generates the family-multiplication and commerce strategies that in turn lead to rapid population growth and diaspora. This is not a haphazard affair. In each case a dynamic strategy is "chosen" because it is the most effective one available in the prevailing physical and social environments.

But how do individuals from the lowest to highest life forms make these choices? There are two existing extremist answers to this question provided by the neo-Darwinists and the neoliberal (economic rationalist) economists. The neo-Darwinists insist it is our genes that decide behavior, while the neoliberal economists insist it is our rational faculties or ideas.[2] Some readers might be tempted to say that the neo-Darwinists are right about animals and the neoliberals are right about humans. This, however, would only maintain the unsupportable dualism in our attitude to life—a dualism that Darwin and, particularly, Wallace tried to eliminate more than a century ago. Neo-Darwinism, therefore, is anachronistic.

Neither the neo-Darwinists nor the rationalists are correct in this matter for *any* life form, high or low. Essentially the **same** process of decision-making is employed by all life forms, and that is determined *neither* by genes *nor* by ideas. Instead it is determined by strategic desire—the desire to survive and prosper. Both genes and ideas, combined in varying proportions by different life forms, merely facilitate desires. They encode and translate the methods by which desires are successfully achieved.

As genes and ideas do not drive animal society but merely facilitate the desires of its members, we need to replace both the neo-Darwinist genetic model and the neoliberal rationalist model with a realist theory of decision making. Through the inductive method employed in my earlier books it has been possible to derive a theory of "decision making" relevant to both low and high life forms and, thereby, finally eliminate the present dualism. I call it the "strategic-imitation" model of decision making.[3]

In reality, decision making is based on the need to economise on nature's scarcest resource—intelligence. This is clearly the case with lower life forms, and it is one of the reasons that neo-Darwinists have opted for the "genetic leash" argument (the other is that they are professional geneticists of one sort or another, and have a vested interest in claiming that genes rule life). But what of our own species? The neoliberal rationalists have adopted a totally unrealistic view of human decision making involving: the construction of mental models about the way the world works; the collection of vast quantities of economic cost-benefit information; and the possession of rapid and accurate intellectual processing abilities.

The strategic-imitation theory rejects both the anti-intellectual view of the neo-Darwinists and the supraintellectual view of the neoliberal rationalists. In the real world, in contrast to the fantasy worlds of these game-playing deductionists, individuals do make choices. But, rather than acting like computers, the great majority of animals, including humans, merely imitate those individuals and those activities that are conspicuously successful. This means that the only information sought by the vast majority of decision makers is that needed to answer the simple, but key, question: who is successful and why? In this way the many follow the successful few.

The "few" are the strategic pioneers and the "many" are the strategic followers. This is how and why religions emerge and flourish so readily. The only information decision makers require is the relatively costless "imitative information", not the prohibitively expensive cost-benefit information; and the only intellectual faculty needed is that required to determine that some of one's peers are more successful than others. Even the strategic pioneers do not employ rationalist techniques when seeking new ways of exploiting strategic opportunities. Rather than using sophisticated techniques to calculate the "best" solution from the large number available, the pioneers believe that their intuitively chosen solutions *are* the best. Only a few will have their universally optimistic expectations vindicated, but it is the "fewest of the few" who are slavishly imitated by the many. While the tendency for animals to imitate each other has received widespread recognition, the strategic-imitation model is the first to employ this act as part of a general dynamic theory—as in my books *The Dynamic Society* (1996) and *The Collapse of Darwinism* (2003).

But what of life forms without any intellectual capacity at all? Organisms in pursuit of survival and prosperity control their dynamic strategies through a number of "strategic instruments", including brains in organisms that possess them and special genes in those that do not. In *The Collapse of Darwinism* and *The Selfcreating Mind*, I call these instruments the "strategic cerebrum" and the "strategic gene". Early life forms were able to pursue the full range of dynamic strategies without the use of central nervous systems or brains.[4] Simple life forms possess a gene or genes that switch dynamic strategies on and off according to the availability of nutrients and the degree of competition. Considerable scientific research has been conducted on this topic.[5] The only matter in dispute is who is in control of this process, the selfish gene or the selfish organism.

There is a sound empirical and theoretical basis for my view that it is the selfish organism that controls its dynamic strategies through the strategic gene. Even genetic structures are shaped by the choices made by organisms in the strategic pursuit. The reason that organisms eventually developed central nervous systems and quickly substituted the strategic cerebrum for the strategic gene was to more effectively supervise their dynamic strategies as they became more complex. The brain is a far more flexible and imaginative instrument of strategic control than the strategic gene. Accordingly the strategic gene was abandoned by more advanced organisms. There can be no doubt where the real power over life lay. This argument was originally presented in *The Collapse of Darwinism* (2003, ch. 12) and developed more fully in *The Selfcreating Mind* (2006: part III).

The Dynamic Mechanism

Strategic desire is a self-starting and self-sustaining force that drives a dynamic mechanism centred on the strategic pursuit. It is a process involving the adoption and exploitation of the most effective available dynamic strategy (or substrategy) by the materialist organism—or materialist man—to achieve its objective of survival and prosperity. A dynamic strategy begins as an individual or a family activity which, if successful, is adopted by successively wider social groups, at first local, then regional and, finally, global. This aggregation process, which involves a progression from the micro- to macro-biological/economic levels, takes place via the strategic-imitation mechanism by which conspicuous success is rapidly copied. In this way, a successful dynamic strategy becomes widespread throughout a population, a species, even a dynasty.

The sequence of dynamic strategies

The choice of dynamic strategy—from four possibilities including genetic/technological change, family multiplication, commerce (symbiosis), and conquest—depends on the underlying material and social conditions, such as the relative abundance of natural resources and the degree of external competition. It is important to realise that organisms "invest" energy and resources in each of these dynamic strategies at different times and under different conditions to achieve the same universal objective—survival and prosperity.

Typically, organisms in a given species will pursue a sequence of strategies from the time they begin to diverge from the parent species or society until they finally go extinct. The "strategic sequence" prior to the emergence of human society 2 myrs ago was typically genetic-change▶family-multiplication (or, alternatively, commerce)▶conquest. Each dynamic strategy is continuously exploited until it is exhausted, which leads to a temporary crisis until a new strategy can be developed and employed in the species' strategic pursuit. If, in a normally competitive environment, a new strategy cannot be found to replace an old, exhausted strategy, that species will collapse and go extinct prematurely. Accordingly, this strategic sequence leads not to a linear development path but—as shown in Chapter 3—to a series of biological/economic waves, which describe the phases of expansion, slowdown, stagnation, crisis, decline and, with a lapse in time, renewed expansion.

Imagine a non-Darwinian world characterised by minimal competition and abundant resources that emerges following the dramatic extinction of an earlier animal dynasty. Contrary to the predictions of Darwin's theory of natural selection, this is precisely the time when surviving organisms invest energy in the "genetic strategy", because they have both the time and opportunity to exploit abundant resources. By creating a new "genetic style" (or species) they are able to gain more intensive access to employed resources and/or new access to unused resources. The resulting increase in biomass per input of resources in nature is equivalent to economic growth generated by technological change in human society.

How, we need to ask, are organisms able to manipulate genetic change and turn it to the advantage of themselves and their families? Basically it involves the new concept of "strategic selection" that is a response to strategic demand. While only a brief outline can be given here, strategic selection is discussed in detail in *The Collapse of Darwinism* (2003: ch. 12). A beneficial mutation that improves an organism's access to resources will attract the attention of those with similar abilities or aspirations. These individuals will cooperate and/or mate with each other, thereby improving the prospects of the existing generation as well as the genetic characteristics of the next. Selection by the organism at the phenotypic level, therefore, shapes the genotype. This is what I mean by strategic selection. It is a form of self-selection—or selfcreation—that replaces the "divine selection" of the creationists and the "natural selection" of the Darwinists. Over very long periods of time this key principle is responsible for the upsurge in speciation that always follows a major extinction—an outcome that Darwinian natural selection cannot explain.

Strategic selection is also the answer to the question that has always been a great embarrassment to the neo-Darwinists: why sex? They are unable to satisfactorily explain the "popularity" of sex as a means of replication, because their central dogma about "reproductive success"—that organisms attempt to maximise copies of their genes in the gene pool—requires that asexual reproduction, which enables individuals to pass on copies of *all* their genes rather than just *half* of them, should be the norm. Clearly this is not the case with sexual reproduction, as sexual individuals thwart the alleged Darwinian objectives of their genes.

The dynamic-strategy argument about sex is that it provides individuals with greater control over their dynamic strategies. This is the concept of "selective sexual reproduction". In the first place, reproduction through sex enables individuals to choose partners that display characteristics, both physical and instinctual, most needed in the particular dynamic strategy they are pursuing. For "genetic-change" one requires characteristics that can provide better access to natural resources; for "family-multiplication", those that provide greater fertility and mobility; for "commerce" (symbiosis), those that enable the monopolisation and exchange of strategic resources; and for "conquest", those that enable "military" success and territorial domination. Organisms are able to pursue and change dynamic strategies more effectively by being able to choose between the different physical and instinctual characteristics embodied in potential mates. Second, sexual reproduction increases the rate of mutation and genetic variety in the family, both of which are the primary material for the dynamic strategy of genetic change and for the diversity of family abilities required to maximise strategic opportunities more generally. And third, sexual reproduction provides the basis for specialisation and division of labor along gender lines in family groups, thereby increasing both strategic efficiency and the probability of strategic success. Essentially, all these matters provide organisms with greater control over life's strategic pursuit.

Once a new genetic style (or species) has fully emerged, the dynamic strategy of genetic change will have exhausted itself. It will, therefore, be more cost-effective in terms of metabolic energy use for an organism to switch investment from the genetic to the family-multiplication strategy. A higher cost-effectiveness in energy use is translated into a higher probability of survival and prosperity. The new dynamic strategy will lead to an exclusive focus by organisms on the procreation and migration needed to fully exploit the new genetic style. In this way the members of our new species can outflank their parent and sibling species by rapidly increasing their populations and spreading throughout the accessible world. All the great diasporas in life have been based on the family-multiplication strategy. It is a strategy that leads to "expansion" (more resources accessed by larger numbers of organisms at the same degree of intensity) rather than "growth" (more intensive resource use), and it occurs during periods of "normal" competition—competition that is neither minimal nor extreme. Indeed, individuals and families are able to escape extreme competition by migrating to unoccupied or under-occupied regions.

This expansion phase is characterised in some species by the individual's pursuit of the more specialised dynamic strategy of commerce or symbiosis. It is a strategy that involves the interaction between individuals in two different species (or societies), each specializing in access to different resources and "trading" with the other for mutual gain. These "commercial" relationships exist between organisms in different species of plants, different animals and plants, and different species of animals. Examples include: algae and coral polyps; algae and fungi (lichens); acacias that house and feed ant colonies in return for protection; ants that culture fungi for food; bacteria in the digestive systems of many animal species—to name just a few. Similarly mutually beneficial relationships also characterise human societies. The great commerce societies of the past—as shown in chapter 7—have included the Egyptians, Phoenicians, Greeks, Carthaginians, Venetians, Dutch, and British.

In both the family-multiplication and commerce strategies, the choice of, and cooperation between, associates and sexual partners is based not on the ability to exploit existing resources more intensively but on the ability either to procreate and migrate, or to monopolise and trade scarce resources/ commodities. In other words, through the operation of "strategic selection", benign mutations in the expansion phase will be ignored (by the selective sexual reproduction mechanism) unless they assist in promoting the family-multiplication or commerce strategies. It is for this reason alone that the genetic profile of a species will approximate what has been misleadingly called "punctuated equilibria" by Niles Eldredge and Stephen Gould.[6]

By the time a genetic style has been exhausted through procreation and migration, resources available to individuals in this species will be scarce, resulting in intense competition for them. This produces a crisis, because the earlier family-multiplication and commerce strategies will have generated levels of population and consumption that can only be maintained by a continuous inflow of natural resources. To prevent going under during such a crisis, individuals search for a new dynamic strategy to replace the old exhausted one. The only possibility in these circumstances is the conquest strategy, because there is insufficient time to employ the dynamic strategy of genetic/technological change. As usual, this new strategy starts at the individual level and, if successful, progresses to the regional, national, and global levels through the strategic-imitation mechanism.

With the exhaustion of any given genetic style (once the family-multiplication strategy has come to an end) individuals in that species will battle fiercely with each other for the diminishing supply of resources as overpopulation damages their ecosystem. In the process, they will turn upon each other to take control of key resources. This type of conquest strategy, which can be likened to civil war, renders a species vulnerable to a takeover of their ecosystem by a closely competing species or to any adverse change in their physical environment. Extinction of the species in these circumstances is highly probably. The fossil record shows that extinction also happens under these conditions in closely interacting groups of species, when the exhaustion of their genetic styles coincides.

When the wider "genetic paradigm" of an era is exhausted, the entire dynasty resorts to the conquest strategy and is plunged into "world war", which fatally damages the environment and ultimately leads to the extinction of the entire dynasty. But as this world war is waged over a period of hundreds of thousands of years, many species employ a limited form of genetic change (limited by time) to support their conquest strategies by developing offensive and defensive biological weapons.[7] This add-on "technology" is a response to changing "strategic demand" as the conquest strategy unfolds. Organisms do not have the time or resources to effect a complete genetic transformation.

Hence the Darwinian world of scarce natural resources and intense competition leads not to "evolution" through natural selection but to conquest and, ultimately, the extinction of the entire dynasty. Only once the *non-*Darwinian world of minimal competition and resource abundance has been ushered in does directional genetic change and speciation occur once more. While Darwinism has collapsed just as surely as the dinosaurs, most scientists pretend not to have noticed.

The reason that the conquest strategy in human society did not lead to the extinction of humanity, was the role played by technological change—an option not open to other species. Conquest in human society is a "Neolithic" dynamic strategy, and its systematic pursuit by a succession of civilisations—such as Assyria, Babylon, Persia, Macedonia, Rome, Parthia, and medieval Europe—is the mechanism by which the neolithic technological paradigm was eventually exhausted, opening the way for the Industrial Revolution and the introduction of the technological strategy. It was the technological strategy that prevented conquest from eventually destroying mankind and his natural environment. Wars in the industrial technological era undertaken by leading nations are self-defeating and short term, because they are not as materially rewarding as the technological strategy. Without the "technology option", mankind would have gone the same way as the dinosaurs.

The dynamic strategies employed in human society are the same as those discussed above for all pre-human dynasties. The main difference is the historical sequence in which these strategies have been utilised. The old sequence, as we have seen, was genetic-change▶family-multiplication or commerce▶conquest; and it was determined by the eternal recurrence of the great wheel of life—of the cyclical process of genetic rise and fall. With the substitution of the new technology option for the old genetic option, a new strategic sequence was introduced. Instead of being cyclical it was progressive, and was advanced by the technological paradigm shifts discussed in Chapter 3. Hence, the earliest human dynamic strategy, which was associated with the paleolithic technological paradigm, was the family-multiplication strategy. The pursuit of this strategy—leading to the great diaspora of mankind—eventually exhausted the paleolithic paradigm (about 10,600 years BP) and opened the way for the Neolithic Revolution of agriculture. During the era of the neolithic technological paradigm the dynamic strategies of conquest and commerce were employed to raise material living standards of the opportunistic/predatory society above the level that could be generated by agricultural productivity. In *The Ephemeral Civilization* (1997) I show just how successful conquest (Rome) and commerce (Egypt) societies were in achieving this objective. The pursuit of conquest and commerce eventually exhausted the neolithic technological paradigm (by the mid-eighteenth century), and opened the way for the Industrial Revolution and the industrial technological strategy. But while the strategic *sequence* of humanity is different to that of non-human species, the objective and basic operation of these strategies is very similar. Even the strategic cerebrum plays only a facilitating role in the strategic pursuit of mankind.

A dynamic form for the new theory
As individual organisms seek to exploit their physical and social environments, which sets in train a mass movement orchestrated through strategic imitation, the dominant dynamic strategy unfolds. By this I mean that the materialist opportunities inherent in the strategy are progressively exploited and, finally, exhausted. This unfolding process generates a great wave of biological/economic output, as discussed in Chapter 2. It is important to realise, however, that there is nothing automatic, inevitable, or teleological about this unfolding process, which is merely the outcome of dynamic strategists exploring and investing in existing strategic opportunities. Herein lies a stark contrast with the metaphysical and teleological theories of Gaia and the Biocosm discussed in my recent book *Dead God Rising* (2010b: ch. 9).

But why and how does the expansion of a species/society lead ultimately to strategic exhaustion? As I show in *The Dynamic Society* (1996: ch. 12) and *The Collapse of Darwinism* (2003: ch. 15), strategic exhaustion is the outcome of the "law of diminishing *strategic* returns". A stage is reached in the expansionary phase of a species/society when each additional unit of metabolic energy/total resources invested by individuals in the dominant dynamic strategy leads to a decline in additional units of resources accessed. Eventually, the extra or marginal unit of energy/resource "revenue" will be driven down to equality with marginal energy/resource costs. At this point in time the dynamic strategy is exhausted and it will be abandoned, because any further expenditure of energy/resources would fail to pay for itself. No life form can afford to expend more energy/resources than it is able to access through its dynamic strategies. Thereafter, stagnation of the species/society sets in, followed by a general decline as many individuals are unable to obtain sufficient resources to satisfy basic requirements.

The rise and fall of a dynamic strategy pursued by individuals in a species/ society, or even a dynasty, traces out a distinctive strategic pathway in terms of biomass/GDP, which can be seen in the fossil and historical record. This strategic process, which has been discussed in detail in my books *The Ephemeral Civilization* (1997) and *The Collapse of Darwinism* (2003), is outlined in chapters 2 and 3 above. What this evidence suggests is that the dynamic-strategy theory expresses itself through a series of biological/economic waves within waves. The great waves of life (of geometrically declining duration), shown in Figure 3.2 (chapter 3), generated by the rise and fall of biological dynasties, encompasses the long waves (of about 30 myrs) generated by the rise and fall of groups of species, which in turn contain the shorter waves (of up to 6 myrs or so) generated by the rise and fall of significant individual species. In human society there are the great economic waves of about 300 years, which contain long waves of about 40 to 60 years, and short waves of about 5 to 20 years. At all levels in both life and society, these waves are generated by the exploitation, exhaustion, and replacement of dynamic strategies (or substrategies), genetic/ technological styles, and genetic/technological paradigms. This pattern of waves within waves, therefore, constitutes the dynamic form of our theory and models. Owing to historical contingency and exogenous influences, the duration of these waves can never be precisely predicted, but they can be identified in a rough and ready, yet workable, way.

Strategic demand and strategic confidence

The unfolding dynamic strategy, driven by the competitive energy of materialist organism/man, plays a central role in our theory. Not only does it provide a realistic dynamic form, but it also gives rise to the two important concepts of "strategic demand" and "strategic confidence". These concepts are important in explaining not only the investment of energy/resources by organisms in the four-fold dynamic strategies, but also the impetus for the fundamental process of strategic selection.

Strategic confidence, which rises and falls with the dominant dynamic strategy, is the cement that binds society together. It is responsible for the dynamic order that underlies the trust and cooperation between individuals in any social group. Rather than having trust in each other—which neither sociologists nor economic rationalists are able to convincingly explain— individuals have confidence in their successful joint dynamic strategy, owing to the stream of resources and income it provides. It is this *strategic* confidence that gives rise to the decisions made by organisms to invest energy/resources in the dominant dynamic strategy. In contrast, when a dynamic strategy is severely challenged or even exhausted, the evaporating strategic confidence contributes to the emerging crisis in the species/society by fracturing the orderly relationship between individuals. Only when a new strategy arises does strategic confidence, and hence order, stability and trust, return.[8]

Strategic demand, which is *the* core concept in the dynamic-strategy theory, also rises and falls as the dynamic strategy unfolds. It comprises the dynamic demand generated by the "strategists", or individual decision makers, for a range of inputs required in the strategic pursuit as a continuum through time. To exploit strategic opportunities, individuals need to invest in infrastructure (the fabric of shelters, burrows, nests, beaver dams, farms, cities, transport and communications, organisations) and "ideas" (both genetic and technological); to pass on acquired knowledge to the younger generation; and to develop and enforce social conventions, organisational relationships, and strategic ideologies. All of this is a response to the strategic demand of the dynamic *logos*.

Strategic demand, therefore, is the central active principle in life. And it is the formal recognition of this critically important fact that makes the dynamic-strategy theory unique in an intellectual world dominated by supply-side theories. Naturally, the supply response in terms of population change, infrastructure, construction, and genetic/technological change—which in turn is influenced by the relative scarcity of these factors reflected in "relative factor prices"—will contribute to the way in which strategic opportunities are exploited. But they do so passively. It is strategic demand that creates its own supply, *not* the other way around as most scientists, both natural and social believe.

At the centre of this strategic demand-supply response is "strategic inflation". In non-monetised human society and animal society, "strategic inflation" takes a non-price form. Yet the role is just the same as for human society (see chapter 11). Those resources that are much in demand for reasons of survival are highly "valued" and competition for them is intense. Where these resources are embodied in certain individuals or groups of individuals, these individuals are highly sought after so that their status in their group and their feelings of self-worth are enhanced. This greater "value", "sense of self-worth", and "status" in non-monetarised societies, whether human or non-human, operates to the same end as strategic inflation in more sophisticated societies. It provides an indication of the urgent requirement of the dynamic strategy being pursued by society. The equivalent of "inflation targeting" in non-monetarised societies would be to suppress the status and sense of self-worth of individuals urgently required by a society's dynamic strategy. Herein lies the irrationality and self-defeating nature of inflation targeting.

The Strategic Struggle

A mechanism central to the "politics" of life is the "strategic struggle". It is entered into by individuals attempting to maintain or take control of their "society", and by groups, populations, and species attempting to replace old genetic or technological styles/paradigms with new ones. To do so, these individuals and groups employ the dynamic tactics of order and chaos. The tactics of order, which are used by insiders to maintain and exploit the status quo, include the threat of punishment or ostracism, and the enforcement of customary "rules". And the tactics of chaos, which are used by outsiders to disrupt the existing order, include attempts to undermine the authority of the existing leader, or even to challenge him to combat (or, in modern political parties, to a leadership challenge in the party room). In each case, the aim is to either maintain or usurp control of the dominant dynamic strategy. Why? Because it is the source of society's ability to survive and prosper and therefore of great personal wealth and power for the strategic leader.

The common occurrence in many species of intimidation and conflict between males is not, as the neo-Darwinists claim, primarily about sex. Males battle for supremacy, we are told with mind-numbing frequency, to maximise the presence of their genes in the gene pool by mating with as many females as possible. But in reality, males battle with each other to gain control over the sources of their society's dynamic strategy, which in the animal world involve territories that provide access to food, shelter, and team support. They battle, in other words, to become the leading strategist in their group. Their conflict is part of the struggle for "political" control of their "society". Having won this battle and maintained/hijacked strategic control, which ensures his survival, the "strategic leader", as head of a herd, tribe or nation, is in a good position to maximise his prosperity, which in turn leads to the consumption of food, sex and, for the time being, leisure. While procreation assumes greater significance when it is a response to the strategic demand generated by the dynamic strategy of family multiplication, even then it is merely a means to a more important end.

The strategic struggle also plays a central role in the rise and fall of genetic/technological styles and paradigms. With the exhaustion of a genetic style, for example, individuals within a species battle with each other for control over the depleting sources of their dynamic strategy. Like warlords in a world of conquest, they attempt to assume strategic leadership to improve their prospects of survival and prosperity at the expense of others in their species. More significant, however, is the strategic struggle that emerges when an entire genetic paradigm approaches exhaustion. In these circumstances, the struggle takes place between the old strategists—the leaders of the old dominant dynasty—and the new strategists—the leaders of the newly emergent or resurgent dynasty. Because the old strategists have been weakened by the exhaustion of their genetic paradigm, the strategic struggle eventually favours the new strategists, such as the triumph of the archosaurs (protodinosaurs) over the therapsids (protomammals).[9] But, as we have seen, this may involve many regional battles throughout the accessible world over tens, even hundreds, of thousands of years. In these battles, the old strategists employ the dynamic tactics of order, while the new strategists employ those of chaos.

As is well known, similar struggles occur in human society during critical times, when technological strategies and paradigms are exhausted. Whenever a human dynamic strategy approaches exhaustion, the old and new strategists struggle for the leadership of their society, as it provides control over the diminishing sources of their wealth. An example is the struggle between the old gentrified commerce leaders and the new industrialists in Britain in the first half of the nineteenth century.[10] More serious, however, is the strategic struggle in societies that have exhausted their entire strategic sequence—such as Rome after 190 AD—because it involves a terminal conflict between groups of strategist within and without its borders.[11] Finally, there is the struggle for global supremacy between leading societies when the prevailing technological paradigm is finally exhausted. The most recent example is the exhaustion of the neolithic technological paradigm in the mid-eighteenth century. This precipitated a struggle for technological supremacy between the leading powers of Western Europe, which ultimately led to the disastrous consequences of the First World War, 1914–1918.

Will there be a similar outcome when the industrial paradigm exhausts itself in the middle decades of the twenty-first century? Only if we fail to learn the lessons, not of the past, but of dynamic-strategy theory and the strategic *logos*. Our future will be the outcome, not of the past, but of the demands of the ever-changing strategic *logos*. And the future can be understood not through the extrapolation of historical trends (simple historicism inevitably resorted to by even the most technical social sciences when predicting the future), but through the development of a general dynamic theory. The often quoted (and, more often, misquoted) cliché that "those who cannot remember the past are condemned to repeat it" (George Santayana, *The Life of Reason* vol. 1, 1905-06), therefore, is wrong. Instead, material failure awaits those who ignore the strategic *logos*.

Strategic Exhaustion

The force constraining life is not the limited supply of natural resources but rather the limitations of society's dynamic strategies. Many readers will have difficulties with this concept. To their minds, natural resources are finite, so that, once a species (including mankind) or a dynasty has "used up" its resources, its ecosystem will crash. This is the flawed thinking behind the currently popular concept of "sustainable development". Fortunately this type of thinking is not correct, otherwise life would have stagnated, or even collapsed, about 3,500 myrs ago when heterotrophic life forms (which are unable to use photosynthesis to manufacture their own food supply) exhausted the supply of free-floating organic molecules to create the world's first "energy crisis". Life was able to continue owing to genetic innovation—owing to the creation of new life forms that could employ existing resources more effectively.

The entire history of life on Earth is a story about organisms employing dynamic strategies to gain access to energy and other natural resources. This access occurs in two ways: a more intensive and a more extensive use of resources. To gain more intensive access to a given stock of resources, organisms employ either the genetic or the technological dynamic strategy.

This requires the creation of new genetic or technological styles and, at the wider level, of new genetic or technological skills. Organisms can extract a greater stream of services from existing resources, thereby increasing output per unit of input or productivity. An obvious example in human society is the application of machinery and fertilisers to agricultural land to increase crop yields; while in the early stages of life on Earth, cyanobacteria (or blue-green algae) by breaking down water to gain hydrogen were six times more efficient than sulphur (or green and purple) bacteria, which obtained hydrogen by breaking down hydrogen sulphide.

To gain more extensive access to the Earth's natural resources, organisms have taken their new genetic or technological styles to previously inaccessible areas by the pursuit of the family-multiplication, commerce, or conquest strategies. For example, before the emergence of mankind, dispersion was made possible by the Endothermic Revolution whereby newly emerged warm-blooded animals could, for the first time, migrate to the planet's colder regions. And in human society, the invention of windmills, for example, enabled the extension of agricultural lands through the draining of marshes. *Hence, the supply of natural resources is limited only by the effectiveness of our dynamic strategies. In other words, the supply of resources can only be defined relatively (rather than absolutely) in terms of the dynamic strategies available to exploit them.*

Strategic exhaustion (rather than natural resource exhaustion) operates at a number of levels. The first of these is at the level of the species or individual genetic style. A new genetic style, which provides improved access to natural resources, is exploited by individuals in that species until its potential is exhausted. With exhaustion, a crisis occurs as population presses heavily upon natural resources. The response by individuals in the species is to opt for the "internalised" conquest strategy (civil war), which is a short-run, zero-sum game that ultimately leads to the collapse of the genetic style or species. This accounts for the so-called "background extinctions" within a dynasty.

In human society, the exhaustion of comparable technological styles (or substrategies) and even the larger dynamic strategies, are usually negotiated through a relatively peaceful strategic struggle in which the casualties are measured in terms of economic loss. But occasionally it does lead to civil war. Here are two examples, discussed in my book *The Ephemeral Civilization* (1997): the English civil war of the 1640s, which was a clash between remnants of the old conquest strategists led by the recalcitrant Stuarts and the new commerce strategists led by the Parliamentarians (Oliver Cromwell); and the American civil war, which was a clash between the northern states pursuing an industrial technological strategy (wanting a protected mega-market for its output) and the southern states pursuing a commerce strategy (wanting free trade with Europe).

A more encompassing type of strategic exhaustion occurs at the levels of the dynasty and even the genetic paradigm. A new dynasty, or collection of closely related species—such as the Permian reptiles, or the protomammals, or dinosaurs, or modern mammals—exploit their joint strategic opportunities until they are finally exhausted. Approaching dynastic exhaustion is reflected in a growing rate of "background extinction" as groups of species exhaust their genetic styles, and in an increasingly depressed "origination" rate as unaccessed global resources decline. The outcome of this process is a growing dominance of the prevailing dynasty by one or two species, which is a sure sign that the dynasty is approaching exhaustion. And the outcome of dynastic exhaustion is the pursuit of conquest, the outbreak of "world war", followed by ecological crisis, collapse and, finally, dynastic extinction. While this is a terribly destructive process, it clears the way for the emergence of a new dynasty that, in its turn, will create a range of entirely new genetic styles to improve its access to natural resources. It may take the rise and fall of a number of dynasties before an old genetic paradigm (such as the ectothermic) is exhausted and a new genetic paradigm (such as the endothermic) emerges to take its place. *The dynamics of life, therefore, is all about unlocking a growing stream of services from the natural resources that were inherited when the Earth was formed some 4,500 myrs ago.*

The same, of course, is true concerning the dynamics of human society. It is sometimes harder to see this in our own lives owing to the greater complexity of our own dominant dynasty and the highly subjective manner in which we usually view it. But there is a major difference. And this concerns the outcome of the exhaustion of a technological paradigm. As suggested above, while exhausting technological paradigms—the paleolithic (10,600 BP), the neolithic (mid-eighteenth century) and the modern (mid twenty-first century)—can lead to major wars, such as the Napoleonic, First, and Second World Wars, they have obviously never resulted in the collapse of our dynasty. And the reason is that technological change provides an escape from a continuous cycle of world war. This is why we must strenuously resist attempts by the "antistrategists" who want to eliminate or constrain growth-inducing technological change in the name of Gaia or climate mitigation. If we fail—as discussed in chapter 13—the outcome could be a global conflagration from which we (like the dinosaurs) might never recover.

Social Organisation and Transformation

Sociobiologists attempt to explain the social interactions between related and unrelated individuals by employing the genetically based kin-selection model. Even if we assume, just for the sake of argument, that their model is correct, sociobiologists are still unable to "explain" social interactions beyond the extended family. In particular they have failed to explain the structure of human society or the way it changes over time. And, as I show in *The Collapse of Darwinism* (2003: ch. 7), they are in fact unable to explain social relationships even in the extended family. Even those sociobiologists who favour coevolution theory are left empty handed. Human nature and action in the coevolution model is seen as the outcome of "epigenetic" rules controlled by genes under the influence of natural selection. In this way individuals are held, according to E.O. Wilson, on a "genetic leash"—an explanation that many find offensive as well as unpersuasive—and social institutions are merely extruded from the human mind.[12] It is just another failed supply-side theory.

Institutionalists of both the old (Veblen and Commons) and new (Hayek and North) varieties have advanced our knowledge little further than the sociobiologists. Both groups view institutions (social rules) as central to the dynamics of human society and focus on "Darwinian" evolutionary-like processes. Despite the long history of this tradition, institutionalism has yet to provide a convincing dynamic theory. The primary reason is that it treats institutional change as a central self-contained mechanism rather than as a response to strategic demand generated by society's unfolding dynamic strategy. Because of their supply-side, evolutionary nature, these models are unable to explain the reversals that commonly occur in the process of sociopolitical change. Democracy, for example, is *not* an evolutionary process (which is uni-directional), as in the past it has undergone dramatic and systematic reversals, as I show in *The Ephemeral Civilization* (1997: ch. 4). Like sociobiology, institutionalism is a supply-side theory in a demand-side world.

How then do we account for the coherence of society in both the animal and human spheres? The dynamic-strategy theory contains a model of individual interaction that I've called the "concentric-spheres model".[13] It is based on the notion of genetically determined desires, but allows for varying degrees of individual choice and action. It shows that the way the self relates to other individuals and groups depends on their potential contribution to maximising the probability of the self's survival and prosperity. This potential contribution is measured in the concentric spheres model (Figure 4.1) by the "economic distance" between the self and all other individuals and groups who occupy different positions on a set of concentric spheres that radiate outwards.

Underlying the dynamics of this model are two balancing sets of forces, one centrifugal and the other centripetal. The centrifugal force is the innate desire of the self to survive and prosper, which leads typical individuals to persistently pursue their self interest. This is the life-energising force of strategic desire, which continually threatens to disrupt social relations. In contrast, the centripetal force, which can be thought of as the economic gravity holding animal society (from the highest to lowest forms) together, is generated by the self's need to cooperate with other individuals and groups in order to achieve its own objectives through the joint pursuit of a common dynamic strategy. While this model was developed primarily to explain animal (including human) behavior, it can also be applied to plant and earlier life forms (bacteria and viruses).

Figure 4.1. The Concentric Spheres Model of Behaviour

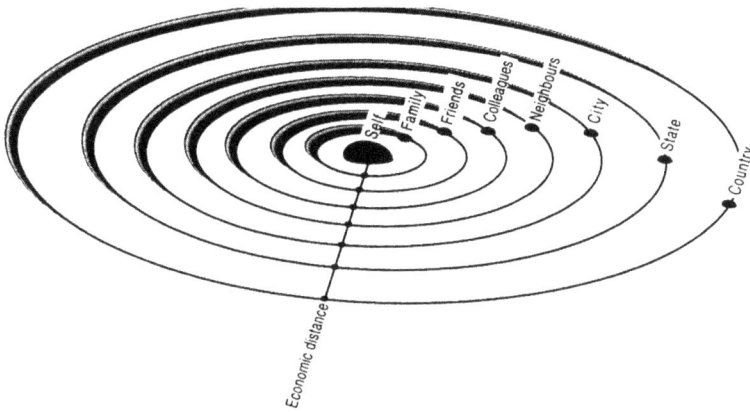

Source: Snooks 1997: 30.

It is through the interaction of competition and cooperation that individuals maximise the probability of their survival and prosperity. And it is in this way that their societies progress towards higher living standards and greater complexity. But it is important to realise that the underlying condition for the "trust" required for cooperation is not "altruism", genetic or otherwise, as argued by sociobiologists and institutionalists. Rather it is, as argued earlier, strategic confidence. This is the confidence that arises from the conspicuous success of the dynamic strategy being jointly pursued by these cooperative but highly self-interested individuals. And the cooperative actions undertaken by these individuals are shaped by strategic demand—a relationship I've recently called the process of "strategic exchange".[14]

Because Darwin's theory of natural selection—or "survival of the fittest"—does not allow for cooperation, neo-Darwinists were forced to invent a fanciful hypothesis about a genetic-based "altruism" to "explain" social relationships. This concept is discussed and refuted in *The Collapse of Darwinism* (2003: chs 7 and 8). Social scientists who have adopted this concept run into difficulties similar to those facing sociobiologists in explaining the real world.

In contrast, the dynamic-strategy theory is able to completely explain the dynamics of social organisation. In my theory, systematic changes in strategic demand provide the incentives, opportunities, and imperatives for the changing structure of animal and human society. The strategic cycle of adoption, exploitation, exhaustion, stagnation, and decline—the complete unfolding process of a dominant dynamic strategy—has a characteristic impact on the organisational and institutional structure of society. Unlike evolutionary theory, the dynamic-strategy theory can explain institutional reversal in terms of the traditional reversal of the strategic sequence—expressed, for example, as: conquest►commerce►conquest. This is discussed in outline in chapter 7, and in detail in both *The Ephemeral Civilization* (1997) and *The Collapse of Darwinism* (2003).

Institutional change, despite the claims of sociobiologists and evolutionary institutionalists, has no life of its own. Nor is it the outcome of the independent action of genes plotting from within their "lumbering robots", "survival machines"—as Richard Dawkins claims—or individual organisms—as you and I recognise them. Institutional change, including religious change, is reactive, not proactive. It has no "evolutionary" logic of its own. Animal society, whether simple or complex, is merely a vehicle for achieving the basic desire of life forms to survive and prosper—a vehicle that owes its vitality to the strategic *logos*. While the dynamic process is eternal, the sociopolitical institutions and organisations of life are ephemeral.

A SELFCREATING ENGINE OF LIFE

Life has an observable pattern and an existential meaning. The rise and fall of species, dynasties, societies, empires, and civilisations; the great genetic and technological revolutions; the great diasporas, civil wars, world wars, and extinctions—all are a part of an intelligible whole. These patterns, outlined in Chapter 3, are the outcome of individual organisms struggling to gain access to nature's resources, through the pursuit of a four-fold set of dynamic strategies, in order to survive and prosper. This is the dynamic core of the engine of life. It possesses a pattern and meaning that can be understood from within life itself— rather than by approaching supernatural beings as society has long attempted— through the dynamic-strategy theory. As we have seen in this chapter, this is a theory about the "selfcreating", or autogenous, nature of living systems.

We are now in a position to travel into completely unknown territory. Life also has an **unobservable** pattern and a **hidden** meaning. This invisible pattern—like the unseen forces determining the structure and dynamics of the physical world—can only be detected indirectly. The indirect method involves using the dynamic-strategy theory to detect the unseen reflected in the seen— akin to detecting unseen planets in far distant solar systems. This invisible pattern, which is generated by the unseen but powerful interactions between organisms and their society, is the universal life-system or, more succinctly, the strategic *logos*. And it is the strategic *logos* that provides the true meaning of life—a hidden but essentially materialistic meaning. The strategic *logos* is the subject of the next chapter.

Chapter 5
Strategic *Logos* — the Ark of the Sun

The logos *is the shaper of life and society.*

Life is the most profound mystery in the Universe. Although scholars take great pride in their major scientific achievements, they don't really understand how life emerged on our planet, how it was able to generate complex genetic and institutional forms, how it was able to sustain itself over the past 3,800 myrs, what the future might bring, or whether intelligent life exists on worlds other than our own. The fundamental reason for these critical uncertainties in human knowledge is that the underlying life-system is a hidden system, which, until recently, has eluded the objective methods of science. Accordingly, the life-system has, over many thousands of years, become the subject of much speculation, myth, and religion. It is my aim in this chapter to dispel the mystery of millennia by revealing the hidden life-system. This is done by introducing the materialist strategic *logos*, which provides the key to understanding not only life and human society, but also the origin, role, and dynamics of mythmaking and religion. The *logos* is the shaper of life and society.

Some readers may have difficulty conceptualising the strategic *logos*, not because this realist concept is difficult, but because it is unfamiliar. New ideas take time to be absorbed into the popular consciousness. It may help, therefore, if I nominate a number of conceptually similar concepts that have been part of our knowledge base for some time. Here are three analogous concepts that are familiar to most of us: the cosmos, the atomic world, and the self-conscious human mind. In each case, a hidden dynamic system comes into being owing to a complex and invisible interaction between its physical elements (which is why it is a materialist system), and disappears forever with the destruction of those physical elements. So it is with the strategic *logos*.

- **In the cosmos** we can observe the pattern of planetary motion, but not the force of gravity that shapes the solar system. And we can observe the dynamics of solar systems and galaxies, but not the forces that drive them, such as the appropriately named dark matter (pull factor), dark energy (push factor), and black holes. Yet, scientists claim that these invisible forces exist, because they can be indirectly and theoretically recognised. The cosmos, therefore, is a hidden **dynamic system** consisting of visible physical objects on the one hand, and invisible forces on the other. And the cosmos, as a dynamic system, lasts only as long as the physical bodies that inhabit it. Our solar system, for example, will last only until the Sun burns up all its fuel. This is a good analogy for the strategic *logos*, which is a hidden system consisting of visible agents and organisations, together with invisible interacting forces that can be indirectly and theoretically recognised. And like the cosmos, the *logos* is ephemeral. Yet, at any point in time many *logoi* (the plural of *logos*) exist.

- **In the atomic world**, it is possible to observe the patterns of atoms and molecules, but not the invisible but powerful nuclear and electromagnetic forces that determine these patterns. Yet, scientists tell us these forces do in fact exist, despite being unable to observe them directly. And we believe them, because it has been demonstrated that, by disrupting the nuclear and electromagnetic forces through "splitting" the atom, a subset of the atomic world can be made to break down violently (nuclear fission), releasing a large amount of energy.

  In a similar way, the strategic *logos* can be made to break down violently by disrupting the "strategic demand–response" mechanism (discussed in chapter 11) through the dictatorial controls of a centralised command economy, such as the USSR or, possibly, a future global command-mitigation economy. Societal breakdown of this type, is indirect evidence of the existence of a hidden life-system, just as nuclear fission resulting from deliberate intervention in the atomic world is evidence of an atomic-molecular system. In the ruins of chaos, we recognise the invisible structure of order.

- Another helpful analogy concerns that complex strategic instrument we call **the human brain**. We can observe its physical composition, but not the interactions taking place between its various component parts—invisible interactions that create the hidden mind. The self-conscious **mind** is invisible and cannot be directly observed by scientists, only experienced existentially by its hosts, or explored analogously through metaphor. The metaphor I have in mind is the **metropolis**, where we can observe the interactions between agents and organisations, even the resulting cultural modes of "self-awareness" (see chapter 9). Both the **mind** and the **metropolis** last only as long as their physical components retain their integrity. Irretrievable damage sustained by a brain or an urban structure will terminally disrupt the network of strategic interactions, and will lead to the demise of the mind or the metropolis as a dynamic system. So it is with the strategic *logos*.

THE VEHICLE OF LIFE

Some natural scientists are fond of telling us that we inhabit a peculiarly "life-friendly" Universe. By this they mean that the laws of physics and the values of the "fundamental constants of nature"—including the cosmological constant, gravity, the velocity of light—are just what is required to enable the emergence of carbon-based life in the Universe.[1] As shown in *Dead God Rising* (2010: ch. 9), these scientists usually have some sort of teleological theory—either the

"Mind of God" or the superintelligence—that they are promoting. In contrast, those scholars studying life-systems in either the natural or human domains are keenly aware that the physical world is extremely hostile to life.

Because the Universe is so hostile to life, all its forms are dominated by the overriding desire to survive and prosper. For example, life forms only exist because they have found ways to defy the second law of thermodynamics. This law tells us that while heat flows *spontaneously* from hot to cold bodies, this inevitable process cannot be reversed, at least not *spontaneously*. The upshot of this law is that all *closed* physical systems are trapped in a one-way trip towards the final state of thermodynamic equilibrium, or "heat death". Stated in slightly different terms, this equilibrium is the outcome of increasing entropy. Hence, all closed systems are moving inevitably from a state of order to a state of disorder.

Entropy is a variable rather than a constant, and the change in entropy (ds), which measures the change in disorder, is related to temperature (T) and heat (dtQ). Hence, an infinitesimal amount of heat absorbed by any system leads to a change in the entropy (disorder) of that system according to the formula:

$dtQ = Tds$ or $ds = dt/T$

Of course, while the entire physical system may be closed—such as the Universe as a whole—any part of it may find ways to decrease its entropy (or increase its order) by absorbing heat released by other parts of the larger system. This, in physical terms, is how order and complexity can be achieved by open biological systems, without violating the laws of physics. It happens when ways and means are found to convert energy from a body like the sun (or from the molten core of a planet in the ocean depths) into work—a less than fully efficient process that loses energy to the environment in the form of heat.

While all of this appears straightforward in physical terms, the trick, and it is not an easy one to master as far as life forms are concerned, is to develop techniques that provide continuous access to energy and other natural resources. These techniques, as discussed in Chapter 4, can be both biological and technological, which are generated by investment of time and energy in new "ideas". Much of my work—generated by metabolic energy derived both directly and indirectly from the sun—over the past few decades has been devoted to showing how this has been undertaken. What should be realised is that biological and technological "ideas" do not just emerge spontaneously in a way similar to the flow of heat from hot to cold bodies. While *disorder* is a spontaneous physical process, the creation of *order* requires considerable energy, effort, and *creative* impulse to be achieved. In other words, life forms need energy not only to survive and prosper, but also to develop a continuous supply of techniques to gain long-term access to sources of energy and other natural resources. But the survival "trick" requires more than this. Energy is also needed to develop "dynamic life-systems" in order to protect and sustain this extremely difficult process of survival and prosperity in a hostile world that is continuously running down. This protective life-system—which I call the "strategic *logos*"— has to be dynamic because it is necessary to continuously reinvent itself in order to gain access to the resources required. A static system would quickly perish in a world running down. The strategic *logos*, which is the vehicle of both life and human society that is fueled by solar energy, is the "ark of the Sun".

Once established, a strategic *logos* operates according not to the laws of physics but to its own internal laws—the laws of life and history—which are discussed in chapter 6. The laws of physics merely provide the background against which agents of the strategic *logos* play out the game of life. While the laws of physics make it possible to play the game of life, it is the players— the individual organisms driven by strategic desire—who decide whether or not to play the game and, if so, how it should be played. And we play this exacting game in the self-contained world of the strategic *logos*; a world which defies the hostilities, difficulties, and mindlessness of the physical world. Because the strategic *logos* operates according to its own internalised rules, scientists are unable to employ the laws of physics to explain life. This is why self-organisational and complexity theory—currently popular supply-side models—which emerged from the natural sciences, are not capable of conveying an understanding of life and human society.[2] To comprehend these amazing entities we must first understand the strategic *logos* and the internal laws by which it operates.

Once a viable strategic *logos*—or dynamic life-system—has been established, it is necessary to defend it against a wide range of external threats. These threats come from both the physical and organic worlds. Physical threats include asteroid attack, volcanic eruptions, earthquakes, tsunamis, floods, typhoons, droughts, fires, and rapid climatic change. Most viable strategic *logoi* are able to withstand these physical threats precisely because they have been shaped over millions of years to do so. There will be times, of course, when extreme events will force a dynamic life-system into a temporary decline, with recovery taking time, energy, and the employment of accumulated wealth. These random events temporarily distort the more cyclical pattern that has been detected (as discussed in Chapter 4) in human and other life-systems.

In contradiction of the claims of most natural scientists and environmentalists interested in this issue, the strategic *logoi* of life and human society are remarkably resilient to the onslaught of random physical shocks. Massive volcanic eruptions can tear holes in a society—such as the Roman cities of Pompeii and Herculaneum in AD 79—but viable societies just repair these holes and continue on with life; major changes in climate—such as those in Egypt from the prehistoric to the Old Kingdom—can provoke viable societies to respond creatively through the introduction of new technologies (irrigation systems) and the adoption of new economic activities (riverine agriculture in place of hunting), but they are not responsible for the collapse of those societies. This is merely a myth propagated by natural scientists and their Green followers, who have not constructed the dynamic theory required to analyse complex living systems. As I have shown in *The Dynamic Society* (1996), *The Ephemeral Civilization* (1997) and *The Collapse of Darwinism* (2003), the collapse of dominant species, societies, and dynasties is the outcome not of random physical shocks, but of the exhaustion of dynamic strategies as well as biological and technological paradigms. The same will be true of human-induced climate change, as discussed in my recent book *The Coming Eclipse* (2010a) and addressed in chapter 13.

What the climate mitigationists don't realise is that the strategic *logos* has evolved over billions of years to survive in the face of rapid climate change. This has been the case throughout the history of life. It has also been the experience of mankind. If we confine ourselves just to the history of modern man, we find that during the past 100,000 years there have been as many as twenty-four occurrences of abrupt and very rapid climate change. These periods were typically characterised by gradual cooling from a warm interglacial period, followed by more abrupt cooling, then a cold interval and, finally, an abrupt and very rapid warming by around *10 degrees C. in only a decade* (Pittock 2006). These occurrences are known to the scientific community as Dansgaard/ Oeschger events. The latest of these, which occurred about 12,800 years ago, is called the Younger Dryas event, and it involved an increase in global temperatures by *8 degrees C. in a decade*. As the strategic *logos* of man has developed in order to survive rapid climate change, there is little doubt it will be able to handle the present global warming event.

More problematical are the threats posed by other life-systems. These more serious threats arise from other strategic *logoi* within the same species and from other species. In our own species, the greatest threat comes from competing strategic *logoi*, particularly those pursuing the dynamic strategy of conquest. For example, Phoenicia was swept away by Alexander the Great; Carthage was finally completely destroyed by Rome; Egypt was seriously challenged by Assyria, Persia, and Macedonia, and finally extinguished by Rome; Venice was challenged by the Ottomans and ultimately felled by Napoleon. Ironically, even the victorious societies in these conflicts eventually collapsed owing to their very success—ultimately they exhausted their dynamic strategies of conquest. And an exhausted, irreplacable strategic *logos* does not survive for long.

Less challenging for the human strategic *logos* are the attacks of other species. Wild animals are annoying because they take human life and generate minor economic loss, but microbiological life forms have had a greater impact. In the past, diseases like bubonic plague—which eliminated between one-third and one-half of the populations of viable societies—and the great influenza pandemic—which killed 20 million people world-wide just after the First World War—have been devastating. But the fascinating thing is that these societies continued as if nothing had happened. In Europe during the mid-fourteenth century, the Hundred Years' War between England and France hardly missed a beat, even when bubonic plague first struck Western Europe; and Europe was ready to engage in a Second World War less than a generation after the great influenza pandemic.[3] The point is that the strategic *logos* is a very effective mechanism for throwing off even large-scale effects of exogenous shocks. And it will be the same with any viral pandemic—whether "bird flu" or "swine flu"—in the future. Individuals are highly vulnerable to the attack of virulent new diseases, but the strategic *logos* is remarkably resilient. It has to be, if life is to survive in a hostile world.

The resilience and success of the strategic *logos* is reflected in the "logological constant" of life discussed in Chapter 3. What it measures is just as remarkable and unchanging as the fundamental constants of the physical world. As we have seen, it shows that over the past 3,800 myrs the global biomass/GDP has not only increased at an exponential rate, but that in geometric (or compound growth-rate) terms it is a constant with a coefficient value of approximately 3.0. This suggests that each biological/technological transformation (taken as a whole) occurs in one-third of the time taken by the previous one. This fundamental constant of life is ample proof of the resilience and effectiveness of the strategic *logos* in the face of both the second law of thermodynamics and the hostile physical and biological world. Hence, it is the strategic *logos* rather than the brute physical facts of the Universe that is "life-friendly". It is the strategic *logos* that confounds the gloomy predictions of the crisis exaggerators—those antistrategists fearful of change.

DEFINING THE STRATEGIC *LOGOS*

We need to formally address the question: what is the strategic *logos*? It is, as suggested above, the dynamic life-system that is essential to our individual and group survival and prosperity. Without the *logos,* life would never have gained a foothold on this planet; without the *logos,* life certainly would not have flourished; and without the *logos* we would all have perished. The strategic *logos* is an entropy-defying, shock-deflecting mechanism. Yet despite its absolutely essential role in our very existence and survival, the *logos* is still a great mystery to the science community, which is incapable of exploring its hidden forces. Instead, scientists think they see complex systems arising spontaneously—like entropy—from the mere interaction of decision-making agents. Life is seen as a form of social physics.[4]

Previous Usage of the Term "Logos"

The Greek word *Logos* (λόγου) has a long history. While this history has in no way influenced the content of my concept of the "strategic *logos*"—the concept was complete before this history was even known to me—it can be usefully surveyed here.[5] In Homer (ninth century BC), meanings of the word *logo* include: "to gather", "to count", "to enumerate", "to enter on a list", "to narrate" and "to say". There was also a sense of wholeness or comprehensiveness about any such enumeration or narration. Likewise the noun *logos*—the plural of which is *logoi*—had, for Homer, the meanings of "collection", "gathering", "assemblage", "list", "calculation", "account", "reckoning", "narrative" and "speech". Soon after Homer's time, the meaning of *logos* became restricted to rationally established and constructed speech.

Heraclitus (around 500 BC), from my reading of his collected fragments[6], employed the term *logos* to denote a mysterious, possibly divine, "system", which had a controlling influence over human society. Its usage implies that our world has unity, coherence, and meaning, which is established through ever present change or flux. Heraclitus was the expert of the ancient world on the dynamics of life and human society, which is why I am so interested in his work, as fragmentary as it is.
Heraclitus tells us:

> For wisdom, listen
> not to me but to the *logos*
> and know that all is one.

The *logos* is also the entity "from which all things follow". Yet he appears exasperated that:

> The *logos* proves
> those first hearing it
> as numb to understanding
> as the ones who have not heard.

(No doubt the same will be true regarding the reception of the strategic *logos* in this book.) Instead, he tells us, the people and their leaders prefer the shallow explanations of "specialists" or experts:

> Although we need the *logos*
> to keep things known in common,
> people still treat specialists
> as if their nonsense
> were a form of wisdom.

He could, of course, be commenting on our own times—particularly regarding the reception of market economists—rather than those of 2,500 years ago. Heraclitus even tells us that these "specialists", deluded by their popularity with the people, attack those who seek to discover and explain the *logos*:

> Dogs, by this same logic,
> bark at what they cannot understand.

After the time of Heraclitus, the word *logos* was employed by Christian theologians—St John the Divine and Philo, for example—to refer to the revelation of Christ. In this context, *logos* is usually translated into English as "Word", meaning the spiritual aspect of Jesus Christ that is alleged to have the power to create and sustain life. And in Western philosophy today, *logos* is taken to refer to the rational principle that governs and develops the Universe; in theology it refers to the divine Word of God made known by Jesus Christ; and in one interesting but eccentric work in sociology (Roy Rapport) it is construed as the "rational order uniting nature, society, individual humans and divinity into 'a great cosmos'", which is established through religious ritual.[7] My use of the term strategic *logos*, as shall be seen, is very different to all these, although in sentiment it comes closest to what we can detect in the fragmented writings (quoted in other ancient works) of Heraclitus.

While the "strategic *logos*" is invisible and its meaning hidden, all ancient societies have been aware of its shadowy presence, and based their mythologies and religions on it. They referred to it as: harmony, order, stability, cosmic balance, security, truth, law of the Universe, unity of nature, "sacred circle" (Sioux).They saw this shadowy reality as the changelessness beneath the superficial flux of everyday life. (In fact, the strategic *logos* is ever-changing.) And they personified the various perceived characteristics of this underlying reality as gods. We can even see the longing for order, balance and stability today in the inflation-targeting policies of economists and central banks, and the climate-mitigation policies of environmentalists.

Some ancient and pre-modern societies even had names for this hidden system of order, balance and stability. As we have seen, the Greeks called it *logos*; but, in addition, this mystery of mysteries was called *maat* by the Egyptians, *Asha* by the Persians, *Rta* by the Vedic Indians, *Nelli* by the Toltecs, *Wakan-Tanka* (or "Great Mystery") by the Sioux, and the "Dreaming" by Australian Aboriginies.[8] All these societies, as well as those who had no special name for this mysterious system underlying life, were extremely concerned to sustain it together with all its life-giving powers. They were convinced that their life-system would be disrupted by inappropriate behaviour, either of omission or commission, and the result would be disorder and chaos. Without understanding the scientific concept of entropy, they had a strong sense of the world running down. Hence, it was essential in their eyes to undertake the appropriate sacrifice and ritual, and to live according to the laws of the *logos*. In this, as shown in chapter 8, they looked to their wisemen and their kings. This was the real origin and purpose of religion.

A WORKING MODEL OF THE STRATEGIC *LOGOS*

The strategic *logos* is a dynamic mechanism that generates a largely invisible process of interaction between human agents and their society. It is a self-generating and self-sustaining life-system that not only protects its members from a hostile world but enables them to progress both technologically and culturally. In the absence of overwhelming external shocks—such as the invasions of the New World in the early sixteenth century and of the Great South Land in the late eighteenth century—the strategic *logos* continues to flourish until its entire sequence of dynamic strategies is completely exhausted. In the case of the world's most successful societies, such as ancient Egypt or Rome, this can last anywhere from one to three millennia. During this time, the *logos* is driven and shaped by its own internal laws—the laws of history—that are independent of the laws of physics.[9] Ultimately, however, the laws of history run their course, the strategically exhausted society enters into terminal crisis, and the strategic *logos* collapses. The heart of this particular human society throbs no more. But, in time it will be replaced by another *logos* and society.

The strategic *logos*, therefore, is ephemeral rather than eternal. It exists only as long as the society with which it came into the world. While a particular *logos* accounts for the rise and fall of a client society, it is also the creation of that society—or, at least, of the collectivity of individuals in that society, who are integrated by their common strategic pursuit. The strategic *logos*, as will be demonstrated, is both the outcome of, and reason for, the creative interaction between the people and their society, which I have called "strategic exchange".[10] Hence, the *logos* is born with the emergence of a particular society and the *logos*, together with its mythical strategic guardians, dies with that society. It is this close and essential relationship that has led human societies to worship the unknown strategic *logos* and to call its strategic guardian God. As each society unknowingly creates, and is created by, its own strategic *logos*, it is not alone; many *logoi* exist at any point in time. It was for this reason, as discussed in chapter 8, that human societies in both the Old and New Worlds had their own home-grown gods. Each society created its own god or gods in order to protect and sustain its own strategic *logos*. Further, it should be realised that while each society has its own strategic *logos*, there is no overarching *logos* for humanity as a whole. Earth's human race is the outcome of the interaction between competing *logoi*.

A Simple Two-Dimensional Model

In an effort to make visible what has for many thousands of years remained hidden, a diagrammatic model of the strategic *logos* is presented in Figure 5.1. This model is based on the dynamic-strategy theory (chapter 4), which in turn was constructed inductively from the close and systematic observation of living systems in both the human and non-human worlds (Chapters 2 and 3). Needless to say, this figure is merely a simple, two-dimensional representation of a complex, three-dimensional process. What Figure 5.1 clearly shows, however, is the fundamental circular nature of interaction between man and society—the selfcreating process of strategic exchange—that lies at the heart of the strategic *logos*. This pattern of concentric circles—this complex mandala—bears a close resemblance to the dominant role that circles and concentric circles played in the sacred art of the paleolithic era. As shown in *Dead God Rising* (2010b: ch. 2), these concentric circles represented the life-system of early hunting societies.

Figure 5.1. The Strategic *Logos*

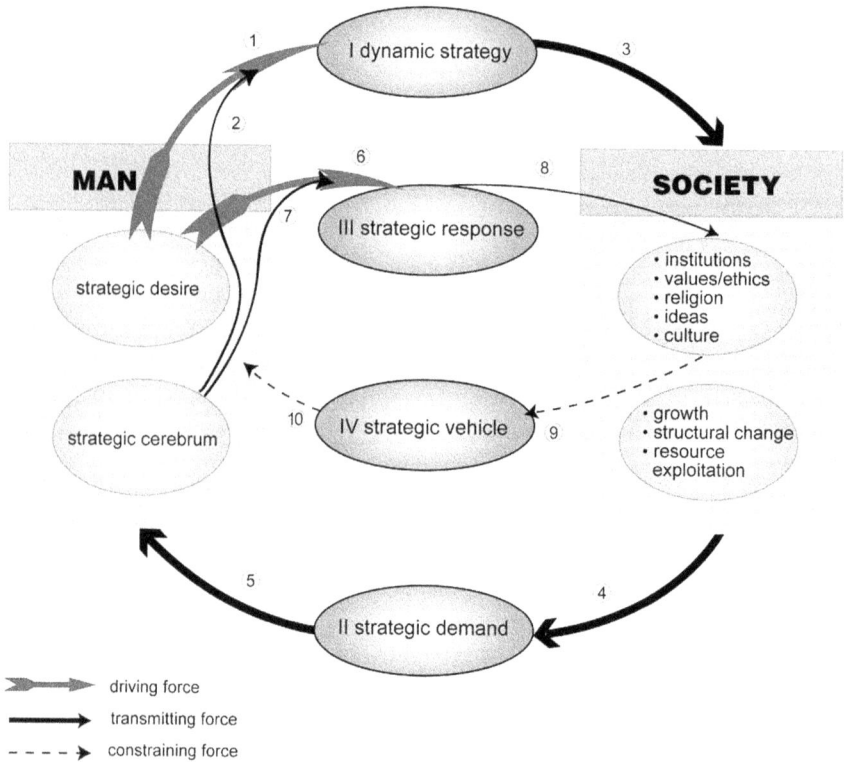

driving force
transmitting force
- - - - ▸ constraining force

Source: Snooks 2010: 322.

The circular process of strategic exchange occurs at four main levels. These include: **I** the dynamic strategy pursued by society; **II** the strategic demand that this unfolding process generates for a wide range of strategic inputs; **III** the individual and collective response to strategic demand; and **IV** the resulting strategic vehicle that carries society forward in its "strategic pursuit". These forces also generate the laws of history (and of life).

The strategic *logos* is driven by "strategic desire", which, as shown in Chapter 4, is the motive force that powers the dynamic circle, or mandala, of life. It is the centre of life's pulsating heart, and it provides this dynamic engine with its self-starting and self-sustaining character. Strategic desire, which is fed both directly and indirectly with energy from the sun, operates primarily by driving both the dynamic strategy being pursued by society together with its "strategic response". In both cases this activity is facilitated by the supervisory and planning role played by the "strategic cerebrum" (discussed in chapter 9).

The great *directing* force in human society is "strategic demand", which continually changes as the dominant dynamic strategy unfolds. This directing force provokes a necessary response from the people, thereby providing the institutional, organisational, and cultural vehicle required to engage successfully in the strategic pursuit. This societal vehicle also provides the medium for natural-resource exploitation, as well as for economic growth and the structural change required to meet the people's strategic objective of survival and prosperity.

Just as the laws of physics are derived from observing physical relationships in the cosmos, so the laws of life and history have been derived from observing societal relationships in the strategic *logos*. These laws shape and regulate the dynamics of life, human society, and civilisation. In *Laws of History* (1998) and *The Collapse of Darwinism* (2003; ch. 15), I derived nine general and universal laws from the operation of the strategic *logos*. These "primary" laws, which are listed here and explained in chapter 6, include:

- The law of motivation in life
- The law of competitive intensity
- The law of strategic selection
- The law of strategic optimisation
- The law of strategic imitation
- The law of strategic struggle
- The law of diminishing strategic returns
- The law of strategic crisis
- The law of societal collapse.

These laws define the entropy-defying nature of the strategic *logos*. Other laws— "secondary" (four in life and five in society) and "tertiary" (four in life and nine in society)—applicable to the major historical eras, have been derived from these eight primary laws by introducing different initial conditions from these eras.

There are four main *logos* types, each generating a different dominant dynamic strategy, namely the hunting *logos* (family strategy), military *logos* (conquest strategy), merchantile *logos* (commerce strategy), and enterprise *logos* (technological strategy). Each *logos* generates, through strategic demand, a distinct institutional and cultural structure (see chapter 7).

With this overview in mind, we can investigate the operation of the strategic *logos* in Figure 5.1. We begin with "Man" in the left-had box. Man is dualistic in his strategic nature. Not only driven by strategic desire to achieve his fundamental joint objective of survival and prosperity, Man also possesses a highly sophisticated instrument—the strategic cerebrum—employed to plan and supervise the strategic pursuit. This was achieved, as we saw in Chapter 4, through the adoption and exploitation of one of a quartet of dynamic strategies— family multiplication, conquest, commerce, technological change—available to that society. As the chosen dynamic strategy unfolds, society increases its access to natural resources, grows economically, and changes structurally. In the process, the "Society" generates strategic demand for an extensive range of strategic inputs, including land, labour, capital, ideas (technological, strategic, other), institutions (societal rules), organisations (societal networks), values, ethics, religion, and culture. The nature of these inputs bears the stamp of the particular dynamic strategy being pursued. All human values, in other words, are initiated outside (although with the participation of) man by the strategic *logos*, not purely by the mind of man as most scholars claim.

The drive behind the strategic response to "logosian demand" is, once again, provided by strategic desire, and is facilitated by the strategic cerebrum. A major outcome of this strategic response is the creation of an institutional, ethical, religious, cultural vehicle capable of carrying the strategic pursuit forward and, thereby, delivering the material success that meets the needs of strategic desire, which initiated the entire process. The completion of this circular interaction, however, doesn't lead to equilibrium, because strategic desire is never satisfied. Accordingly, the circular interaction becomes an upward spiral that continues until the strategic *logos* collapses, sending the whole process into reverse.

While this diagrammatic model of the strategic *logos* provides a convenient two-dimensional sketch of a complex dynamic engine of society, its limitations are obvious. First, Figure 5.1 is merely a cross-section of the entire circular process of strategic exchange. The missing third dimension is time, which is needed to show how the *logos* allows a society not only to exploit the founding dynamic strategy, but also how its exhaustion, which threatens the continuing viability of the *logos*, opens the way for the adoption and exploitation of a further dynamic strategy from its four-fold armoury.

By adding time, a three-dimensional model would demonstrate the strategic sequence, which would burrow into the surface of the page at level **I**. Such a sequence would show how a changing strategic demand impacts on the strategic vehicle we call civilisation. One need only reflect, for example, on how different was Greek civilisation under the conquest strategy (400–100 BC) from that under the commerce strategy (800–500 BC). Of particular interest in this example, is how the strategic sequence of conquest▶ commerce▶ conquest led ancient Greece to advance toward and, later, retreat from democratic ecosociopolitical forms— see my book *The Ephemeral Civilization* (1997: ch. 8). This unfolding strategic sequence was presided over by the Greek *logos*—transforming itself from military to merchantile to military—which was recognised but misinterpreted as the divine *Logos* by Heraclitus around 500 BC.

Secondly, the strategic *logos* should not be thought of as being confined by fixed dimensions as Figure 5.1 probably suggests. By adding the missing variable of time, the *logos*, as a dynamic engine, grows larger (or smaller, if in decline), more complex (representing a spiral rather than an ellipse), and it generates greater (or lesser) levels of population, GPD and GDP per capita. In a more partial and ad hoc manner, these issues can be dealt with by employing conventional "timescapes" that show changes in the variables by which the success (or failure) of societies and civilisation are usually measured. What is important to note here is that these performance variables feed back into the decisions made by agents through "strategic confidence". Also we need to remember that all three outcomes are generated by the strategic *logos*, which is not to be simplistically confused with the crude representations of it made in Figure 5.1.

Finally, it is important to realise that in life, dynamics—or, in the words of Heraclitus, "flux"—is deep and abiding, not superficial and intermittent. Not only is life in constant flux, but the system of life that generates this flux is also dynamic in itself. In other words, the dynamic engine that is the strategic *logos* acts upon itself as well as on life and society. The *logos* is not absolute, eternal, and changeless in the way that gods are supposed to be, but rather it is ephemeral and in a state of continuous change. The strategic *logos* changes as its dynamic strategy unfolds; and it is transformed as the global genetic/technological paradigm shifts occur. *Both the moved and the mover are dynamic*. This reality is in stark contrast to the theological idea that arose to explain this mystery of mysteries—the fanciful idea of the unmoved mover.

The strategic *logos* depicted in Figure 5.1 can be generalised to embrace all "societies" in life. They would differ largely in terms of degree of sophistication of the strategic cerebrum (or, in its absence, the "strategic gene"), of complexity of the strategic vehicle, or of the type and magnitude of material outcomes. As discussed in *The Collapse of Darwinism* (2003), even simple, single-cellular life adopts and pursues the generalised quartet of dynamic strategies available to human society. Hence, the strategic *logos* accounts for the origin and growing complexity of the entire "society" of life. The *logos* is, in other words, the dynamic machine responsible for the selfcreating—or autogenous—process that can be detected in all species of life.

It is the strategic *logos* which provides the protective environment that life and human society require to flourish in a difficult environment. It is the vehicle of life, the ark of the Sun. But to undertake this critical function, the *logos* requires above all else, sustained loyalty and dedication by society's members to the cause of survival and prosperity. It can only do its work if there are no serious divisions in society—if the inevitable emergence of antistrategic elements are restricted to a tiny minority in a sea of enthusiastic strategic supporters. The vast majority of the population are required to support the strategic ideology of their society. In the past, the strategic ideology may have been pagan, Zoroastrian, Christian or Islamic, but today it is scientism—the belief in the role of science and technology in the successful strategic pursuit. While the *logos* is blind to colour, race and creed, it demands complete support for the prevailing strategic ideology. Those antistrategists working against the *logos* from the inside include, most obviously, local terrorists involved in destructive activities in support of the conflicting ideologies of external organisations and societies; but also include, less obviously, those internal groups supporting ideologies that surreptitiously and seriously undermine the viability of the *logos* in the name of a pseudo scientism. In the immediate future, the latter will be of greater danger to our civilisation, as they are becoming a significant and influential minority in societies that have failed to understand the nature of the strategic *logos*.

HISTORICAL REALITY AND ULTIMATE REALITY

What are we to make of the strategic *logos*? There are, in my philosophy of life, two forms of reality. First, there is "historical reality", which consists of *objects* and physical relationships between objects that can be perceived through the senses over time. And, second, there is "ultimate reality", or the strategic *logos*, that is the outcome of a complex set of invisible relationships between *forces*—such as strategic desire and strategic demand—that cannot be perceived through the senses, despite having materialist origins. Only the agents (or "strategists") and outcomes (institutions, organisations, infrastructure, and material wealth) generated by these invisible forces can be detected by the senses. The discovery of the strategic *logos* is similar in nature to the discoveries in science.[11]

The invisible pattern of forces described in the diagrammatical representation (Figure 5.1) of the strategic *logos* can only be comprehended by developing a general dynamic theory (Chapter 4) that can explain and predict the recurring visible patterns in historical reality (Chapter 3). Ultimate reality in life, therefore, is the hidden dynamic system responsible for generating biological life together with all its observable vehicles of change.

Interestingly, the dynamic-strategy theory outlined in Chapter 4 was developed not in pursuit of the strategic *logos*—the existence of which I had not initially considered—but rather to explain and predict the recurring patterns found in historical reality. Only once this theory had been constructed was it possible to detect the existence of the *logos*, precisely because it is not directly accessible to the senses. Hence, it is historical reality that leads the way to life's ultimate reality; and it is the dynamic-strategy theory that provides the link between them.

This theoretical link between levels of reality should be Janus-like—it should work in both directions. Here it might help to play a mind game that has nothing to do with reality. If one could apprehend only ultimate reality—the strategic *logos*—it would still be possible to develop the underlying dynamic-strategy theory (and the laws of history) by analysing the relationships between strategic forces. In turn this dynamic theory could be used to discover the patterns in historical reality (had they been unknown to us). Of course, we would have to be very different beings to work in this way. Remember, this exercise is only a game, but a game with a serious point to make: which is that historical reality and ultimate reality are linked through the exercise of "strategic thinking"—see chapter 9—whereby observable patterns are identified and employed as the basis for inductive theory making. The nature and role of strategic thinking, which is contrasted with deductive thinking, has been discussed at length in *The Selfcreating Mind* (2006). The implication of this argument is that the strategic *logos* could not have been discovered in any other way—such as by deductive thinking—by beings like us. The history of philosophy over the past 3,000 years attests to this.

THE MEANING OF LIFE

The strategic *logos* is the only source of hope for life in a hostile world. It is the meaning of life. This existential fact clearly has been understood by all societies in the past for which evidence is available. All societies have been only too aware of their precarious circumstances in this world. The ruins of former, once flourishing, societies and civilisations are there for all to see. In Mesoamerica for example, the Aztecs saw their life-system as the Fifth Sun, as they were acutely aware that four other life-systems, or "Suns", together with their gods, had flourished in their world for a time, and then collapsed. And in Egypt, every night was a time of potential crisis, as the sun god Re and his divine retinue passed through the underworld, for the ancient Egyptians believed that as their ordered world (*maat*) had emerged from a watery chaos (*nun*) so it would end in a watery chaos. Today there is a widespread fear that climate change will irreparably harm our own life-system. Such concern can be appreciated, because, if our strategic *logos* were irreparably damaged, there would be no hope for societal progress or individual survival. But unfortunately, in an attempt to "save" our life-system—without understanding what it is or how it works— "experts" (of the Heraclitian kind) are advocating massive intervention that will merely destroy the focus of their concern. Environmentalists, inadequately informed by the realist social sciences, have associated planet Earth, rather than the strategic *logos,* with the ark of the Sun.

Chapter 6
Laws of the *Logos*

The laws of life triumph over the laws of physics.

It is a remarkable fact that none of the sciences possesses a set of *general* laws that can explain the origins and dynamics of the real world. Science has only been able to develop laws that are restricted to either subsets of the dynamic whole or to static relationships. Usually the latter. This is just as true of the physical and biological sciences as it is of the social sciences. While law-making is most advanced in the physical sciences, even in this less complex field of intellectual endeavour there are no general laws bridging dynamic relationships between the smallest and greatest levels. Why? Because there are no general dynamic theories that can embrace both the micro and macro worlds. Until now.

A recent breakthrough has been made in the social sciences. This may come as a surprise to some because the social sciences in general and history in particular are widely regarded as more backward in law-making than their more precocious siblings in the natural sciences. Indeed, physical scientists are usually less than impressed with even the most "scientific" of the social sciences—neoclassical economics; and biological scientists have long been threatening that they are on the verge of colonising their less-scientific brethren.

The social sciences possess a longstanding set of **static** microeconomic laws, but few in macroeconomics and none in history. What they have always lacked is a set of general **dynamic** laws. This may be surprising to some, as philosophers and historians have been searching for the laws of history for thousands of years. In *The Laws of History* (1998a), I devote five chapters to examining the investigations of the "law seekers", who are divided into two groups: the "metaphysical historicists", including Hesiod and Heraclitus (about 500 BC), Plato (427–347 BC), Hegel (1770–1831), Marx (1818–1883), Spencer (1820–1903), Spengler (1880–1936), and Toynbee (1899–1975); and the "positive historicists", including Comte (1798–1857), J.S. Mill (1806–1873), Buckle (1821–1862), the nineteenth-century historical economists, and Rostow (1916–2003). Unfortunately, no one from either group of historicism was able to uncover the laws of history: the metaphysicists because they employed the unrealistic method of deductivism; and the positivists because they were unable to develop an inductive method that could be employed to construct a realist general dynamic theory.

In contrast to metaphysical and positive historicism, the method of "existential historicism" that I have developed in my global dynamic-systems approach, has made possible the construction of both a realist general dynamic theory and the discovery of the laws of history and of life—the laws of the strategic *logos.*[1] This research provides the basis for the "social dynamics" that John Stuart Mill (1843) attempted to develop but was later forced to abandon as a failed intellectual enterprise. This development in the social sciences, therefore, occurred from within rather than without, as had long been predicted. Why? Because the life sciences in general and sociobiology in particular were never in the race. Darwinists of both the original and sociobiological kind have failed to develop a general dynamic theory despite their longstanding claims to the contrary. It was one of the objectives of my book *The Collapse of Darwinism* (2003) to show why.

What accounts for the recent success of the social sciences? This success is curious because the history of the social sciences consists of either a retreat into story-telling (a role with which most historians appear to be comfortable), a preoccupation with deductive fantasy by those employing pseudo physical-science methods (pursued by orthodox, neoclassical economists), or a slavish imitation of the flawed Darwinist theory (adopted by less orthodox institutional economists). These matters are discussed in detail in my books *Economics Without Time* (1993: ch. 1), *The Ephemeral Civilization* (1997: ch. 4), and *Longrun Dynamics* (1998b: pt II). This breakthrough in the social sciences came from a rejection of story-telling, of deductive game-playing, and of neo-Darwinian mimicry. By embracing a new inductive approach—what I call "existential historicism"—it has been possible, as shown in chapter 4, to reconstruct the general dynamic mechanism underlying the historical patterns not only of human society but also of all life. The laws of life and history—the laws of the strategic *logos*—are derived from modeling this dynamic mechanism. As argued in chapter 1, the laws of life triumph over the laws of physics.

A NEW METHOD OF LAW-MAKING—EXISTENTIAL HISTORICISM

Historicism has had a remarkably bad press. This is largely due to the politically motivated attack made in the middle decades of the twentieth century by a number of extreme deductivists under the intellectual influence of Karl Popper.[2] But it is also an outcome of the limited imagination of the old historicists as a group. The old historicists in the social sciences treated the patterns they detected in history as the dynamic mechanism itself rather than merely the outcome of the *underlying* process of change. They were, therefore, easy targets for extreme deductivists such as Karl Popper (1902–1994) and Friedrich Hayek (1899–1992). In the biological sciences the historicists (or paleontologists) are also afflicted with the same problem, which is exacerbated by their refusal to abandon the flawed Darwinian framework. Curiously, even the deductivists (including Popper himself!)[3] resort to simplistic historicist models—extrapolating recent trends into the distant future—when dealing with the big dynamic issues facing humanity today, owing to the inadequacies of their static deductive models. This can also be seen in the case of climate mitigation, which I discuss in detail in my book *The Coming Eclipse* (2010a) and outline in chapter 13 here.

In *The Laws of History* I argue that while the "problem of induction" does exist—there are no mechanical rules for working from observation to law making—philosophers have overlooked the "problem of deduction"—the failure to embrace the totality of reality—and that this problem is even more of a handicap in science. This situation is reflected quite clearly in the failure of the deductivists in either the biological or social sciences to construct realistic general dynamic theories. I have also argued at length in *Laws* that the problem of induction can be reduced to manageable proportions through employing what I call the "existential quaternary method".[4]

The existential quaternary method—the four steps of induction—includes the following stages:

- identification of "timescapes" or historical patterns;
- construction of a general dynamic model that explains these patterns;
- derivation of the historical dynamic mechanisms underlying these timescapes;
- construction of a model that explains the dynamics of institutions and organisations.

This is the realist method that underpins the development of the dynamic-strategy theory. It is the method of existential historicism—a type of historicism, ironically, that falsifies Popper's "poverty of historicism" hypothesis. As Popper failed to recognise this form of historicism, the poverty of the imagination that he ascribed to his methodological opponents must also be shared by him. Rather than exposing the poverty of historicism, Popper was responsible for its perversion.

The laws of life can be derived using the "quaternary system of analysis". To do so we must focus not on the timescapes—the fallacy of the old historicists—but on the underlying general dynamic model, the historical dynamic mechanisms, and the dynamic model of institutional change. The reason for excluding timescapes—the patterns of the past—as a basis for law-making is that they merely show the pattern of *outcomes* generated by more fundamental dynamic processes, and the pattern of outcomes can suddenly change (even go into reverse) as the dynamic mechanisms unfold. It was the old historicists' fatal mistake to view this pattern of outcomes as laws in themselves that could be universalised and extrapolated into the future. They did not, in other words, allow for structural change. Indeed, it did not occur them, or to antihistoricists like Popper, that dynamic mechanisms might underlie these patterns, and that these mechanisms could predict future structural change. Unfortunately, the real lessons arising from the failure of naïve historicism in the past have not been learnt, because the climate mitigationists are currently employing the same methodology to extrapolate recent changes in climate a century or so into the future.

Table 6.1 The Laws of Life—A Checklist

The Primary Laws	
1	The law of motivation in life
2	The law of competitive intensity
3	The law of strategic selection
4	The law of strategic optimisation
5	The law of strategic imitation
6	The law of strategic struggle
7	The law of diminishing strategic returns
8	The law of strategic crisis
9	The law of societal collapse
The Secondary Laws	
10	The law of cumulative biological/technological change
11	The law of genetic revolution
12	The law of (biological) eternal recurrence
13	The law of technological revolution
The Tertiary Laws	
14	The fundamental law of institutional change
15	The law of social complexity
16	The law of social cohesion
17	The law of institutional economy

Source: see text.

Just as there are three sources for the laws of life, so there are three categories of laws, each operating at a different level of biological activity. A checklist of these laws is provided in Table 6.1. The laws derived from the general dynamic model are the "primary laws of life". They are the unchanging laws that govern the behavior of organisms as they pursue their objectives of survival and prosperity by investing in the most effective of the four main dynamic strategies. They also govern the way species/societies/dynasties respond to the dynamic strategies—as outlined in chapter 4. The "secondary laws of life" are derived from the dynamic mechanism underpinning the historical eras both before and since the exhaustion of the "genetic option" discussed in chapter 3. As these historical mechanisms were reconstructed by applying the general model to the quantitative timescapes, the secondary laws can be thought of as being derived from the unchanging primary laws. Finally, the "tertiary laws of life" are derived from the dynamic-strategy model of institutional change outlined in chapter 7. These laws can be thought of as being derived from both the primary and secondary laws.

THE PRIMARY LAWS

The primary laws, as indicated above, have been derived from the general dynamic-strategy model developed in chapter 4 using the historical (or inductive) method. As we (should) know, laws must be derived not from patterns in the historical record but from the underlying dynamic mechanisms. By constructing and employing this basic model—the general dynamic-strategy model—it is possible to explain the general nature of the dynamic process operating beneath the surface of life. It is self-evident that if the general model of life is valid, as I claim, then it must be based on a set of unchanging laws that can be isolated here and employed in other contexts. The easy part is deriving the laws. What is difficult—the outcome of decades of intensive effort—is constructing the general dynamic model. Indeed, as I show in *The Laws of History*, scholars have struggled with this problem for the past two thousand seven hundred years—ever since the time of Hesiod.

It should also be possible to reverse this process of model-construction▶ laws, to become one of laws▶model-construction. Starting with the laws of life it would have been possible, in consulting the timescapes, to reconstruct the dynamic-strategy theory. It is possible, therefore, to work both ways between laws and general dynamic theory once we have identified the historical patterns of life and human society. What is essential to both law-making/model-building processes is an understanding of the **real world** of existential historicism rather than the **virtual world** of deductivism.

The primary laws are highly general and involve universal and necessary relationships that are strongly supported both empirically and logically. Derived from the general dynamic-strategy model, the fundamental laws can be set down in the following nine interrelated propositions.

1 *THE LAW OF MOTIVATION IN LIFE* states that the constant preoccupation of organisms throughout the history of life is the struggle to survive and prosper under varying degrees of scarcity.

Discussion

1.1   This law, which underpins the dynamic-strategy theory, was derived from a historical examination of life over the past 3,850 myrs and of human society over the past 2.4 myrs. As scarcity is demand-determined this condition will last as long as life itself.

1.2   This law provides the driving force in life that is both self-starting and self-sustaining. It accounts for the origin and dynamics of life on any habitable planet in the Universe. It drives the strategic *logos*.

1.3   This law implies that life in general and human society in particular will never be based on altruism. This does not, however, involve a rejection of cooperation (very different from "altruism"), which is often necessary for the achievement of self-interest. Indeed, cooperation is the outcome of "strategic exchange"—the interaction between strategic demand and strategic response in society's core dynamic mechanism.

1.4   The counterfactual conditional for this law is that the only alternative to the struggle for resources is poverty and, ultimately, extinction.

2   THE LAW OF COMPETITIVE INTENSITY states that the fundamental activity of organisms, involving the selection and pursuit of dynamic strategies, varies according to the intensity of competition for scarce resources at any given level of genetics/technology. It defines the *logos*.

Discussion

2.1   In life, intense competition—the Darwinian scenario—leads not to the genetic strategy and speciation but to the conquest strategy and extinction. Ironically it is the non-Darwinian scenario of minimal competition that leads to the genetic strategy and speciation. Moderate competition is the forcing ground for the family-multiplication and commerce strategies (see chapter 4).

2.2   Complete isolation (the absence of external, but not internal, competition), a rare and temporary condition, leads not to genetic (or technological) change—as neo-Darwinists of the "peripheral isolates" persuasion (Mayr 1963; Eldredge and Gould 1972) believe—but to stagnation and, on recontact with more open societies that have pushed ahead, to extinction. This can be seen most clearly in human history, particularly, in the New World, Australasia, and the Pacific, where long-isolated societies (lacking external pressure) were devastated by more technologically developed societies once contact was renewed.

3   THE LAW OF STRATEGIC SELECTION states that organisms focus on and develop those specific physical and instinctual characteristics—a product of inheritance and mutation—that assist their strategic pursuit, while ignoring the rest.

Discussion

3.1   This law, which is central to the dynamics of life, governs genetic change that is an outcome *not* of "divine selection" or "natural selection" but of "strategic selection"—self-selection writ large. It covers both the emergence of new species in response to the genetic strategy and the development of add-on "technology" in support of non-genetic strategies. Genetic change, in other words, is a dynamic strategy that is deliberately pursued by organisms, but only when circumstances are favourable (see Law #2).

3.2   This law also governs the selection of physical and instinctual characteristics that support non-genetic strategies—such as fertility and mobility (together with sexual and adventurous drives) in the family-multiplication strategy and offensive and defensive weapons (together with aggressive drives) in the conquest strategy. Hence this law is far more general than Darwin's concept of natural selection purports to be.

3.3   Strategic selection is made possible in both intelligent and non-intelligent life through the mechanism of strategic imitation (see chapter 4).

3.4   This law accounts for the non-Darwinian genetic profile of most species, which reflects relatively rapid genetic change followed by much longer periods of minimal genetic change. While this pattern has become known as "punctuated equilibria" (Eldredge and Gould 1972)—although it was recognised by some of Darwin's peers—the causal implications of the name are totally misleading. This is an example of investing a timescape with bogus theoretical status. It has nothing to do with stasis (long-run equilibrium) as claimed by Eldredge and Gould, and everything to do with dynamics—the dynamics of strategic selection by organisms (see my book *The Collapse of Darwinism*, 2010a: ch. 5).

4   ***THE LAW OF STRATEGIC OPTIMISATION*** states that a competitive "society" will adopt the dynamic strategy that promises to satisfy its materialist objectives most efficiently.

Discussion

4.1   Efficiency is measured in terms of the benefits and costs of metabolic energy and other resource use as between alternative dynamic strategies. This is worked out by organisms through trial and error, not by rational calculation. The optimum strategy is widely adopted within a society/species/dynasty through the "strategic-imitation" process. This is the reason that in the modern technological world, conquest (as pursued by Nazi Germany) will always fail—it is a materially inefficient strategy in comparison with that of technological change. Just a word of caution: conquest as a dynamic strategy should not be confused with military action undertaken to defend the technological strategy.

4.2 Efficiency is a relative, not an absolute concept. In other words organisms adopt the most efficient dynamic strategy in a particular environment, not the most efficient strategy in a timeless sense.

5 *THE LAW OF STRATEGIC IMITATION* states that successful strategic innovators who pioneer new dynamic strategies and who earn supernormal "profits" will be followed by a swarm of imitators, at first in a limited locality, but eventually on a widening front until the entire society/species/ dynasty embraces the new strategy.

Discussion

5.1 The strategic pioneers are the first to respond to changes in the strategic environment—in relative factor "prices"—by investing in new strategic opportunities. This is a trial-and-error process, during which the many will fail and the few will succeed.

5.2 It is through strategic imitation that the "desire" of organisms to maximise their probability of survival and prosperity is achieved. In life, imitation is just as important as innovation.

5.3 This is the mechanism by which successful individual "choice" is transformed into the dynamic strategies of life. Imitation is the real basis of animal and human "decision-making." It is the outcome of the remarkable survival instinct of organisms. This mechanism makes nonsense of rational choice theory.

5.4 It is also the way in which strategic selection becomes manifest in a society/species/dynasty (Law #3).

6 *THE LAW OF STRATEGIC STRUGGLE* states that organisms, in an attempt to achieve their materialist goals, struggle with each other for control of the dominant dynamic strategy and, hence, access to natural resources.

Discussion

6.1 The strategic struggle in most species is played out by the males who, using the tactics of order and chaos, battle with each other for control of "family" and higher social groups. It is through these groups that the various dynamic strategies are pursued. The primary reason, therefore, for the struggle between males is not for sex to maximise the presence of their genes in the gene pool but for control of the sources (natural resources) of survival and prosperity—for control of the strategic pursuit. Sex and other pleasures are by-products.

6.2 Strategic struggle is also the mechanism by which an unfolding dynamic strategy is translated into ecosociopolitical change (see chapter 4).

7 *THE LAW OF DIMINISHING STRATEGIC RETURNS* states that the investment of energy and resources in a dominant dynamic strategy will ultimately experience diminishing returns as the strategy is exhausted. This leads to a deceleration and eventual cessation of life/societal dynamics.

Discussion

7.1   Stagnation will occur when the marginal return (generated by access to natural resources) and marginal expenditures (of energy and resources) of the dominant dynamic strategy are finally equated. At this stage the dominant strategy will have been exhausted and stasis will result, if only temporarily.

7.2   This law also implies the existence of the countervailing law of increasing strategic returns experienced in the early stages of an unfolding dynamic strategy.

7.3   This more general law replaces the classical (assuming a fixed supply of land in the longrun) and neoclassical (assuming that all "factors of production" are fixed in the shortrun) economic laws of diminishing returns. Diminishing strategic returns in reality arise not from the exhaustion of resources but from the exhaustion of dynamic strategies that provide access to resources that cannot be regarded as fixed. For a detailed discussion see my books, *The Dynamic Society* (1996: ch. 12); *Ephemeral Civilisation* (1997: part II); *The Laws of History* (1998a: 202–3); and *The Collapse of Darwinism*(2003: ch. 10).

8 *THE LAW OF STRATEGIC CRISIS* states that the exhaustion of a dominant dynamic strategy in a competitive world leads not to the stationary state (longrun equilibrium) but to a strategic crisis that threatens the very existence of the society/species/dynasty. The strategic *logos* is endangered.

Discussion

8.1   The reason that stasis turns into crisis is that the earlier exploitation of a viable dynamic strategy leads a society/species/dynasty to attain levels of population and consumption that can only be maintained by a continuous inflow of natural resources. Once the inflow dries up, the over-nourished society is forced to down-size, and ultimately it collapses. And this inflow dries up completely with strategic exhaustion.

8.2   The more general dynamic law of strategic crisis displaces the flawed concept of Malthusian crisis (central to Darwin's natural selection concept), because strategic crisis is an outcome not of continued population pressure on resources but of the exhaustion of strategic opportunities. Population change, which is a direct response to strategic demand, is never an independent cause of strategic crisis.

9   *THE LAW OF SOCIETAL COLLAPSE* states that any species that
exhausts its genetic style, any dynasty that exhausts its genetic paradigm,
or any human society that exhausts its dominant dynamic strategy, **and
is unable to replace it with a new dynamic strategy**, will collapse. The
strategic *logos* is finally extinguished.

Discussion

9.1   In nature, crisis will lead to collapse only when the strategic potential
of a species (its genetic style) or a dynasty (its genetic paradigm)
has been entirely worked out. The only recourse for individuals
faced with strategic exhaustion is the zero-sum dynamic strategy of
conquest, which can lead only to the extinction of the species and,
ultimately, of the dynasty.

9.2   In human civilisation, collapse of mature societies will occur
whenever the old, exhausted strategy cannot be replaced with a
new strategy. But under the technology option the adoption of the
conquest strategy, in the final phase of an exhausted paradigm, will
not necessarily lead to the extinction of our species because we can,
under normal circumstances, transcend the exhausted technological
paradigm through the development of a new paradigm. Changing
technological paradigms leaves a society changed but intact. This
was not possible under the genetic option of the pre-human era,
where a new genetic paradigm (a new dynasty) can only take place
following the collapse of the old genetic paradigm (literally over the
dead bodies of the old dynasty). By the middle decades of the twenty-
first century a new technological paradigm will be required.

9.3   It is possible, however, that the collapse and extinction of our species
could occur through a misguided global attempt in the twenty-first
century to ban growth-inducing technological change in the mistaken
belief that it will prevent the destruction of the physical environment
or solve the problem of climate change. This would occur if we were
foolish enough to block the emergence of the next technological
paradigm shift on environmental, climate-change, or any other,
grounds. See my books *The Dynamic Society* (1996: 427–30) and
The Coming Eclipse. See also chapter 13.

THE SECONDARY LAWS

The primary laws of life operate at a very general level. Their purpose is to
explain the general behaviour of organisms, the strategies they employ to meet
their objective of survival and prosperity, and the general consequences of these
actions for the society, species, or dynasty. In order to explain the dynamic
processes dominating specific historical eras, we need to apply these primary
laws to our timescapes—the patterns of the past. This enables us to reconstruct

the underlying historical dynamic mechanisms. The secondary laws, in turn, are arrived at inductively from these dynamic mechanisms, not from the timescapes (historical patterns) as the old historicists mistakenly thought and the climate mitigationists still believe. In effect, if not in practice, the secondary laws are derived from the primary laws.

By employing both the timescapes and the general model, we can identify and explain the three great interlocking mechanisms that have been operating over the past 3,500 myrs. The general dynamic-strategy model, therefore, generates distinct but related processes of change under different historical circumstances, namely whether the genetic or technology options are operative. As shown in chapters 2 and 3 these historical mechanisms are the "great genetic paradigm shifts", the "great wheel of life", and the "great technological paradigm shifts". The first leads to biological progress (in terms of output and "productivity"), the second to the eternal recurrence, and the third to economic progress. The secondary laws are derived from those mechanisms that are specific to either the genetic or technology options.

The four laws underlying the historical mechanisms that have dominated the changing fortunes of life over the past 3,850 myrs are as follows.

10 *THE LAW OF CUMULATIVE BIOLOGICAL/TECHNOLOGICAL CHANGE* states that the relationship between a series of genetic/technological paradigm shifts is geometric owing to the cumulative effect generated when the "technological" (either genetic or industrial) output of one paradigm becomes the input of the next in the strategic *logos*.

Discussion

10.1   Not only does the time lag between paradigm shifts (both genetic and technological) decline exponentially, so too does the period of both the transition and the global dispersion of organisms. The pace of the dynamics of both life and human society has been and is accelerating. A major implication is that the next technological paradigm shift in human history—the Solar Revolution—will appear soon (probably beginning in the middle decades of the twenty-first century) and will take no more than a generation to unfold. See my books *The Dynamic Society* (1996: ch. 13) and *The Coming Eclipse* (2010a: ch. 6), and chapter 13 here.

10.2   The geometric relationship for biological change appears to be quite regular and precise. Each great wave of biological activity is approximately one-third the duration of the wave preceding it. In other words, this relationship approximates a log-linear function. I have called this the "logological constant" (which has a coefficient of 3.0), which can be thought of as equivalent to the "cosmological constant", but more precisely explained.

11 *THE LAW OF GENETIC REVOLUTION* states that once the potential for an increase in biological output at the global level has been exhausted, a new genetic revolution (paradigm shift), which causes a quantum leap in *potential* access to natural resources, will occur *provided the "genetic option" (the capacity for further access to resources through systematic genetic change) has not already been exhausted.*

Discussion

11.1 The reason that an exhausted genetic paradigm is followed by a new one is that paradigmatic exhaustion leads to extinction and, thereby, to the removal of intense competition for natural resources. It is in this non-Darwinian world of minimal competition and abundant resources that speciation occurs under the driving influence of the genetic strategy (chapters 2 and 3). This is the law that delivers the *coup de grâce* to natural selection—the Darwinian theory of "evolution." Rather than a process of *evolution* it is a process of *revolution.*

11.2 The series of genetic revolutions will not occur indefinitely. Once the "genetic option" has been exhausted—once genetic change can no longer provide better access to natural resources owing to the saturation of all possible habitats in the most effective possible way— subsequent dynasties will merely invent different biological ways of achieving the same level of biological output and productivity (output per unit of input). This introduces the "great wheel of life", or the "eternal recurrence" discussed in chapter 3.

12 *THE LAW OF (BIOLOGICAL) ETERNAL RECURRENCE* states that, when the "genetic option" for life on any habitable planet has been exhausted, all future dynasties will merely repeat the biological achievement of the past in slightly different ways.

Discussion

12.1 This law operates the "great wheel of life" (Figure 3.6) that turns unobserved in time without gaining any upward traction. The substitution of the great wheel for the great steps of life marks the end of biological progress, as measured in terms of total biomass and of output per unit of energy input.

12.2 This dynamic should be regarded as the normal outcome for life on habitable planets throughout the Universe (chapter 3). The only way the eternal recurrence can be broken is if one species in any dynasty is able to pass the brain-size threshold required to replace the exhausted genetic option with the unanticipated "technology option" before the dynasty of which it is a part collapses and goes extinct.

The probability (as suggested in chapter 3) of life on any planet doing so is very low.

12.3 Life on Earth defied the odds through a long chain of unlikely and unsought events to generate the Intelligence Revolution (chapters 2 and 3). *As this Intelligence Revolution is an outcome of pure chance rather than of the desire of organisms to survive and prosper, there is no law governing its emergence, only its future course once under way.*

13 *THE LAW OF TECHNOLOGICAL REVOLUTION* (which only comes into operation when the "technology option" has replaced the exhausted "genetic option") states that, once the potential for an increase in material living standards (real GDP per capita) at the global level has been exhausted, a new technological revolution (or paradigm shift) will occur, causing a quantum leap both in *potential* access to natural resources (including energy) and in *potential* material living standards.

Discussion

13.1 With great good luck, life on Earth escaped the eternal recurrence—that biological black hole—and was able to substitute the "technology option" for the long (80 myrs) exhausted "genetic option". This enabled one "fortunate" species to continually improve its access to natural resources through an endless sequence of technological revolutions (or paradigm shifts). In this way the human species was able to transcend the habitat limitations of genetic change and to generate ever increasing material living standards.

13.2 Unless we build barriers to this law—by banning growth-inducing technological change in favour solely of climatic adaptive and mitigation technological change—human society will not collapse until the life-supporting mechanism in the Universe does, because there is no other limit to the technology option. Unless, that is, we damage the driving force in ourselves through genetic engineering.

13.3 With the introduction of the "technology option", an analogous set of laws—the laws of history—were introduced. These new laws of the strategic *logos* have governed the dynamics of human society ever since, and will continue to do so until the *logos* of life is finally extinguished. The laws of history, which are discussed in detail elsewhere (Snooks 1998a), include additional secondary laws on: the optimum size of societies; human dispersion; economic progress; and economic regression.

13.4 The introduction of the technology option limits the size and complexity of the brain of the leading species. Brain size and complexity will only increase to the threshold level that enables the leading species to successfully negotiate a series of technological paradigm shifts. See *The Selfcreating Mind* (2006) and chapter 9.

THE TERTIARY LAWS

As there is no independent mechanism underlying institutional/organisational change, there can be no independent laws to govern it. The modern quest by sociobiologists and evolutionary institutionalists to discover an independent general theory of societal rules and organisations, therefore, is similar to the medieval quest for the holy grail. Both are searching for something that does not exist. While there certainly are regularities, or recurring patterns, in institutional/organisational structures throughout time and space, they are the outcome of the fundamental mechanism captured by the dynamic-strategy theory and not of any independent institutional/organisational mechanism. The laws governing institutional change, therefore, are merely derived from the fundamental laws of the dynamics of life. And the ephemeral nature of animal and human institutions can only be understood in terms of the eternal forces that drive life.

There are four laws governing institutional change, which constitute the tertiary laws of life.

14 *THE FUNDAMENTAL LAW OF INSTITUTIONAL CHANGE* states that all institutions and organisations, no matter how simple or complex, change in response to the unfolding and replacement of the dynamic strategies and substrategies of life.

Discussion

14.1 This is the law from which all other laws of institutional change follow. Its rationale is discussed in chapters 4 and 7.

14.2 The nature of the strategic sequence is the key to understanding very longrun institutional change. If the strategic sequence is reversed (owing to changes in the underlying dynamic forces), then institutional change will be reversed. There is no such thing as institutional "evolution" in some sort of Darwinian sense. It is a Victorian myth that survived into the twentieth and twenty-first centuries; a myth that must now be abandoned.

14.3 The nature of all institutions/organisations changes according to the requirements of the strategists. It responds, in other words, to changes in the strategic demand of the *logos*.

15 **THE LAW OF SOCIAL COMPLEXITY** has a Janus-like structure: the first form states that, as the dynamic strategy unfolds, the societal vehicle carrying it forward will increase in size and complexity; and the converse form states that, if the dynamic strategy is exhausted or derailed, the vehicle of societal change will be transformed in the reverse direction.

Discussion

15.1   The explanation behind this law is that, as the dynamic strategy unfolds, both the requirements for and the capacity of new genetics/ technologies make larger and more complex societal structures and rules necessary as well as feasible. As this can be reversed—the law is Janus-like—it is impossible to treat institutional change as "evolutionary."

15.2   While this law applies to both nature and human society, it can be seen working most clearly in the latter case. For example, with the unfolding of the commerce strategy, tribal kingdoms were transformed into city-states (ancient Greece) and nation-states were transformed into empires (Britain); with the unfolding of the conquest strategy, tribal kingdoms (Rome and Tenochtitlan) and city-states (Greece and Venice) were transformed into empires; and as the technology strategy unfolds, nation-states are being transformed into mega-states (the European Union). And in the past, when ancient strategies were exhausted, empires (Rome and Venice) were transformed back into city states and even tribal kingdoms (Western European monarchies). See my book *The Ephemeral Civilization* (1997) and chapter 9.

15.3   This law explains why human institutions are not evolutionary, but instead are a response to the strategic demand of the *logos*. A good example is the institution of democracy, which advances as the dynamic strategies of commerce and technological change unfold; but retreats if these strategies are replaced with conquest. As shown in chapter 7, English democracy advanced because of the fortuitous strategic sequence of conquest▶commerce▶technological change; rather than the ancient Greek sequence of conquest▶ commerce▶conquest.

15.4   For complex modern societies there are other institutional laws— such as the "law of democratisation"—that have no counterpart in simple pre-human society. See *The Laws of History* (1998a: ch. 10).

16 *THE LAW OF SOCIAL COHESION* states that social structures, both simple and complex, will emerge and be viably maintained only while the dominant dynamic strategy is unfolding successfully.

Discussion

16.1 The explanation of this law (chapter 4) is that social cohesion is generated by strategic confidence, which is an outcome of a successful dynamic strategy. Strategic confidence generates the social cement that is commonly called "trust." Trust, therefore, is a product of neither human nature, intellect, nor institutional evolution as is usually claimed.

16.2 Strategic confidence is the "economic gravity" in the concentric-spheres model of behaviour that, in a viable "society," balances the centrifugal force of the maximising self (chapter 4 and Figure 4.1).

16.3 When a dynamic strategy exhausts itself strategic confidence collapses and trust vanishes, thereby unleashing the centrifugal forces that generate social unrest and endanger the future of society.

17 *THE LAW OF INSTITUTIONAL ECONOMY* states that the form of the institution/organisation chosen to facilitate strategic demand will be the one that does so most economically.

Discussion

17.1 The explanation of this law is that organisms—the dynamic strategists—attempt to maximise the probability of survival and prosperity by organising their activities so as to get the best returns from energy/resource use.

17.2 This is not to say that institutions will take the most economical or efficient form in any timeless sense, only in a relative sense taking into account the backdrop of past "choices." This is a trial-and-error process in which mistakes and associated costs are involved.

LAWS AND THEIR USES

An integrated set of laws governing the dynamics of life has been presented in this chapter. This was only possible because of the prior construction of a general dynamic model—the dynamic-strategy theory. The difficult part in this process is not the derivation of the laws of life but rather the reconstruction of the dynamic mechanism underlying the fluctuations of life over the past 3,850 myrs. This is something that Darwin and the neo-Darwinists in the biological sciences, and a long line of philosophers, economists, and historians in the social sciences stretching back thousands of years, have failed to do. The natural selection hypothesis is not a realist dynamic theory and, not surprisingly, it is completely unable to explain the patterns in either the history of life or of human society. Hence, there are no operational or testable Darwinian laws, which is why Karl Popper regarded the theory of natural selection as unscientific. The ability to generate an integrated set of laws is a critical test for any theory of life. Darwinism is not on its own in failing that test.

The laws of life provide the opportunity to construct a new generation of models capable of analysing detailed aspects of biological change, genetics, directed mutation, and of the "societies" of animals and humans. Some progress has already been made in this respect regarding the economic and political development of both First World and Third World societies.[5] It also enables us to make sensible predictions about the future not only of life on Earth (including that of human civilisation) but of life on any habitable planet in the Universe. These predictions are not about individual events but rather about dynamic processes and their outcomes. While the future is visited in the final chapter, we turn now to the "ephemeral civilisation"—the citadel of the *logos*—to discover how the laws of history operate in human society and culture.

Chapter 7
Citadel of the *Logos* — The Ephemeral Civilisation

Institutions provide the vehicle, not the engine of progress.

Civilisation is an enigma. We are all caught up in its vibrant surface but have little understanding of its hidden depths. Even civilisation-watchers cannot agree as to whether its essential characteristics are cultural, social, political, economic, or some combination of them all. Not surprisingly there is no consensus on the most basic questions asked about civilisation. Questions such as: Why do civilisations rise and fall? What accounts for the dominance of Western civilisation in the modern world? Does Western civilisation have a future? How real is the so-called "clash of civilisations"? While these questions have attracted many and varied answers, none has been very persuasive. In this chapter I will provide a strategic model of institutional and cultural change that explains the nature of civilisation, and illustrates how the laws of history operate. It is shown that institutions are the vehicle, not the engine of progress.

A CASE STUDY IN INSTITUTIONAL CHANGE: ENGLAND 1000–2015

The more abstract discussion that follows can better be understood within the context of a case study—England/Britain, 1000–2015 as the early leading representative of the rise of the West—condensed from a much larger account in my book, *The Ephemeral Civilization* (1997). While England/Great Britain, as the first technological society, is the subject of our focus here, it should be realised that the rise of Western civilisation was the outcome not of the actions of a single state, but of all European states interacting closely with each other. For the past millennium Western Europe has been a highly interdependent entity owing to the fiercely competitive environment both within and without its boundaries.

England or, after 1707, Great Britain, provides a fascinating case study, which can be sketched only in the barest of outlines here. For some seven centuries this society struggled desperately with its neighbors for political survival in the pressure-cooker environment of Western Europe. In the process, England was so transformed that in the early seventeenth century it suddenly broke out of its immediate environment into all parts of the globe to form the largest, most widespread empire the world has ever known. Yet within just three centuries the British Empire—on which the sun never set—rose, flourished, basked in its own glory for a brief season, and then fell. While the ancients would have been impressed by the speed and range of the rising British Empire, they would have been astounded, not by the rapidity of its fall, but by the unique fact that after the dust had settled, Great Britain was still a viable society with a standard of living higher than during the greatest days of empire. And still growing.

The ancients would have been astounded because Britain had achieved what no former empire could ever hope to achieve—a life after empire. In the ancient world a collapsing empire meant a collapsing society. Why had Britain survived? Because part way through the process of empire-building Britain, for the first time in the history of mankind, adopted the industrial technological strategy which, as far as long-run prosperity was concerned, rendered imperialism redundant. It led to the awakening of Albion.

To fully understand the rise and fall of the British Empire we need to go back to the very beginning of the kingdom of England in the late tenth century. England's "strategic pathway" traced out three great waves between 1000 and 2015 AD, each being up to 300 years in duration. As can be seen from Figure 7.1 these great waves of GDP surged forward during the periods 1000 to 1348, 1480 to 1750, and the 1760s to 2015, and were generated by three very different dynamic strategies—conquest, commerce and technological change. In turn each of these strategies was composed of a series of substrategies. With the exhaustion of each of these strategies, England was fortunate enough to be able to replace them—albeit after a period of apprehension during which economic stagnation or decline was experienced—with a new dynamic strategy. Hence England was able to avoid the collapse that had occurred in all ancient societies. Yet this was due more to fortunate timing, coming as it did at the very end of the neolithic paradigm, than to superior strategic skills.

Figure 7.1 The Great Waves of Economic Change—England/Britain, 1000–2000

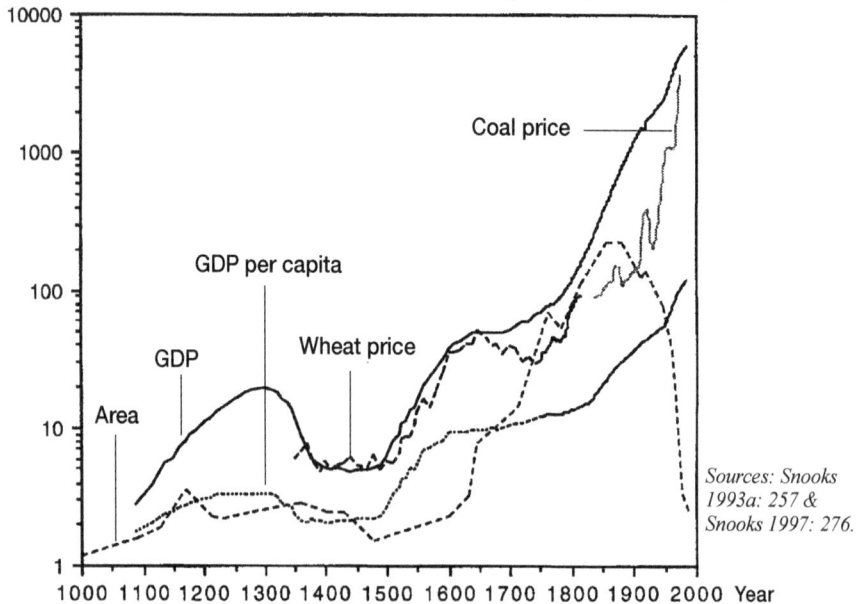

Sources: Snooks
1993a: 257 &
Snooks 1997: 276.

These great waves provide a timescape depicting the unfolding and transformation of England's dynamic strategies throughout the past millennium. And it is this strategic unfolding and transformation that generated the demand for institutional change to facilitate the materialistic pursuit of survival and prosperity. When analysing the impact of an unfolding dynamic strategy in a conquest or commerce society, it is possible to represent the strategic pathway with a graph showing fluctuations in territorial acquisition, because this was central to their success. In the case of a technological society, however, an index of territorial acquisition is totally inadequate. Instead, we need indexes of real GDP and real GDP per capita, because efficiency rather than territorial acquisition is central to the success of the technological strategy. In other words, technological change, broadly conceived, can generate the extraordinary profits relentlessly pursued by mankind without the need to acquire additional territory. If such territory is acquired, it is for very different reasons—the defense of their technological strategy.

The pattern of real GDP and territorial acquisition shown in Figure 7.1 shows how these two variables interacted during three main periods: 1000 to 1450, 1450 to 1780, and 1780 to 2015. The first period, 1000 to 1450, was the conquest strategy phase. While there is a long-run correlation between these two measures of growth, there are shorter periods when a slump in one is compensated for by a boom in the other. As we shall see, before 1300 the difficulties of pursuing a conquest strategy in a highly competitive environment required the generation of the surpluses needed to finance wars through increases in productivity and trade. After 1300 the slump in the wool trade led England to focus to a greater degree upon territorial acquisition. The second period, 1450 to 1780—the commerce strategy phase—also saw a change in leadership between these two variables. Until 1600, commerce-generated increases in real GDP per capita outstripped increases in territorial acquisition, whereas thereafter, as Britain won its struggle against the Dutch and French, the roles were reversed, culminating in territorial gains in India. Only during the third period, 1780 to 2015—the technological strategy phase—was it possible to achieve a long-run inverse relationship between these two variables, demonstrating for the first time in human history that prosperity no longer depended upon territorial acquisition. From the mid-nineteenth century, although continuing to acquire territory (to defend the technological strategy), Britain granted self-government to its European-settled colonies. Despite granting self-government, real GDP per capita continued to increase rapidly, and when Britain completely dismantled its empire after the Second World War, the growth rate actually accelerated.

And throughout the ebbing and flowing of these great waves of economic change, prices echoed the long-run fluctuations in aggregate demand or real GDP (see Figure 7.1). The most representative prices before the Industrial Revolution are wheat prices, and thereafter coal prices. Before about 1400 even wheat prices are too unreliable to be employed here. The so-called "price revolution" of the sixteenth century was merely part of this overall pattern, which is driven by demand rather than supply (usually identified as the amount of gold and silver brought back from the New World) forces. Our evidence shows that prices had been rising rapidly for about two generations *before* the flow of Spanish silver reached "full flood" in the 1560s, and that the supply of silver was not sufficient to satisfy demand, thereby requiring the use of gold (not previously used) as well. The dynamic mechanism envisaged here, which is different to all previous explanations, is of real GDP being driven by the pursuit of a sequence of dynamic strategies by decision-makers attempting to maximise their prospects of survival and prosperity. In other words, aggregate demand in the economy at any point in time is the static outcome of strategic demand, which in turn is the dynamic outcome of the unfolding and replacement of a society's dynamic strategies. And prices are driven in the longer term by changes in aggregate demand. In the shorter term it is possible that a sudden increase in bullion—the pursuit of which is driven by the unfolding dynamic strategy—might lead to an increase in prices but in the longer term the money supply will adjust to the requirements of strategic demand. Money is merely a facilitating institution, which responds to the requirements of the *logos*. This discovery—first presented in my books *Economics without Time* (1993) and *The Ephemeral Civilization* (1997)—was the foundation for my theory about the key role of inflation in the strategic demand-response mechanism discussed in chapters 4 and 11.

From this case study in *The Ephemeral Civilization* (1997: ch. 10), a number of institutional themes emerged. It was observed there that the British economic system transitioned from tribal to feudal to mercantile to industrial, as commodity and factor markets developed; that the system of strategic control shifted from tribal chief and his kin, to regional and national kings and their baronial councils, to king and his parliament, to limited parliamentary monarchy, to constitutional monarchy with restricted and then universal suffrage; that the rise and fall of different strategic classes—in terms of wealth, education, and influence—emerged and declined as different dynamic strategies unfolded and were substituted one for the other (including a feudal landowning aristocracy, a commercial gentry, and an industrial middle class and proletariat); that strategic ideologies were transformed with the rise and fall of Christianity and, more recently, the emergence of the secular faiths of Marxism, scientism, and environmentalism; and that feudal law emerged and was eventual replaced by a flexible common law that has progressively protected the property rights of the commerce and industrial strategists.

If we stand back far enough and merely observe the superficial outlines of these institutional changes, we might convince ourselves, as many have done, that this is an evolutionary process. But if we examine these changes carefully and search for the underlying causal influences, as attempted in *The Ephemeral Civilization*, we will notice that these institutional transitions were characterised by significant discontinuities. And also we will discover that it was driven not by Darwinian-like evolutionary forces, but by the coincidental conjunction of three separate dynamic strategies to form a conquest►commerce►technological-sequence. As this sequence is not inevitable—it is determined by fundamental economic forces that owe nothing to the institutional forms to which they give rise—the institutional transition is not an evolutionary process.

A different sequence would have generated an institutional transition similar to that in earlier civilisations. Such as the conquest►commerce►conquest sequence in ancient Greece, or the commerce►conquest sequence of Venice. Modern institutionalists have been misled by their observational position in historical time. There is no way that ancient Greek observers, from the vantage point of mid-fourth century BC (that is, just after the time of Alexander the Great), would have seen institutional change as evolutionary. They would have recognised that it was driven along a tortuous path that has many discontinuities and reversals.

This non-evolutionary reality can be illustrated convincingly with one key institutional transformation, namely the emergence of modern democracy in England. (An entire spectrum of institutional transformations can be found in my book *The Ephemeral Civilization,* 1997: Ch. 10). The recent (2015) celebration in the United Kingdom of 800 years since the sealing of Magna Carta, has focused on the "evolution" of political democracy and associated liberties that are thought to have begun with this event. They include: Magna Carta 1215, the Montfort parliament 1265, the Poor Law 1601 (big gap!), the Petition of Right 1628, the Putney Debates 1647, the Bill of Rights 1689, (now it gets a roll on!) Abolition of the Slave Trade 1807, Catholic Emancipation Act 1829, Great Reform Act 1832, Factory Act 1833, Tolpuddle Martyrs 1834, the People's Charter 1838, Female Suffrage 1918, and the Race Relations Act 1965.

While these important changes are seen by most as the outcome of unidirectional evolutionary forces (**evolution cannot reverse itself** and was regarded by Darwin as a **slow and steady process**), they were in fact responses to the episodic changing requirements of the dynamic strategies pursued by England/UK. To start with, Magna Carta was not about the rights of the English people, but about the power of a handful of barons—leaders of the conquest strategy—exercised against a strategically unsuccessful king, who managed to lose all their lucrative manors in France. And had not the conquest strategy of England exhausted itself and been replaced by the dynamic strategy of commerce from the mid-fifteenth century, under which the wealthy commercial strategists were much more numerous than the former conquest strategists, political power and "rights" would have remained in baronial hands. And even the limited democracy achieved during the era of commerce would have been **reversed** had the exhausting commerce strategy in the mid-eighteenth century been replaced by a new conquest strategy (as had happened regularly in the ancient world), as appeared to be happening during the generation prior to the

Industrial Revolution. As explained in chapters 3 and 4, only the coincidental exhaustion of both England's commerce strategy and the world's neolithic technological paradigm, provided the UK with a more economically viable alternative (the technological strategy) to conquest.

This was the first time in history that a society which had exhausted its commerce strategy was able to avoid using conquest as a means of preventing stagnation, decline, and collapse. English democracy, therefore, did not evolve, but responded to the strategic coincidences of history. And the implication is clear, if the forthcoming Solar Revolution is derailed by radical groups (possibly climate mitigationists), the only strategic alternative for the Dynamic Society will be the adoption of the ancient strategy of conquest. In such a scenario, all our institutions, including democracy, will be thrown into reverse and will return to earlier authoritarian forms, which will be even more repressive as they will be exercised with electronic efficiency.

A STRATEGIC MODEL OF INSTITUTIONAL CHANGE

In order to examine the process of interaction between the fundamental dynamics of human society and institutional change, we need to abandon the deductive approaches of the new institutional economics and neo-Darwinism, and to adopt the existential approach advocated in chapter 4. By doing this we will be able to distinguish between the primary and secondary mechanisms of societal dynamics. The primary dynamic mechanism was analysed and modelled in *The Dynamic Society* and chapter 4 above, and the secondary dynamic mechanism, by which institutions emerge and change in response to these more fundamental processes, is explained in detail in *The Ephemeral Civilization* and sketched briefly here. This strategic approach involves an examination of the relationship between dynamic strategies and tactics on the one hand, and human institutions and organisations on the other, in forging the citadel of the strategic *logos*. As Plato says, the state arises out of the needs of mankind. It is important to realise that this new model of institutional change has been derived inductively from an extensive historical analysis undertaken in my books. The model explains why civilisation and its underlying strategic *logos* are ephemeral.

The Real Nature of Institutions and Organisations

The basic argument in this chapter is that institutions and organisations emerge and change primarily in response to changing dynamic (strategic and tactical) demand generated by an unfolding dynamic strategy. Only their superficial, ephemeral forms are shaped by what I have called "relative institutional prices". Hence, in a competitive environment, dynamic demand for both institutional and organisational support will be met in the most efficient way possible at the time, given the relative costs of various possible alternatives that reflect factor endowments and prior historical developments.

"Societal rules", both formal and informal, will be established and constantly altered to carry out the dynamic strategies by which decision-makers attempt to maximise their chances of survival and prosperity and to impose the dynamic tactics by which competing groups attempt to control the distribution of society's wealth. These rules are required in order to economise on that scarcest of resources, the intellect. Similarly, "societal organisations" of all types— economic, political, social—also respond largely to these dynamic strategies and tactics, rather than to institutions as Douglass North argues.[1] Hence, the incentives to which organisations respond are to be found in the strategic and tactical opportunities rather than the opportunities provided by institutions. Societal rules do not provide opportunities or incentives of their own volition, they merely communicate the opportunities generated by the strategic *logos*. There will, of course, be a degree of interaction between these demand and supply forces, but causality flows overwhelmingly from the former to the latter.

It is in the process of "strategic imitation", by which the vast majority of decision-makers emulate the action of the successful strategic pioneers, that societal rules are employed. Institutions are needed to economise, not on information as academic institutionalists claim, but on intelligence. Rules are required also by those who attempt to achieve their objectives through order and control. Hence the rule-makers are the "strategic followers" and the apostles of order, while the rule-breakers are the "strategic pioneers" and the apostles of tactical chaos. As the former constitute the vast majority of decision-makers, rules are essential to the dynamics of human society even though they are purely derivative of it.

While these variables will be modelled more fully later in the chapter, enough has been said to provide a framework for categorising institutions and organisations in order to see how institutional change occurs. They can be divided into two broad groups: strategic institutions and organisations and tactical institutions and organisations. Institutions and organisations are dealt with here together because both respond to dynamic demand in similar ways, and because the new institutionalist focus on institutional rules is too narrow. They are jointly determined by dynamic demand, and any *independent* interaction between them is relatively minor.

Strategic institutions

Strategic institutions are those formal and informal rules of conduct that are required to support the emergence and development of the dynamic strategies of family multiplication, conquest, commerce, and technological change. These institutions, which operate at both the macro/micro and national/regional levels, cover the full societal spectrum of economic, social, and political activities. They include the economic and political system; the rules by which business is conducted; the way goods, services, and factors of production are bought and sold; the way business is financed; the rules of money supply; the way property rights are allocated; the way politics is conducted; and the way people interact at a social level. The type of dynamic strategy pursued by a particular society has a characteristic and predictable impact upon all these institutions.

In simple societies the demands made upon intellectual faculties are *relatively* light and, hence, the role of formal rules is relatively unimportant; informal rules and customs are sufficient. As the society becomes increasingly complex, "strategic costs" (interpreted by institutionalists as transaction costs) will rise with the increasing demands made upon intellectual resources. This will lead to the growing importance of formal institutions or rules. This is not, as some have argued, a result of declining "mutual trust"[2]; nor does it endanger the viability of that society. What endangers society and its underlying strategic *logos* is the exhaustion and non-replacement of the dominant dynamic strategy. This eventuality leads not to a reduction in trust, but to a decline in "strategic confidence". Any decline in confidence in the prevailing strategy by decision-makers leads to less cohesion than before, because there is no longer the same degree of strategic leadership which the bulk of agents normally follow.

The variable nature of society's strategic institutions can be seen in Table 7.1, which has been compiled from the historical studies reported in both *The Dynamic Society* and *The Ephemeral Civilization*. The four main dynamic strategies, arising from four distinct *logos* types, generate demands for different types of societal rules in order to facilitate very different approaches to the eternal pursuit of survival and prosperity. A few examples taken from Table 7.1 will suffice to illustrate my point. As far as the economic and political system is concerned, a conquest strategy will lead to central economic and political control by a military strongman (king or dictator) because of the monopoly of economic ownership; the commerce strategy will see the emergence, owing to a more widespread ownership of economic resources, of a regulated market system with a wider political franchise which, depending on the era, will range from elected merchant princes in democratic city-states to parliamentary systems with an upper middle-class franchise in nation-states; and the technological strategy results in a market system with a parliamentary democracy based upon universal franchise owing to the universal system of economic democracy. While this set of relationships between the dominant dynamic strategy and the economic and political system is not entirely precise at the detailed level, it is quite clear in bold outline. The same is true of the different systems of exchange, of property rights, of law, and of social intercourse. The historical reasons are discussed in detail in *The Ephemeral Civilization*.

These relationships are not accidental. Different strategies can best be implemented with different economic and political systems. A society that switches from a commerce or a technological strategy to a conquest strategy, for example, will see the emergence of a new ruling elite; it will experience significantly less freedom of political or economic expression; control over its rules of exchange will pass from private (free markets, private monopolies, guilds) to public (forced labour, plunder, state distribution) control; its property rights will change from a widespread to an elitist basis; its guarantees to individuals will change from a universal to a restrictive and authoritarian basis; and its democratic rules of social exchange will be replaced by autocratic decree. Changes of this nature can be seen throughout the historical record, as in the case of Carthage (after 300 BC) and of Greece (after 338 BC) as they turned increasingly from commerce to conquest; and in the case of Germany and Japan after the mid-1930s as they turned from the technological to the conquest strategies. These reversals, which are due to changing dynamic strategies, cannot be explained by evolutionary institutionalism.

Tactical institutions

Tactical institutions are even more ephemeral than strategic institutions, because they are deliberately employed by ruling elites and their opponents to gain control of the dominant dynamic strategy and to effect short-term changes in the distribution of wealth. But this is a relative matter as the same tactics may be successfully employed over decades, generations, even centuries.

Just as the dynamic tactics can be divided into the categories of order and chaos, so can the institutions that are required to facilitate them. Institutions of order are demanded by the ruling elite to maintain the existing distribution of wealth. They are employed to ensure the compliance of all members of society. These orderly constraints include rules governing finance (particularly taxation); criminal and civil law; enforcement of these laws; economic, social, and political exchange; property rights; and ideology, both established religion and propaganda. Institutions of chaos, on the other hand, are demanded by those who wish to break down the existing order and to change the existing distribution of wealth. This involves negating the rules governing order through the deregulation of commodity and factor markets, reform of political and social structures, rebellions, and the propagation of radical ideology (such as Christianity in the late Roman Empire, Marxism in late nineteenth century Europe, and capitalist 'economic rationalism' in the Western world during the 1980s and 1990s). These tactics, and the rules relating to them, fluctuate within the opportunistic boundaries provided by the fortunes of the dominant dynamic strategy.

Strategic organisations

As in the case of institutions, the various dynamic strategies call forth a set of characteristic and predictable organisations. These have been outlined in Table 7.2 that, like the earlier table, is based upon my detailed historical investigations. I have divided strategic organisations into two main categories—major strategic organisations and support organisations. The major strategic organisations are those demanded by decision-makers to implement and expand society's dominant dynamic strategy. For societies pursuing the family multiplication

Table 7.1 Strategic Institutions—Past 100,000 years

Dynamic Strategy (*Logos* type)	Political System	Ruling Elite	Economic System	Constitutional and Legal System	Commodity Exchange	Factor Exchange	Property Rights	Risk Control	Social Intercourse
Family multiplication (Hunting *logos*)	Hunting band Tribal kingdom • Head of family Tribal chief	Hunter/warriors	Subsistence Barter	Tribal rights and privileges Family rights and privileges	Rules of barter	Nil	Traditional rights of land use Protection by tribal force	Kinship support Gift-giving Invoking of spirits	Taboos Tribal & family customs & codes of behaviour
Conquest (Military *logos*)	Kingdom Empire • Monarchy Dictatorship Oligarchy	Warrior elite Land-owning aristocracy	Centralised systems: Feudal/manorial Totalitarian	Divine right of kingship King's court Lords' courts	State marketing system Barter	Labour: coercive labour systems Capital: plunder Land: state control and distribution	Right of conquest Elite rights Protection by armed forces	Religious support Benevolence of elite Regional diversification	Codes of elite conduct Religious codes and laws
Commerce (Merchantile *logos*)	City-state Nation-state Empire • Merchant princes Councils elected by merchant elite	Merchant elite Upper middle class	State-controlled market systems	Limited constitution Courts for middle classes	Private monopoly marketing system Guilds Codes of merchant conduct	Regulated markets: Labour: master & servant regulations Capital: usury laws Land: ownership restrictions	Extensive rights for middle class over real & financial capital Protection of law— restricted	Charity Insurance on mercantile operations Limited state assistance	Criminal & commercial laws Religious codes & laws
Technological (Enterprise *logos*)	Nation-state Mega-state • Parliamentary democracy Universal franchise	Business/labour interests Consumer class	Free market system Various degrees of state intervention	People's constitution Universal court system	Free markets State regulation: tariff protection prices surveillance consumer protection	Free markets State regulation: wages policy workers compensation immigration central banking money markets	Universal rights over all forms of property Protection of law— universal	Widespread insurance against loss, damage, etc, of all types of property, life, contingencies Extensive state compensation Welfare Economic regulation	Criminal & civil laws Arbitration & small claims regulations Family laws Secular codes of conduct

strategy this involves the kinship teams required for hunting and gathering; for those pursuing conquest it covers military and imperial organisations; for those pursuing commerce it includes trading and financial organisations together with state naval and foreign service organisations; and for those societies pursuing the technological strategy it encompasses industrial and commercial organisations together with a comprehensive state bureaucracy.

Table 7.2 Strategic Organisations—Past 100,000 years

Dynamic Strategy (*Logos* type)	Major Strategic Organisations	Support Organisations
1. Family multiplication (Hunting *logos*)	• Kinship hunting & gathering teams • Kinship & tribal raiding parties	• Initiation & hunting rituals • Toolmaking groups • Trading groups • Witch-doctors
2. Conquest (Military *logos*)	• Military system – armed forces – engineering division – logistical division • Imperial administration – central organisation – local governors	• Training organisations – military skills – engineering techniques – leadership and administrative skills • Arms factories • Military technology • Prophets & oracles
3. Commerce (Merchantile *logos*)	• Commercial system – trading networks – financial organisations – shipping firms – insurance firms • State navy • State foreign service	• Training organisations – business & commercial skills – navigation – naval skills • Ship-building organisations • Transport technology • Religious & scientific guidance
4. Technological (Enterprise *logos*)	• Industrial system – factory organisation – multinational corporation • Commercial system – finance firms – insurance firms • State bureaucracy	• Training organisations –scientific technological skills – commerce skills – higher education • Research & development organisations • Economic forecasting

Any society changing its dominant strategy would also need to change its major strategic organisations. A society, for example, switching from commerce to conquest—such as Athens during the Peloponnesian wars—would gradually replace its commercial organisational structure with a military structure; while a society switching from commerce to technological change—such as Western Europe between the eighteenth and nineteenth centuries—would replace its commercial structure with an industrial system. And we could expect to see a massive change in our present organisational structure if, under pressure from a climate-mitigation dictator, the technological strategy collapsed and, by default, was replaced by the conquest strategy. A possibility discussed in chapter 13. In this event the industrial–commerce complex would be subordinated to a military–imperial system. The effect would be similar to that achieved partially in both Europe and Asia in the 1930s and 1940s, when dictators pursuing irrational objectives such as racial purity emerged briefly but destructively.

Support organisations also depend upon the type of dynamic strategy pursued by any society. Table 7.2 suggests that the nature of education and training, the type of manufacturing concerns, the character of research and development, and even the forecasting methods employed (compare the non-scientific forms employed in both Nazi Germany and ancient Rome) depend on the dominant strategy. Once again this can best be seen in a society switching its dynamic strategy. With a shift from commerce to conquest—which can be seen in Carthage in the third century BC, Greece in the fourth century BC, and Venice in the early sixteenth century—the support organisations shift from a preoccupation with the development of skills and the production of goods required in trade to a focus on activities and skills needed for war.

Quite clearly, the strategic and support organisations of society depend upon the opportunities and incentives generated not by institutional constraints, as argued by Douglass North and other "new" institutionalists, but by its dynamic strategies. And changes in these organisations are driven not by forces on the supply side, as favoured by these institutionalists, but by the forces of logosian demand generated by an unfolding dynamic strategy. The role of supply forces—relative institutional prices—is limited to considerations of organisational design.

Tactical organisations

Tactical organisations are a response to the demand generated by those employing the dynamic tactics of order and even chaos. I say "even" chaos because this tactic involves a breaking down rather than a building up of societal structures. Those wishing to break down an existing orderly structure require organisations to do so, as political strength comes from numbers. Quite clearly, individuals working on their own are unable to change society. And, as the dynamic-strategy theory shows, even groups can only act as agents of strategic change if and when required by the strategic *logos*.

Tactical organisations of order are demanded by the ruling elite so as to force or persuade the rest of society to comply with their wealth-distributional objectives. Clearly some of these institutions have a joint purpose in that they are employed both for strategic and tactical ends. The sharpest distinction between strategic and tactical organisations occurs in societies controlled by "antistrategists" (criminal organisations, terrorist groups, and radical interventionists), who pursue rent-seeking tactics rather than profit-seeking strategies. In most societies, however, strategies and tactics reinforce each other. They include state-controlled organisations: to raise revenue; to make and supervise civil and criminal law; to enforce all kinds of laws, regulations, and the whims of the ruling elite; and to generate and disseminate the ideology of order. Revenue-raising organisations have included the royal household, the exchequer (the first modern finance department, established in England in the twelfth century), and modern taxation departments. Law-making organisations have included royal councils, military cabals, and elected parliaments. And organisations supervising the resulting laws have included the formal courts of kings, lords, and the people. Organisations enforcing these laws have included the armed forces of kings, lords, and military strongmen, and, more recently uniformed police, secret police, and, in the last resort, the army. Finally, ideological organisations have included state religions ranging from ancient sun worship to the modern religions of Judaism, Christianity, Islam, Buddhism, and Marxism, together with bureaucratic departments responsible for creating and disseminating official propaganda. Clearly some of these organisations are also employed for strategic purposes, such as the use of state religion to involve the entire population in the dominant dynamic strategy (for example, the gods of war in Rome and Tenochtitlan, the Christian god in Western Europe, and the god of Islam in the Middle East).

Tactical organisations of chaos, or dissent, are demanded by those who wish to change, or even overthrow, the existing order so as to alter the distribution of wealth. These organisations attempt to marshal resources, ideas, and human support to effect the reform of existing institutions, to deregulate commodity and factor markets, to create and disseminate dissenting ideology, and even to overthrow the existing system. They include groups at the local, national, and even international levels that are concerned with such diverse issues as the abolition of slavery, the release of political prisoners, the promotion of feminism; groups concerned with land rights, wage justice, financial deregulation; and groups holding and promoting dissenting political, religious, and environmental schemes, some of which may be illegal and forced to operate underground.

The essential point to realise is that the tactical institutions and organisations of both order and chaos are instruments in a "strategic struggle". They are used by competing groups to alter, in their own favour, the distribution of wealth generated by a society's dynamic strategies. The boundaries of this continuous strategic struggle, therefore, are defined by the degree of success of the dynamic strategies both old and new. Realisation of this point is essential because the literature of institutionalism, both old and new, gives the impression that society is a holistic entity which adopts institutional constraints on the freedom of individuals in order to reduce the costs of exchange. This is an unrealistically static and narrow conception that is totally rejected by the dynamic strategic/ tactical approach adopted here.

Changes in Institutions and Organisations

The key to understanding institutions is the realisation that they can only achieve the objectives of those who employ them, at both the strategic and tactical levels, if they are relatively stable. It is not possible to conduct business successfully if the rules of the game, such as property rights and market regulations, are constantly changing. Continuous revolution, as the Chinese discovered in the 1960s and 1970s, is bad for business. Institutions, therefore, are of no use unless a workable degree of stability can be attained. But we know that they do change over time. The argument developed in *The Dynamic Society* (1996) is that this change in the longer term is driven by dynamic demand—generated by the strategic requirements of the *logos*—and shaped by relative institutional prices. As we have seen, dynamic demand depends upon the long-run strategies and the short-run tactics of society, and it changes when, and only when, there is a change either in the fortunes of a strategy or in the balance between the forces of order and chaos. Hence, those periods of relative stability in society's institutions reflect the stability of dynamic demand rather than the stasis that, we are told by the evolutionary institutionalists, is supposed to characterise the Darwinian process of institutional change. Relative institutional prices, which are the costs of alternative institutions that can be adopted to facilitate both strategies and tactics, change owing to changes in economies of scale and technology that arise from the dynamic processes of the real economy. *This, therefore, is the basis of the great paradox of human society: what is static is ephemeral, and what is in flux is eternal.* This paradox is at the centre of my wider research programme.

This model is seen as radical and revisionist. It is seen as a realist alternative to existing models of institutional change that are extensions of supply-side neoclassical models (North 1990) or of biologically inspired supply-side evolutionary models (Veblen 1919; Hayek 1988; Hodgson 1993). The major driving force in my theory of institutional change is dynamic demand, although supply-side forces do help to shape the form of changing institutions. And on the supply-side I acknowledge the important work undertaken by the institutionalists. But my theory is very different from theirs. Institutional change is *not* the primary mechanism of societal dynamics operating through either "group selection" or path-dependence. Rather it is part of a secondary mechanism that responds to the dynamic process of the real economy. This is not to deny some feedback between institutional change and the primary dynamic mechanism, just that it is a secondary and minor force.

Dynamic demand

Dynamic demand for institutional and organisational structures is, as indicated above, generated by the dynamic process of the real economy and consists of both strategic and tactical demand. "Strategic demand", which exerts a long-run influence, is an outcome of the major dynamic strategies of family multiplication, conquest, commerce, and technological change that are pursued within the strategic *logos*. Shifts in strategic demand occur in response to the changing fortunes—or unfolding—of the dominant dynamic strategy, and to the transition from one strategy to another. In turn these developments depend upon changes in relative factor endowments and in the wider competitive environment. "Tactical demand" operates in the short-run, changing with the balance between groups struggling for strategic control. The most powerful and enduring of these shaping influences, therefore, is strategic demand and, as such, it dominates our historical reinterpretation. As will be seen, dynamic demand is very different to the neoclassical concept of aggregate demand, which is merely an outcome of the dynamic system at any point in time. Aggregate demand could be thought of as "static demand", which is both narrower than and derivative of dynamic demand.

We need to consider both the nature of strategic demand and the forces that cause it to shift over time. The outcomes of strategic demand for institutions and organisations are outlined in Tables 7.1 and 7.2. These outcomes are achieved by human agents wanting to invest in the dominant dynamic strategy and needing to establish stable rules and organisations to do so. The demand for relevant organisations is quite straightforward. Individuals form associations with each other—such as trading, financial, shipping, insurance, industrial, and military organisations—to enable investment in, and the operation of, the dominant dynamic strategy. The demand for institutions, however, is more complex because the procedure involved is less direct. To change the formal strategic rules it is necessary to influence those who hold political power. This can be achieved either by tempting or pressuring the political leaders. Temptation can be exercised by giving the political leaders a share of the strategic profits either through bribery or through legal business arrangements. Political pressure is exercised by lobby groups who threaten to divert the political support of their strategic backers to the political opposition.

The strategic struggle

The central mechanism by which strategic and tactical demand are converted into institutional change is the competitive struggle between various groups in society for control of the dominant dynamic strategy. These competing groups in society can be classified as follows:

- strategists (or profit-seekers)

- old strategists—supporters of the traditional strategy

- new strategists—supporters of the emerging strategy

- nonstrategists (or coerced workers and dependents)

- antistrategists (or rent-seekers, terrorists and criminals)

As the strategic-struggle hypothesis presented here is entirely different to the prevailing concept of class struggle developed by Marx, and branded upon modern consciousness, we need to introduce an entirely new terminology to express this new theory.

The "strategists" comprise the dynamic group in society who invest time and resources in pursuing and profiting from one of the four dynamic strategies. As the largest profits are to be obtained from the dominant dynamic strategy, it will attract the attention of the most ambitious, risk-taking strategists. The less ambitious and more risk-averse, however, will find some material comfort in the supporting or secondary dynamic strategies. But the dynamic strategists should not be thought of as a homogenous group. Indeed, during certain phases in the unfolding of the dominant dynamic strategy a deadly tension will be generated between different subgroups among the strategists. In particular, as the dominant strategy approaches exhaustion and as the more adventurous strategists begin seriously exploring the possibility of developing new strategies, greater tension and conflict will emerge between different strategist groups. I have called those supporting the traditional strategy the "old strategists", and those supporting the emerging strategy the "new strategists". It is the struggle between the old and new strategists for control of society's resources that has led to major transformations in institutions (for example, the shift from an absolute to a constitutional monarchy) as well as to the transfer of strategic control. And when this transfer did not take place smoothly it led to revolutions such as the English civil war, together with the French, Russian, and Chinese revolutions.

The role of the "nonstrategist" changes dramatically between various dynamic strategies and technological paradigms. Once again there is nothing evolutionary about this. Quite the reverse. During the paleolithic epoch most adults were participants in and beneficiaries of the dominant dynamic strategy of family multiplication. The family controlled the economic activities of hunting, gathering, and raiding, and, as there was no surplus to fight over, few were forced into the role of nonstrategists. After the Neolithic Revolution, which generated substantial agricultural surpluses, ruling elites emerged to garner, protect, and trade these new commodities as well as to plunder the storehouses of their neighbours. The ruling elites and their supporters are the "strategists", and the dependent labourers and slaves are the "nonstrategists". In ancient and early medieval conquest societies the nonstrategists represented the vast bulk of the population, while the strategists, who maintained political control through a monopoly of military power, were a tiny minority.

Only in those ancient societies that pursued the commerce strategy did the proportion of nonstrategists fall to lower levels, usually restricted to the underclass of slaves. Commerce was the reason for "democracy" (restricted to free male citizens) in ancient Greece, as it was in Western Europe from the late medieval period. But even by the mid-eighteenth century when the commerce strategy in Western Europe had been exhausted, the ratio of strategists to nonstrategists was not high and was restricted to wealthy males. Only the pursuit of the technological strategy from the late eighteenth century led to a widening political involvement of the bulk of the population. As the modern strategy unfolded, this political inclusion embraced the lower middle and working classes beginning with adult white males and extending, in America, to black males and finally to adult women. Today, as in early hunting societies, the nonstrategists in technologically advanced nations have virtually disappeared, being limited to minors, the poverty-stricken, and prisoners. *Hence the last twelve thousand years have seen not an evolutionary progression but a great circle.* And we should not regard the present as unalterable. If, as the radical ecologists of the late twentieth century insisted, or as the climate mitigationists of the early twenty-first century are demanding, growth-inducing technological change were to be abandoned, then war and conquest would re-emerge and the proportion of strategists to nonstrategists would fall dramatically as a ruling military elite would emerge to meet the new challenge, as they did towards the end of ancient Greece and, indeed, in Nazi Germany and Imperial Japan.

Our final category is the "antistrategist", which takes a number of forms. First, they comprise those ruling elites who assume control of societies during times of crisis and who engineer repressive economic and political systems. These command systems are designed to eliminate existing strategists, to prevent the re-emergence of potential strategists, and to facilitate the pursuit of rent-seeking. Examples of societies dominated by antistrategists include Rome from the time of Claudius, Soviet Russia, Nazi Germany, and Communist China. Control by antistrategists is the outcome of a military-backed takeover by a small band of professional revolutionaries. A vulnerable time for any society is the transition from a traditional strategy to a new strategy. If the new strategists do not possess sufficient economic power to overwhelm the old strategists quickly, the way is opened for a small band of professional revolutionaries with military support to hijack the "strategic transition". The most successful antistrategists are those who manage to involve potential strategists in the rent-seeking command system, because it widens the network of people who have a vested interest in its survival. Examples include Rome's public service system from the time of Claudius, and Stalin's command system. But eventually they fail in their endeavors because antistrategic societies cannot compete with strategic societies in the longer term. This is why the West won the cold war of the twentieth century.

Second, antistrategists encompass terrorists, such as the supporters of Al-Qaeda and ISIS, who attempt to destroy existing strategic societies. And third, they include less politically motivated or radical antistrategists who have no wish to destroy the strategic system, merely to exploit it. They are society's criminals. The psychology of antistrategism is discussed in chapter 10.

The defining characteristic of the strategist is whether he or she invests in either (or both) physical or human capital (skills and experience) required for the pursuit of a society's dynamic strategies; whether they make a proactive contribution to the viability of the strategic *logos*. This includes the supporting as well as the dominant strategies. It has nothing to do with Karl Marx's concepts of class and class struggle which are based on ownership of the means of production—of "capitalists" and "labourers". An illustration of this difference is furnished by Western society from the late nineteenth century. All "classes" of the technological society—including "capitalists" and "labourers"—became strategists of one sort or another because they all invested time and resources in the dynamic strategies and benefited from the surpluses they generated. The reward did not depend on the type of means of production that one owned, as Marx argued, but on the amount and the quality of the investment and the way in which that investment was exploited. In contrast to Marxism, there is no fundamental conflict in the strategic-struggle model between "capital" and "labour", because both accept, pursue, and benefit from the technological strategy. The objective of the struggle between these sub-groups over their degree of control of the joint strategy is to marginally influence the distribution of the strategic surpluses. They are both on the same side in the strategic struggle against the rent-seeking antistrategists. They are both "new strategists". This is the reason there has been no real proletarian revolution—only an antistrategic takeover of middle-class revolutions—in any technological society. This is the reason that both "capitalists" and "workers" in every European nation joined forces to fight to the death in support of their country's strategic *logos* during the First World War, despite calls by Marxist ideologues for "workers of the World to unite". This is the reason Marx was wrong. He incorrectly saw all capitalists as rent-seekers, as exploiters of labour, rather than profit-seekers (although he used the term profit rather than rent).

All societies at any time contain representatives of these strategic groups, who are involved in a continuous struggle for influence or control over the sources of income and wealth. As we have seen, the ratios between these groups have changed remarkably. Not as a simple progression over time but as a complex function of changing strategic and paradigmatic variables.

The dynamic mechanism of institutional change

Hence, the nature of the struggle between these groups, who demand and employ new institutional changes, depends upon the type of dynamic strategy pursued, the point reached in strategic development, the nature of the prevailing technological paradigm (pre-paleolithic, paleolithic, neolithic, industrial), and the point reached in paradigmatic development. The unfolding of a society's dynamic strategy, via "strategic pathways", is outlined by the timescapes presented in chapter 3. It should be realised that the pathways of an unfolding dynamic strategy are not smooth. There can be disruptions on both the demand and supply sides, with a resulting loss of strategic confidence and, hence, a fall in investment. This is discussed more formally in chapter 11.

At the beginning of a dynamic strategy the "new strategists" will be in the ascendancy as the successful pioneers are followed by packs of imitators (strategic imitation) who will generate an effective demand for a wide range of new institutions. By the middle development phase there will be a healthy balance between strategic groups and the increasing exercise of order, resulting in a slow-down, even stagnation, in institutional change. Hence periods of rapid institutional change will be followed by periods of stability. But this is not equivalent to the biological concept of "punctuated equilibria" as some have claimed. It is due to forces on the strategic demand side rather than on the evolutionary supply side.

As the society approaches strategic exhaustion, the conflict between the old and new strategists will increase, with each resorting to tactics of order and chaos respectively. Ultimately there will be a transfer of political control from the old to the new strategists, either peacefully or through revolution. There are, however, two possible alternative scenarios. First, if the new strategists are sufficiently powerful to create a revolution, but not to quickly overwhelm the old strategists, the chaos resulting from the unplanned involvement of nonstrategists may lead to victory for the professional revolutionaries or antistrategists. Seizing their opportunity, the antistrategists, initially with the support of the nonstrategists, ruthlessly eliminate all the existing strategists, both old and new, and construct a command system that not only enslaves the nonstrategists and prevents the reemergence of the new strategists, but maximises the extraction of rents from all the people. The second scenario will emerge if, as society approaches strategic exhaustion (as in the case of Rome during the first century AD), there is no available new strategy. In this case the old strategists, or profit-seekers, will reinvent themselves as antistrategists, or rent-seekers, and will construct oppressive institutions. The type of institutions and organisations demanded and employed by the strategists in all these phases will depend (as can be seen in Tables 7.1 and 7.2) on which of the four dynamic strategies is being pursued.

The nature of this strategic struggle also depends upon the point reached in the prevailing technological paradigm. In their early phase, human societies are involved in establishing a radically new technology through the construction of a network of very different and far more sophisticated institutions, such as those established during the Neolithic and Industrial Revolutions. This involves a struggle for the control of resources between the old "paradigmists" and the new "paradigmists" as the new technological frontier rolls over the face of the occupied world.

During the middle phase of an unfolding paradigm, our main interest is in the strategic sequence experienced by the society. It is in this phase that "strategic reversals" are possible: such as the conquest►commerce►conquest sequence in ancient Greece, or the family-multiplication►conquest►family multiplication sequence in China after c. AD 500. This leads to a reversal of the earlier victory of one group of strategists over another, such as merchants over warriors followed by warriors over merchants as in Greece, with a corresponding reversal in institutional development. And, finally, as paradigmatic exhaustion is approached there is a struggle between those new strategists/paradigmists who wish to push on beyond this paradigm into the next, and those antistrategists (such as the radical ecologists of the late twentieth century and the climate change mitigationists of the early twenty-first century) who wish to retreat from this threshold. As always, the resolution of these strategic struggles determines the nature of institutional change.

Institutional supply

While the primary dynamic mechanism of the strategic *logos* generates a changing demand for institutions and organisations to facilitate the objectives of the dynamic strategists, their design is shaped by supply-side forces. Basically these forces involve costs associated with the range of feasible rules and organisations that could be employed in any particular society to meet the change in dynamic demand. The forms chosen will depend upon which of the available alternatives meet the prevailing dynamic demand most efficiently and hence maximise material advantage. This process must take into account past decision-making and the general cultural context. In other words, the most efficient institution or organisation "available" to a particular society at any point in time is not necessarily the most efficient form available in a timeless sense. While a society's history of decision-making does not lock it into a particular development path, as many under the influence of recent ideas about "path-dependence" claim, it does affect the costs of alternatives.[3]

Within the limits provided by the strategic-demand framework, changes in institutions and organisations will also occur as relative institutional prices change. Relative institutional prices change whenever there is a change in technology broadly conceived to include ideas relevant to the structure of human society. But even these changes depend upon the primary dynamic mechanism. Enough has been said about the supply side, as this has been discussed at length in the works of the new institutional economics. Yet a new perspective and orientation that gives pride of place to strategic demand is required in institutional analysis. Until now we have lacked a persuasive account of the demand side.

Only strategic demand can solve the puzzle in Douglass North's work about why apparently inefficient institutions persist in the longer term. The model developed here suggests that "inefficient" institutions persist in societies where formerly successful dynamic strategies have been exhausted, or where dynamic strategies have never been successful. In these circumstances of "*strategic* failure" the most profitable *tactic* for the ruling class is rent-seeking. And this rent-seeking generates a demand for tactical instruments—rules and organisations—that are, in comparison with societies employing successful dynamic strategies, relatively inefficient. Rent-seeking is a tactic rather than a strategy because it aims not to increase prosperity through the growth of real GDP per capita but merely to redistribute wealth more inequitably.

While the institutions associated with rent-seeking might seem inefficient to the successful dynamic strategist, they are effective instruments in the hands of either failed strategists (as in many Third-World societies today), or dedicated antistrategists (as in the former USSR or in Communist China) in their attempt to gain a greater share of existing wealth. This model can, therefore, effectively account for those differences in institutions, organisations, and economic performance between England and Spain in the pre-modern period, or between developed and Third World countries in the late twentieth century, that have puzzled North.[4] (Or between the West and the Soviet block of countries before 1989). Consider the case of early-modern Spain.

Spain's earlier successful conquest strategy had been exhausted by the early seventeenth century and, in the competitive circumstances of the time, could not be replaced with the commerce strategy so effectively used by England throughout the sixteenth and seventeenth centuries. This produced in Spain a level of performance and an efficiency of structure that compared unfavourably with England's, particularly as the exhausted commerce strategy in the eighteenth century gave rise to the technological strategy we know as the Industrial Revolution. The Spanish ruling elite, however, was able to use new and existing institutions quite effectively in redistributing wealth in their own favour and in maintaining the existence of a less efficient economic system. North's explanation, that Spain's poor performance was the result of its culturally determined inefficient institutions, is not at all persuasive. It is not valid to use the coincidence of poor performance and inefficient institutions as evidence for the institutional hypothesis for societal dynamics. Both are jointly determined by the dynamics of the real economy. The same is true for the continuing contrast between First and Third World nations. The astute reader also would have understood the implication of supply-side institutional models that attempt to explain performance differences between countries in terms of cultural differences: in the absence of a demand side to these models, the only explanation can be racial differences. My demand-side dynamic-strategy model avoids this moral trap.

Summing up

The process of institutional change, therefore, is a derived process—derived from the demands generated by the real dynamic process. To sum up, the primary dynamic mechanism generates a demand for institutional and organisational support and operates primarily through the process of strategic struggle between various groups in society. This involves both strategic and tactical demand. Strategic demand is of a more enduring nature and involves the search for rules and organisations that will facilitate investment in a society's dominant dynamic strategy, which, in turn, leads to very longrun growth. Tactical demand, which aims to influence the redistribution of existing wealth, is of a more ephemeral nature and is generated by the balance between the forces of order and chaos in the struggle for strategic control. Only the *form* of the institutional response will depend upon the institutional costs of the various possible alternatives. Of all possibilities, the most efficient will be employed and its superficial characteristics will be determined by the dominant culture. While there may be some interaction between institutions and organisations, this is not sufficiently important to generate the independent process of institutional change hypothesised by North and other institutionalists. Both institutions and organisations are jointly determined by dynamic demand.

Dynamic demand provides the incentives, opportunities, and imperatives for the changing structure of civilisation. As we have seen, the strategic cycle of adoption, expansion, exhaustion, and decline have a characteristic impact upon observed changes in the strategic and tactical structure of society. Institutional change has no life of its own. It cannot evolve in isolation from what is happening in the real economy. It is reactive, not proactive. It has no evolutionary logic of its own. It zig-zags rather than evolves. Accordingly, if, as suggested in *The Dynamic Society*, Western civilisation were to adopt the conquest strategy by default, owing to determined efforts to abolish growth-inducing technological change, then there would be a reversal in the development of Western institutions. This, of course, is not possible in the evolutionary model of institutions where change is irreversible. In the end it must be recognised that human civilisation is merely a vehicle—albeit a vehicle of dazzling form—for achieving the basic desires of mankind, and that while the dynamic process is eternal, the institutions of civilisation—the citadel of the strategic *logos*—are ephemeral.

A GENERAL MODEL OF CULTURAL CHANGE

We are now in a position to outline a general model of cultural change. By cultural change I mean changes that take place in the entire fabric of human society, including the arts, industrial crafts, sciences (natural and social), humanities, popular culture, religion, and sport, in addition to the economic and political institutions that we have been discussing. In other words, cultural change encompasses everything that contributes to the complex structure of human civilisation. It will be argued that cultural change is an outcome rather than a driving force in the strategic *logos*.

A distinction can be made between cultural change on the one hand and institutional and organisational change on the other. As we have seen, institutional change is a direct outcome of changing dynamic demand. It is required to facilitate changes in productive forces that are to be found at the very centre of the strategic *logos*. There is, of course, another type of demand generated by this dynamic process with which economists and historians are more familiar. It is private and public consumer demand. Clearly this is the end-product of the dynamic process. While consumer demand is a derivative of the dynamic process, it does directly influence the production of those final goods and services consumed by materialist man and, as such, is the object of his desires. These goods and services are the products of the leisure, entertainment, artistic, scholastic, health, and welfare industries that feed into the process of cultural change.

Figure 7.2 General Model of Cultural Change

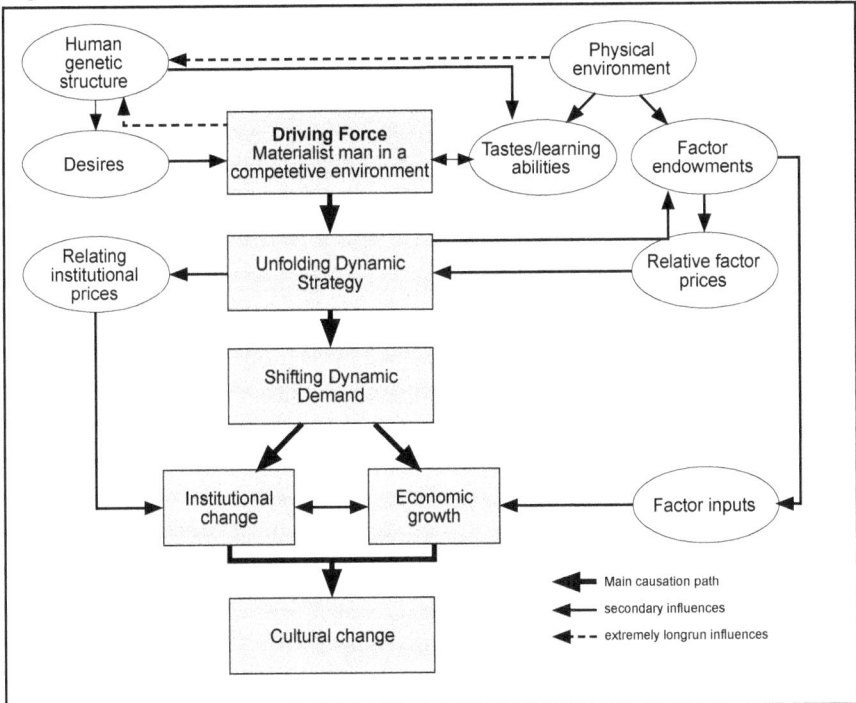

Source: Snooks 1997: 69.

A general model of cultural change is presented in diagrammatical form in Figure 7.2 It shows the main causal thrust in the development of human civilisation, proceeding from the driving force of materialist man to the dynamic strategies of family multiplication, conquest, commerce, and technological change. In turn the dynamic strategies generate dynamic demand that leads to economic growth on the one hand and to institutional and organisational change on the other. There is a degree of interaction between growth and institutional change. Finally, both economic growth and institutional change influence cultural change through increasing consumer demand and changing societal forms. Needless to say, there are a variety of feedback effects, particularly from technological change to relative prices, but these do not alter the causal path shown here.

A few comments are also required about the influences on the driving force embodied in materialist man, the forces determining the dynamic strategies, and the way these impact upon institutional and organisational change. As shown in Figure 7.2, materialist man is a product of his animal desires, tastes, learning abilities, physical and intellectual faculties, and his physical and social experiences. In turn, mankind's desires for survival and for satisfaction of the appetites are shaped by its genetic structure, while mankind's tastes, learning abilities, and physical and intellectual faculties are influenced both by its genetic structure and its physical and social environment (particularly its competitive environment). "Genetic structure", as demonstrated in chapter 4, is the outcome of an endogenous selfcreating system, rather than being exogenously determined.

As shown in *The Dynamic Society*, the dynamic strategies are determined by relative factor endowments of land, labour, and capital expressed through relative factor prices in a competitive context where materialist man is attempting to maximise his material advantage. In turn the nature of factor endowments is determined both by the physical environment and the driving force of mankind.

Finally, as is argued in this chapter, institutional change is a response to strategic and tactical demand. In the process by which the institutional forms are shaped, relative institutional prices—the costs associated with alternative institutional and organisational arrangements—play a more minor role. The forms chosen will, at any point in time, tend to be the most efficient available. This is not to say that optimal institutional arrangements are ever achieved. That is a timeless analytical concept in neoclassical economics that requires perfect knowledge and perfect computing abilities. Abilities that materialist man neither possesses nor requires.

Culture embodies the spirit of the strategic *logos*. It carries the vital principle of the age. The reason is that cultural activities, both "high" and "low", respond to the needs of the dynamic strategists and reflect the technology of the time. The culture of a society changes as its dominant dynamic strategy unfolds and, particularly, as one strategy is replaced by another. This is reflected, for example, in the changing nature of entertainment in Europe, from the aristocratic war games of the conquest strategy, to the middle-class interest in the performing arts of the commerce strategy, and to the electronic entertainment for the masses under the technological strategy.[5] But while culture embodies the spirit of human civilisation, it does not play a determining role in the fundamental dynamic process. There is no independent feedback from culture to the unfolding dynamic strategy. Cultural ideas that pursue an independent path fail to flourish because there is no strategic demand for them. Cultural ideas developed in the scholarly/artistic ivory tower are neglected by society and remain unutilised until, if ever, the *logos* generates a strategic demand for them; and even then they will probably need to be reinvented. And once all dynamic strategies have been exhausted, the culture of a society goes into inevitable decline.

The role of culture is, nonetheless, essential. It both transmits and transcends the materialism of the dominant dynamic strategy. Cultural activities such as religion, higher learning, the arts, and sport translate the vital principle of the age into forms that people can understand and respond to. By doing so, cultural activities draw the people into the prevailing dynamic strategy, inspire them to cooperative action, and provide hope for the future in a meaningless material world. This reinforces the dynamic principle in society. But more than this. By giving the dynamic principle aesthetic shape, cultural activities are able to transform the crude and joyless pursuit of survival and prosperity into an almost spiritual experience. At the very least they entertain and divert us from the grossness, harshness, and repetition of life.

Culture, of course, can be manipulated by society's leaders for their own benefit. It can be employed consciously to achieve compliance with leadership objectives. Religion and the associated arts (such as the decoration and visual "messages" in temples and cathedrals, together with religious music and plays) have long been used in this way. Where this has been undertaken by **strategic** leaders, where these cultural forms actually embodied the spirit of the age, the outcome is much more than mere propaganda. It satisfies a genuine need in society. But, where societies have been hijacked by **antistrategists**, the attempt to employ the arts (religion is usually eliminated and replaced with an antistrategic ideology) solely for propaganda purposes—such as the crude social realism in the visual and performing arts in Nazi Germany, the USSR, and Mao's China—invariably fails, precisely because antistrategic art does not embody the dynamic spirit of the time. Antistrategic art is without soul or meaning. Purely propaganda, it is unable to transmit or transcend the dominant dynamic strategy. It is unable to involve the people. A culture devoid of the spirit of the age is just marking time.

In simplifying the main lines of interaction in this general model much of the complex detail has been suppressed. That complexity is discussed in much greater depth both in *The Dynamic Society* and in *The Ephemeral Civilization*.

The intention here is merely to show how institutional and cultural change—that is dynamic civilisation—is an outcome of the central dynamic process in the real economy of the strategic *logos*. Institutional change is not a causal force in that central dynamic. It is the vehicle not the engine of societal dynamics. Accordingly those theories in economics, social science, and sociobiology that focus on social evolution are of little or no use in explaining reality. And they fail to even recognise the ultimate reality that is the strategic *logos*.

Chapter 8
Ideology of the *Logos* — from Religion to Scientism

Dead gods also rise.

There are many mysteries in life, which are gradually being driven back by modern science. Some of these mysteries are more important to us than others. What we have never been able to comprehend, and what is infinitely more important to us than any other mystery, is the nature of the universal life-system, or "strategic *logos*". Why? Because it enables us to survive and prosper. It makes the improbable possible. In *Dead God Rising* I argued that the supreme, yet unsuccessful, attempt by mankind to understand the strategic *logos* has been responsible for the world's great myths and religions. Religion and its successor, scientism, are the instruments employed by our species to understand and manipulate this great mystery of mysteries. Religion and scientism form the bases of logosian ideologies.

THE HIDDEN LIFE-SYSTEM AND ITS MYTHS

Mankind has always been aware that its very existence is the outcome of a hidden system of forces. But because it is hidden, we have, until now, not been able to understand it in a rational manner. And this lack of understanding has led to a concern that this vital system might break down, leading to the destruction of our society, even our species. Our greatest priority throughout history, therefore, has been to understand the universal life-system, gain access to the forces controlling it, and to exert some influence over its processes. The underlying fear that has driven this great quest has been fuelled by the evidence all around us of human societies that have failed. Yet despite the failure of individual societies, the human race as a whole has prospered, owing to the underlying robustness of the strategic *logos*.

As the strategic *logos* has remained a mystery throughout human history—as it has resisted rational exploration—the only way in which it could be accessed was through myth; through the exercise of our story-making imagination. Karen Armstrong in her small book entitled *A Short History of Myth* (2005) also eloquently makes this point. She tells us that:

> Myth is about the unknown; it is about that for which initially we have no words. Myth therefore looks into the heart of a great silence ... all mythology speaks of another plane that exists alongside our own world, and that in some sense supports it. Belief in this invisible but more powerful reality, sometimes called the world of the gods, is a basic theme of mythology ...

> ... mythology is an art form that points beyond history to what is timeless in human existence, helping us to get beyond the chaotic flux of random events, and glimpse the core of reality.[1]

Myth, of course, is not truth. It is the imaginative equivalent of truth in a fictional parallel world. It may encourage us to think that we are approaching the "core of reality" and, thereby, are able to exert some mystical influence over it, but to really understand and shape the strategic *logos* we must employ science not myth. We must operate within the real world not a virtual parallel world.

The original authors of these sacred myths clearly understood what they were attempting to do. They knew they were groping for an understanding of their life-system through the use of metaphor rather than reason. Their "gods" were ephemeral "strategic guardians" of their particular *logos*, not eternal lords of the cosmos. It was only much later that generations of professional "priestly philosophers"—or metaphysical thinkers—turned these founding strategic myths into what we understand today as religion. In *Dead God Rising* I argued that this was the outcome of persistent "strategic failure" followed by intense and prolonged "strategic frustration" in societies occupying the borderlands—Syria, Palestine, and Arabia—between the ancient superpowers of Egypt, Mesopotamia, and Rome. In the process, the early strategic guardians were transformed into "gods". Rather than treating the early strategic myths as metaphor, the priestly philosophers—or metaphysicians—employed them as factual statements about reality. For this reason, any discussion of the role of religion in society is really an exploration of man's vision of the hidden strategic *logos*.

Contemporary commentators on ancient religions, however, fail to understand the origin of these mythologies as metaphors for the hidden life-system. Here is what an otherwise perceptive Egyptologist, Erik Hornung, in *Conceptions of God in Ancient Egypt* (1996), has said of this issue:

> Of course we no longer attempt to 'explain' gods — the farther we penetrate into the world of these ancient images the less we can explain what a god is.[2]

Scholars have, in the main, abandoned the attempt to explain the origin of gods and religion because, like the priestly philosophers, they have been unable to comprehend the strategic *logos* in either rational or mythical terms. Religion is seen merely as a reflection of the cultural attainment of the society that gave rise to it. In contrast, explaining what gods *are* was the very purpose of *Dead God Rising* and it is the focus of this chapter.

MANKIND'S EXISTENTIAL ANXIETY

Mankind has an intense desire to understand, manipulate, and sustain its life-system. This is an outcome of the need to survive and, having survived, to prosper. Prosperity, at its most basic, is insurance against future crises. The driving force in this process is, as shown in chapter 4, "strategic desire". It is a concept discussed in detail in my earlier books *The Collapse of Darwinism* (2003) and *The Selfcreating Mind* (2006). There are two dimensions to this basic need of mankind that are central to our exploration of the nature and role of religion. The first and most important is the desire of the entire society to understand the mystery of mysteries to ensure its longevity and prosperity; and the second is the longing of the individual within this society for personal peace and security.

Mankind has always been concerned about the viability of its societies. Human society is a fragile and ephemeral entity.[3] Hear what the Anglo-Saxon poet (6th to 9th centuries) had to say on this matter:

> Where has gone the steed? Where has gone the man? Where has gone the giver of treasure? Where has gone the place of the banquets? Where are the pleasures of the hall? Alas, the gleaming chalice; alas, the armoured warrior; alas the majesty of the prince! Truly, that time has passed away, has grown dark under the helm of night as though it had never been … Here wealth is ephemeral; here a friend is ephemeral; here man is ephemeral; here kinsman is ephemeral; all this foundation of the earth will become desolate.[4]

Such ephemerality has always been obvious to mankind as the evidence of failed societies lies all round. We need only reflect on the haunting lines of Percy Bysshe Shelley's (1792–1822) well-known poem "Ozymandias" (a personal name of Ramesses II):

> I met a traveller from an antique land,
> Who said — "two vast and trunkless legs of stone
> Stand in the desert … near them, on the sand,
> Half sunk a shattered visage lies, whose frown,
> And wrinkled lips, and sneer of cold command,
> Tell that its sculptor well those passions read
> Which yet survive, stamped on those lifeless things,
> The hand that mocked them, and the heart that fed;
> And on the pedestal these words appear:
> My name is Ozymandias, King of Kings,
> Look on my Works ye Mighty, and despair!
> Nothing beside remains. Round the decay
> Of that colossal Wreck, boundless and bare
> The lone and level sands stretch far away.

In the past, the very greatest of societies—such as Egypt, Greece, and Rome—arose from and eventually returned to obscurity over long periods of time, whereas lesser societies only briefly made their mark before being engulfed by oblivion. Even today, in living memory, well-established empires like Britain and the USSR have suddenly collapsed after giving impressions of permanence, while lesser ones like Nazi Germany and Imperial Japan have emerged and collapsed in a handful of years. Smaller societies in the Pacific, Southeast Asia, the Middle East, and south-eastern Europe are forever forming and foundering. Even the superpower of today, the United States of America, will be eclipsed this century.

Why this is so has always been a great mystery to the leaders, citizens, and scholars of the many societies of mankind, both past and present. This widespread and profound failure to understand the sources of the emergence, the expansion, and the collapse of societies has generated an intense anxiety in the breast of man. It is an anxiety that leads to an overwhelming need to achieve order and balance (or equilibrium) in human society—a need never realised. In the past, ancient societies like Egypt judged the living and the dead by their contribution to the mystical *maat*, or worldly and cosmic order; and today we are fixated with the desire to achieve economic equilibrium through the equally irrational "war on inflation", or, alternatively, to intervene massively in order to "fix" global recession and even halt climate change. Why irrational? Because inflation plays a vital and positive role in the dynamic processes of the strategic *logos,* and because massive interventions disrupt and distort the dynamic mechanism of the *logos*.[5]

In the past, the priestly philosophers were regarded by their societies as experts concerning the mystery of mysteries—concerning the life-systems underlying the prosperity of their societies. In today's modern world these experts are considered to be the worldly philosophers or economists. Both groups of so-called experts have focused their attention upon the same objective—order and equilibrium. Interestingly, today's worldly philosophers, who are inadvertently attacking the very dynamic mechanism that underlies their society's strategic success—see chapter 11—are no closer to understanding the mystery of mysteries than were the priestly philosophers of the past.

In the past, this great anxiety about whether order and stability would emerge from the mystery of mysteries led to the creation of comforting myths about strategic guardians—myths that were ultimately turned into religions about creator gods, even a supreme creator God of the Universe. The vast number of gods—tens or hundreds of thousands—and their associated religions, together with the massive investment of time and material surpluses required to maintain them, is testament to the great anxiety of mankind in the face of the mystery of mysteries. In the contemporary world this anxiety has led to the creation of a body of metaphysical knowledge called neoclassical economics, which is attended to by a "priestly" class of experts called economists, who have captured the ears of politicians throughout the Western world. These economists, as shown later in the chapter, are responsible for creating new myths about the mystery of mysteries in order to assuage our existential anxiety. But as they do not understand the *logos* or its dynamic processes, they do more harm than good. Hence they merely add to our fears.

Existential anxiety is not just a collective experience. Individuals in any society also harbor intense personal fears about the future. If their society is uncertain, how can they, as individuals, hope to survive and prosper. As our study of history shows, individuals also look to the strategic guardian or gods of their society to soothe their existential anxiety. Initially, the strategic guardians were called upon by a society's wisemen or shamans for the benefit of the entire community. But, later, in the hands of the professional priestly philosophers, these strategic guardians were transformed into creator gods that could be sought out by individuals, as well as by communities through their kings and priests. This "democratisation" of access to the gods was an outcome of the ever-present pressure in human society for the masses to partake of the privileges of their leaders as well as achieving a greater share of society's wealth.

Transformation of strategic guardians into personal gods, however, had an ironic twist. Initially, as I have suggested, the strategic guardians were required to ensure the material success of their society. But in the course of this successful "strategic pursuit", individual members of a given society were required to do things that their rational faculties told them were wrong. The source of this problem—as I show in *The Selfcreating Mind* (2006) and chapter 9 here—is that individuals are composed of a body, driven by strategic desire, together with its facilitating strategic instrument, the mind, ruled by reason. What the body craves, the mind both facilitates and, sometimes, questions. This problem has led to a compartmentalisation in the personal lives of human beings—a separation of what we need to do on a daily basis to survive, from what we believe we should do. I call this compartmentalisation of the mind, "existential schizophrenia".[6]

In some people, existential schizophrenia works quite well. They are able to participate fully in the strategic pursuit—which involves, at least, intense competition with others and, at worst, systematic killing—and still regard themselves as morally upright and entirely justified in what they need to do to survive and prosper. Sanity is retained by refusing to integrate reality with their distorted perception of themselves. Other individuals, however, are not so "fortunate". In some of these, as I show in *The Selfcreating Mind*, existential schizophrenia leads to pathological schizophrenia,[7] while in others the only resolution of this fundamental dilemma of life is forgiveness from a supernatural being. What these guilt-stricken people cannot forgive in themselves, requires forgiveness from the gods. This is where the ironical twist comes in. These individuals are led to call on gods, which arose from the need to ensure strategic success, in order to obtain forgiveness for actions committed in the course of achieving that strategic success. Perhaps it is fortunate they are unaware of the origins of their gods.

EMERGENCE AND TRANSFORMATION OF THE GODS

In *Dead God Rising* I argued that it was mankind's attempt to penetrate the mystery of mysteries and to come to grips with the life-system underlying everyday life that led to the emergence of strategic guardians in paleolithic societies. The recognition of these strategic guardians, and the attempt by shamans to contact and influence them, enabled these early hunter-gatherer societies to participate in the strategic pursuit with greater confidence. While they did not rationally understand how their life-system, or strategic *logos,* worked, they did achieve a sense of *rapprochement* with it by employing a simple "strategic ideology", or mythological explanation.

The Strategic Guardians of Paleolithic Societies

Early religious beliefs and rituals can be reconstructed from the evidence left by paleolithic societies on the walls of caves and rock shelters. But these sacred sites provide only a glimpse of a religious activity that included dance, song, and rites of various kinds. These religious activities can be found in all societies of modern humans (*Homo sapiens*) and there are even tantalising suggestions in the archeological record that they were performed also by *Homo neanderthalensis* (0.3 myrs ago) and possibly even *Homo erectus/ergaster* (1.2 myrs ago).

While *H. erectus/ergaster* and *H. neanderthalensis* appear to have employed art for religious purposes, it is not until about 40,000 BP that we have any detailed information about the nature, role, and significance of these activities. The oldest, most detailed, and continuous stream of evidence for sacred art comes from Aboriginal Australia, where an unbroken tradition has existed for over 30,000 years. This ancient culture is of particular significance as it has been directly observed and interrogated by our own age. While Western European cave paintings can also be dated back to over 30,000 BP, we know considerably less about the culture that produced it. In Eastern Europe and Siberia, art objects—including ceramics, textiles, and ivory sculptures—can be dated back to 26,000 BP, and personal ornaments to 42,000 BP.

There are also many prehistoric art sites in Africa—some 30,000 sites in the Republic of South Africa alone—dating back to more than 10,000 BP, but few have been adequately examined and studied. Art objects, such as ostrich egg-shell beads, have been dated to 35,000 years of age, with some, such as cross-hatched lumps of hematite, being dated "controversially" to 77,000 BP. Painted religious symbols on rock shelters throughout southern Africa are at least 28,000 years old; and some of these can, as in the Kalahari and in Australia, be discussed with the direct descendants of the prehistoric artists. Much of this art is thought to be associated with shamanism. In the Americas, Californian rock paintings have been dated conservatively to 9,300 BP, and petroglyphs (or rock engravings) controversially to 19,000 BP. Much of this symbolic representation is thought to be shamanic in origin and nature. Brazil possess rock paintings that are about 12,000 years old; and in Alaska, representational objects have been dated to over 3,000 years.

The stone-age societies of both Western Europe and Australia—the case studies employed in *Dead God Rising*—have, at their deepest levels, much in common. They both employed the dynamic strategy of family multiplication—of procreation and migration to gain greater access to natural resources—which was expressed through hunting and gathering. They were both isolated for vast periods of time—300,000 years during the Neanderthal Mousterian, and 60,000 years during the Aboriginal Dreaming—during which they expanded geographically to exploit the animal and plant resources of these unoccupied lands using advanced stone-age technology. Once they had fully occupied and exploited the natural resources of these lands at opposite ends of the globe, they both achieved states of "dynamic equilibrium"—a dynamic balance achieved in the face of slowly changing geographical and climatic conditions. They both attempted to understand and influence their mysterious life-systems, or strategic *logoi*—in order to survive and prosper—by devising strategic rituals. These rituals were led by shamanic figures in order to penetrate these mysteries so as to negotiate with the various spirits and ancestors—with the **G**uardians **O**f their **D**ynamic **S**trategies (or **GODS**). Both societies, therefore, gave birth to the **GODS**. And they both extrapolated an understanding of their hidden life-systems onto the visible physical Universe. In this way the *logos* and the cosmos—the strategic and the religious—became one.

The Many Gods of Neolithic Societies

With the neolithic technological paradigm shift (or agricultural revolution) beginning about 10,600 years ago in the Old World and about 7,700 years ago in the New World, not only was there a strategic demand for a more sophisticated strategic ideology but also surpluses were generated that could be used to support a professional class of priests and priestly philosophers, and to invest in great temples and pyramids as working models of the mystery of mysteries. Over several millennia, simple ideas about strategic guardians were reworked into complex myths about the gods—whereby the **G**uardians **O**f **D**ynamic **S**trategy, or "**GODS**", were transformed into universal deities, or "gods"— which provided a protective shield under which the society could progress strategically. This was the work of the priestly philosophers, who responded to strategic demand generated by the *logos* of neolithic communities—such as Egypt and Mesopotamia—for a more sophisticated strategic ideology. In this transformational process, the ritual of the strategic ideology became more elaborate and responsibility for it was assumed by the strategic leader, or king, the ruling social elite, and the professional class of specially trained and educated priests. This elaborate system of strategic ideology in support of the *logos* was the outcome of strategic success in the ancient world. As seen through the eyes of ancient neolithic man, the great strategic success of Egypt and Mesopotamia was a reflection of the power of their gods and the efficacy of their strategic ideologies in eliciting the support of these strategic guardians. A brief survey of the dynamic strategies and strategic ideologies of Egypt and Mesopotamia will clarify this argument.

The agricultural revolution in the Fertile Crescent was the driving force for changes in the perception of the gods. Agriculture first appeared in Syria and Lebanon, with Natufian hunter-gatherers harvesting wild cereals by 10,500 BC.

By 9,000 BC villagers were cultivating "domesticated" wheat and barley using dry-farming techniques throughout the Middle East. In Egypt, farming along the Nile did not begin until about 5,000 BC, some three millennia later. To facilitate the development of these farming communities, long-distance trade emerged in the Fertile Crescent in the eighth millennium BC. Eventually, a number of these agricultural societies adopted commerce as a dynamic strategy that would lift their standards of living far above the levels that existing agricultural technology could support. Others adopted conquest.

Not until the development of large-scale irrigation techniques around 5,500 BC did Near Eastern farmers move from the foothills of the Zagros Mountains onto the rainless plains of Mesopotamia. Together with the invention of the plough around 4,500 BC, large-scale irrigation enabled, for the first time, urban civilisation to emerge and flourish. Many vibrant city states—such as Eridu, Ur, Uruk, Nippur, Lagash, Umma, Kish, Agade—emerged on the rich alluvial plains between the Tigris and Euphrates rivers. They formed the land of Sumer (non-Semitic) in the south and Akkad (semetic) in the north, and created a new form of strategic *logos*. In these walled cities—fortifications were essential to protect their new wealth from raiding nomads—all the essential instruments of civilisation were soon developed, including: writing by 3,400 BC (cuneiform by 2,900 BC); the measurement of time; advanced mathematics (and other deductive thinking); the invention of bronze (particularly for weapons); the development of specialised professions (military, political, legal, religious) and crafts; and, most important of all, the construction of temples as "homes" for their strategic guardians. This remarkable new civilisation became the citadel of the strategic *logos*.

Between 4,300 and 2,334 BC, the world's first civilisation, the Sumerian, flourished and provided an example for the rest of the Old World. At its base was a highly productive agricultural system. But the greater wealth of cities like Uruk—which by 2,900 BC had a population of about 50,000 people—was generated by the dynamic strategies of commerce and, increasingly, conquest. In a climate of escalating competition for, and conflict over, control of commerce, one city leader, King Lugalzagesi of Umma, conquered all of Sumer, for the first time, in 2,350 BC. Yet this was soon followed—just sixteen years later—by the assault of the Akkadian king of Kish, who not only conquered Sumer but fashioned the world's first empire that extended from the Persian Gulf to the Mediterranean Sea. Political stability was to be an elusive goal in the Near East, as the subsequent ancient history of Mesopotamia consisted of relatively short-lived empires of conquest, dominated successively by Ur, Assyria, Babylon, the Hittites, the Kassites, Neo-Assyria, Neo-Babylonia, the Persians, and finally the Macedonians.

Egypt, which was isolated from such intense competition, took a different strategic path. Once the various agriculturally based "confederacies" along the Nile had been forged militarily into a unified kingdom—probably by King

Narmer around 2,900 BC—Egypt pursued the dynamic strategy of commerce rather than conquest. Military action was used only to extend and defend the highly lucrative commerce strategy, or to reunify Egypt as a commerce society after periods of chaos—the so-called "intermediate" periods.

How were the gods viewed by Mesopotamian and Egyptian priestly philosophers? Both societies had thousands of gods. Of these, the main ones were associated with various aspects of their dynamic life-systems. In Mesopotamia, Inana, goddess of fertility and war, represented both the "primal drive" in their life-system, as well as the dominant dynamic strategy of conquest, which was responsible for the Ur's great wealth and prosperity. Other major gods included An (Anu), god of heaven and supreme creator god, responsible for the cyclical nature of seasons; Utu, the sun god, who was judge of the gods and responsible for the eternal recurrence of day and night; Enlil (Ellil) of Nippur, god of winds and agriculture, who invented the hoe, and was responsible for the prosperity and abundance of his chosen city in war and peace (but who could also be highly destructive if displeased, as in the Great Flood); Enki (Ea) of Eridu, god of wisdom and sweet water of the life-giving rivers, who was a creator god engaged in the primordial battle between good and evil, was god of artists and craftsmen, and was responsible for the well-being of the natural world; Marduk who, under the Babylonians, replaced An and Enlil as the chief deity and leader of the forces against chaos; and Assur, who was the national deity of the Assyrians, replaced Marduk as the hero god.

As the social structure of Mesopotamia changed from a collection of competing city-states to a conquest empire—owing to the unfolding of the Mesopotamian "strategic sequence"—the roles of the gods and the relationships between them changed as suggested above. At first, the various patron gods of the city-states were regarded as equals; but when Nippur built its empire, Enlil became the supreme god of Sumer—later superseded by the Babylonian god Marduk and then the Assyrian god Assur—and the Sumerian pantheon was reorganised. In other words, the gods, in their role as guardians of the dynamic strategies, were responsive to changes in the Mesopotamian *logos*. But, at the same time, the material success of the *logos* provided the priestly philosophers with the freedom to employ their imaginations to reshape their stories about the gods and to indulge in ever more elaborate religious ritual. Over time, these metaphysicians, in response to the emergence of empire, elevated one of the many city gods to be the chief amongst his peers, clearing the way for the chief god to become the one and only God of all creation.

Like the gods of Mesopotamia, the Egyptian deities were regarded as representatives of the major characteristics and dynamic forces of their life-system. There was, for example, Maat, the centrally important winged goddess, responsible for cosmic and earthly order; Re, the sun god, responsible for the daily cycle of life; Nun, the god of primeval waters, responsible for the creative ferment underpinning the eternal recurrence; Thoth, god of the moon and wisdom, responsible for the development of knowledge and for discovering the laws of *maat* (order); and so on down to ever more detailed and mundane levels of human life. As shown in *Dead God Rising,* Egyptian ideas about their gods contain the most elegant and complete mythological analysis of the strategic *logos.* This was largely the outcome of a strategic system that remained intact for three millennia—a strategic system that was subjected to close scrutiny by an intellectual class that remained faithful to its dictates and resisted the temptation to divorce the idea of their gods from the reality of the strategic *logos* of which they were the custodians.

Monotheism in the Borderlands

The transformation of neolithic strategic ideologies—centred on a multiplicity of gods—into what we would recognise as modern religion—centred on a single divine being—was a product not of strategic success, but of strategic failure. In the ancient world, the most difficult region to build a successful strategic society was the land of Canaan—what we know today as Palestine and Syria—lying in the borderlands between the superpowers of Egypt in the south and Mesopotamia in the north and east. The greater material wealth, population, and, hence, power of Egypt and Mesopotamia, was generated by richer agricultural systems arising from the flooding and irrigation of the Nile and Tigris-Euphrates rivers. Canaan was a land dominated by these superpowers.

The small societies in this rich corridor of commerce—the reason it was so attractive to the superpowers of the ancient world—only prospered on the rare occasions that both superpowers were otherwise distracted. In the absence of superpower attention, small Palestinian or Syrian states quickly expanded. But never quickly enough, because the returning superpowers just swept them away and imposed their hegemony on the local peoples. This geopolitical reality generated a depressing sequence of long periods of oppression and exploitation, followed by short periods of liberation and prosperity, followed in turn by long periods of oppression and exploitation. This vicious cycle generated intense and prolonged strategic frustration—a type of individual and collective neurosis— as discussed in *The Selfcreating Mind* and chapter 9.[8]

Judaism

In the eighth century BC, Josiah, king of the small society of Judah, attempted to take advantage of the temporary absence of the superpowers, by developing plans to expand his kingdom into northern Palestine and Syria under the protection of the strategic guardian YHWH—the tribal god of Abraham, Moses, and David. To this end, Josiah's priestly philosophers reworked the local myths of YHWH into a sophisticated strategic ideology, later revised and called the Hebrew Scriptures (or, to Christians, the Old Testament). But even before his plans were executed, Josiah was captured and killed by the Egyptians returning to control this commerce corridor. The subsequent destruction of

Judah by the Babylonians, the fall of Jerusalem, and the Exile in Babylon, led the captive priestly philosophers to transform Josiah's strategic ideology of conquest (under the conquest strategic guardian, YHWH) into a religion—a spiritual (nonstrategic) rather than a materialist (strategic) ideology—later known as Judaism. This transformation was an outcome of strategic failure and intense strategic frustration. In the subsequent three centuries of superpower oppression by the Mesopotamians and Macedonians (586–301BC), the Egyptians (301–200BC), and the Mesopotamians again (200–107BC), Judaism could only survive as a religion—a spiritual ideology—as there was no scope for the exercise of an independent strategic ideology.

With the revolt of the Maccabees in 167 BC at a time of superpower withdrawal, the Jews experienced a rare period of independence. For about a century, Judaism was employed both as a religion and a strategic ideology for a short-lived conquest strategy that led to the Hasmoneans occupying all of Palestine. Predictably, however, this period of independence and prosperity was brought to a sudden and final end in 63 BC by the expansion of the Roman empire under Pompey. Once again the people of Palestine experienced deep existential frustration arising from this strategic failure. The response was varied. Some Palestinians attempted to accommodate themselves to Roman occupation, others looked to apocalyptic prophets, others rebelled, and yet others attempted to construct a new **nonstrategic** community within their oppressed land.

Christianity

The solution chosen by Jesus of Nazareth and his followers—a path determined by strategic frustration—was the building of a nonstrategic community. In the hands of the priestly philosophers in the centuries after Jesus' death, however, this minor nonstrategic ideology was transformed into a new monotheistic religion called Christianity, which Jesus of Nazareth certainly would not have recognised.

Ironically, Christianity, with its **nonstrategic** origins was later adopted by the Roman emperor Constantine as a new **strategic** ideology. Owing to the exhaustion of Rome's conquest strategy in the late second century AD, the old gods of war had lost favour and the empire was desperate to find a new strategic ideology and a new strategic guardian. Constantine, who attempted to revive the flagging fortunes of the empire, adopted the Christian God to lead his conquest strategy and Christianity as the new strategic ideology. Christianity also served as the new religion of Roman citizens owing to its surprising but temporary success. With the collapse of Rome in the early fifth century, Western European societies, employing the conquest strategy, continued the use of Christianity as both strategic ideology and state religion. And the Eastern (or Greek) Roman Empire employed Christianity as ideology for their successful commerce strategy.

Islam

The other great monotheistic religion, Islam, also emerged in the borderlands between superpowers, this time—in the early seventh century AD—consisting of the Eastern Roman empire (later called Byzantium) and the Persian empire. Like the Palestinians of earlier times, the Arabs had long experienced strategic failure, intertribal warfare, and intense strategic frustration. With the examples of Zoroastrianism (Persia), Judaism, and Christianity (Roman empire) surrounding him, Muhammad wanted to fashion a monotheistic strategic ideology that would unite his people and enable them to succeed and prosper like the surrounding superpowers. Owing to fortunate timing—the Roman and Persian empires had fought each other to a standstill—the Arabs were remarkably successful.

Within the space of a generation, they had conquered the Persian empire and made themselves and their Islamic ideology masters of Egypt, Palestine, Arabia, Mesopotamia, and Iran. Islamic forces even went on to challenge the survival of the West with its Christian strategic ideology—a challenge that was only finally eliminated by the industrial technological paradigm-shift effected by Western Europe in the nineteenth century. Almost overnight, the advanced Islamic societies (together with other formerly great societies, such as China and India) were rendered economically backward. Only the fortuitous possession of vast oil reserves required by the industrial societies has lifted parts of the Islamic Middle East out of obscurity, even if only until their oilfields are drained or made uneconomic by shale oil supplies in the Americas.

The "death of God" and the rise of scientism

The Industrial Revolution, beginning in the late eighteenth century, marked the end not only of the Islamic challenge but also, ironically, of Christianity as a strategic ideology, if not a religion, in the most advanced societies. The underlying reason is that the new technological strategy was based on science rather than religious mysticism. The advanced Western societies in both the Old and New Worlds looked to technology and science to sustain their strategic *logoi*, rather than to the old metaphysical mythology. As is discussed in more detail below, the technological-paradigm-shift mechanism is a "god breaker" as well as a "god maker". In these circumstances Christianity as a strategic ideology became irrelevant, encouraging intellectuals like Friedrich Nietzsche (1844–1900) to proclaim, in the last quarter of the nineteenth century, that "God is dead". Even as a religion, Christianity has been declining in strategically advanced societies and, like Islam, has only made new converts in the Third World. The new ideology in the industrialised world is "scientism". Where this ideology has taken the form of environmentalism and the cult of Gaia, it has become a new religion for some.

The new priestly philosophers of scientism initially believed that, armed with their new strategic ideology, they would be able to finally penetrate the mystery of mysteries where their religious predecessors had failed. But this has not been the case. The reason is that once they leave the realms of the natural sciences, the priestly philosophers of scientism—including orthodox economists—approach human society with metaphysical reasoning (deduction) rather than "strategic thinking" (induction). A breakthrough in this respect had to wait until the more difficult inductive methodology could be successfully employed in the realm of human and other living systems. Only with the identification and understanding of the strategic *logos* has the mystery of mysteries been penetrated in an intellectually rigorous and scientific way. Yet, even in the era of science and technology, religion, in the form of scientism, has re-emerged, owning to the persistence of metaphysical thinking. For as long as there are priestly philosophers and materially frustrated citizens, there will be religion of some kind or another. Yet this need not worry us as it clearly worries the new atheists, such as Richard Dawkins, who bizarrely sees religion as an "evil virus". It is essential to emphasise that it is material rather than spiritual issues that determine human motivation. As my work clearly shows: desires drive, while ideas, whether religious or otherwise, merely facilitate those desires.

GOD-MAKER AND GOD-BREAKER

The great transforming mechanism driving strategic ideology, or religion, is what I have called the "technological paradigm shift". In other words, the technological-paradigm-shift mechanism is the "god-maker/god-breaker" of human society: it is the driving force behind **dead god rising**, by which one major ideology is replaced by another. This mechanism was, as already suggested, responsible for the birth of the gods as guardians of the strategic *logos* of early man, for the transformation of these strategic guardians into gods of the cosmos during the early phases of civilisation, for the death of the old god in the nineteenth century, and for the rise of the deity of science in our own age. It will also determine the nature of "gods" in the future, both on this planet and beyond. We should focus more closely on this mechanism of cultural transformation, which shows why dead gods also rise.

While a general outline of the wider genetic/technological paradigm shift mechanism, operating over the past 4,000 myrs, is provided in chapters 3 and 4, we need to focus here in greater detail on the way it has operated over the past 2 myrs and, in particular, over the past two centuries.[9] We will also consider the future. The underlying dynamic mechanism represented in Figure 3.5 (chapter 3)—the god-maker/god-breaker—involves the exhaustion of an existing technological paradigm, the adoption of an entirely new technological paradigm through a major economic revolution (or technological paradigm shift), a transformation of the strategic *logos* of the pioneering society, and a global strategic transition affecting the *logoi* of all societies. In turn, the transformed strategic *logos* generates a changing strategic demand for a wide range of economic, institutional (social rules), organisational (social networks) and cultural inputs. Also, the new *logos* causes a transformation in the nature and societal role of the strategic guardians—commonly called gods.

From Figure 3.5, we can see that the paleolithic technological paradigm shift—paleolithic shift for short—coincided with the birth of the simple strategic guardians discussed briefly above; the neolithic shift coincided with the transformation of simple strategic guardians into complex gods of the cosmos that eventually gave rise to the One God; and the modern shift coincided with the death of the old God and the rise of scientism. As we shall see, this god-making mechanism also has implications—even if unknown—for the future.

At the risk of some repetition, Figure 3.5 requires a brief explanation. Each of the paradigm shifts that it portrays opens the door for an extended period of material expansion through the exploitation of the new technological capacity it provides. The new and higher level of technological capacity is represented by the "potential" curve, and the exploitation of this potential is shown by the "actual" curve. When the two curves coincide, the paradigm is exhausted. In other words, at this point the entire technological capacity of the paradigm has been fully exploited.

The paleolithic shift, as we saw in chapter 3, involved a substitution of a hunting for a scavenging technology. This caused a major change in the strategic *logos* of human society, which in turn generated a significant change in strategic demand for material, institutional, and cultural inputs for humanity's strategic pursuit. Of particular importance for this chapter is the new demand for assistance from strategic guardians in sustaining this more complex life-system. In this new, unknown and frightening world there was an urgent need for assistance from beings more knowledgeable and powerful than themselves. Such a being had to be greater than any human being precisely because mankind was unable to understand or directly influence the mystery of mysteries on which their survival and prosperity depended. These strategic guardians, as shown in *Dead God Rising*, were directly responsible for sustaining key aspects of the strategic *logos*, by ensuring regular patterns of rainfall; adequate numbers of wild herds, plants, and fruit; appropriate human fertility; and effective protection from predators, both animal and human. For this reason, the gods can be numbered in the hundreds and thousands. But, as yet, strategic guardians were not cosmic beings.

The neolithic shift involved the substitution of an agricultural/herding technology for a hunting technology. Once again this technological paradigm shift was responsible for transforming the strategic *logos* of mankind. And the transformed *logos* generated a changing strategic demand for a wide range of strategic inputs, including a more complex understanding and mastery of the mystery of mysteries and its protective strategic guardian. To provide this greater understanding and mastery, a professional class of priestly philosophers emerged, financed by the surplus that could now be generated through agricultural production. And the greater the scale on which this agricultural production and associated commerce or conquest strategic pursuit occurred—the greatest examples being in the irrigated lands of Egypt and Mesopotamia—the greater the investment in the infrastructure of strategic ideology. In these agricultural societies the strategic guardians were transformed into gods that not only sustained the strategic *logos* but also took on cosmic significance. The most impressive strategic ideology was developed by the ancient Egyptians, who came closest to understanding and mastering the mystery of mysteries, owing to the great longevity—some 3,000 years—of their civilisation. They finally failed because, in the end, metaphysics and mythology are self-referential not existential.

The transformation of strategic ideology into metaphysical mythology or religion was, as suggested earlier, a product not of strategic success but of "strategic failure". Religion emerged in those societies located in the borderlands of the superpowers of the ancient world. In the process, the vast numbers of strategic gods were displaced by a sole, universal God. This was the case with the exasperated Judahites in the sixth century BC, the frustrated Galileans in the early first century AD, and the marginalised Red Sea Arabs in the early seventh century AD. It was the Christian form of this One God that was, ironically, adopted as a strategic ideology by the failing Roman empire and, thereby, transmitted to the European kingdoms that emerged in the West. From the seventh century AD it was the Judeo–Christian–Islamic God that provided the model for the strategic guardians that dominated the societies of Europe, Asia Minor, the Fertile Crescent, and North Africa for the next two millennia. It also provided the basis for the spiritual needs—as compensation for the highly inequitable distribution of material surpluses—of its people.

The technological paradigm shift that has shaped our own strategic *logos* is the Industrial Revolution (Figure 3.5). This modern shift involved the substitution of an industrial for an agricultural technology. And at the core of this technology was the use of fossil fuels and inorganic construction materials, which replaced the old technology centred on organic fuels and materials. Science played a central role in this more complex process of substitution, particularly as the industrial paradigm unfolded—as the Industrial Revolution passed from its initial pioneering mechanical phase (in Britain, 1780 to 1830) into its more sophisticated chemical and electrical phases (in Germany and the USA during the later nineteenth century).

With the rise of science, some of the mystery of the strategic *logos* seemed to dissipate. Governments and the educated public believed that science was the solution to the age-old problem of how to sustain a vital life-system and, thereby, how to maximise the probability of survival and prosperity. As belief in science rose, faith in the old strategic God fell. Accordingly, governments, businesses, and individual consumers shifted their expenditure on "strategic insurance" from the infrastructure of religion to the infrastructure of science. Since the nineteenth century, the most strategically advanced societies have invested a substantial proportion of their GDPs—in the vicinity of 7–8 percent (OECD 2003)—in the fields of science, technology, and education, in the belief that this will guarantee their strategic success. Success in sustaining their strategic *logos* and, thereby, maximising the probability of their survival and prosperity.

At the same time, investment by advanced societies in the infrastructure of religion has declined dramatically. Can anyone imagine a modern strategic society building the contemporary equivalent of the Great Pyramid (which absorbed 10 percent of Egypt's GDP at the height of its building program[10]), Notre Dame Cathedral, or St Paul's Cathedral? Instead we construct great universities, scientific institutions, and research establishments. This shift in the relative importance of religion and science is also reflected in the numbers of trained professionals entering both fields; in the relative status, prestige, and remuneration of these professionals; and the relative importance of science and theology in the halls of higher learning. But, of course, neither field is as prestigious or as well remunerated as strategic activities. This has always been the core of our strategic *logos* throughout the course of human history. It is a reflection of the dynamic-strategy maxim that "desires drive, ideas facilitate".

What of the future? In *The Dynamic Society* (1996) I argue that owing to the exponential pace of technological paradigm transformation—identified and measured by the Snooks-Panov algorithm[11]—the next great shift will occur from the middle decades of the twenty-first century.[12] I have called this the "solar shift" or "Solar Revolution".[13] It will completely transform the strategic *logos* of humanity and, therefore, will generate a very different strategic demand for cultural institutions and strategic ideology. However, at this distance we are unable to predict what form the new strategic guardian might take. Certainly our ideas about the universal life-system and the natural and social sciences that will attempt to explain, model, and predict it, will change dramatically. Perhaps that revolution in thinking will be influenced by the radical ideas about the strategic *logos* presented in this book.

THE RISE OF MODERN SCIENCE: A NEW EXPLANATION

Just as the dynamic strategy theory can explain the emergence of the gods and their transformation over time, so it can account for the rise of modern science. It can even explain the precocious emergence but ultimate stagnation of ancient science. Essentially, science is a strategic instrument and, like other strategic instruments, it is a response to the changing strategic demand generated by an unfolding dynamic strategy. Where there is a strategic demand, there will always be a supply response. But when that strategic demand levels off or even disappears, the supply response will eventually wither. In other words, science does not possess an internal driving mechanism — it does not have a momentum of its own. At least, not in the long run. Ancient Greek and Chinese (Song era) science illustrates this argument.

While all four dynamic strategies generate a dynamic demand for new techniques, only in the commerce and technological strategies is this demand sufficient to give rise to an integrated body of knowledge that could be called "science"—from the Latin *scientia*, meaning knowledge. For example, the paleolithic family-multiplication strategy generated a dynamic demand for (stone) tools for hunting, and simple devices for transport (rafts and canoes); while the conquest strategy generated an unfolding demand for military equipment, siege machines, engineered infrastructure (roads, aqueducts, ports, docks and buildings), naval equipment, transport and communications. Owing to the lack of writing in paleolithic societies, simple technological ideas were passed from parent to child, with the result that no independent body of knowledge was built up. In conquest societies—particularly before the time of the Greeks (1000–150 BC)—manuals containing military technology were written, but the knowledge they contained remained practical rather than abstract or theoretical. Changing techniques were a direct response to strategic demand and existed as a working collection of inventions. Conquest societies had little need for abstract ideas about the natural world.[14]

The world of commerce was an entirely different matter. The unfolding commerce strategy generated a dynamic demand not only for new strategic techniques—such as larger and faster ships, better naval protection, efficient wharfs and docks, lighthouses, better handling and storage techniques, more effective forms of communication—but also for abstract ideas about the natural world. As merchants needed to travel large distances over dangerous seas and deserts, they required effective navigation techniques, accurate maps, sextants, chronometers, and mathematical systems. Their businesses also generated a demand for effective accounting techniques, business forecasting, together with systems of balances, weights, and measures.

To meet these demands for specific strategic instruments, commerce societies—from the Egyptians, Greeks and Phoenicians in the ancient world to the Arabs, Italians, Portuguese, Dutch and British in the pre-modern world—found it necessary to develop abstract bodies of knowledge about the natural and human spheres. These scientific fields included observational and theoretical astronomy; mathematics; accounting; cartography; the accurate measurement of time, dimension, and mass; the theory and craft of precise instruments; and the chemistry of metals, clays, glazes and dyes. Commerce societies, in contrast to conquest societies, regarded intellectual activities as an acceptable male pastime alongside the more familiar war games of gladiatorial combat, jousting, wrestling, archery, and hunting. The reason, of course, was that the outcomes of new intellectual activities fed into the viability of the commerce strategy, which in turn generated material prosperity. And, finally, the growing surpluses of commerce societies created middle classes with the leisure and private resources to engage in these intellectual activities.

In the ancient world, the normal strategic sequence for societies inhabiting an internationally competitive environment was conquest▶commerce▶conquest. Each of the Greek strategies in this sequence was exploited for about 300 years before they were exhausted. When the initial conquest strategy had been exhausted, it was replaced with the commerce strategy, and when the commerce strategy had been exhausted it was replaced with conquest.[15] Hence, while the Greeks developed science during the commerce phase (800–500 BC), once this strategy had been exhausted, the development of classical science was brought to an end. Science was not a requirement of their conquest strategy.[16] As the role of science declined, that of religion and the dark arts rose.[17] Only societies that were effectively shielded from intense and aggressive international competition for millennia—the chief example being Egypt—were able to focus largely on commerce and the development of their sciences in a more sustained fashion.[18]

Greek experience in the field of science can be contrasted with that of Western Europe. Take the case of Britain, which was the pioneering society in the industrial technological paradigm shift that began in the late eighteenth century. It embarked on the classical strategic sequence, for a society exposed to intense international competition, of conquest (1000–1300) followed by commerce (1480–1750). And Britain would have reverted to conquest—there are signs that in the mid-eighteenth century it was preparing to do so—except that its commerce strategy fortuitously exhausted itself at the very time that the neolithic technological paradigm was also exhausted. For the first time in history, the strategic sequence became, in the case of Britain: conquest▶commerce▶technological change (1780 to date). This, with individual variations, became the general experience of Western Europe. So the rise of pre-modern science in Western Europe, which was a response to their commerce strategy, continued to rise in the modern era owing to the adoption of the technological strategy. Had the industrial technological paradigm shift not occurred after 1780, the so-called "science revolution" that began in Western European commerce societies, would have been aborted. Just as it had in the ancient world when conquest replaced commerce. Science has no long-term internal dynamic; rather it is a response to changes in strategic demand.

Another mystery for scholars without a realist general dynamic theory, is why China failed to forge an industrial revolution on the basis of its technological advantage over the West in the Song period (960–1279). As I made clear as early as the mid 1990s in *The Dynamic Society* (1996: 322–24) and particularly *The Ephemeral Civilization* (1997: 466–71), China, because of its relative isolation from global competition, adopted a family-multiplication strategy, which was unable to provide the necessary strategic demand for sustained technological change. By achieving a form of dynamic equilibrium, China did not exhaust its neolithic technological paradigm before the West did. China's strategic experience contrasted with the highly competitive environment of Western Europe that provided the driving force for the adoption, exploitation, and exhaustion of a sequence of the more combative dynamic strategies of conquest and commerce. In this way, by the mid-eighteenth century, the West had exhausted the underlying neolithic technological paradigm, thereby opening the way for the emergence of the new industrial paradigm. Hence, the so-called "Needham puzzle" (Needham 1958; Hartwell 1996; 1997) is only a puzzle for historians unfamiliar with my general dynamic theory developed during the early 1990s. New ideas travel slowly in communities of conservative scholars.

The unfolding technological strategy of the West generated a dynamic demand for a new and more sophisticated range of technological and scientific ideas. It is interesting that the pioneering British Industrial Revolution did not at first make great demands on the scientific community, precisely because the scientific developments of the nineteenth century were a response to, rather than the cause of, this technological paradigm shift. The British Industrial Revolution was the result of practical and resourceful men attempting to find new ways to maintain their profits in the face of an exhausting commerce strategy.[19] Innovations in the textile, iron and steel, coal-mining, and transport industries were generated by men familiar with the practical aspects of their industries. One of the few partial exceptions to this generalisation is the work that James Watt (1736–1819)—whose employment as a scientific-instrument maker led to an interest in improving Thomas Newcomen's (1663–1729) atmospheric steam engine—undertook in developing the modern steam engine. Even in this case, the invention of the steam engine gave more to science, in the form of the theory of thermodynamics, than science gave to steam technology. It was not until the pioneering phase of the Industrial Revolution was over (by 1830) that the transformed science profession made a significant contribution to the further unfolding of the technological strategy, particularly in the fields of alloy steels, chemistry (artificial dyes), electricity, and magnetism (the electric dynamo and motor).

From the mid-nineteenth century there was a growing interaction—a symbiosis—between science and the unfolding technological strategy. It was at this point in history that God died. It must be understood that the driving force in this relationship was the motivation underlying the strategic pursuit. If, at any time in the future, the industrial technological paradigm exhausts itself *without* being replaced by a new paradigm—a possibility if a global climate-mitigation command society emerges—the rise of science will cease, stagnate, and then fall, because there will be no further demand, and no further funds, for scientists or their ideas. As in the rest of life: desires drive and ideas merely facilitate. That is the central maxim of the strategic *logos*.

SCIENTISM — A NEW STRATEGIC IDEOLOGY

While science is a strategic instrument employed by the modern strategic *logos*, "scientism" is the strategic ideology of advanced, twenty-first century societies. Scientism, therefore, is the equivalent of state religion in the pre-industrial age.

But what is scientism? In a *Scientific American* article, appropriately called "The shamans of scientism", Michael Shermer defined scientism as follows:

> Scientism is a scientific worldview that encompasses natural explanations for all phenomena, eschews supernatural and paranormal speculations, and embraces empiricism and reason as the twin pillars of *a philosophy of life* appropriate for an Age of Science.

> Scientism's voice can best be heard through a literary genre for both lay readers and professionals that includes the works of such scientists as Carl Sagan, E.O. Wilson, Stephen Jay Gould, Richard Dawkins and Jared Diamond. Scientism is a bridge spanning the abyss between what physicist C.P. Snow famously called the 'two cultures' of science and the arts/humanities (neither encampment being able to communicate with the other). Scientism has generated a new literati and intelligentsia passionately *concerned with the profound philosophical, ideological and theological implications of scientific discoveries.*

> Although the origins of the scientism genre can be traced to the writings of Galileo and Thomas Huxley in centuries past, its modern incarnation began in the early 1970s with mathematician Jacob Brownowski's *The Ascent of Man*, took off in the 1980s with Sagan's *Cosmos* and hit pay dirt in the 1990s with Hawking's *A Brief History of Time*.[20]

Shermer makes the additional points that: "cosmology and evolutionary theory ask the ultimate questions that have traditionally been the province of religion and theology"; "this being the Age of Science, it is scientism's shamans who command our veneration"; and "we are also storytelling, mythmaking primates, with scientism as the foundational stratum of our story and scientists as the premier mythmakers of our time". Shermer sees himself as an exponent of scientism.

This is an interesting starting point for our exploration of scientism as a strategic ideology. We can agree that scientism provides a science-based worldview; that it has spawned a popular literature advancing a scientific philosophy; that it asks ultimate questions about the beginning and end of the Universe, which was once the sole province of religion; and that the public advocates of scientism are the shamans of the modern world. But there are also distinct points of disagreement and differences of focus.

As demonstrated in *Dead God Rising*, the worldview of scientism may be based on science, but that is not enough to make it scientific. Even Shermer makes the point that the advocates of scientism are both the "shamans" and the "premier mythmakers of our time". Mythmaking, however, is not a scientific activity that necessarily "embraces empiricism and reason as the twin pillars of a philosophy of life appropriate for an Age of Science". Secondly, it is hardly correct to assert that scientism is a bridge between science and the arts in any meaningful sense. Science in the hands of advocates like Edward Wilson has failed, as shown in my book *The Collapse of Darwinism*, to embrace the arts, despite its intention to do so, precisely because of its own scientific limitations. Sociobiology has failed to colonise the social sciences because of its own difficulties in coming to an understanding of biological transition.[21] There is just no way that sociobiology (which has its origin in Edward Wilson's study of ant colonies) can identify let alone analyse the nature and role of the strategic *logos*. The same can be said for those who make claims about social physics.[22] Despite the twentieth century's science "revolution", the truth is that scientists are no closer to understanding the universal life-system than are theologians. Advocates of scientism—in contrast to science—are the new priestly philosophers; the new metaphysicians of the modern world.

Third, we must be careful employing a term like the "Age of Science", because this age is not the creation of science. Rather it is the outcome of the industrial technological paradigm shift and the ongoing dynamic strategy of technological change, which are driven by desires not ideas. Fourth, it is not correct to say that the *modern* form of scientism can be traced back only to the 1970s. Its roots go back to the mid nineteenth century when the Industrial Revolution was being pioneered. Its advocates, as discussed in *Dead God Rising*, included Lyell, Darwin, Wallace, Nietzsche, Marx, Buckle and so many more, who attempted to substitute a scientifically based world view for the monotheistic world view at a time when science began to have a systematic influence on the unfolding industrial technological paradigm.

Finally, it will be clear from his view of its origins, that Shermer's definition of scientism is far too narrow. It is not the worldview of just those who write and read the popular works of articulate scientist such as Sagan, Wilson, Gould, Dawkins, Hawking (not that the latter's work could be regarded as readable); rather it is the worldview, however inadequately articulated, of all those who *believe* in the power of science in the struggle to survive and prosper—just as in the pre-modern world ordinary people *believed* in the power of religion to do the same thing. Climate-change science is the prime contemporary example.

The modern article of *faith* is that science will guarantee the survival and prosperity of our life-system. Because of this *belief*, modern society has invested massively in the infrastructure of science, technology, and higher learning. This is not just a simple belief that investment in science will generate an increase in incomes and wealth. It is a belief that science is able not only to detect looming crises—such as climate change—but also to resolve them. A massive leap of faith is involved here, because mankind has demonstrated repeatedly that our intellectual models of society and nature are so simplistic that they are totally incapable of analysing complex dynamic systems in the past and present, let alone predicting how they might work themselves out in the future. Even if we were able to make accurate predictions about the emergence of future crises, our track record of remedial intervention is so abysmally poor, that the outcome of significant interference is likely to be more catastrophic than the crisis itself. To make a life-system operate more sustainably, we need to understand the nature and processes of that system. As I have shown in this book, neither natural nor social scientists have any effective understanding of the strategic *logos* that they are determined to substantially alter. To change one or two parameters in a complex dynamic system is likely to send that system spiralling out of control. These issues are discussed in my recent book *The Coming Eclipse* (2010a).

There are a number of classical examples of instability caused by large-scale interventions. The first of these is the attempt by the USA after September Eleven to secure oil supplies in the Middle East by invading Iraq and deposing Saddam Hussein. The problem seemed simple and tractable. Certainly it was a simple matter to destroy the conventional military forces in Iraq and to eliminate the antistrategic leadership of the Hussein family and the Bathist party, but it proved to be impossible to predict and shape the longer term outcomes of interference in a complex sociopolitical system. All the USA was able to achieve was the destruction of the old Iraqi strategic *logos*, without being able to replace it with a more satisfactory one. The Bush administration had no conception of the complexity of what they were attempting because they, and their "expert" advisors, had no understanding of the workings of the strategic *logos*. Recall what Heraclitus said about "experts":

Although we need the *logos*
to keep things known in common,
people still treat specialists
as if their nonsense
were a form of wisdom.

And they still do!

On a smaller, but still significant, scale is the misconceived policy of inflation targeting in advanced strategic societies. These societies—such as the USA, Britain, other EU countries, and Australia—have charged their reserve (or central) banks with keeping inflation under control. The governors of these reserve banks are usually people trained in orthodox neoclassical economics, with working experience somewhere in the financial sector. The problem is that neither the discipline of neoclassical economics nor financial experts understand how the strategic *logos* operates. Indeed, they have no idea even of its existence. Nor do they understand the dynamics of complex living systems. Their discipline employs a comparative static methodology with a focus on equilibrium solutions. While they have no body of theory to explain the role of inflation in a dynamic society, they have a vague fear that it will lead to instability and away from equilibrium. Like the priestly philosophers of Egypt, modern deductive (metaphysical) economists are concerned to maintain order and stability. Their solution is to eliminate inflation—or at least reduce it to low levels—by increasing interest rates so as to slow the growth process and to deflate the economy. Hence, the economy alternates between phases of growth and inflation and stagnation (even negative growth) and deflation. As I show in *Longrun Dynamics* (1998b), *Global Transition* (1999), and *The Global Crisis Makers* (2000), *strategic* inflation plays a positive role in the dynamic process by orchestrating the strategic demand-response mechanism. While it is possible to eliminate inflation by deflationary policies, to do so successfully in the long run would also eliminate economic growth. My discovery of the growth-inflation curve demonstrates that inflation is a non-accelerating function of economic growth.[23] Hence, owing to their ignorance of the dynamic mechanism of the strategic *logos*, orthodox economists and gullible politicians run the risk of reducing the efficiency of, even derailing, the dynamic process of advanced strategic societies.

What unintended impacts will current attempts to control climate change have on the complex living systems on this planet? The simple truth is that because these systems are so complex and the existing models of natural and social sciences so simplistic, scientists cannot answer this question. But the *belief* in the power of science is so strong that these "experts" believe they can manipulate the dynamic systems of the planet, together with the life-systems of all its species, despite not recognising or understanding the nature of the strategic *logos* and how it interacts with climate change. What man once did in the name of God, he now does in the name of science. Science itself has become our highest deity. To continue in this myopic way is to invite disaster—a disaster that the deity of science will not be able to deflect.

Scientism also invites a belief in the ability of science to deliver an endless stream of new ideas that will continue to drive the increase in wealth and living standards. This view is based on a fundamental misunderstanding of the role of science—and of ideas in general—in modern society. As emphasised throughout this book, desires drive and ideas merely facilitate. The occasional suggestion that a "national ideas summit" (as in Australia in early 2008) will somehow improve our strategic pursuit and/or our sociopolitical system is totally naive. Such an event is merely a forum for egoistic self-promotion by "celebrity" intellectuals. (Needless to say, nothing of a strategic nature emerged from the 2008 Australian talkfest.) Strategic demand creates its own ideas, but ideas never create their own strategic demand. Ideas without a demand for their application will merely wither on the vine. Ideas summits are all about elitist feelings of self-importance. The only way that human society will continue to generate innovations is if the strategic *logos* continues to require them. Human society solves its problems strategically rather than scientifically. This is true of issues like climate change as well as material living standards. Indeed, climate change will only be resolved—to the extent that it can be resolved—if it becomes part of the strategic calculus of mankind. It will be resolved, in other words, through the operation of desires rather than ideas.

Scientism also fulfills the secondary function of strategic ideologies down through the ages—that of a personal religion. Some people have always needed something greater than themselves to believe in. Just as every society needs to believe in a strategic guardian that knows more than its people do about the life-system that sustains it, so individuals need to believe in something greater than themselves to give their lives meaning in an apparently meaningless Universe. In the pre-modern world, strategic guardians were transformed into personal gods; while in the modern world, in the absence of a deity of scientism acceptable to a "sophisticated" modern, many people have looked to a personified nature. This is the outcome of a romantic approach to scientism, which is similar to eighteenth-century Romantism in the West. Today the so-called "green movement" has revived the Romantic attitude to nature, by providing it with a sensible personality. Some, such as James Lovelock, have gone as far as to regard the Earth—rechristened Gaia—as a living organism worthy of veneration.[24] Others have projected the same quality onto the cosmos, thereby generating a sort of cosmotheology.[25] Just like religious fundamentalists, the radical ecologists/environmentalists, and followers of Gaia have unwittingly become "antistrategists" dedicated to undermining the strategic *logos*.

The ancient Egyptians called their antistrategists (such as Akhenaton and his family) "criminals", while the ancient Romans called them "atheists". What will future generations call the destabilising climate mitigationists: heroes or knaves? This is considered further in the final chapter.

Chapter 9
Strategic Awareness of the *Logos* — the Selfcreating Mind

Strategic awareness inhabits both the mind and the metropolis.

To understand how the strategic *logos* shapes human society, it is necessary to explore one of its major instruments—"strategic awareness"—in more detail. As will be shown, strategic awareness inhabits both the mind and the metropolis. It has already been suggested—in chapter 5—that the strategic nature of mankind is dualistic. While driven by "strategic desire", we also possess a highly sophisticated instrument, the "strategic cerebrum", in order to be able to supervise the strategic pursuit. Strategic dualism is examined in detail in the present chapter.

The human brain, composed of 100 billion nerve cells, is the most complex object in the known universe. As such it is a source of endless fascination for the layperson as well as the specialist. Yet despite the rapidly growing attention it has received over the past few generations, the mind remains a great mystery. We still do not fully understand the mind's role in life, how it emerged from inchoate matter, how it has become conscious of itself, or why it continues to malfunction in a significant minority of people. Unravelling these mysteries of the mind was the purpose of my book *The Selfcreating Mind*. An overview of the emergence and role of strategic awareness is provided in this chapter.

UNRAVELLING THE MYSTERIES OF THE MIND
Philosophers ever since the ancient Greeks, Indians, and Chinese have speculated about the role and function of the mind. And the schools from which they came have offered explanations and treatments for mental disorders. It is interesting that while laymen were entrusted with healing the body, only the wisemen and priests were considered capable of treating the mind. Clearly the mysterious mind has always been treated with the awe and respect reserved for the gods. Indeed the mind has often been regarded as that part of the divine that is in man.

The argument underlying this chapter is that the human mind can only be understood at a deeper level by placing it within the dynamics of life; and, conversely, that the dynamics of human society can only be fully understood by exploring the mind. To do this we need to examine the relationship between the mind and those systematic forces driving and shaping life, which can only be achieved by observing the mind in history. Not by philosophising about it or even by carefully recording its physical processes. In other words, we must employ not the deductive logic of philosophy nor the experimental method of the natural sciences[1], but rather the inductive method of the historical sciences if we are to negotiate the current impasse.

In this and the following chapter, the emergence, role, function, and malfunction of the human mind are explored using a general dynamic theory derived from the historical evidence of both life and human society. The meaning of the mind, in other words, has been examined using the historical method. It is a method, as we shall see, that has a very long history, grounded as it is in the type of thinking—"strategic thinking"—that organisms with brains have always used. It is the type of thinking that is central to successful participation in the "strategic pursuit"—the drive for survival and prosperity. But while this method has been adopted by successful strategists, it has been spurned by the "experts"—those, who in the words of Heraclitus, "bark at what they cannot understand".

Strategic thinking involves the recognition of patterns in reality, the development of schematic explanations (or models) to make sense of those patterns and to predict their future, and the adoption of those that appear to provide the greatest success in the strategic pursuit. It was to employ this type of thinking that the human mind emerged through a remarkable "autogenous"—or "selfcreative"—process. In contrast, deductive thinking, which is of more recent origin, was developed by the "strategic brain" to enable more precise calculation of rational outcomes. It is based on mankind's rule-making abilities that first emerged in response to the need—or "strategic demand"—for institutions (customs and laws) to facilitate the unfolding of our early "dynamic strategies". In other words, deductive thinking was a non-biological way of extending the strategic brain. As such it is subordinate to strategic thinking. Indeed, as will be demonstrated, deductive thinking is the thinking process of robots—the rational calculators—rather than the thinking process of "strategists"—the imaginative pattern-interpreters.

We need to think about the mind in an entirely new way. And to do so requires a completely new theory about the way the human mind has emerged and how it functions. We need to consider the "selfcreating mind"—a mind that arises from an autogenous process of "biotransition". The theory of the selfcreating mind is part of a more general dynamic theory—the dynamic-strategy theory—that has been employed in this book to explore the fluctuating fortunes of life and human society. As we have seen, it is a realist theory—based on strategic thinking rather than deductive thinking—in which organisms, driven by "strategic desire", struggle to survive and prosper by selecting the "dynamic strategy" (one of a total of four) that is most likely to maximise the probability of their survival and prosperity. By alternatively exploiting and exhausting these dynamic strategies, organisms generate biological/economic change and institutional transformation.[2]

The focus of this chapter is on "biotransition", which involves the mind as well as the body. While biotransition occurs largely as an outcome of the pursuit by individual organisms of the dynamic strategy of genetic change, it can also occur as a by-product of the pursuit of any of the other three dynamic strategies. Biotransition—my preferred term for "transmutation" or "evolution"[3]—is the outcome of my newly discovered mechanism of "strategic selection", first presented in *The Collapse of Darwinism* (2003) and discussed in chapter 4. This mechanism, which is autogenous in nature, replaces the unworkable concept of natural selection.

Strategic selection operates in response to strategic demand, which changes as the dynamic strategy of their society unfolds. This is the demand—generated by organisms exploiting a dynamic strategy—for a wide range of inputs including natural resources, labour, capital, institutions (rules), organisations, and "ideas" whether genetic, technological, cultural, or strategic. The human mind, like all other strategic instruments, has emerged in response to strategic demand. This is why strategic awareness—examined below—inhabits both the mind and the metropolis.

THE STRATEGIC BRAIN

The brain is a "strategic instrument". It is, in other words, a biological device "employed" by the unconscious organism to supervise its participation in the strategic pursuit, so as to maximise its probability of survival and prosperity. Herein lies the essential characteristic of mankind—"strategic dualism." And it is a relatively recent device, because (as outlined in chapter 3), prior to the emergence of animals with central nervous systems about 500 million years (myrs) ago, its job was undertaken by the "strategic gene". Even today there are many life forms—including bacteria, viruses, and the entire plant kingdom—that still "employ" the strategic gene to ensure their survival and prosperity.

The role played by the brain—which I call the "strategic cerebrum"—as a strategic instrument has had an important impact on its structure and operation. These physiological features are very different from those that would have emerged as an outcome of Darwinian or neo-Darwinian natural selection. While the Darwinian brain—if it ever existed at all—must be thought of as a highly specialised and inflexible modular system, the strategic brain is a general, creative, plastic, flexible, and complex organ. The Darwinian brain is often envisaged by its supporters as akin to a "Swiss-army knife", whereas I see the strategic brain as resembling a teeming metropolis.

What is the Strategic Cerebrum?

Of the brain's 100 billion neurons (or nerve cells), about 30 billion are housed in the cortex alone. The cortex itself comprises a million billion synapses (or neural connections)—which would take 32 myrs to count at the rate of one per second—together with a host of neural circuits that number 10 followed by at least a million zeros, greatly exceeding the number of particles (10 followed by 79 zeros) in the known Universe. As the average human brain cavity is only about 1,350 cubic centimetres, these vast numbers of neurons, together with all their circuits, are packed together at incredibly high levels of density and complexity.

It is essential to realise that the brain, even in the most primitive of organisms that possess one, is *always* the strategic cerebrum. The brain emerged at that stage in life when some organisms "discovered" they could pursue their dynamic strategies more effectively in an increasingly complex social environment by substituting the strategic cerebrum for the strategic gene. Right from the beginning, the brain was a complete and effective strategic instrument, even if it was not very powerful. Subsequent development merely resulted in a more sophisticated and powerful strategic instrument required by an organism to survive and prosper in a more sophisticated world.

At every point in time in the historical development of the brain, all its various parts and functions were (and are) highly integrated and subordinated to the strategic pursuit. In other words, although various parts of the brain might be responsible for movement, sight (colour, shape, movement), hearing, problem-solving, and so on, they are not autonomous modules as Darwinists usually argue. They work not in their own interests—nor were they developed to do so—but rather in the strategic interests of the organism.

Why is this so? Because only those inherited and mutated features of the brain that further the strategic interests of the organism are subject (as shown in chapter 4) to "strategic selection". All other inherited and mutated features are, through the mechanism of "strategic imitation", ignored. Hence, any expansion in cognitive abilities, achieved through an increase in the size and complexity of the brain, merely increases the strategic capability of the organism. Before the expansion in cognitive abilities the brain was a strategic instrument, whereas after this expansion it was a *more effective* strategic instrument. This essential point must be recognised if we are to understand both the structure and functioning of the brain, and the nature and purpose of consciousness.

It is important, therefore, to abandon any temptation to think of earlier versions of the brain in the history of life as incomplete or partial in the strategic sense. Each version—an artificial construct because until the emergence of *homo sapiens sapiens* the brain was changing continuously—was an effective strategic instrument within its social and physical environment. Even the first species that developed rudimentary brains were able to effectively participate in the strategic pursuit. And as the strategic pursuit became more complex with the passage of time, the strategic cerebrum also needed—as was communicated to organisms by strategic demand—to become more complex. The strategic brain continued to do the same job over the 500 myrs following its first emergence, just at an increasingly higher level of sophistication in an increasingly complex social environment.

The strategic perspective has important implications for the way we view the growing complexity of the brain over very long periods of time. Any small generational increase in brain complexity was directed towards the improvement *not of a particular activity per se but of overall strategic effectiveness*. This means that any physical addition to the brain, bringing with it modest improvements in the various physiological activities of the organisms in a species, had to be effectively integrated into the existing strategic cerebrum. If this cerebral integration was not achieved, these mutations and, hence, the individuals carrying them would either be ignored, shunned, or destroyed by other individuals in the same social group who had been more successful in this key respect. This way of viewing the brain contrasts with the prevailing concept in evolutionary psychiatry of the Darwinian modular brain—see *The Selfcreating Mind* (2006: ch. 13).

The implication of this argument is that all those improved inputs—seeing, hearing, speaking, motor and other skills—required by the unfolding dynamic strategy can be thought of as a "strategic package". In hominids, this strategic package included precise control of the digits, improved vocalisation and language formation, better navigational abilities, improved organisational skills, better technical ideas and their application to tool-making, and more sophisticated strategic thinking. All of these developments had to take place at the same time—during periods of tens or hundreds of thousands of years—*in an integrated way*, rather than sequentially as suggested by Darwinian adaptive modules, if their family-multiplication strategy was to continue to unfold.

These changing cognitive and physical abilities had to develop together in a slow but steady manner through small overall modifications to the existing strategic cerebrum. Clearly this process must have required a close dialogue between the improved cerebral features and the existing brain structure. Hence, it is the strategic function of the brain that accounts for both the complex interaction between its various parts, and the fact that individual functions are governed by a large number of centres within this structure.

There was adequate time for hominid "strategists" to select for mutations that improved the *combined* performance of their strategic techniques. As discussed in chapter 3, the size of the human brain increased *each generation* by only 0.005 cc between 3 myrs and 2 myrs BP, 0.007 cc between 2 and 1 myrs BP, and 0.01 cc between 1 myrs and 150,000 years BP. It also increased at a similar rate in complexity, as measured by the increasing surface area of the cortex within a given cranial capacity, through "wrinkling": over the past 4 myrs, total brain size increased at the rate of 35.5 per cent per million years, and complexity increased at the rate of 41.4 per cent per million years.[4] Finally, the density of neuron connections would also have been increasing steadily throughout this period to support the integrated nature of the strategic cerebrum.

What type of information is processed by the strategic cerebrum? As the brain's role is to act as a strategic instrument for the organism, everything else is subordinated to this function. For this reason the brain processes information that improves its ability to participate in the strategic pursuit. Essentially there are two types of information processed by the strategic brain: information required for pattern recognition, and information required for imitation. "Pattern-recognition information", which is supplied by all the senses, is used in two main ways. First, all functional organisms in a society require simple information about their world in order to find their way around, to carry out their necessary daily activities and, hopefully, to survive in the short term. These are the "strategic followers" discussed in chapter 7. Second, a few exceptional individuals will also employ this information to analyse their world and to explore new strategic opportunities. They are the "strategic pioneers" who blaze new trails in the generation and application of new ideas.

"Imitative information" is sought and processed by the strategic cerebrum in order to achieve long-term survival and prosperity. As the brain is a strategic instrument rather than a rational machine, it seeks out imitative information about who is successful and why, rather than benefit–cost information. It does so in order to imitate conspicuous success. This is the process of strategic imitation, discussed in chapter 4, by which the successful dynamic strategies of the few are imitated by the many.[5] The modern human brain employs the same type of information and operates in the same strategic way that animal brains have always operated.

The strategic theory presented in this work contrasts with the various Darwinian theories discussed in greater detail in my book *The Selfcreating Mind* (2006 ch. 10). In view of what we know from neuroscience about the structure and function of the human brain, the Darwinian hypothesis held by the evolutionary psychiatrists—that the brain "evolved" through natural selection by "bolting-on" new sections in the form of "autonomous domain-specific" modules (or "mini-computers")—makes little sense. The alleged "bolting-on" procedure could not possibly generate an effective instrument for the survival and prosperity of the organism. In the absence of a central controlling system in the brain (which is rejected by Darwinists), it is just not possible for autonomous modules responding at different times in history to changes in the *natural* environment to become part of a highly integrated organ. Each module in a Darwinian "brain" is an adaptive unit responsible for a single function. As there is no adaptive module for integration, the Darwinian "brain" could not operate as a unified system. It would always be at odds with itself. And it certainly could not account for the brain's complex systems of reciprocal interaction between neuronal groups. Even pragmatic neuroscientists are unable to explain how natural selection could possibly account for the interactive, unified brain revealed by their empirical studies. They prefer to remain silent on this key issue.

The favourite metaphor of those who subscribe to a Darwinian modular brain structure is the Swiss-army knife.[6] As is well known, this useful instrument includes a large number of single-purpose tools that operate quite independently of each other. It is only possible to employ its autonomous and highly specialised tools one at a time in separate operations. And, of course, these tools can only be operated at all because the knife is employed by an external agent—its human owner. A major problem for the evolutionary psychiatrists who employ this metaphor is that there is no central controlling agent in the brain equivalent to the Swiss-army-knife "owner". Ironically, this metaphor is an excellent reflection of the **limitations** of the Darwinian modular theory of the brain, rather than the reverse as intended by the Darwinists.

In contrast to the Darwinian approach to the mind, the strategic theory views the development of the brain as the outcome of a more general and dynamic process in which new neural circuits are added to the existing structure in order to improve a wide range of existing functions that are required to develop a more sophisticated strategic instrument. As layers of new circuits are laid down they are closely integrated into the existing structure by establishing reciprocal pathways between old and new neuronal groups. Both steps—the creation of new neuronal groups and their integration with older structures—take place at the same time under the shaping influence of strategic demand. This is a response to changes in the *social* rather than natural environment—to the strategic *logos*.

It is because of this dual process that any individual function, say speech, is governed by different parts of the brain through the forging of preferential connections. An existing function, which is an integral part of the strategic cerebrum, will be improved over time by the addition of new circuits in separate but convenient parts of the brain, which are simultaneously connected with existing circuits governing that function. *Because of the historical development of the brain there can be no single location for single, increasingly complex, functions. And because of the strategic purpose of the brain these single functions cannot be autonomous.*

It is true that the human brain structurally reflects is historical development. At the macro level, it consists of the reptilian brain (brain stem and cerebellum), the mammalian brain (limbic system), and the human brain (cortex and neocortex). But the evidence from neuroscience shows that these historical features are highly integrated rather than largely self-sufficient as claimed by some scholars.[7] They remain as distinct regions because each marks a distinct and consolidated stage in the historical development of our brains.

The reptilian brain, for example, began to emerge some 500 myrs ago and then consolidated itself over the next 400 myrs. Then the mammalian brain built upon these well-established foundations by gradually developing the limbic system in a fully integrated way from existing tissue. After its initial emergence about 200 myrs ago, the mammalian brain consolidated itself during the 60 myrs following the collapse of the dinosaurs around 65 million years BP. And, finally, the hominid brain, or cortex, developed from the membrane covering the mammalian brain, eventually laying down six cortical layers. The human brain has been constructed on these foundations over the past 4 myrs. Each of these three main stages, consolidated over vast periods of time, was closely integrated into the existing structure by the simultaneous development of communication pathways under the shaping influence of strategic demand. The objective throughout these 500 myrs has been to fashion an increasingly sophisticated strategic instrument to cope with an increasingly complex social environment. Clearly the natural environment had not become more complex over this period of time. If a metaphor helps us to think about the nature of the brain, I suggest we think in terms of the modern metropolis. This metaphor is developed later in the chapter; and, as we shall see, it is more than a metaphor.

Figure 9.1 Structure of the Humn Brain

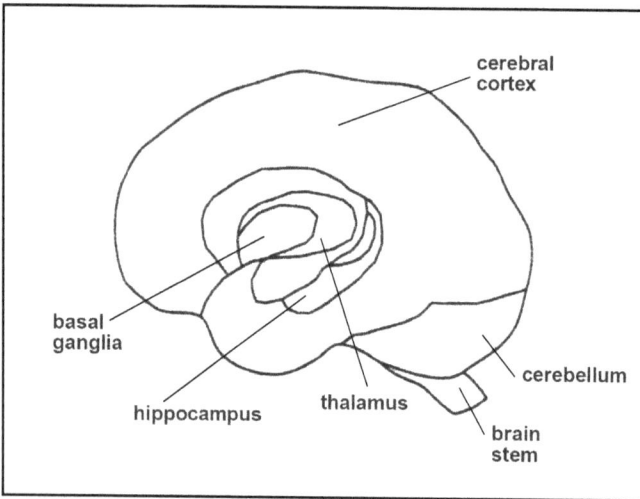

Source:
Snooks 2006: 118

Cerebral Integration

Why does the brain act as an integrated whole? The answer, which has been completely overlooked in the literature, is quite simple. Despite its three distinct historical stages and the variety of regions responsible for the organism's everyday functions, the brain acts as an integrated whole because of the shaping influence of "strategic demand". Strategic demand of the *logos* is responsible for both the historical and the lifetime development and structure of the brain.

As shown in the section below on the historical development of the brain, its various parts have been integrated by a vast number of interconnections to form a strategic instrument. The lifetime development of the brain—the development of a unique set of neuronal circuits in the head of a single person—is also an outcome of the response of the individual, with his genetic inheritance (itself a response to strategic demand through strategic selection), to the society's unfolding dynamic strategy. Each child is trained by its parents, extended family, school, local community, and wider society to play a role within the changing strategic framework. Training for this strategic role helps to create and maintain, within broad genetic parameters, a particular and unique pattern of neural connections in the individual brain. In the young individual, new activities will forge new neural connections, continuing activities will maintain existing neural connections, and abandoned activities will allow earlier connections to wither. Each person, therefore, will create a different neural pattern because they not only play different roles in society, but they also respond differently when fulfilling the same role owing to different outlooks and personalities. Hence, the neural pattern as well as the massive connectivity of the brain is a response to changing strategic demand. This is why even identical twins (who share the same DNA) display different lifetime aptitudes and preferences.

The Darwinists have no convincing explanation for the unique neural pattern displayed in the individual brain. Most merely assume that it is the outcome of the genetic inheritance of the individual that has been shaped by natural selection. And they leave it at that. More sophisticated Darwinists, such as Edelman and Tononi,[8] talk of "experiential selection"—a part of "neural Darwinism"—in which lifetime neural connections are the outcome of "behavioural experience". This is fine as far as it goes, but they have no general dynamic theory to explain the underlying patterns of behavioural experience. Their approach is partial and *ad hoc*. Indeed, if they were able to realistically explain behavioural experience, they would find that these explanations would completely undermine their comforting concept of natural selection. The neuroscience dilemma is that the role and structure of the brain cannot be understood by focusing solely on the physiology of the brain. We need to study the brain as a strategic instrument within the dynamic context of both human society in particular and life in general—as part of the strategic *logos*.

An approach that rises above naive Darwinism is that employed by sociobiology. Edward Wilson claims that the structure of the individual brain is the outcome of "epigenetic rules", which allegedly are the genetically determined constraints that are supposed to operate on the "anatomy, physiology, cognition, and behaviour of organisms".[9] This, of course, is the usual supply-side approach that is resorted to in the absence of an effective dynamic theory of life and human society. While Darwinism cannot provide such a theory, the strategic approach can, and in this book, has.

Another supply-side approach is complexity theory. Complexity theorists claim that cerebral integration is the outcome of "self-organisation" that arises from the interaction of neurons according to the laws of physics. This hypothesis merely begs the question: Why do neurons interact? Essentially, complexity theorists have no persuasive answer to this question. Their usual response is that neurons have an "inherent" tendency to interact, as there is no "self" in self-organisation. This supply-side model of brain organisation is metaphysical rather than realist. In contrast, the dynamic-strategy theory explains the interaction between neurons as a response to changes in strategic demand. Quite clearly, "self-organisation" and "selfcreation" are very different concepts with starkly different explanatory powers.

Perhaps a metaphor will help illustrate my argument. The structure of neural circuits between neurons and groups of neurons is, I suggest, similar to the structure of social, economic, and political connections between individuals and groups of individuals in densely concentrated parts of human society. What I have in mind is the metropolis of any civilisation. In the metropolis, these connections are shaped by the unfolding dynamic strategy operating through strategic demand. As strategic demand changes over time, the connections between individuals and groups in the metropolis also change. An individual's changing strategic role leads him to sever some old societal connections, to maintain and even strengthen others, and to forge new connections with other individuals and groups of a social, economic, and political nature. The same is true of the brain. As the individual's strategic role in society changes over time so do the neural connections.

Quite clearly, what I am arguing is that strategic demand—which is an active force generated within the social environment rather than a passive Darwinian filter responding to the natural environment, or a metaphysical force underlying the interaction between agents—is the shaping force that determines the changing nature of individuals, groups, and "societies", and of the connections between them, no matter what the level of organisation of life. It is, in other words, strategic demand that explains the nature not only of global relationships, nations, regions, cities, towns, and villages, but also the nature of the bodies and brains of the individuals inhabiting them. This suggests that the metropolis concept transcends metaphor—a subject taken up later in this chapter.

Characteristics of the Strategic Brain

The strategic role played by the brain has led to the development of a number of characteristic features. These include its general and creative nature, its plasticity, and its flexibility. None of these qualities could have arisen in the modular brain generated by the adaptive process of natural selection.

First and foremost, the strategic brain is a **general** instrument. As its role is to facilitate and supervise the organism's participation in the strategic pursuit, the brain must be able to respond to any future circumstance, even if it is unable to predict what that circumstance might be. Herein lies a critical difference between the strategic cerebrum and the Darwinian brain. As the Darwinian brain merely "bolts-on" modules in order to adapt competitively to new environmental circumstances as they arise, it would be unable to adjust to sudden and lethal changes in nature. The highly specific Darwinian brain with its finite number of purpose-built "tools", would not survive *sudden and unexpected* changes in climate, sea levels, massive volcanic eruptions, or asteroid attacks. Indeed, if "biotransition" had to depend on natural selection it would never have got under way in the first place.

Of course, the strategic cerebrum is also unable to anticipate future changes in the natural, or more importantly, the social environment. This is why the *general* nature of the strategic brain is so important. Rather than developing in order to adapt to specific problems in the natural environment, the strategic brain emerged to enable the organism's successful participation in the strategic pursuit, *no matter where that pursuit might lead*. From the very beginning of life on Earth, the strategic pursuit has called for a *general* approach by successful organisms. What organisms had to be good at was detecting the most fruitful strategic opportunities and adopting the most appropriate dynamic strategy. It was because the "strategic gene" experienced problems coping with the growing complexity of the *social* environment that the more general strategic instrument, the strategic cerebrum, was developed.

No Darwinist squarely facing this issue is able to explain why humans, who are supposed to have "evolved" through natural selection, were able to adjust to the outbreak of civilisation, which was without precedent in the history of life on Earth. Edward Wilson, for example, has puzzled over how natural selection, which he admits cannot anticipate future needs, prepared humans for civilisation before it suddenly burst onto the world. Our species took to civilisation like ducks to water, despite the fact that we had no previous experience of this way of life and could not, in the time available, have developed an adaptive cerebral module to enable us to do so. Reflecting on this amazing feat, Wilson writes: "This is the great mystery of human evolution: how to account for calculus and Mozart".

It is a mystery easily penetrated by the dynamic-strategy theory. The strategic cerebrum had long been accustomed to responding to major changes in strategic demand. Just consider the way our early ancestors adopted a meat-and-marrow version (substrategy) of the older hominid family-multiplication strategy, and how, as a result, they massively increased the size and complexity of the human brain, substituted technological for genetic change, migrated to all the natural environments in the known world, and became the dominant predator on Earth. This was a revolutionary change of no lesser significance than the emergence of civilisation some 11,000 years ago. The point is that both revolutions were effected by the strategic cerebrum, but only because it was a *general* strategic instrument able to respond to any change of circumstance. Neither revolution would have been possible with the highly *specific* modular brain of Darwinian fantasy. As for "calculus and Mozart", they were the fortuitous outcome of the "tool-and-rule" approach (to be discussed in the next section of this chapter) that man had developed to generate the technology and social organisation required by early man as he adopted the meat-and-marrow substrategy.

Because natural selection cannot explain the emergence of civilisation, most Darwinists regard it as "artificial". Somehow this ploy is supposed to justify the Darwinian failure to explain the most complex species in life. Of course, there is nothing artificial about civilisation—as shown in chapter 2 it emerged quite naturally out of life—but this cannot be said about the concept of natural selection. *The bottom line is that any general dynamic theory that cannot explain **both** nature and human society cannot explain either.*

The strategic brain is also a **creative** instrument. It has to be in order to respond effectively to unpredictable changes in strategic demand. In early human society, greater creativity was required than formerly in the pursuit of an increasingly sophisticated dynamic strategy. Those groups of hominids that were unable to respond in a creative way were quickly swept away in rapidly changing times. This creativity involved being able not only to recognise patterns in reality—something that all animals are able to do—but also to manipulate these patterns in the mind so as to create new configurations and arrive at new resolutions. The strategic brain, in other words, is able to detect connections between variables that are not immediately obvious (and to make predictions about likely outcomes), in order to develop new ways of achieving its strategic objectives.

New ways of this type, involve different combinations of natural resources to enable the generation of even greater surpluses. And they are based on new ideas that are generated by this inductive, or strategic thinking. These new ideas can be of a strategic, technological, or institutional kind. "Strategic ideas" embody new ways of combining *all* the instruments of capital, labour, land, institutions (rules), and organisations in order to develop more effective dynamic strategies and substrategies. Clearly these types of ideas were essential to the revolutionary changes in lifestyle that took place as our ancestors began their global diaspora, and again when they began building civilisation. "Technological ideas" are new ways of employing the more narrow group of resources of land, labour, and capital in the productive process to increase efficiency—to get a greater surplus from the same amount of resources. And "institutional ideas" involve new rules and organisations to better facilitate the strategic pursuit.

The dynamic-strategy argument, therefore, is that human creativity at any point in time is a response to changes in strategic demand both at that time and in the more distant past. At any point in time the generation of new ideas is the outcome of a creative response by individuals to contemporary changes in strategic demand as the dominant dynamic strategy unfolds. But the *ability* to respond in this creative way to contemporary changes in strategic demand is the outcome of alterations to the strategic cerebrum that have occurred over very long periods of time—hundreds (even thousands) of thousands of years in duration—owing to the response of organisms to changes in historical strategic demand through the medium of strategic selection.

In other words, both the demand for, and supply of, creative ideas at any point in time are shaped by strategic demand in time present and time past. Hence, human creativity can be explained endogenously by using the dynamic-strategy theory. The outcome is not deterministic, because strategic demand is the outcome of human individuals systematically but *freely* exploring strategic opportunities under the influence of strategic desire and brought together socially through "strategic imitation".

The Darwinist, on the other hand, has great difficulty in explaining cultural creativity. As the Darwinian brain consists of adaptive modules, it is difficult to see how it could develop the capacity for creativity. It is not sufficient to say that a module for cultural creativity "must have evolved". It is essential to show *how* cultural creativity improves one's "fitness" in the Darwinian struggle for survival, when it is not intuitively obvious that it does. As we have seen, the great self-confessed mystery of life for the Darwinist is to account for "calculus and Mozart". This, however, is not a problem for the "stratologist": once the creative faculty of the strategic cerebrum has emerged fully developed in response to historical strategic demand, it can be employed not only for strictly strategic purposes, but also in the pursuit of intellectual and artistic ends, to render joyful the austerity of our fundamentally materialistic life.

The strategic brain possesses a remarkable degree of **plasticity**. There are three main manifestations of this important quality. First, the human brain retains its unity even after suffering damage through strokes and accidents. Functions normally undertaken by one hemisphere of the brain will, after damage to that hemisphere, be taken over, in part at least, by the undamaged hemisphere. Experiments on animals, involving the systematic removal of parts of the brain, show that it continues to operate as before, only less powerfully.[10] Hence, it is the plastic nature of the brain that enables it always to act as a strategic instrument even when damaged. Minor damage may diminish the overall effectiveness of the brain, but it remains a strategic instrument until finally incapacitated. Partial damage to a Darwinian modular brain would completely eliminate specific functions, thereby terminating the individual's involvement in the strategic pursuit (even assuming that such involvement was possible).

The second manifestation of the brain's plasticity is reflected in its ability to accommodate new layers of neural circuits as the social environment becomes more sophisticated. This accommodation takes the form of connections— reciprocal neural pathways—between the existing cerebral structure and the new groups of neural circuits that have been recently laid down. These new circuits, which add to the strategic capabilities of the organism, are able to link up with existing groups of neural circuits that control similar functions. Once again this plasticity exists to serve the strategic purpose of the brain. Indeed it is necessary to ensure that the changing brain is always a strategic instrument rather than an *ad hoc* collection of Darwinian, domain-specific modules.

Finally, the plasticity of the brain can be seen reflected in the lifetime changes made in the individual brain's neural connections. As we have seen, the changing strategic role played by an individual during the course of its lifetime leads to a change in older circuits and to the forging of new ones. Only a plastic brain can respond to changing strategic demand. There is no way that these forms of plasticity could exist in the Darwinian brain—yet we know they do exist in real brains—because there is no proven module for plasticity.

The strategic cerebrum is also highly **flexible**. It is able to adapt quickly to any of the quartet of dynamic strategies and to the much larger number of substrategies. The outcome, in the case of modern man, is a host of very diverse cultures, which are responses to different substrategies pursued in widely varying social and physical environments. Yet despite this sociopolitical variability they all have at their core the universal principles of dynamic strategy. Sociopolitical institutions are required, as shown in chapter 7, to facilitate the strategic pursuit, and are a response to a changing strategic demand, which is capable of reversing back on itself whenever a society's "strategic sequence" is reversed—such as the conquest▶commerce▶conquest sequence that occurred in most ancient societies. Only a flexible strategic brain could enable this cultural response.

For the Darwinian brain to generate the cultural diversity we see in history it would be necessary to construct a large number of brain types—one for each type of culture—consisting of different combinations of domain-specific modules. There are no universal principles underlying the Darwinian brain, because each module is an adaptive response to a specific change in the natural environment. Hence, it would be impossible to successfully transplant an individual with a particular brain type from its original environment (say tribal Africa) to an entirely new social environment (say colonial America). Of course, we know that this is not so. An infant transferred between cultures is just as capable as locals, *ceteris paribus*, of responding effectively to the new culture, provided it is given the same social support. It is the flexibility of the strategic cerebrum as a general instrument that makes this possible. And it is this flexibility of the human brain, as is shown in *The Selfcreating Mind*, that makes nonsense of the Darwinian explanation of psychic problems by evolutionary psychiatrists.

The Historical Development of the Human Brain

The selfcreating brain is the outcome of individual organisms exploring their strategic opportunities in a competitive environment. While this is true of non-human as well as human organisms, our attention here focuses on the latter. To participate fully in the unfolding dynamic strategy of family multiplication, early hominids needed to become highly mobile. This required, as discussed in chapter 2, a shift from the highly localised nut-and-tuber substrategy to the universal meat-and-marrow substrategy. Only by developing non-biological weapons and tools—as hominids lacked biological ones as well as the time needed to acquire them through strategic selection—together with new means of communications and social organisation, could such a shift of substrategy be achieved. Thus began the reliance of hominids on technological change—a concept that includes all types of innovative ideas—which heralded an unprecedented era in the history of life on Earth. An era that could only be negotiated by the strategic cerebrum.

The "technology option", however, could only be introduced fully if hominid brain power increased sufficiently to enable the *simultaneous* development of precision-made tools and weapons, together with improved skills in navigation, social organisation, and communication. This was achieved, as with all directional genetic change in the past, through strategic selection in response to strategic demand—the facilitator of the selfcreating mind. What I am arguing is that the autogenous development of the strategic cerebrum needed to be able to cope with the emergence of a whole host of physical and intellectual changes in response to strategic demand. These changes can be thought of as the inputs required to exploit the increasingly sophisticated strategic opportunities. Hence, as we have seen, the brain had to be a general rather than a specific strategic instrument.

How, then, did the strategic mechanism work? The attempt by one line of hominids to pursue a universal form of their family-multiplication strategy generated strategic demand for the following group of *combined* inputs:

- improved hunting weapons and tools;
- improved biological systems of navigation;
- more effective economic and social organisation;
- better means of communication for both hunting/gathering and social organisation;
- strategic thinking;
- tactical thinking.

It is essential to realise that these inputs required by the strategic pursuit were not separate and autonomous adaptations; rather they were simultaneous and integrated changes in response to a general strategic demand. This was an autogenous process because strategic demand was an outcome of individuals actively exploring strategic opportunities, and the response to it was mediated through strategic selection based on individual choice. Owing to limitations of space, I will focus on the last three: communication, strategic thinking, and tactical thinking. They are the most complex and controversial strategic inputs; the others, which involve more straight-forward responses to strategic demand, are discussed in detail in *The Selfcreating Mind* (2006: ch. 8).

Communication skills

Some observers suggest that "the reason for the emergence of language is mysterious", and they look for clues in the structure of the brain itself.[11] This is a myopic approach. Although we must discover as much as we can about the physiology of the brain, the only way to explain its emergence is within the context of the history of mankind.

The unfolding family-multiplication strategy for hominids required improvements in communication in order to coordinate scavenging and, particularly, hunting teams; to prepare group plans; to issue instructions and suggestions; to train the young in scavenging and hunting techniques; to organise family and clan groups; to draw lessons for the group from past experience; and to arrange future undertakings and meetings. To avoid ambiguity, even primitive forms of communication had to employ grammatical rules, just as rules (institutions) were required in even primitive society to facilitate the strategic pursuit. Once again there is a gender dimension here: as gathering was a more social activity than hunting, females developed greater language skills than males. It is thought that early systems of gestures and grunts were replaced about 1.5 myrs ago with more formal sign language and, about 100,000 years ago, with spoken language.[12] Language, therefore, emerged in response to strategic demand, just as did a number of other skills required by the strategic pursuit. Hence, it is not correct to argue, as many have been tempted to do, that language played an independent role in the development of mankind's large brain. Nor is it correct to claim, as the postmodernists have done, that language plays an independent role in human culture—that "everything is literature and literature is everything". This is the usual supply-side theory advanced by those with no understanding of the dynamics of life.

It will be clear to readers interested in linguistics that the dynamic-strategy theory of language also presents a powerful challenge to Noam Chomsky's supply-side theory—a fashionable theory that has taken the discipline of linguistics by storm. Chomsky claims that language is generated by "a dedicated language module" in the human brain, which is acquired at birth as "a common human possession".[13] It is, in essence, a system of universal principles, which is characterised by "parameters" or "choice points" that can be set (or "fixed") by reference to "incoming linguistic data" to produce specific language, such as Chinese, Italian, French, or English. Chomsky even claims that this language module is an "optimally designed system", at least in its interaction with other brain modules. Obviously, this modular theory of language is similar to the Darwinian modular theory developed by evolutionary psychiatrists.[14] All supply-side theories, particularly of the modular kind, fly in the face of historical evidence. Language is not the "holy grail" that many linguists believe it to be—it is not the objective of life—but rather is merely one of the many "institutions", or societal rule systems, that have developed in response to strategic demand. The brain is a general pattern-recognising, rule-creating system, not a "domain-specific" system of adaptive modules.

The area of the brain that accommodated these changes was the left hemisphere, particularly Wernicke's area (which renders spoken language comprehensible), Broca's area (which generates speech), and the angular gyrus (which is concerned with meaning). It is thought that once primitive language had taken hold in the brain of *Homo habilis*, it developed rapidly, pushing the visual functions to the back of the cortex and appropriating much of the left hemisphere previously devoted to spatial skills. As a result, the visual-spatial skills were focused in the right hemisphere. This may have been the beginning of hemisphere specialisation that characterises the modern human brain.[15] But, as we have come to realise, this occurred in a totally integrated way, as all these language, visual, and spatial skills were performed together in the increasingly sophisticated strategic pursuit. Neanderthals also clearly had the power of language, despite the claims of those anthropologists (such as Steven Mithen) seduced by evolutionary psychiatry.[16]

Strategic thinking

As the human brain is a strategic instrument, its main function is to recognise patterns in reality through observation and experience, and to draw generalisations from these observations in order to survive and prosper. This ability to recognise patterns and to generalise about them—a process that I call "strategic thinking"—focused upon the dynamics of the local natural environment, one's own and competing societies, and the constellations in the night skies.

At the local, or micro, level, pattern recognition involves observing and assessing clues about the presence and passage of animals and other hominid/ humans, which are employed to develop simple *inductive* theories about the activities of their prey and competitors. Strategic thinking, at various levels of sophistication, had to be undertaken by all active members of the society of early man. This involved the exploration of memories of patterns of the recent past, and the projection of those patterns onto the present and the future. It was an intellectual process that assisted with their hunting/gathering and raiding activities.

Some—the wisemen and priests—were interested in bigger, or macro, issues. They searched for longer-term and more complex patterns to be seen in the rise and fall of animal populations as well as the societies of their competitors. They also pondered the changing patterns in the night skies, seasons, and weather, and systematically recorded their observations on pieces of bone (e.g. the Ishango bone, 18,000–20,000 BP). The generalisations that the few drew from these macro patterns were used to tell stories about the origins of their tribe, other life forms, and the heavens and earth; and to tell stories about the future. They were concerned with the bigger issues of life and death that were overlooked by the many; they were concerned to avert impending disasters and to seek new strategic opportunities.

Strategic thinking, therefore, involves an imaginative response to the changing natural and social environments, in order to develop new and better ways to survive and prosper. This is achieved, as we have seen, by developing entirely new dynamic strategies and substrategies when the old ones have been exhausted. It involves both individual and group responses. The successful strategic pioneers—the few—are followed by the many through the process of strategic imitation that was explained earlier. This is the process by which individual decision-making is transformed into the dynamic strategy of the entire society.

Both micro- and macro-strategic thinking is, as we have seen, based largely on induction—generalising from patterns recognised in reality. By this I mean that induction is the main source of information employed by the strategic cerebrum. This is not to say that it is the only source, because deduction, which is based on a set of logical rules, is also employed. But deducting thinking suffers from what I call the "problem of deduction": the information embodied in its conclusions is only as good as the information contained in its initial assumptions—rubbish in, rubbish out. Deduction is notorious for what it leaves out, rather than famous for which it includes. There is just no substitute for effective pattern recognition and inductive generalisation for understanding what is happening in reality, particularly if one's life depends on it.[17] This is discussed further in chapter 6.

The strategic cerebrum is a master of pattern recognition and inductive generalisation—of strategic thinking. It was developed by the unconscious organism through the autogenous process of strategic selection precisely for that purpose. Sustained deductive thought, on the other hand, was not natural to early man and is a specialised activity even today. Deductive thought requires a level of sophistication that only emerged in civilisations over the past 6,000 years. Indeed, it was strategic thinking that gave rise to human civilisation, which in turn enabled the development of systematic deductive thought. The rule-based nature of deductive or logical thinking arose from the institutional response— the development of social rules—to changes in strategic demand. This rule-making ability was employed much later to develop logical systems of thought, eventually expressed in mathematical form. Why? Because rule-based thinking made possible the more precise calculations—as opposed to "rules of thumb" based on practical experience—required in the more exacting task of building cities rather than nomadic shelters.

The reality is that even modern humans are not good at logical thought. Intelligent people who are not rigorously trained in the rules and procedures of deductive thought, consistently fail tests of "rational" ability.[18] It is for this reason that for thousands of years, human society has trained experts— analytical philosophers and mathematicians—in logical thought, and why more recently we have invented rational machines, or computers, to do the hard work of logical thinking for us.

We continue to do what we are good at—strategic thinking based on pattern recognition and inductive generalisation. This is a highly subtle and imaginative art form. An interesting possibility is that as rational machines become more sophisticated they will displace the deductive experts. But what machines will never do is to displace the inductive thinking of the strategic cerebrum. To do so it would be necessary to build machines that are independently capable of surviving, prospering, and reproducing in the course of the strategic pursuit. This will never happen because machines are not driven by strategic desire. We will never have to compete strategically with machines. The essence of humanness, therefore, is our integrated embodiment of strategic desire and the strategic cerebrum.

The need to think strategically in the increasingly complex social environment of hominids and, in particular, early man, stimulated the expansion in size and complexity of the prefrontal cortex. In humans the prefrontal cortex is much enlarged in comparison with that of surviving primates. This part of the human brain is thought to be associated with proactive abilities and the development of novel plans or strategies using information from the general environment. Susan Greenfield, in discussing the behaviour of people who have undergone a leucotomy, in which the fibres that connect the frontal lobes to the rest of the brain are severed, tells us that

> these patients became changed characters, lacking in foresight and emotionally unresponsive. In line with this apparent inability to be proactive, patients with damaged frontal lobes are less able to develop novel strategies or plans to tackle a particular problem. They cannot use information from their environment to regulate or change behaviour; instead they perseverate [endlessly repeat old responses].[19]

There can be little doubt, therefore, that the development of the prefrontal cortex was a response to the need for pattern recognition and strategic thinking in order to engage more effectively in the strategic pursuit.

Tactical thinking

Success in life requires tactical as well as strategic thinking. With the emergence of a formal social structure required to pursue a dynamic strategy, comes the need for tactical thinking by those wishing to gain political power. Through political power an individual, or alliance of individuals, is able to control their society's dynamic strategy and, hence, its material resources and wealth. In this way they hope not only to survive and prosper but to do so indulgently. While this is clearly in the interest of the successful individual, or group of individuals, it is also in the interest of society as a whole. The reason—as shown in chapters 4, 7, and 11—is that those who succeed in the tactical power struggle must provide appropriate "strategic leadership", which is essential for a healthy society.[20]

I have called the fierce competition between individuals striving for control of their society the "strategic struggle".[21] It is the strategic struggle that generates a derived demand for tactical thinking—derived from the unfolding dynamic strategy and, hence, strategic demand. Quite clearly, individuals who can second-guess their rivals will find themselves in a better position to take advantage of the struggle for political control. By second-guessing, or "mind reading", his rivals, an ambitious individual hopes to be able to predict how they might respond to his political initiatives. Tactical thinking, therefore, developed through strategic selection as hominids and early man formed social groups to facilitate their strategic pursuit.

It is this type of cognitive activity that is the focus both of game theory in economics (and, more recently, biology) and of "theory of mind" analysis in psychology. Game theorists are mistaken, however, in calling these tactics and associated tactical thinking, "strategies" and "strategic thinking". They are no more than short-term tactics that arise between competing individuals, groups, or nations. Strategies involve longer-term and broader objectives. And advocates of "theory of mind" are mistaken in believing that tactical thinking is *central* to the development of the prefrontal cortex or that it is a prime mover in the emergence of consciousness.[22] Indeed, as shown in the next section, theory-of-mind abilities—or tactical thinking—can only take place *after* the emergence of both strategic thinking *and* consciousness. Tactical thinking is, as I have explained, a response to a derived demand. Nevertheless, the need for tactical thinking probably contributed *marginally* to the development of the prefrontal cortex, which was already under way owing to the driving force of strategic thinking. In the strategic cerebrum all these matters are highly integrated so as to produce an effective strategic instrument.

CONSCIOUSNESS—THE METROPOLIS OF THE MIND

Consciousness is a curious condition. Although we all experience consciousness directly, there is no consensus about what causes it or how it emerged during the historical development of the brain.[23] Philosophers have long debated the relationship between consciousness and the material brain. This is the essence of body–mind dualism famously highlighted by René Descartes (1596–1650). Yet although most modern thinkers emphasise the material rather than the divine basis of consciousness, there is little agreement about the neuronal processes underlying this state of experience.

While the state of experience we call consciousness might arise from the operation of the physical brain, it has no material or objective existence. It can only be experienced subjectively. How then can consciousness be studied scientifically? My view is that while such study is necessary, it is not sufficient if we wish to fully understand the historical emergence and role of consciousness in life. In this section we will explore the existential state of consciousness within the operational context of complex organisms and their social networks. Consciousness has no meaning when divorced from this wider strategic context.

Cultural Awareness in the Metropolis

As argued in *The Selfcreating Mind*, the best *description* of consciousness is that by Edelman and Tononi. They have shown consciousness to be supported by three characteristics of the brain: first, that there is widespread neural activity in the thalamocortical system; second, that this activity is highly integrated owing to rapid and effective reciprocal (or "reentrant") interactions; and third, that these interactions are highly differentiated and, hence, informative. These characteristics, I suggest, are not unique to the brain and consciousness, but exist in all living dynamic systems. The metropolis is one of these. The metropolis' counterpart of the brain's consciousness is what I call "cultural-awareness". Cultural-awareness is the outcome of widespread strategic activity in the metropolis, which is generated by a high degree of reciprocal interaction between highly specialised strategists and the specialised introspective cultural critics that they support. Clearly the mind is not unique in this respect.

Strategic interaction operates throughout the social, economic, and political spectrum. Individuals come together at various times and various places in different configurations to exchange goods, services, and surpluses of a material and non-material kind. This is made possible by the considerable infrastructure for intra-city transport and communications that was gradually but deliberately developed as the metropolis grew from insignificant origins. Like the brain, the metropolis has operated as an integrated system—a strategic instrument—at all times in its historical development. And like the brain, the metropolis has laid down integrated networks of interaction between strategists. It is also continually strengthening many of their existing connections, dissolving others, and creating entirely new ones.

Individual strategists in a large and sophisticated metropolis are highly specialised. They are, in other words, highly diverse in terms of their temperaments, interests, physical and intellectual skills, training, and experience. While this differentiation is an outcome of the variation of inheritance and environment between individuals (that is, of comparative advantage), it is brought into play by the size of the city. In small villages, individuals tend to employ general skills and experience, but as these social entities grow into towns, cities, and metropolises, it becomes more efficient to increase the degree of specialisation and division of labour according to comparative advantage. Even those gifted individuals who can accomplish all tasks better than the rest, will specialise in what they do best, because they can, thereby, increase their own material well-being. The efficiencies generated by specialisation are known as economies of scale. And with an increase in specialisation—or "differentiation"—the culture of the metropolis becomes more sophisticated and more able to support those who specialise in reflecting upon this achievement. The outcome is "cultural-awareness".

Contact between strategists throughout the metropolis is many-faceted. Individuals come together in groups of many kinds. Economic interactions take place in markets, shopping precincts, business districts, stock exchanges, finance houses, ports, and industrial estates; political activities occur in city halls, parliament houses, and in popular rallies and protests in city plazas and streets; and social intercourse takes place in theatres, concert halls, cinemas, dance halls, churches, restaurants, coffee houses, shopping malls, schools, universities, and homes. These widespread and multi-faceted interactions between strategists have been performed in cities since their beginnings some 8,000 years ago. Once these cities passed a certain threshold size, specialisation began and cultural-awareness emerged.

More recently the need for strategists to meet in groups has been reduced by the development of electronic communications. Landmark innovations include radio, television, VCR, DVD, telephone (and now, mobiles or cell phones), computers, and the Internet. Increasingly, economic, social, and political interactions are being conducted electronically. Instead of moving out of the residential sectors each morning and into the business, social, and political precincts of the metropolis, strategists are increasingly remaining in their homes and interacting electronically. While this trend will never be complete, because people enjoy physical interchange and need it to retain their sanity, it will become highly significant. Interaction in the metropolis of the future will be conducted largely by electronic pulses rather than by the movement of people. In this way the metropolis is becoming even more like the human brain in which neurons are largely fixed, with the interaction between them taking place through a vast network of electrochemical pathways.

Cultural-awareness is generated by a remarkably similar process to that underlying consciousness. It occurs in a widespread manner throughout the metropolis, but it is neither coextensive with the city nor is it confined to one particular district. While most citizens of the modern metropolis are involved in the strategic activity that supports cultural-awareness at some time, they are not involved all the time. Just like neurons in the brain. When actively involved, they are strategists; when not involved, they are nonstrategists; and when actively undermining the metropolis' dynamic strategy (as criminals or terrorists, which are like cancer cells in the brain), they are antistrategists. At any given time, those strategists actively involved in interactions supporting cultural-awareness can be regarded as part of the "strategic core" of the metropolis.

The "Dynamic-Strategy Core" and Consciousness

My "strategic-core concept"—which is discussed at the global level in *Global transition* (1999)—is similar to the dynamic-core concept—which is discussed at the brain level by Edelman and Tononi (2000). Indeed, I could quite easily have called it the dynamic-strategy core, given the nature of my dynamic-strategy theory. There is, however, an essential difference, which is reflected in my use of the word "strategic". This usage reflects the *theoretical* content of my concept in contrast to the *descriptive* content of Edelman and Tononi's concept. I argue that the dynamic-strategy theory can be used to explain not only cultural-awareness at the city, national, and global levels, but also consciousness at the level of the individual brain. I will return to this issue soon.

The "strategic core", which represents a changing cluster of strategists interacting with each other at different times and in different places in the metropolis, supports cultural-awareness. And the vitality of cultural-awareness depends on the extent, pace, and diversity of the interaction of strategists in the strategic core, and on its ability to draw in those existing on the city's "strategic fringe". In turn, the vitality of the strategic core depends on the scale and pace at which the metropolis' dynamic strategy unfolds. The same is true for the brain's dynamic core, which supports consciousness: the vitality of consciousness depends on the interaction of neurons in response, albeit indirectly, to strategic demand for cerebral inputs generated by the unfolding dynamic strategy of the outside world.

Like consciousness, the sustainability of cultural-awareness depends on the continued viability of the strategic core—of the activity of dynamic strategists. Just as individuals can lapse into unconsciousness, or experience dissociative disorders (hysterical blindness, fugue states, multiple personalities, amnesia), a city's cultural-awareness can "slumber" during the early hours of the morning when the diversity of interacting strategists falls below some critical level, and it can be temporarily disordered by the disruption of power supplies and communications (through strikes and civil disputes) and even by damage to the underlying infrastructure (through terrorism, war, and revolutions). And like consciousness, cultural-awareness possesses a unity that even extensive damage to the underlying infrastructure cannot fragment. In the human brain a hole torn in the cerebral infrastructure by strokes or accidents is immediately surrounded by the individual's consciousness; and in the metropolis, a hole blasted in the urban infrastructure is just as quickly engulfed by cultural-awareness. The damage done by the September 11 terrorists to the central business infrastructure of New York was quickly bridged by that city's cultural-awareness.

The metropolis and the mind are similar in another important respect: they are both instruments that serve the larger body, of which they are a part, in relations with the outside world. As we have seen, the human brain is an instrument "employed" by the unconscious organism to enable it to interact successfully with the strategic *logos*. In the same way the metropolis is the instrument "employed" by the wider national society to interact with other national societies through its leading strategic groups in the economic, political, and social spheres. In both cases this relationship is a strategic one. *The metropolis is the "conscious mind" of the nation, and, therefore, of the strategic* logos.

The Decentralised Nature of Consciousness

The metropolis-of-the-mind metaphor is able to shed some light on the way the brain works. Like the free metropolis, the brain has no central processor or controller. Strategic activity, which supports cultural-awareness, is the outcome not of central decree but of individuals participating voluntarily in the strategic pursuit in response to strategic demand. Occasionally, reckless experiments in command systems by totalitarian regimes—in which antistrategists hijack the strategic pursuit in order to oppress the strategists and siphon off their surpluses—have been undertaken, but without exception these have quickly failed. Rome flourished for a thousand years, whereas Stalin's Moscow and Akhenaten's Akhetaten (14th century BC Egypt) lasted less than a lifetime.

The primary reason for the failure of command metropolises is that they do not possess the ability to respond flexibly to changing strategic opportunities. Why? Because they replace innovative profit-seeking strategists with conservative rent-seeking bureaucrats or antistrategists. In effect they displace or cripple the strategic *logos*. Ultimately these antistrategic societies (such as the former USSR) are unable to compete with the more innovative strategic societies (such as Western civilisation), they fail to grow as rapidly as their strategic competitors, and they collapse.[24] The only way a command, or antistrategic, society could compete successfully with a strategic society is if it were possible to anticipate how the existing technological paradigm was going to unfold and how the resulting strategic demand could be responded to optimally. Clearly this is impossible—which is why the brain developed as a general strategic instrument. Only democratic societies, in which strategists are free to constantly and innovatively explore strategic opportunities, can hope to achieve anything approaching optimal long-run growth rates. Only free, strategic societies, therefore, can continue to survive and prosper in the modern world.

It is for the same reason that the human brain does not possess a central processor or controller. In order to respond flexibly to changes in strategic demand for cerebral inputs, it would be essential for any central processor of the brain to accurately anticipate the unfolding of the existing technological paradigm and its associated dynamic strategies. Any central processor would need, in other words, foreknowledge of the way in which the brain had to develop. This is just not possible. The human brain, as even sociobiologists such as E.O. Wilson admit, was unable to anticipate the sudden emergence of civilisation some 6,000 years ago. As there is no way to obtain such foreknowledge, the emerging human brain needed to develop a structure that would maximise its flexibility in responding to changing strategic opportunities.

In a dynamic world—and this is the only world that has ever existed—the most effective societal system is one based on flexible markets in which individuals compete to exploit strategic opportunities. Similarly, in the same dynamic world, the most effective strategic brain is one in which neurons are free to respond to strategic demand in competition *and* in cooperation with each other. A central processor would inevitably make the wrong decisions and preside over an inflexible and ineffective strategic instrument. Such a processor would end up, like the command hierarchy, controlling and oppressing the activity and development of neural groups. Even if central processors had emerged in some brains in the past—as command economies have—these "antistrategic brains" would have been unable to compete effectively with "strategic brains" and would, therefore, have been eliminated. Before its demise, the central processor, like the command hierarchy, would exert a tyranny over its unconscious organism. This, of course, defeats the purpose of a strategic instrument in either human society or the human organism.

But to operate effectively without a command hierarchy, a strategic society must consist of highly specialised individuals who are able to communicate rapidly and effectively with each other. They must have ready access to imitative and pattern-recognition information in order to respond effectively to strategic demand. This is what I have been arguing about human society for the past few decades. The evidence provided by Edelman and Tononi suggests that the human brain operates in a similar way. And, I need to add, it does so for similar reasons.

The human brain, for similar reasons, can only operate effectively in the absence of a central processor if its neurons are highly specialised and interact rapidly and effectively with each other. They too need to communicate imitative information about successful neural interactions that will lead to the strengthening of some existing circuits and the development of new circuits, as well as information about less successful interactions that will cause other circuits to be shut down. This is the process of "cerebral strategic imitation". And through this process, the brain is able to respond effectively to strategic demand.

Consciousness Explained

The metropolis-of-the-mind metaphor can also be employed to cast light on how, in the past, consciousness emerged in mammals and, in particular, hominids. My argument, as will be quite clear by now, is that cultural-awareness is a function of the size and, hence, complexity of the metropolis. As a village grows into a town, a town into a city, and a city into a metropolis, this organisation finally passes some threshold size at which strategic activities are able to support cultural-awareness—a selfconscious and self-sustaining cultural flowering that pulsates throughout the metropolis. This involves a cultural sophistication at the social, economic, and political levels, generated by a high degree of specialisation and division of labour according to comparative advantage. Underpinning this cultural flowering and cultural-awareness is a successful strategic pursuit.

There are strong parallels here with the historical emergence of consciousness in life. The highly differentiated (specialised) neural activities that support primary consciousness only occur in brains that have passed some size/complexity threshold; and the achievement of higher-order (or self-) consciousness requires the passing of an even higher size/complexity threshold. As discussed in chapter 2, the growth in the size/complexity of the hominid/human brain was a response to the unfolding of an increasingly complex family-multiplication strategy. The dynamic core in the thalamocortical system identified by neuroscientists was, therefore, also a response to changes in strategic demand. Hence, the "dynamic core" is a dynamic-strategy core. *This means that consciousness, which is supported by this dynamic-strategy core, is the unintended consequence of strategy-driven brain size/complexity.*

We have seen the metropolis emerge in this chapter as a metaphor for the mind. Yet it is more than metaphor. The reason that this metaphor throws so much light on the function, operation, and emergence of the human brain is that the metropolis and the mind are different dimensions of the same reality. Both are outcomes, at different levels, of the general and universal principles of strategic organisation in living systems. Both contribute to the construction of the strategic *logos*. Neurons in the brain, and individuals in the metropolis organise themselves in remarkably similar ways in response to strategic demand. Hence, the same general theory, which is developed in the next section, can be used to explain both cultural-awareness and consciousness. They are both manifestations of the more general principle that I call the "strategic-awareness" of the *logos*.

A GENERAL THEORY OF STRATEGIC-AWARENESS

It is now possible to construct a general theory of "strategic-awareness" that encompasses both individual consciousness and cultural-awareness at the metropolitan, national, and global levels. Also in this section of the chapter, our general theory is employed to explain the higher function of the generalised strategic instrument, the historical emergence of strategic-awareness, and the mechanism and role of this higher function.

Strategic Instrument of the *Logos*

The "strategic instrument" (whether gene, brain, or metropolis) is employed by the strategist (whether organism or society) in the pursuit of its dynamic strategy. Its purpose is to monitor the changing social environment, to adopt appropriate dynamic strategies in order to exploit that environment, and to initiate an effective response to "strategic demand".

The strategic instrument has been developed over a very long period of time. At the beginning of life on Earth, the "unconscious organism" employed the "strategic gene" for this purpose. This continued until about 500 million years ago when some pioneering species substituted the "strategic cerebrum" for the strategic gene. Some 6,000 years ago, the metropolis joined the strategic cerebrum in the organism's armoury of instruments to facilitate the strategic pursuit, this time at the societal level. In retrospect it can be seen that these developments were steps taken blindly on the way to strategic-awareness at the levels of both the individual and the society. None of this, of course, was inevitable, merely the unforeseen outcome of individual organisms struggling to survive and prosper by exploring their strategic opportunities. The final achievement of strategic-awareness transformed the strategic instrument into a highly flexible and effective tool for survival and prosperity.

Emergence of Strategic-Awareness

Strategic-awareness, therefore, operates at both the individual and societal levels. Individual awareness could occur only once the strategic cerebrum had been substituted for the strategic gene and once it had reached some size/complexity threshold level. Once this had occurred, the organisms concerned were able to "generate a mental scene in which a large amount of diverse information is integrated for the purpose of directing present or immediate behavior".[25] This form of awareness is usually called "primary consciousness" and is found in animals with brain structures similar to our own. "Higher-order consciousness", which requires an even larger and more complex brain, involves a sense of self, together with the ability to imagine and connect past and future, as well as present, scenes. This is strategic-awareness at the highest individual level.

What does strategic-awareness at the societal level mean? Essentially, that a society is conscious of its role in the strategic pursuit at the economic, social, and political levels. Strategic-awareness, in other words, occurs when a society passes a size/complexity threshold level that enables the generation of an ecosociopolitical culture that is self-reflective—that reflects upon and analyses its objectives, activities, and achievements. This self-reflection, which can be seen in the history, philosophy, critical cultural (in the broadest sense) studies, literature, and fine arts of the society, is built on the foundations of a sophisticated strategic pursuit. This strategic awareness also involves a notion of a hidden life-system—a strategic *logos*—that is responsible for sustaining the achievement of survival and prosperity. But this notion—as shown in chapter 8—has always been difficult to develop clearly and precisely.

Strategic-awareness is not the objective of the individual strategist or the strategic society. It is no more, or less, than a remarkable outcome of the response by organisms to the changing strategic demand generated by the unfolding of an increasingly sophisticated dynamic strategy. As we have seen, the growth in the size and complexity of the brain was a response to the strategic demand for cerebral inputs into the strategic pursuit. Organisms played a critical part in this process through "strategic selection". Once the brain achieved the necessary size/complexity threshold to allow the emergence of a "strategic core", primary consciousness emerged; while further increases in brain size/complexity led to the fortuitous emergence of higher-order consciousness. Nothing that had gone before, in terms of the general increase in brain size, gave any indication that it could or would lead to strategic-awareness. Consciousness and selfconsciousness were the great unexpected bonuses of life.

While not sought after nor "expected", strategic-awareness at the individual level proved to be a great advantage in the strategic pursuit. It enabled one species of hominids to dominate life. By being able to imagine past and future scenarios, as well as reflecting on the one unfolding before them, human beings have been able to develop more sophisticated and demanding dynamic strategies, particularly that of technological change. Technological change, and its offspring civilisation, would not have been possible without the emergence of selfconsciousness. And civilisation itself has led to an even more sophisticated form of strategic-awareness at the metropolis level, based on formal systems of thought, that I call cultural-awareness. Cultural-awareness is a non-biological form of consciousness based on human "strategic thinking" (pattern recognition and generalisation) and rule-making skills developed initially to facilitate the unfolding dynamic strategy. To be strategically aware is a great advantage in the strategic pursuit called life.

The Mechanism of Strategic-Awareness

The dynamic-strategy theory offers an explanation of the mechanism of strategic-awareness. The strategic-awareness mechanism is an outcome of the role played by the strategic instrument, which operates at the individual, societal, and global levels. As the dominant dynamic strategy unfolds, a changing strategic demand leads to growing specialisation among "strategic agents" and to an increase in the channels of communication between them. These strategic agents, which form a dynamic strategic core through their interaction, can be neurons in the brain, individuals in the metropolis, metropolises in the nations, and nations in a global context. The main source of information that the strategic agents exchange is "imitative information", which is an amalgam of sensory and other data. At its most basic level, what the strategic agents need to "know" is: Who and what is successful and why? It is not too difficult to see how this operates at the individual and societal levels.[26] At the level of the brain, think in terms of the widespread conclusion that "neurons that fire together, wire together". Like individuals, neurons "imitate" the successful networking of others in response to strategic demand.

The increasing reciprocal interaction between highly specialised strategic agents within the strategic core leads to a growing awareness of the outside world and of its own group activity, together with a growing reflection on both. But what is it that underlies this growing awareness? Strategic theory tells us that the abundance of highly specialised strategic agents, which is the outcome of strategic success measured in terms of surpluses of wealth or intellect, enables a proportion of them to specialise in reflecting upon the strategic processes they are pursuing. This implies that consciousness is the outcome not just of the diversity of neural interactions, as argued by Edelman and Tononi. While their observations and speculations are insightful, these authors do not appear to realise that individual consciousness is only one manifestation of the wider condition of strategic-awareness; or that the brain is just one strategic instrument among several. Only by observing the dynamics of life at all levels can we hope to understand the human mind.

What we need to discover is who or what these agents are that generate strategic-awareness. Strategic agents are bodies—cells, organisms, metropolises, nation-states—that transmit imitative information within the dynamic core of a strategic instrument, which in turn is employed by a more encompassing body in the pursuit of survival and prosperity. The central strategic agent in this hierarchy is the individual organism, because it embodies the driving force in life. It is the individual organism that employs the strategic cerebrum together with various societal organisations required in its strategic pursuit.

The population of potential strategic agents consists of strategists, nonstrategists, and antistrategists.[27] This is true, however, not just at the various societal levels but also at the level of the individual brain. It is the interaction of the strategists that defines the strategic core at all levels, while the nonstrategists occupy the strategic fringe, and the antistrategists (cancer cells as well as deviant individuals) are to be found in the borderlands.[28]

Membership of both the strategic core and its fringe, however, is not static. It changes constantly in both the shortrun and longrun. A given agent will change from nonstrategist to strategist and back again during the course of its lifetime. In difficult times it may even become a destructive antistrategist. The same agent in the shortrun will regularly cease to be a strategist when it temporarily retires from direct involvement in strategic activity. This occurs for individuals when they cease their daily work, and particularly when they sleep; for neurons when they pass from involvement in the brain's conscious to its unconscious routines; and for nations when they switch from globalisation to isolationist policies.

The strategic core, in response to strategic demand, will also range relatively widely through the space provided by the physical boundaries of the strategic instrument, whether brain, metropolis, nation-state, or globe. It is never coexistent with the whole of this space nor is it limited to any one part or module of it. The vitality of the strategic core depends on the extent, pace, and diversity of the interaction between its participating strategic agents, which in turn depends on strategic success. Hence, strategic-awareness ultimately depends on the way in which the strategic agents are able to respond to the unfolding dynamic strategy. While agents at the individual and societal levels respond directly to their particular strategic demand, those at the level of the brain respond indirectly through their individual host, who shapes lifetime neural connections through the activities he pursues.

It is necessary for the strategic core to maintain the diversity of its activity or it will experience a lapse of strategic-awareness. In effect, it will lose those strategic agents who specialise in introspection. The central question, therefore, is: How can this diversity of strategic activity be maintained? The answer is that it all depends on how successfully they participate in the strategic pursuit. When the dynamic strategy is unfolding rapidly and profitably, the interaction between strategic agents is maintained at a high and diverse level, with the result that strategic-awareness flourishes. But, when the dynamic strategy has been exhausted and the strategic *logos* falters, the interaction between strategists declines and strategic-awareness falters and fails.

At the individual and societal levels, the failure of strategic-awareness is the outcome of falling material surpluses and, hence, a decline in funding for those—historians, philosophers, social and cultural critics—who specialise in reflective activities. And at the level of the brain, this failure is an outcome of depression and other disorders that result in reduced psychic energy. What I am saying is that strategic-awareness is not the outcome of some Darwinian accident of adaptation that may have affected the connections between neurons (how could it affect those between individuals in society or societies within the world?), or of Edelman's "neural Darwinism". Rather it is the outcome of successful participation by strategic agents in the dominant dynamic strategy.

During sleep, however, the individual withdraws only temporarily from active involvement in the prevailing dynamic strategy. This leads to a decline in the diversity, if not the rate (as shown by similar patterns of sleeping and waking brain waves), of interaction between neural strategic agents, which generates a loss of consciousness or strategic awareness. Sleep appears necessary for the organism to recover from its strategic exertions and for the brain to consolidate the day's experiences by replaying recent experiences, discarding irrelevant information, laying down long-term memories, and *undertaking virtual strategic exercises*. The hippocampus plays a central role in this process by sending these memory reconstructions to the cortex, where they are experienced as dreams. Dreaming, therefore, is the outcome not of an independent unconscious mind as Freud and his followers claim, but of the pattern-forming activity of the strategic brain temporarily disengaged from the strategic pursuit. It is, in other words, an outcome of *virtual strategic thinking*.

The fascinating characteristic of the strategic instrument is that it is not controlled by a central processor. In this, it is important to realise, the brain is not unique. Strategic agents are coordinated not by decree, but by an exchange of information. This is widely understood. What is not known is that the key information exchanged is "imitative information" and that it is in response to changes in strategic demand. The coordinating principle, therefore, is the mechanism of strategic imitation in which the opportunistic many follow the successful few, and the successful few anticipate the strategic unfolding. As we have seen, this coordinating principle provides strategic agents with the freedom they need to explore the changing opportunities of their dynamic world. A central processor—or command system—would repress this freedom and lead to the ossification of the strategic instrument; and there is no such thing as "spontaneous order" or "self-organisation" (a construct of deductive supply-side fantasy). In the brain, successful neurons and neural groups responding to the strategically determined needs of the organism, initiate responses from other neurons and groups of neurons. The outcome is the strategic coordination of neural activity.

THE ENDANGERED SELF

There can be no doubt that selfconsciousness is an important asset in life. It has enabled members of our species not only to monitor their participation in the strategic pursuit, but also to learn from past experiences and to make predictions about the future. In this way we have been able to participate successfully in increasingly sophisticated dynamic strategies. On this foundation, humanity has been able to construct remarkable cultures embodying complex systems of abstract thought and artistic imagination.

Yet despite all its advantages, selfconsciousness can also undermine our ability to survive and prosper. It is indeed a double-edged sword. Selfconsciousness has endowed the strategic cerebrum with the ability to pursue an agenda that conflicts with the interests of the unconscious organism that "employs" it. Owing to the faculty of selfconsciousness, the strategist has become vulnerable to a take-over by its own strategic instrument. In fact, the conscious self has come to regard itself—in effect the thalamocortical system—as the real individual, and the body as an ever present danger. In doing so the conscious self has in some unfortunate individuals, become the endangered self.

Strategic Dualism

While rejecting Cartesian duality, through the affirmation of the mind's material basis, I embrace the new concept of "strategic dualism".[29] This new form of dualism is based on the distinction between the strategist (unconscious organism) and its strategic instrument (brain). It is the strategist that embodies the driving force arising from "strategic desire", and the strategic instrument that plans and supervises the strategic pursuit. Problems arising from strategic dualism are discussed in the following chapter.

Of course, the strategist and its strategic instrument developed in a highly integrated manner. Both body and brain became increasingly sophisticated as they developed in parallel fashion to exploit more complex dynamic strategies and technological paradigms. As is well known, improvements in physical abilities, such as the manual skills required for precise tool-making, could only occur in step with the further development of those regions of the brain that controlled these activities. Both strategist and strategic instrument became highly dependent on each other. Today neither can exist without the other. A person who suffers massive and irreversible brain damage is unable to exist without an artificial life-support system, despite a perfectly sound body. The reverse is also true.

Yet despite the close integration of body and mind, the latter is able, and sometimes willing, to undercut the viability of the organism. This can, and does, lead to mental disorders—such as schizophrenia and eating problems—and even to mutilation and suicide in some susceptible individuals. Such deviant action by the mind defeats the entire purpose of the unconscious organism, which is to maximise the probability of survival and prosperity. It is unfortunate that the conscious self opens the way for the endangered self. To understand why this happens, we need to examine the conflict between desires and ideas, the ways in which humans have attempted to resolve this conflict, and what happens when these attempts break down.

The Conflict between Desires and Ideas

There is much truth in the old saying that reason is the slave to desire. In reality, as I have been attempting to show in a series of books on the strategic pursuit in which we are all involved, desire drives and reason facilitates. It is this reality that underlies the different roles played by the strategist and the strategic instrument. But this reality is not achieved without internal tension, psychological damage, and even premature death.

The reason for this internal tension is that the conscious self is, in most cases, unwilling to accept the nature of the driving force in life. A world driven by strategic desire is a world populated by organisms that, on average, will stop at nothing in order to survive and prosper. Their defining characteristic is a determined self-centredness. In the pursuit of their dynamic strategies most people, if they feel they have no alternative, will systematically destroy the careers and even the lives of those who possess the resources they desire.

The dynamic strategy of conquest is the most obvious example of this systematic ruthlessness. In the Old World, Rome, the most successful of all conquest societies, systematically killed, raped, enslaved, plundered and oppressed their neighbours for 1,000 years. In the New World, the Aztecs ritually slaughtered tens of thousands of captured warriors whenever they dedicated major public buildings. Their conquest strategy was abruptly cut short, not by a change of heart, but by the Spaniards who destroyed their civilisation, as well as that of the Incas, for a few rooms filled with gold. This is typical of what conquest strategists were prepared to do to earn their daily bread.[30]

Other dynamic strategies—commerce and technological change—were only less blood-thirsty because such systematic brutal acts were not required to earn a living. This did not, however, prevent outbreaks of extreme violence whenever their dynamic strategies were threatened. We only have to recall the commerce wars of Carthage, Venice, Britain, and Holland, or the First and Second World Wars in the technological era.[31] Even in today's technological world, ruthless acts are undertaken in "respectable" organisations—such as corporations, the public service, and universities—by which the careers of individuals and groups are systematically targeted and destroyed by managers and "colleagues", in order to hijack the resources they command. It is a form of bloodless, but not painless, conquest.

These ruthless acts are the outcome of strategic desire—the obsession of individuals to survive and prosper. For an organism without any sense of self, this does not pose a problem. Desire is triumphant. But for the conscious self these ruthless acts are not so easy to accept. The conscious mind has a very different view of its role in life. It is dominated not by desire but by reason. Since the emergence of civilisation, at least, the mind of man has turned to philosophical and artistic reflections. This has led to the creation of abstract notions of what life *should* be like. In these abstract worlds of our own making, ideas take on a reality of their own. There is a confusion between what the world *should* be like and what it *is* like. Consequently it is difficult for a reasonable mind to accept its involvement in ruthless, self-centred, and brutal activities in order to survive and prosper at the expense of one's fellows.

Because of these difficulties experienced by the rational mind in the face of reality, there has arisen a tension between strategist and strategic instrument, between desires and ideas, between pattern recognition and logic, between induction and deduction, and between reality and ideality. While some individuals reject reason for desire and revel in depravity, most attempt to resolve the tension and to lead normal "decent" lives. Some fail to achieve such resolution and, as a result, experience mental disorders and, even, premature death. In the next section I deal with the mechanism employed by those who successfully resolve the tension between desire and reason and, in chapter 11, I focus on the psychological problems of those who fail.

Resolving the Existential Dilemma

A variety of methods has been employed to resolve the tension between reason and desire, or what I call the "existential dilemma" of mankind. Essentially, people either refuse to recognise that their actions are anything less than altruistic, or they recognise the role of desire in life and attempt to banish it from their own lives.

The main response is to pretend that, whatever the rest of the world might be like, one's own actions are largely altruistic. Since 1996 I have called this response "existential schizophrenia", a non-pathological condition required to resolve man's biological dilemma.[32] Very few seem able to squarely face this dilemma, to accept it, and to divert strategic demand into creative rather than destructive avenues. Instead, the great majority deny the reality of their everyday lives. They do this by dividing their lives into mutually exclusive compartments. In one compartment they place the actions, thoughts, and justifications that are necessary to survive and prosper. In reality this compartment demonstrates that they are irrational, selfish, and ruthless in competitive situations. The other compartment contains their views and aspirations about themselves. They like to see themselves as essentially rational, compassionate, and altruistic. Over thousands, if not millions, of years we have become experts in keeping these two compartments apart and in resolving the existential dilemma through sleight of hand. We are experts in deluding ourselves.

The second, less widespread, response to man's existential dilemma involves recognising the suffering inflicted by desire and attempting to eliminate it. This is the approach taken by a number of great thinkers, such as

Plato and Schopenhauer in the West, and great saints such as Buddha and other Hindu thinkers in the East. Essentially this is an attempt to negate the driving force in life. In reality the only way to eliminate desire is by opting out of the competitive—the strategic—world. In turn this can only be achieved, ironically, by relying upon the wealth and patronage of others who continue to be driven by desire. This is a false existence because those taking this path can survive only as long as their supporters remain in the rat race. If everyone turned their back on desire, human society would collapse. In the end, to live this false life requires the same degree of self-delusion—of existential schizophrenia—as that practiced by the rest of humanity.

The third response is to adopt the approach favoured by mainstream religion. Adherents do not attempt to eliminate desire, merely to develop rules to define the boundaries of what might be called "reasonable desire". For example, various mainstream religions have in the past placed limitations on materialistic desire in the form of usury laws and regulations concerning fair prices and wages; on sexual desire in the form of marriage (as is well known, St Paul said that it was "better to marry than to burn"!); on selfishness in the form of social responsibilities (such as "good works" and charity for the poor). And, knowing in advance that these rules will be broken, they have developed further rules for forgiveness involving confession and restitution. While this does help to resolve the tension between reason and desire, it is based on the self-delusion that, with the assistance of divine intervention, one can balance the materialistic and the spiritual. In the end it is also a form of existential schizophrenia—of placing desire and reason in separate compartments. But, unlike Buddhism, it is strategy-affirming, which is why religions such as Christianity and Islam have been adopted by strategic leaders and their followers in leading strategic countries. The real nature of religion is analysed in chapter 8.

It is only when these resolution mechanisms break down that the conscious self becomes the endangered self. At such times, mental disorders and suicide seem, to some susceptible people, to be the only solution to a life dominated by strategic desire. Various methods of treating this critical problem of tension between body and mind have been developed over thousands of years. In the East this has been attempted by reintegrating the body and mind through meditation and disciplines such as Tai Chi, and in the West through the "talking cures" of psychoanalysis. A more viable alternative—a strategic alternative—is proposed in the next chapter.

Chapter 10
Restoring Damaged Consciousness — A Strategic Psychology

Mental disorders arise from strategic malfunctions.

A viable self-consciousness is central to the pursuit of survival and prosperity. Hence, this chapter is concerned with the problem of restoring damaged self-awareness in the *logos* via a new strategic psychiatry. But what could possibly be new in the world of abnormal psychology? The symptoms of mental disorders have been extensively investigated over the past 150 years and have been carefully described and categorised. Despite this, there is little agreement about the systematic causes of mental disorders. While there are a variety of psychological theories—ranging from the psychoanalytic to the Darwinian—they possess severe limitations. Once again the problem is that none of these theories is able to provide a satisfactory account of the dynamics of life and human society. And without this it is not possible to understand the real causes of mental disorders or the most appropriate way to treat them.

Essentially, psychological illness emerges in individuals who suffer malfunctions in those psychic mechanisms that enable them to participate in the "strategic pursuit". Without an understanding of the strategic mechanisms in life, we cannot hope to know the causes of, or the real relationships between, the mental disorders that the psychiatric profession has so painstakingly described and classified. The dynamic-strategy theory, therefore, provides the first real opportunity to understand the *ultimate* causes of these mental disorders, because it enables us to place the human psyche within the wider context of the dynamics of life and human society. It also enables us to explore the role that mental disorders have played in the emergence of religious ideas (see chapter 8). But before doing so, we will consider further the "strategic dualism" of human nature.

STRATEGIC DUALISM

As suggested briefly in the last chapter, strategic dualism has nothing in common with Cartesian dualism. René Descartes (1596–1650), as is well known, made a distinction in his philosophy between "extended substances" or matter/bodies, and "thinking substances" or minds/souls. Only bodies, he claimed, are subject to the mechanical laws of natural science. Bodies, according to Descartes, are machines. Minds or souls, which remain beyond the reach of scientific laws, are subject only to divine laws and are released when machine-like bodies die. Cartesian dualism, therefore, involves a distinction between the material body and the non-material mind.

Strategic dualism, by contrast, does not draw this mystical distinction. The strategic mind, which is an outcome of the material brain, has no independent existence. It is subject to the laws of natural science and is extinguished when the body dies. Strategic dualism arises from the different roles played in life by the body and the brain. While the body is the embodiment of "strategic desire"—the fundamental driving force in life—the brain, and hence the mind, is the instrument employed by the "unconscious organism" to satisfy this desire through successful participation in the strategic pursuit. The complex relationship between body and mind in man is discussed in chapter 9.

What are the main implications of strategic dualism? Essentially, it suggests that human nature is the outcome of a complex dialogue between body and mind, strategist and strategic instrument, strategic desire and reason. It is this dialogue that defines our strategic power and, hence, our nature. This contrasts with the rationalist view that reason is the "governor" of the passions; with the neo-Darwinist view that the body and mind are *both* instruments of the selfish gene; and with the sociological view that the body and mind are fashioned by society. Strategic dualism is also the source of tension within individuals that sometimes leads to the breakdown of the psychic unity that normally prevails in human beings. This is discussed later in the chapter.

The dialogue between the different sources of human nature operates at a number of different levels. The first and most commonplace of these takes place at the level of body and mind. It is the level most familiar to the layperson in all societies. Most people are aware of the interaction and tension that exist between the body and mind in daily life. Culture, both popular and refined, is based on the obvious unequal conflict between the passions and the intellect. The dominance of sex and aggression in our daily lives is the staple fare of television melodrama and grand opera alike.

The second level of tension is the philosophical dialogue between reason and desire. In contrast to popular commonsense, the dominant philosophical view of this dialogue is the Platonic one in which reason dominates desire. If reason failed to govern desire, Plato argued, the ideal society would unravel and descend into chaos. In Plato's republic, the "guardians"—Plato's moral police—were to ensure that this did not happen. Even Aristotle, who was less disturbed than his teacher by the passions, still viewed the rational mind—the self or *kyrios* ("dominant one")—as the core of individual personality. While this philosophical tradition has its critics, it remains the mainstream.

By contrast, the dynamic-strategy theory shows that strategic desire is the driving force in life, while reason is employed to facilitate and rationalise our acquiescence in this role that we share with the rest of life. While other life forms are not bothered by the desires that drive them, mankind has achieved such a degree of selfconsciousness and intellectual sophistication that it is difficult for us to accept our true nature. While we are able to see and understand what we are, we invariably do not like what we see, and we look the other way.

It is in order to live with ourselves—to cope with our dual nature—that we have learnt to "look the other way". We pretend to ourselves that we are not like other animals—that we, being intellectual beings, are not driven by desire. We have even developed complex arguments to convince ourselves not only that we are dominated by positive personality traits but that we have somehow transcended the rest of life. This self-deception is, as discussed later in the chapter, a survival mechanism. If we were forced to see ourselves as we really are—to acknowledge our true nature—many more people would not only develop debilitating disorders but also take their own lives. As this would prevent us achieving our objective in life of maximising the probability of survival and prosperity, we have adopted strategic mechanisms to prevent it.

The third level of tension is between the strategist and the strategic instrument. Unlike the other levels of dialogue, this has been raised for the first time in this work. It is a perspective involving a number of important issues. First, human nature—indeed the human individual itself—is the product of a symbiotic relationship between the unconscious organism embodying strategic desire, and the strategic cerebrum embodying the facilitating function of reason. As we have seen, until some 500 myrs ago the unconscious organism was an independent entity and, unlike the brain, was able to exist on its own. But over the intervening years the strategist and its strategic instrument have developed together and become so interdependent that neither can survive on its own, at least not without artificial life-support systems. There is no going back. They survive or perish together.

Second, the strategic instrument has come to view itself as the dominant partner in this relationship. To the conscious mind, *it* is the individual's true self. This is reflected in the generally accepted definition of individual death, which is said to occur when the brain has ceased to have dialogue with both its own body and with the outside world. It is at this juncture that artificial life-support systems are usually turned off and the body is allowed to die. In contrast, the individual who has lost control of his entire body (such as a quadriplegic or a person in an iron lung), but whose mind is undamaged, is automatically kept alive. A recognition of strategic dualism should cause us to think more closely about this matter. If it is the body that embodies the driving force in life, and if that body is undamaged, should strategic desire be terminated when the brain is badly damaged? Surely the strategist has as much right to live as its strategic instrument.

Third, the emergence of strategic dualism has made it possible for the mind to hijack the strategic pursuit and endanger an otherwise healthy organism. There are numerous examples. Individuals willing to destroy themselves for an idea have been as numerous in the past as they are today. No one at the beginning of the twenty-first century needs reminding of the suicide bombings around the world that reached a peak in the terrorist attack on New York on September 11, 2001, and which have continued in a disturbing way to the present time (2015). It is strategic dualism that makes suicidal terrorism possible.

Suicide is the hollow triumph of the confused strategic instrument over the materialist strategist. The strategic cerebrum, which is supposed to facilitate the desire of the unconscious organism to survive and prosper, breaks the historical "contract" with its "employer" and terminates their symbiotic existence in the pursuit of an abstract idea that owes nothing to existential reality. It is an idea that emerges deductively rather than inductively—from rational rather than strategic thinking—in the minds of individuals alienated from their bodies. Other examples of the mind hijacking the strategic pursuit include the self-destructive quest for cerebral sensation through the use of chemical substances, the imposition of starvation owing to extreme views of body image, the removal of limbs that the mind refuses to recognise as part of the "self", and the suicide of depressed individuals who have lost touch with reality. In all these cases, the mind forces the body to abandon strategic desire by employing its drive and energy against itself.

MENTAL DISORDERS

Owing to the previous lack of a general theory of human nature and its role in life there has been no compelling way to classify the various recognised mental disorders. In the last century, mental illness was often divided into neurotic disorders and psychotic disorders, but neither category is mutually exclusive and together they are not exhaustive. Accordingly, the psychiatry profession has recently abandoned these terms in their categorisation of mental disorders. Instead, in the American *Diagnostic and Statistical Manual of Mental Disorders* (*DSM*), they merely list, in a largely arbitrary way, the large number of recognised illnesses.[1]

In order to show how the dynamic-strategy theory can explain the emergence and persistence of mental disorders, it is necessary to briefly outline the most important of these. The principle employed here to group these mental disorders together is the degree to which they disrupt the participation of individuals in their society's strategic pursuit. This has led to my use of two main categories: the "strategy-challenging disorders", and the "strategy-terminating disorders", which are outlined in Table 10.1. This table is meant to be illustrative rather than exhaustive. The important point is that all recognised disorders can be categorised in this way.

While the strategy-challenging disorders tend to be of the neurotic kind and the strategy-terminating disorders of the psychotic kind, this is not necessarily true of every type of disorder. The antisocial personality disorder (psychopathology), for example, is extremely destructive of the strategic pursuit for both the individual and the society, but it is not psychotic in nature. The considerable overlap between those old and new classifications is due to the fact that patients suffering neurotic disorders usually retain both insight into their condition and contact with reality, whereas those suffering psychotic disorders experience delusions and hallucinations, resulting in a loss of contact with reality.

Table 10.1 A Strategic Classification of Mental Disorders

Strategy Challenging (S-C) Disorders	Strategy Terminating (S-T) Disorders
1. Mood disorders	1. S-T personality disorder
2. Anxiety & phobic disorders	• antisocial
3. S-C personality disorders	• paranoid
• avoidant	• schizoid
• obsessional	2. Schizophrenia & other psychotic disorders
• narcissistic	
4. Eating disorders	

Source: Snooks (2006: p. 190)

Strategy-Challenging Disorders

Strategy-challenging disorders include those mental illnesses that are painful and distressing but do not usually prevent the individuals concerned retaining their grip on reality. They suffer, sometime intensely, but are usually able to continue their social and employment activities, even if with less efficiency and enjoyment. In other words, with the exception of extreme cases, they are able to maintain their participation in the strategic pursuit. These disorders challenge strategic participation but usually do not terminate it.

Mood disorders

Mood disorders basically include both depression and mania (euphoria), but can be subdivided, as in *DSM*, into a large number of categories, including alternation between both states. It is important to distinguish between mild and clinical forms of these conditions, because in their mild forms they actually assist in the strategic pursuit: mild mania provides an incentive to continue the current dynamic strategy, while mild depression is an emotional indication that a change in circumstances or in strategy is required.

The main features of clinical depression include lowered mood, reduced energy and pleasure, diminished ability to think and concentrate, pessimistic attitudes, and disturbed sleep and appetite.[2] In the main, those suffering from depression—the probability for women is twice that of men—continue to participate in the strategic pursuit. Only in extreme cases will the reduction in psycho-motor activity lead to depressive stupor and mutism. Depressive moods are usually subject to a diurnal rhythm, with the afflicted individual being at their worst in the morning, but gradually improving in the afternoon or evening.

Owing to the tendency of depressed individuals to retreat from social engagement, the depth and widespread nature of this mental disorder was not generally recognised until recently.[3] Increasingly, support organisations are emerging to provide greater support and recognition to those suffering from this distressing disorder. It has been said that "in its severest form it is possibly one of the most dreadful afflictions humanity can suffer".[4] But, as we shall see, in its more moderate form it plays a positive strategic role in encouraging individuals to abandon deteriorating strategies and circumstances.

Mania—and its milder form, hypomania—is the very opposite of depression. The mood is euphoric, energy levels are high, and self-esteem is inflated. Those experiencing mania tend to view the future with excessive optimism. Accordingly they make over ambitious plans and take on excessive commitments that often require a lavish use of economic and personal resources. Mania sufferers also tend to overestimate their abilities and are intolerant to criticism.[5]

There are various degrees of mania. Mild forms, usually called hypomania, can help individuals to achieve outstanding feats of an intellectual, physical, commercial, or military nature; whereas, severe forms can lead to a loss of reality and almost certain failure in any of these ventures. Severe mania, therefore, will lead to strategic failure and, often as a result, to the onset of depression. This is known as bipolar disorder.

Anxiety and phobic disorders

Anxiety is a natural part of life. It prepares the individual to respond quickly and effectively to danger. Yet, while it is a universal response to the uncertainties of life, in extreme forms it can be highly debilitating. While general anxiety takes the form of a vague, unpleasant emotional state characterised by apprehension, dread, uneasiness, and distress, a panic attack involves a discrete period of intense fear or discomfort. These anxiety states are accompanied by a range of physical sensations of varying intensity, including accelerated heart rate, palpitations, sweating, trembling or shaking, shortness of breath, chest pains, nausea, dizziness, chills or hot flushes, and so on. And panic disorders take the form of recurrent, unexpected, and intense anxiety attacks.

Phobic disorders—from the Greek for fear or dread—produce the same symptoms as anxiety but they are associated with particular objects or events. The trigger for phobias include a variety of threatening circumstances, such as open spaces (agoraphobia), confined spaces (claustrophobia), heights (vertigo), crowds, social situations, and all sorts of dangerous animals (spiders, snakes, sharks) and man-made devices (aircraft, elevators, busy roads, tall buildings). A particularly costly disorder from a strategic point of view is social phobia or social anxiety disorder, which is characterised by an excessive and persistent fear of having to perform in social situations that might lead to acute embarrassment. The fear is that others will judge them to be stupid, incompetent, weak, or anxious. While social phobia is thought to be debilitating for 3 to 13 per cent of the population, many more experience excessive anxiety in social situations.[6] Clearly for a social species like human beings, this disorder adversely affects the efficiency with which these individuals can participate in the strategic pursuit.

Anxiety and phobic disorders are exaggerations of responses that are essential to the survival of individuals in all the higher animal species. To survive, an individual must be alert, vigilant, and sensitive to the dangers around him. This response is the province of the limbic system in the unconscious mind. Although it is possible to moderate these unconscious responses indirectly through the conscious mind, it is usually done with difficulty, because the limbic system has the upper hand in such matters owing to the greater one-way connectivity between the limbic system and the cortex than the other way around. Most individuals find it extremely difficult to control their phobias or to prevent panic attacks once they start to emerge, even when they understand the nature of the problem. This is why the attempt by Freud and other psychoanalysts to eliminate anxiety by encouraging patients to face the underlying traumatic causation rarely succeeds. Indeed by interfering with the normal defense mechanism (of dividing one's life into "watertight" compartments that I call "existential schizophrenia"), they often exposed their patients to even greater danger in the form of psychotic disorders.

Strategy-challenging personality disorders

A personality disorder is defined by the *DSM* as "an enduring pattern of inner experience and behaviour that deviates markedly from the expectations of the individual's culture, is persuasive and inflexible, has an onset in adolescence or early adulthood, is stable over time, and leads to distress or impairment".[7] Grouped together in this definition are the following disorders: paranoid, schizoid, schizotypal, antisocial, borderline, histrionic, narcissistic, avoidant, dependent, and obsessive-compulsive disorders. It will be clear that some of these disorders are essentially neurotic in nature and others are psychotic. More importantly, some are strategy-challenging (avoidant [0.5–1.0% of the general population], dependent, obsessional [1.0%], narcissistic [1.05], and histrionic [2–3%]), and others are strategy-terminating (antisocial, paranoid, schizoid, and schizotypal). These disorders are discussed in greater detail in my book *The Selfcreating Mind* (2006).[8]

The important point to emphasise is that all these personality disorders are exaggerations of characteristics that are necessary to successfully participate in the strategic pursuit. These characteristics include self-love, and the abilities to win the support of others, to control situations, and to attend to important detail. Only when these characteristics take extreme forms do they become a liability to the individual and a challenge to their participation in the strategic pursuit.

Strategy-Terminating Disorders

Strategy-terminating disorders include those mental illnesses that are not only painful and distressing but also lead to the termination of the individual's participation in the strategic pursuit. These illnesses include personality disorders of the antisocial, paranoid, and schizoid kind, together with schizophrenia and other psychotic disorders. They are strategy-terminating because they lead either to antistrategic activity (antisocial personality disorder) or to psychosis and a loss of reality (schizophrenia).

Antistrategic disorders

"Antistrategic disorders" are mental illnesses that affect not only the sick person's strategic role but also the viability of his society's dynamic strategy. This is most evident in criminal activity that undermines a society's success. The main disorder of this type is known as antisocial personality disorder. This disorder is characterised by a persistent and pervasive disregard for, and violation of, the rights of others. Formerly it was known as psychopathy (Britain), sociopathy (United States), and, more recently, dissocial personality disorder. It is thought to afflict about 3 per cent of males and 1 per cent of females in the general population, and 80 per cent of the criminal population.[9] Hysteria, which is largely confined to females, is regarded by some as a mild form of psychopathy.

Those suffering from antisocial personality disorder are (some combination of) untrustworthy, deceitful, impulsive, highly irritable, aggressive (either physically or sexually), and prone to theft (of intellectual as well as physical property) and destructive acts. And they feel no remorse for their antisocial actions. They have a high threshold for fear and anxiety, and experience low pulse rates in stressful situations. How many of your colleagues (office or university) fit this description? These antisocial characteristics can be traced back to childhood, when they may have been truant, delinquent, disruptive, or hyperactive. Despite their antisocial nature, these individuals can also be superficially charming and charismatic.

The questions that all existing approaches to mental disorders—particularly the Darwinian—have difficulty explaining are how and why such a destructive personality type has been able to persist in human society. Later in the chapter I will provide a dynamic-strategy explanation. For now I merely wish to make the significant point that this personality type underlies what I have called the "antistrategist", who attempts to survive and prosper by undermining and negatively exploiting their society's dynamic strategy.[10]

Antistrategists can be divided into conservative and radical, and legal and illegal. The conservative antistrategist has no wish to destroy the existing dynamic strategy, merely to exploit it. This can be done either legally through rent-seeking activities that exploit legal loopholes in existing regulations (such as tax laws), or illegally through criminal activities. The combination of both charm and disregard for the rights of others is a powerful armory for the conservative antistrategist in a law-abiding world. These evil people exist in all the organisations of normal society and have been responsible for the destruction of the lives and careers of many good people who have failed to gain the support of those that are ultimately responsible for these organisations.

We are familiar with the sexual and psychic abuse that exists in corporations, bureaucracies, universities, and churches.

The radical antistrategist, on the other hand, is more ambitious and idealistic than his conservative counterpart. He wants to destroy the existing strategists and their dynamic strategy in order to build an antistrategic organisation or society (as in the USSR, 1917 to 1989) that will deliver the entire surplus of the organisation or society to the antistrategists at the expense of the oppressed strategists. While the conservative antistrategist will weaken their organisation or society, the radical antistrategist will eventually destroy it. As antisocial personality disorder is the most socially dangerous mental illness of them all, it is essential that we are able to understand and treat it effectively.

Psychotic disorders

This is a collective category for a number of severe mental disorders. The defining characteristic of a psychotic disorder is the gross impairment of an individual's ability to relate successfully to the external world—to reality. This is because psychotic individuals make incorrect inferences about the external world, make inappropriate evaluations about the accuracy of their internal thoughts and perceptions, and fail to correct these initial responses even when confronted with contrary information.

Classic psychotic symptoms include delusions, hallucinations, severely regressive behaviour, entirely inappropriate moods, and markedly incoherent speech. Psychotic sufferers, in other words, are unable to participate in social activities or, more importantly, in the strategic pursuit. They tend to withdraw from life and they commit suicide at twelve times the average rate, thereby undermining "strategic desire", the driving force in life.[11] A number of mental disorders are usually grouped together in the psychotic category, including, in order of increasing disorientation: paranoid personality disorder, schizoid personality disorder, and schizophrenia.

First we consider the **paranoid personality disorder**. The main feature of this disorder, which affects 0.5 to 2.5 per cent of the general population, is a pattern of pervasive distrust and suspiciousness of others, who are thought to be malevolent. Paranoid sufferers harbor unjustified suspicions that others are exploiting, harming, or deceiving them; they are wracked with unreasonable doubts about the loyalty of friends and associates; they are reluctant to confide in others for fear that this information will be used against them; they interpret benign remarks or events as threatening; they bear unreasonable grudges; they are quick to counterattack (often through the courts); and they are unjustifiably suspicious of their sexual partners. Of course, in a hostile world it pays to be wary of others, this is a natural defense mechanism, but when taken to extremes this approach merely disrupts one's successful participation in the strategic pursuit.

In stressful situations, individuals suffering paranoid personality disorder may also experience brief episodes of psychosis, or may develop schizophrenia, or even a full paranoid delusional disorder. Clinical evidence suggests that families experiencing this disorder are also prone to delusional disorders of the persecutory type and to chronic schizophrenia.[12] This disorder also shares traits of suspiciousness, aloofness, and paranoid ideation with schizotypal personality disorder, but not the latter's magical fantasies, odd perceptual experiences, or peculiar thinking and speech; and it shares characteristics—regarded by others as strange, eccentric, cold and aloof—with schizoid psychotic disorders. It is because of these associations that I have included paranoid personality disorder in the psychotic group.

Schizoid psychotic disorder centres on a pervasive detachment from social relationships, with a limited range of emotional expression. Schizoid sufferers exhibit an emotional coldness, withdrawal, solitude, and secretiveness. They present a bland exterior that reflects little or nothing of their inner thoughts and feelings. Not surprisingly they are unable to develop intimate relationships. Accordingly they tend to reject the external world in favour of an internal life of their own creation. In rare cases, however, this internal world may be both ingenious and of considerable benefit to mankind. These rare examples are said to include Isaac Newton and René Descartes,[13] but one would want to see more documentation than these cases have received.

Schizoid personality disorder appears to be related to schizophrenia despite not presenting psychotic features. It presents, for example, an increased incidence in families suffering from schizotypal psychotic disorder and schizophrenia. And schizoid sufferers sometimes experience periods characterised by psychotic symptoms. Classification depends on the stage in the illness at which psychotic symptoms are experienced. In any case, schizoid sufferers experience the split between emotional and intellectual functions that characterises schizophrenia.

Schizotypal psychotic disorder, which affects 3 per cent of the general population, can be distinguished from schizoid personality disorder by the presence of cognitive or perceptual distortions and marked eccentricity or coldness. Schizotypal sufferers may be superstitious or obsessed with paranormal phenomena that are outside the norms of their culture; they may believe they have special powers to foretell events, to read thoughts, and to control others through magic; they experience unusual perceptions such as bodily illusions; they exhibit odd thinking and speech; they tend to be suspicious and even paranoid; they have inappropriate or restricted emotional reactions; they experience excessive social anxiety; and their behaviour and/or appearance is odd or eccentric.

There is a strong association between schizotypal psychotic disorder and schizophrenia. We have already noted that it is more prevalent among the first-degree biological relatives of individuals with schizophrenia than among the general population. Also when subjected to stress, schizotypal sufferers may experience brief psychotic episodes lasting from minutes to hours. And while this condition is relatively stable, a small proportion of sufferers regress completely to schizophrenia or other psychotic disorders.

Schizophrenia is a general term for a number of psychotic disorders with associated cognitive, emotional, and behavioural characteristics. This term, which was coined by Eugen Bleuler in 1911 to replace the existing term "dementia praecox", literally means "splitting in the mind". The "splitting" refers not to multiple personalities, a very different and rare disorder[14], but to the dissociation between emotion and cognition. Unlike the split between desire and reason in my concept of "existential schizophrenia", the split between feelings and thinking in "pathological schizophrenia" is involuntary. It is as if the voluntary splitting procedure involved in the normal survival mechanism has run out of control. This, I believe, is the solution to pathological schizophrenia, which has been called "the great unsolved mystery of psychiatry"[15]—a solution examined later in the chapter.

Schizophrenia is characterised by a pattern of psychotic features, including thought disturbances, bizarre delusions, hallucinations (usually auditory), a disturbed sense of self, and a loss of reality. Essentially this loss of reality involves a loss of the strategic abilities of pragmatic pattern recognition and generalisation. The resulting symptoms have been classified by the *DSM* as "positive" and "negative". We are told that

> The positive symptoms appear to reflect an excess or distortion of normal functions, whereas the negative symptoms appear to reflect a diminution or loss of normal function. The positive symptoms ... include distortions in thought content (delusions), perceptions (hallucinations), language and thought processes (disorganised speech), and self-monitoring of behaviour (grossly disorganised or catatonic behaviors) ... Negative symptoms ... include restrictions in the range and intensity of emotional expression (affective flattening), in the fluency and productivity of thought and speech (alogia), and in the initiation of goal-directed behaviour.[16]

As we shall see, the dynamic-strategy theory demonstrates that these positive and negative symptoms are an outcome of the malfunction of the normal existential-schizophrenia mechanism.

There are three main schizophrenia subtypes: the paranoid, disorganised, and catatonic. The "paranoid type" experiences delusions of a persecutory nature and/or auditory hallucinations, while their cognitive and emotional functioning is relatively unaffected. Onset of this disorder occurs later in life than other types, and the affected person may adopt a superior and patronizing manner and be disposed to anger and violence. The "disorganised type" experiences disorganised speech and behaviour, together with flat or inappropriate emotional responses. Their daily activities—such as bathing, dressing, and meal preparation—are usually disrupted. Onset is early and there are no significant remissions. Finally, the "catatonic type" experiences complete immobility or excessive activity, extreme negativism, mutism, eccentric movements, and repetition of the words (echolalia) or actions (echopraxia) of others. The latter, in terms of the dynamic-strategy theory, suggests a malfunction of the central "strategic-imitation" mechanism by which the vast majority in any society follow the successful few.

Schizophrenia is a terribly debilitating disorder that impacts upon every society throughout the world. It is thought to affect 0.5 to 1.5 per cent of the general adult population, with an incidence higher among urban-born than rural-born individuals. This suggests that stress might be a trigger. It is also clear that genetic factors play a role, with first-degree relatives of sufferers having a risk factor tenfold greater than individuals in the general population. But the genetic role should not be exaggerated, as suggested by the "substantial discordance rate in monozygotic [identical] twins"[17]—a significant proportion of identical twins with a schizophrenic sibling are free from this disorder.

The relatives of schizophrenic sufferers also experience higher than average incidence of other mental disorders that are part of what is called the "schizophrenia spectrum". In this respect, the *DSM* notes that:

> Although the exact boundaries of the spectrum remain unclear, family and adoption studies suggest that it probably includes Schizoaffective Disorder and Schizotypal Personality Disorder. Other psychotic disorders and Paranoid, Schizoid, and Avoidant Personality Disorders may belong to the schizophrenia spectrum as well, but the evidence is more limited.[18]

We return to this later in the chapter, when it is suggested that the "schizophrenia spectrum" is an outcome of the various worsening stages in the malfunction of the normal existential-schizophrenia mechanism.

The onset of schizophrenia usually occurs in individuals between their late teens and mid thirties. In men, who have a higher incidence of schizophrenia owing to strategic roles that place greater pressure on the normal existential-schizophrenia mechanism, the modal age of onset is between 18 and 25 years, and in women between 25 and 35 years with a second peak later in life. Men and women also differ in the type of schizophrenia they suffer: men tend to exhibit more "negative" symptoms (flat emotions, inability to initiate and maintain goal-directed activities, and social withdrawal); whereas women exhibit more "positive" symptoms (paranoid delusions and hallucinations). This, I will suggest, is largely due to the different strategic roles that men and women have historically undertaken.

The course taken by schizophrenia is highly variable, but complete remission "is probably not common in this disorder".[19] Women, however, have a better prognosis than men. The usual progression of the disorder is from negative symptoms early in the illness to positive symptoms at a later stage. As positive symptoms are responsive to treatment they may eventually diminish, but negative symptoms remain prominent.

The onset of schizophrenia, therefore, leads to severe social and occupational dysfunction: in other words they are prevented by their disorder from further participation in the strategic pursuit. There is a tragic irony here. Conscious beings are only able to participate in the strategic pursuit and live with the consequences of following their desires on a daily basis by employing the *normal* mechanism of "existential schizophrenia". But such a mechanism, which involves voluntary distortions in perception and evaluation, opens the door for a pathological divorce between desire and reason. In which case, self-delusion becomes involuntary and psychotic. It is the fundamental strategic dualism of mankind that accounts for the persistence of the "schizophrenia spectrum" in human society.

STRATEGIC MALFUNCTION

Human nature developed through the "autogenous" process of strategic selection to enable mankind to participate more effectively in an increasingly sophisticated environment. The outcome of this dynamic process was a delicate balance in man between strategist and strategic instrument, body and mind, and desire and reason. This balance was rendered even more delicate by the emergence of selfconsciousness.

In the normal individual, however, the strategist dominates its strategic instrument and reason is the slave to desire. Yet, in order to render the objectives of desire compatible with the rationality of the conscious mind, it was necessary to develop a psychological mechanism that could compartmentalise the pragmatic realism of the strategist from the rarefied idealism of its strategic instrument. As suggested in the last chapter, this is the mechanism of "existential schizophrenia"—a voluntary splitting of the mind between desire and reason. Without this mechanism, the conscious mind, unable to readily accept the materialistic objectives of its own desire, would have broken down or destroyed itself through mass suicide.

Essentially, the central psychological problem of mankind arises from its strategic dualism. If existential schizophrenia, which is responsible for **strategic integration** in man, malfunctions, affected individuals will develop psychoses and be unable to participate in the strategic pursuit. This strategic malfunction lies at the heart of many mental disorders. Indeed, mental disorders are really "strategic disorders".

While there are other causes of mental disorders, they all emerge from difficulties experienced in strategic participation. These causes include the malfunction of the central mechanism of **strategic imitation**, which is responsible for societal (rather than individual) integration, and the emergence of "strategic frustration". While these problems cause much mental anguish in affected individuals, and challenge their participation in the strategic pursuit, they do not usually terminate it as psychoses do. Instead, these strategic problems lead to the emergence of neuroses, such as anxiety and phobic disorders, mood disorders, and a variety of non-psychotic personality disorders. Our focus in the remainder of the chapter will be on these major "strategic malfunctions" and their psychological outcomes.

Breakdown in Strategic Integration

A breakdown in "strategic integration" involves a major disruption to the essential balance between strategist and strategic instrument, body and conscious mind, and desire and reason. It is an outcome made possible, as we have seen, by the strategic dualism in human nature. The loss of balance between the two main aspects of human nature renders the individual incapable of participating in the strategic pursuit. Treatment of this tragic problem should be aimed, therefore, at preparing the sufferer to rejoin the strategic pursuit whenever this is even a remote possibility. What we are dealing with here is the capacity that an individual possesses for strategic participation. The main force that can dramatically reduce this capacity is a malfunction in the mechanism of existential schizophrenia.

Malfunction of existential schizophrenia

The price we pay for the important strategic instrument of selfconsciousness is an acute awareness of our uncompromisingly materialistic nature. As already suggested, in order to live with ourselves we compartmentalise our emotional and rational lives. This compartmentalisation takes place in the conscious mind, and does not involve a division between the conscious and unconscious mind as claimed in the theory of unconscious fixed ideas developed by dynamic psychiatrists. In the dynamic-strategy theory the unconscious part of the brain has no proactive role to play. We are able, through existential schizophrenia, to think warmly of ourselves as altruistic and rational, while living from day to day in an entirely selfish and materialistic way. We congratulate ourselves on not being like other human beings who are prepared to go to any lengths—including destroying other people psychologically and physically and expropriating their possessions—in order to survive and prosper.

Today we claim to be unable to understand how other societies are able to survive and prosper by pursuing the dynamic strategy of conquest, which requires systematic killing, looting, and enslavement. But, of course, the citizens of conquest societies—such as Rome, medieval Europe, Mesoamerica, Nazi Germany, and Imperial Japan—thought of themselves in the same way. Like us they saw their societies as civilised, just, and altruistic. But, in view of their bloody occupation, how could they? The answer is: just as we do, through the normal mechanism of existential schizophrenia—through separating out what we do from what we like to think we do. It is a voluntary "splitting of the mind", by compartmentalising our desires from our intellectual view of ourselves. We conveniently "look the other way".

Existential schizophrenia is a very effective survival mechanism. Despite our self-centredness and greed, we see ourselves as altruistic; despite our cruelty and brutality, we see ourselves as kind and just; despite our gross materialism, we see ourselves as spiritual beings. We are masters of self-deception and of justifying ourselves to ourselves. While we are quick to point out the imperfections of others, we have great difficulty seeing in ourselves those very same flaws. And we are fortunate that this mechanism of self-deception is so effective. Without it we would run the risk of opting out of the strategic pursuit in disgust, which would lead to the self-destruction of our species. Of course, a very small minority do just that. Existential schizophrenia, therefore, is essential to our survival both as individuals and as a species.

There appear to be varying degrees to which individuals in the normal range of psychological characteristics have control over the mechanism of existential schizophrenia. At one end of the normal range are individuals who possess a relatively good understanding of their own nature and the role that desire plays in their lives. While even these people are not free from self-deception—possibly reflected in their belief and pride that they fully understand their own motivation—they are more able than most to distinguish between their convenient constructions of "reality" and the real thing. The price of this ability is a degree of anguish that emerges as they approach the truth about themselves. Truth is a vivisector.[20]

At the other end of the normal spectrum of self-knowledge are those who appear to have at least some difficulty in distinguishing between their constructions of convenience and reality itself. This difficulty sometimes leads them into faulty decision-making, but at least they experience less anxiety about their existence. The price of bliss, it would seem, can be counted in terms of the number of strategic decisions they get wrong owing to self-deception. It is only a few steps from this extreme "normal" position to the psychotic states discussed above, where the grasp on reality is lost entirely.

While the existential-schizophrenia mechanism has been overlooked by other social scientists and psychologists alike, clinical psychiatrists are aware of the techniques that their patients employ to protect themselves against discomforting and potentially damaging memories and ideas. These techniques are widely known as "defense mechanisms". This is a throw back to Sigmund Freud's early theory of neurosis, in which the "defences" were seen as a barrier to eliminating neurotic symptoms. In this tradition the 2000 edition of *DSM*, which summarises these defense mechanisms in an appendix, is considering the possibility of including them in their classification of mental disorders, but as yet has "insufficient information to warrant inclusion of these proposals as official categories".[21] It is somewhat ironical that these defense mechanisms, which are essential to the operation of the *normal* mechanism of existential schizophrenia, are currently considered by the psychiatry profession as potentially classifiable as mental disorders. No doubt some psychiatrists do treat them—as Freud did—as disorders in their patients. This merely demonstrates the dangers that arise from the lack of a general theory of mental problems.

What are these "defense mechanisms"? According to the *DSM* they are "automatic psychological processes that protect the individual against anxiety [emotional conflict] and from the awareness of internal or external dangers or stressors".[22] It is the objective of psychoanalysis to expose the traumas that underlie these defense mechanisms. The *DSM* identifies defences operating at a number of levels, ranging from, at one extreme, the "high adaptive level"—enabling "optimal adaptation in the handling of stressors" through sublimation, suppression, self-assertion, self-observation, humour, altruism, affiliation, anticipation—to the level of "defensive dysregulation", at the other extreme, owing to the failure of the usual defences and a break with reality *leading to delusions and psychotic denial and distortions*. Intermediate levels include those called "mental inhibitions" (displacement, dissociation, intellectualization, isolation of emotions, reaction formation, repressing, undoing), "image distorting" (devaluation, idealisation, omnipotence, fantasy, self-image splitting), "disavowal" (denial, projection, rationalisation), and "action" (acting-out and withdrawal).

These clinically observed defense mechanisms are, in fact, the various ways that the conscious mind is able to compartmentalise its participation in, and philosophy of, existence, in order to avoid facing up to the driving force of desire—Conrad's "the horror, the horror" in *The Heart of Darkness*. It is evidence at the clinical level for my central mechanism of existential schizophrenia (a voluntary "splitting of the mind")—which was originally derived from historical observation[23]—and for its breakdown leading to pathological schizophrenia. Individuals experiencing breakdown or malfunction of this mechanism become part of the "schizophrenia spectrum" and cease to participate in the strategic pursuit. They only continue to survive, at least in wealthy countries, because of the protection they receive from family or state.

What does this malfunction in the mechanism of existential schizophrenia consist of? Essentially the voluntary "split" of our instinctual and emotional life from our conscious and rational life becomes involuntary. The normal attempt to manipulate our own perceptions of reality gives way in susceptible individuals operating under sustained pressure to an inability to relate appropriately to reality. Carefully shaped self-delusions are replaced by uncontrollable delusions; conscious manipulation of perceptions is replaced by involuntary hallucinations; and individuals faced with these frightening illusions retreat from the everyday world into themselves to live grossly disorganised lives in which language and other forms of communication break down. Unless these degenerative processes can be reversed, affected individuals will never again participate in the strategic pursuit. What begins with the emergence of psychotic symptoms ends in strategic failure.

Figure 10.1. The Schizo-Spectrum

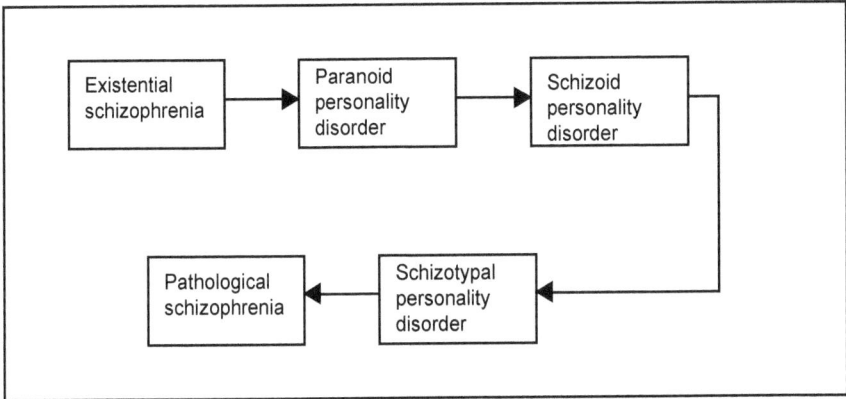

Source: Snooks 2006: 206.

This breakdown in the existential-schizophrenia mechanism forms a spectrum of schizoid states, reflecting increasing psychotic conditions and decreasing strategic involvement. As can be seen in Figure 10.1 my "schizo-spectrum" begins with the normal condition of existential schizophrenia and passes through a number of personality disorders (paranoid, schizoid, schizotypal) until the pathological condition of involuntary schizophrenia is reached. It needs to be emphasised that this schizo-spectrum represents the progression of schizoid states existing in the population, not necessarily in the individual.

In essence, the schizo-spectrum reflects the progressive breakdown of the survival mechanism employed by the selfconscious organism. It witnesses the transformation of strategic integration into strategic fragmentation. This is only possible because of the dual basis of human nature. Strategic dualism in selfconscious life forms, therefore, explains what the evolutionary psychiatrists cannot: why schizophrenia persists in human society despite the fact that the fertility rates of schizophrenics—and hence their ability to pass on their psychotic susceptibility—are much lower, and suicide rates are much higher, than those of normal individuals. While schizoid states are higher amongst individuals in certain families, they keep emerging in previously unaffected families. The irony of existence is that, given the strategic duality of human nature, as a species we can only survive and prosper by continually placing a minority of individuals at risk. *Schizophrenia is the ever-present price we pay to employ the highly beneficial strategic instrument of selfconsciousness.*

Under-active existential schizophrenia

Mental disorders arise not only when the existential-schizophrenia mechanism malfunctions but also when it is under-active. These disorders, however, are of a strategy-challenging rather than a strategy-terminating kind. While they cause considerable pain and discomfort they do not usually prevent an individual participating in the strategic pursuit. These disorders include anxiety and various phobias. They arise because of an individual's inability or refusal to compartmentalise sufficiently the ingredients of his daily existence—of placing what one does and what one thinks one does in different boxes. An under active mechanism, therefore, leads individuals to worry excessively about the things they are driven to do by strategic desire, and about the consequences of their actions. What we widely understand as the human conscience is in reality not some sort of innate or learned moral "voice" but merely the outcome of an under-active existential-schizophrenia mechanism.

Malfunction of strategic control

In a normal person, strategic integration is maintained, despite the dualism of human nature, by the dominant role played by the "unconscious organism". As we have seen, it is the strategist that controls the strategic instrument, rather than the other way around. A variation on the central strategic maxim is: "desire drives and reason facilitates". The physiological reason for the control exercised by the unconscious organism is the greater one-way connectivity between the limbic system and the cortex than the reverse. If, however, this pattern of connectivity were disrupted in the brains of some individuals, then the conscious mind might not only regard itself as the strategist but also have the power to hijack the unconscious organism.

The malfunction of strategic control by the unconscious organism could be the source of a number of mental disorders. These disorders, which arise from the oppression of the body by the mind, include masochism and various eating disorders. In extreme cases it can lead to the mind's destruction of the body through mutilation, starvation, and suicide. We have recently witnessed a resurgence of individuals being persuaded by charismatic leaders to advance their cause by sacrificing their lives. This may take the form of mass suicide among religious sects, terrorist suicide bombings, or suicide missions in wars. Except where individuals are forced into taking this extreme action, they are the outcome of a malfunction of strategic control by the unconscious organism, which is normally driven by strategic desire. In view of these problems associated with the malfunction of strategic control, it is not difficult to see the danger in Joseph LeDoux's (1998) suggestion that, in the future, man can expect to exert greater cortical control over the limbic system. Of course, it should be realised that suicide also occurs in cases of extreme depressive disorder and schizophrenia, which have different origins, when the conscious mind is subject to intense distress.

Breakdown in Strategic Imitation

Another central mechanism in the dynamic-strategy theory is that of "strategic imitation". It is the process of decision-making by which individuals participate in their society's dominant dynamic strategy. As discussed in detail elsewhere, individuals do not employ a rational method to decide what path they should pursue in life in order to survive and prosper.[24] They do not, in other words, employ a benefit–cost framework to calculate how best to employ their time and resources. This would require the collection of a vast amount of information, the construction of abstract mental models of reality, and the rapid and accurate processing of these data. As suggested above, the human mind has not been developed to work in this way.

Instead, the human brain economises on rational intelligence and data collection by merely pursuing the questions: Who and what is successful and why? The vast minority of people—the "strategic followers"—merely identify those—the "strategic pioneers"—who have been successful in the long term and the methods they have employed to achieve their success. The strategic pioneers employ "strategic thinking" rather than rationalist thinking, based on "pattern-recognition information" rather than benefit–cost information. The strategic followers merely imitate the strategic pioneers. This is the mechanism of strategic imitation by which the great majority of individuals are able to participate in their society's strategic pursuit.

Of particular importance in the psychological context are the personal values that contribute to longrun strategic success. The personal values of honesty, truthfulness, responsibility, predictability, even-temperedness, generosity and concern, generally prevail in human society not because of the role of religious or ethical institutions, but because it is the only way to achieve long-term strategic success. They are, in other words, a response to strategic demand. These characteristics, therefore, are "strategic values". Collective activity can only be maintained if the individuals concerned can rely upon one another. Therefore, when a strategic follower asks who is successful and why, he is evaluating not only the material success of the various strategic pioneers but also their "moral" characters. Those with doubtful moral characters are unlikely to be effective role models, because they are unlikely to achieve long-term material success. This can be seen in the regular corporate failures that occur because of the limitless greed and dishonesty of their CEOs, or in the self-destructive outcomes of excessively indulgent popular entertainers.

Equally, those followers who possess doubtful moral characters are unlikely to choose the right strategic role models. It is this deficiency that leads to a breakdown in the strategic-imitation mechanism in some individuals. Instead of imitating reliable pioneers, who are likely to achieve and spawn long-term strategic success, these followers imitate highly doubtful characters, who are bound to achieve and spawn antistrategic and, hence, antisocial failure. Such followers participate not in their society's dynamic strategy but in antistrategic activities (fraud, tax evasion, insider trading, corruption, corporate theft). In addition, these antistrategists develop the antisocial personality characteristics of deceitfulness (repeated lying, use of aliases, con-man techniques), unreliability, aggressiveness, recklessness, and lack of empathy, concern or generosity. This is the basis of antisocial personality disorder.

There are other causes of breakdown in the strategic-imitation mechanism, which generates other mental disorders. These include—as discussed more fully in *The Selfcreating Mind*—dependent personality disorder, obsessive-compulsive personality disorder and catatonic schizophrenic disorder.

Strategic Frustration

While psychotic disorders are an outcome of the malfunctioning mechanisms of human nature—namely a loss of strategic integration—neurotic disorders are largely an outcome of "strategic frustration". By strategic frustration I mean the psychological response of individuals and groups of individuals to persistent barriers raised against their participation in the strategic pursuit. This frustration leads to distressing mood disorders, which are strategy-challenging rather than strategy-terminating. It is the opposite of "strategic satisfaction", which is the balanced state of mind attained by individuals and groups of individuals when they are able to participate successfully in the strategic pursuit.

Strategic frustration arises from problems that can affect entire societies, social groups, and individuals. Essentially, strategic frustration at the societal level, which is an age-old phenomenon, arises from "strategic failure". This can be the outcome of either the failure of strategic leadership—a major problem for advanced societies in the contemporary world—or, as shown in chapter 8, the oppression of small societies by the superpowers of the day; a problem in all times.

The failure of leadership today is due to the obsession of contemporary governments with *deductive* neoclassical economic theory, owing to their loss of strategic perspective—first analysed in my book *The Global Crisis Makers* (2000). The problem is that this theory has lost all contact with reality and has nothing to say about the dynamics of human society. In particular it denies that governments should play a proactive leadership role in market economies. This failure of neoclassical economics to resolve the economic crisis of 2008-09 has led social democrat governments to shift to the other extreme—massive government intervention rationalised by reference to Keynesian economics. The problem for citizens of advanced democratic societies is that while the electorate can change governments that are unable or unwilling to provide strategic leadership, it cannot change strategic policies owing to the fact that *all* major political parties take their advice from orthodox economists. The refusal of governments to provide proper leadership causes strategic frustration throughout society, which ultimately leads electorates to flirt with far-right political parties. This is likely to lead, on the one hand, to "societal neurosis" of the type experienced in interwar Germany (which re-emerges in Europe from time to time) and, on the other, to mood disorders in individuals suffering economic difficulties, such as unemployment and bankruptcy. Similar problems are experienced in small societies dominated by the superpowers of the day— such as Iraq and Afghanistan. They are subjected to strategic failure and, hence, suffer strategic frustration, which in turn leads to the rise of religious fundamentalism, terrorism, and the rise of terrorist "states".

In normal individuals, mood swings involving hypomania and mild depression play an important role in fostering the strategic pursuit. As we have seen, feelings of elation arising from successful strategic participation provide the emotional incentive to continue with past strategies, whereas depressed feelings arising from unsuccessful participation provide the emotional incentive to abandon past strategies and circumstances and to seek out new, more profitable ones. These emotional mechanisms are important, because in their absence, individuals lack the drive and ability to devise and carry out successful plans.

These emotions can only be regarded as disorders if they become extremely intense and persistent to the point where they bear little relationship to their strategic causes. Mood disorders can be found both in the individual and in society. Attention has already been drawn to the persistent and widespread frustration that arises from strategic failure. This lack of leadership, which in contemporary society cannot be rectified by changing governments (owing to the widespread acceptance of neoliberal economics), disrupts society's dynamic strategy and, hence, leads to slow, or negative, economic growth, failed businesses, and increasing unemployment. The widespread frustration that people feel in these circumstances leads to intense and persistent psychological depression throughout society. It should be regarded as a form of societal neurosis.

The second source of depression is the lack of flexibility of some individuals in the face of difficult circumstances. It arises from an inability to respond appropriately to a systematic attack—in the form of denial of promotion, demotion, or redundancy—on one's participation in the strategic pursuit. There are always a number of options open to the frustrated individual. They can fight, submit, withdraw to the periphery, or resign and start anew. Some individuals may not be able to make the appropriate choice that would ease their strategic frustration and, hence, they suffer depressed feelings. For whatever reason, they are unable to respond to this emotional mechanism that provides an incentive to improve their participation in the strategic pursuit.

Viewed through the lens of dynamic-strategy theory, depression is the outcome of being unable, or unwilling, to find an appropriate role in what I have called the "strategic struggle". It is through the strategic struggle that individuals battle to gain control of—at least aspects of—their society's dynamic strategy and, hence, of its sources of wealth and income. The inability to participate in the strategic struggle may lead either to deep and prolonged depression or to the direction of frustration and anger at others (sadism) or oneself (masochism). Sadism is a perverted acting out of the shadow of the power to which the frustrated individual unsuccessfully aspires. It is a form of play-acting in the shadow of the strategic struggle—involving mental, physical, and/or sexual abuse—in order to relieve their frustration. On the other hand, masochism is an acting out of losing the strategic struggle and suffering the (self-inflicted) consequences.

Finally, we should consider the strategic frustration that arises from an inability to adjust one's innate drives to the prevailing dynamic strategy. A heightened sexual drive, for example, is essential to the family-multiplication strategy but not to the mature phase of the technological strategy. Instead of being a pillar of society one may instead be branded as a sexual deviant. Or again, a heightened aggressive drive is essential for the conquest strategy and for war to defend the other strategies, but not for a technological strategy during peacetime. In a non-conquest society in peacetime, the warrior/hero type is likely to be regarded as a dangerous thug. These strategic misfits will always exist in human society, because human nature has been fashioned so that it can respond to the demands of *any* dynamic strategy. In these examples, the strategically frustrated individual, unable to understand why he or she is so out of tune with their society, will lash out at that society (and be regarded as a psychopath), retreat into deep depression, or internalise these instincts and suffer from feelings of guilt and even masochism. It is, once again, the price we pay for our strategic success as a species in an unpredictable world.

A NEW PSYCHOLOGY AND PSYCHIATRY

The dynamic-strategy approach to life and human society provides the foundation for a new psychology. Unlike existing approaches, whether psychoanalytic or Darwinian, strategic psychology attempts to account for mental disorders as the outcome of the dynamics of life. As orthodox theories cannot explain the full range of mental disorders that afflict mankind, their supporters are forced to adopt various *ad hoc* arguments to "explain" each illness. In contrast, the dynamic-strategy theory employed in this book can explain the major psychoses and neuroses as breakdowns in, or inadequate responses to, the strategic mechanisms that make life possible. And it provides the principles of a new psychiatry, which are explored in *The Selfcreating Mind.* Essentially these suggest that strategic disorders can be overcome through the reversal of the process of "strategic malfunction" and the reabsorption of affected individuals and societies back into the strategic pursuit.[25]

Chapter 11
Understanding the Modern *Logos* — Societal Dynamics

Imitation not innovation drives society.

The single most important characteristic of any leading modern society and its underlying strategic *logos,* is its dynamic nature. Therefore, in order to understand modern society, and to ensure that it performs at a desirable level, it is essential to adopt a realist dynamic model. In this chapter I have employed the general dynamic-strategy **theory** presented in earlier chapters, to develop a model specifically for modern societies. I begin by discussing the limitations of orthodox economic theory in analysing modern dynamics, and conclude by outlining the dynamic-strategy **model** derived from my general theory.

THE LIMITATIONS OF ORTHODOX ECONOMICS

There are many issues that can be illuminated by orthodox economics. But only of the marginal (small), short-run, and static kind. What it cannot do is to analyse the big, long-run, dynamic issues. And these are the only issues of critical importance to human society. The bottom line is that orthodox economists have failed to develop a realist general dynamic theory of human society. And without a realist dynamic theory it is impossible not only to resolve the big issues facing human society—such as poverty in the Third World, and global climate change—but also to make any real sense of the current circumstances in relation to recessions, depressions, and financial crises, or to sort out the relationship between issues such as economic growth and inflation. Not surprisingly, policies designed to shape these matters have become a matter of faith rather than science. In this section of the chapter, therefore, a range of misconceptions by orthodox economics will be briefly reviewed, before outlining a realist approach to societal dynamics that affords a more rational and effective approach to economic policy.

On Economic Growth

Economic growth is not an escalator carrying consumers ever upward. While this truth will appear to be obvious to those with any understanding of history, it has been overlooked by many younger economists trained in the neoclassical tradition. The Australian economy, for example, has grown in a rapid and sustained fashion for the past generation, which is a time frame longer than the working lives of many younger economists. As these practitioners have been schooled in neoclassical growth theory, which is concerned with a smooth upwardly directed equilibrium pathway, and as these days they are not taught any economic history, they have come to believe that modern economic growth (and they know no other) always proceeds positively and continuously. Hence, when faced with the prospect of even brief economic townturn or recession, they regard the situation as abnormal, even unprecedented.

Modern economic growth occurs in a fluctuating manner. This cannot be avoided, and should not be regarded as abnormal. The role of policy is not to prevent regular ephemeral downturns, as these are the outcome of dynamic exhaustion resulting from a successfully exploited dynamic strategy/ substrategy/strategic project. The role of policy is twofold: to minimise the impact of the ephemeral downturn on the most vulnerable groups in society; and to facilitate a rapid transition from an exhausted (or exhausting) to a new and vital dynamic strategy. In other words, the public budget should be spent on "strategic policy", rather than the traditional counter-cyclical policy.

Keynesian counter-cyclical policy, which became fashionable (by default) again in the 2008/09 financial "crisis", is merely ephemeral in its impact. While government expenditure will have a multiplied effect (over and above the initial expenditure, provided it is spent and not saved), this effect is of limited duration and soon seeps away, requiring further government expenditures. This cycle of multiplied expenditure and economic seepage, will continue until the budget is exhausted, unless a new dynamic strategy is embarked upon. The fatal flaw in Keynes' *General Theory of Employment, Interest and Money* (1936) is, as I show in *Longrun Dynamics* (1998b), that it has no encompassing general **dynamic** theory.[1]

Keynesian counter-cyclical policy is a bootstraps approach to recovery, and in the end it will fail, just as the Roosevelt "New Deal" failed to generate economic recovery in the USA during the 1930s. Had the Second World War not occurred, it seems highly likely that America would have plunged back into depression in the late-1930s and early-1940s. America's problem was that its earlier dynamic substrategy of supplying an expanding internal mega-market with industrial products had been exhausted by the *mid*-1920s, and until it was able to reorient itself from the internal to the world market—which was achieved through world war and the Marshall Plan—no amount of pump-priming would generate sustained recovery. Truman's Marshall Plan, unlike Roosevelt's New Deal, was a highly effective **strategic** policy.

On Recessions, Depressions, and Financial Crises

Recessions and depressions are not caused by panic on the floor of the stock exchange or by the greed and incompetence of finance managers. This truth is less obvious, but no less important, than that about economic growth, because its establishment requires more that systematic observation. It requires careful historical reconstruction and theory building.

Wall Street crash 1929

The "evidence" referred to by orthodox economists, when claiming that real economic crises originating on the stock market and in the financial sector cause economic recessions and depressions, is the 1929 Wall Street crash. This— to paraphrase William Cunningham's 1892 attack in the *Economic Journal* on Alfred Marshall's methodology—amounts to a "perversion of economic history". The conventional "wisdom" among orthodox economists is that the excessive speculation, panic by traders, and collapse of stock-market prices was the prime cause of the Great Depression in America. In fact, as I show in *The Ephemeral Civilization* (1997), causation ran in the reverse direction.[2] The Great Depression was the outcome of the exhaustion, as early as the *mid*-twenties, of the American dynamic strategy of the previous half-century. This strategy involved basing their industrialisation process on an expanding internal mega-market, protected from cheaper European imports by an extensive system of tariffs. When the internal market ceased growing geographically—when the expanding western frontier was finally closed around 1890—American strategists expanded their sales by introducing new techniques of mass production and distribution. But even this source of economic growth had been exhausted by 1925. The depression in America, therefore, was the outcome of the collapse of the long wave of economic growth that had gained its energy from an expanding domestic mega-market. The reason the depression was a protracted affair in America, was because of the difficulty of developing a new dynamic strategy, whereby the USA ultimately became the workshop of the world. As suggested above, this was finally achieved with the assistance of world war and the Marshall Plan.

In order to continue receiving high returns, American capitalists increasingly shifted their funds from productive to speculative activities. In the process, speculation became the ocean rather than the bubble—to employ a Keynesian metaphor—and the stock market crashed once the majority of speculators finally realised that the situation was unsustainable. This only occurred *after* the real economy, which had been declining since the mid twenties, turned down sharply at the end of the decade. Owing to the precarious structure of the international economy generated by the consequences of the Versailles peace treaty (in which the USA played a leading part) following the First World War, America's strategically determined depression spread rapidly around the world.

East Asian "crisis" 1998

Recessions and depressions, therefore, are outcomes of exhausting dynamic substrategies and strategic projects. The activities of stock market or property speculators and undisciplined finance managers are merely a speculative response to dynamic changes in the real economy. Some economists have a vague supply-side model of the way a struggling financial sector impacts on the real economy via a "contagion" or "disease", which is supposed to spread from the institutional periphery to the real core of the economy. This can be seen in the way economists attempted to extrapolate the temporary financial difficulties in East Asia to the world in the late 1990s. Meetings of the G7 and G22 countries (as they were called) in 1998 were preoccupied with discussions about how to prevent the "East Asian meltdown" causing a global economic crisis. In effect, the agendas of these meetings were hijacked by those people who were involved in the East-Asian speculation and were seeking government protection. Here is what I said at the time in my book *The Global Crisis Makers* (2000)[3]

Some Myths about the [1998] Global "Crisis"

Myth The global economy is on the verge of a crisis of its own making.

Reality The apparent "crisis" to which the neoliberals refer is in reality just part of the normal dynamic process of strategic exploitation and exhaustion experienced by a number of nations in the global community...

Myth The current global "crisis" is the outcome of financial problems in East Asia that have their origins in the corruption and cronyism of political leaders, financiers, and wealthy businessmen. It is a crisis that can only be resolved by financial, political, and moral reform.

Reality Financial problems in East Asia are an outcome of the exhaustion or derailment of the dynamic strategies of the countries involved. They are, in other words, the result rather than the cause of real economic problems. Recovery in these countries will only occur when new dynamic strategies replace the old exhausted ones, or where derailed strategies are put back on track. Financial, political, and "moral" difficulties will resolve themselves as institutions respond to this strategic revitalisation rather than to neoliberal intervention.

Myth The present global "crisis" is an Asian crisis. It is the outcome of the "East Asian meltdown".

Reality There is no "East Asian meltdown, just as earlier there was no "East Asian miracle". The mythical sequence of "miracle" and "meltdown" is merely the normal process by which dynamic strategies are exploited until they are finally exhausted. After a hiatus—popularly known as a recession/depression—a new strategy will emerge. Each of these aspects of the dynamic process is a new wonder only to an intellectual discipline that has no general dynamic theory.

Myth World leaders and their economic advisors are deeply concerned about the global crisis.

Reality Recent (1998) meetings of the G7 and G22 countries to discuss the global "crisis" were hijacked by representatives of the "global gamblers" and their backers, the "global casino financiers". The global gamblers are those individuals and groups that are speculating in the currencies and paper assets of East Asia. Through their neoliberal supporters they have succeeded in persuading world leaders that a *real* global recession/depression is about to occur. It is not surprising to discover that President Clinton's main economic advisors are former money-market participants (Alan Greenspan and Robert Rubin) and his favourite economic authors are successful market speculators (George Soros). What is the motivation of the global gamblers? Narrow self interest. If the speculative boom bursts the global gamblers will be ruined…

Myth   There will be a spillover from the east Asian "meltdown" to the rest of the world, probably extending into the new millennium.

Reality As the downturn in East Asia is, it will be shown, a normal outcome of the pursuit of a successful dynamic strategy, there will be no spillover into the rest of the world…

As we know with hindsight, East Asia did not slip into a long and deep depression, but recovered quickly and strongly as, on the basis of the dynamic-strategy theory, I claimed it would; there was no spillover to the global economy and, as I predicted in the face of orthodox opinion, there was no global crisis; and the financial "crisis" did not bring down international financial institutions. While there was never going to be a global economic crisis, this did not stop the market economists claiming credit where none was due. As I said at the time:[4]

> Probably the most remarkable example of neoliberal hagiography is a front page article in *The Times* (15 February 1999) on Alan Greenspan (chairman of the US Federal Reserve), Robert Rubin (secretary of the US Treasury), and Larry Summers (deputy secretary of the US Treasury), entitled "The Committee to Save the World". This article paints a glowing picture of three white knights who, through their financial interventions (a central neoliberal inconsistency) at the national and global levels, have been successful in "saving the world" from collapse. We are told with bated breath that these three men from the worlds of finance and academia, who have "outgrown ideology" despite their "faith in markets" (another inconsistency), are not only "inventing a 21st century financial system" but are single-handedly responsible for "fighting off one collapse after another" and preventing "a near thing becoming a disaster". This has been due to their "intellectual honesty" and their success in "defending their economic policy from political meddling". This is no less than the "great (neoliberal) man" view of history.

Only a decade later, with the emergence of another panic among the global gamblers, was this evaluation revised. At that time, Greenspan was blamed for **not** inventing a twenty-first-century financial system that could forever abolish financial crises. Even the ex-Federal Reserve chief has admitted to Congress (in October 2008) that: "I made a mistake in presuming that self-interest of organisations, specifically banks and others, was such that they were best capable of protecting their own shareholders and equity... I was partially wrong ... in the regulation of derivatives... we were wrong quite a good deal of the time". But, of course, at the time, Greenspan helped to shore up the global casino. In early 2009 it was the turn of a new generation of market economists and neoliberal academics in the US treasury and Federal Reserve to pretend they understood the dynamics of the global economy. Needless to say, despite their self-serving rhetoric to the contrary, they were no more insightful, or in control, than their predecessors.

Global financial crisis 2007–08

We need a new approach to recessions, depressions and financial crises. The dynamic-strategy theory suggests that the so-called Global Financial Crisis (GFC) of 2007/08 had similar economic origins to the Wall Street crash of 1929. The GFC was an institutional response to the exhaustion of the dynamic substrategy pursued by the USA during the second half of the twentieth century. During this period, the USA had become the workshop of the world, which in turn generated the wealth and political influence that enabled it to become a major world power. But like all dynamic substrategies, this one was exhausted after about 50-60 years (by the first decade of the twenty-first century) owing to growing competition both from a re-energised Europe and a rapidly industrialising Asia. This process of strategic exhaustion was exacerbated by the inflation-targeting policies of governments and RBA, which damaged the underlying dynamic mechanism and blocked the emergence of a new dynamic substrategy (see below).

Owing to the declining investment opportunities in the US real economy, financial institutions, fuelled by increasingly abundant funds from China, redirected financial resources into more speculative activities, particularly the US housing market. As always happens in the wake of strategic exhaustion, financial institutions with over-abundant funds dramatically reduce their lending standards. By 2007, mortgages were routinely and knowingly granted to individuals with low incomes and poor credit histories—the so-called "sub-prime" mortgages. This generated an unsustainable speculative bubble in the US housing market.

For anyone with a sound understanding of history, the economic outcome was predictable. In mid-2007, two funds associated with the US financial company Bear Sterns announced major problems with their holdings of mortgage-backed securities. This warning signal sparked panic throughout the US financial sector, which in turn led to a contraction of credit, a rise in interest rates, and a malfunction in the operation of the credit market. In March 2008, a collapsing Bear Stearns was only saved by a rescue mission led by J.P. Morgan; in September 2008 the major US securities company Lehman Brothers was declared bankrupt; and at the same time the US Government decided (quite inappropriately) to bail out the large insurance company AIG together with two major mortgage agencies Fannie Mae and Freddie Mac (whose names aptly reflect their flippant attitude to financial operations).

These financial collapses in the US generated the usual panic reaction throughout the global financial system. But unlike the early 1930s, when Europe was still struggling with the economic aftermath of the First World War, the international economy in 2009 was far more robust. In particular, international financial markets were relatively sound compared with the 1930s, and the giant Chinese economy continued to power ahead, even if at a slightly slower rate. This, more than the response of world governments and central banks—which reduced interest rates, guaranteed bank solvency and deposits, and implemented sizable fiscal policies—was responsible for ensuring the world's real economy experienced only a short, if sharp, recession, rather than another great depression. Interestingly, Australia continued to grow impressively throughout this period, not because of the Keynesian policies of the Rudd Government (which were irresponsibly and wastefully conducted by politicians with little understanding of economics), but because of the stimulating impact of the rapidly growing Chinese economy on Australia's mining sector.

Strategic not Keynesian or monetary policies

As my dynamic-strategy theory (as well as a study of history) shows, Keynesian policies will be ephemeral in their impact on the real economy. Once the stimulus of government expenditure ceases—which it must, due to budget realities—so too does the recovery. As the recession/depression is the outcome of the exhaustion of the old substrategy, a sustained recovery will only occur once a new substrategy has taken its place. What is required from governments, therefore, are **strategic** not Keynesian—dynamic not static—policies involving investment in the infrastructure of strategic knowledge and technology in order to encourage the emergence of new dynamic substrategies. This is what happened in the US after the Second World War (owing to the Marshall Plan), and appears to be happening in the second decade of the twenty-first century owing to a strategic resurgence in the US and to the resumption of growth in the developed world. The so-called GFC, therefore, was both caused and resolved by the strategic dynamic mechanism, not independently by financial (i.e. institutional) factors. Financial factors merely responded to strategic forces.

Hence, in the face of orthodox confusion about the cause and consequences of economic and financial crises, it needs to be emphasised that *the real economy is driven by demand-side forces rather than supply-side institutions.* In sophisticated societies, any supply-side restriction is quickly resolved through innovation responding to strategic inflation. Accordingly, when the economic problem confronting us is the outcome of strategic exhaustion (a demand-side phenomenon)—which it usually is—then neither the monetary (supply-side) nor pump-priming (Keynesian expenditures) measures adopted in the West in 2008/09 will help at all. Just as they were unable to help during the Great

Depression. What is required are strategic policies aimed at facilitating the emergence of a new dynamic substrategy.

On Societal Confidence

The societal confidence that matters is not confidence among speculators on the stock exchange—the global casino—or even confidence among players in the financial sector, but confidence of the entire community in the strategic pursuit. This fundamental form of confidence—"strategic confidence"—is generated by the successful unfolding of a society's dynamic strategy and the material prosperity it brings. As will be shown theoretically in the next section, strategic confidence is the force that binds society together, whereas its absence causes society to fly apart.

A successful dynamic strategy spins an effective network of competitive and cooperative relationships, together with all the rules and organisations required to facilitate the strategic pursuit. As I show in chapter 4, individuals involved in societal transactions relate directly to the successful strategy (via its material outcomes), and only indirectly to each other. By this I mean that trust is a product of confidence in the wider dynamic strategy in which all society's members are involved, rather than confidence in other individuals or institutions. Trust, in other words, is derived from strategic confidence. Once a previously dominant dynamic strategy has been exhausted and cannot be immediately replaced, strategic confidence declines and, in extreme cases, evaporates completely. And as strategic confidence declines, so too does trust and cooperation. Strategic confidence is communicated directly to individuals in human society by the rise and fall of material standards of living.

Accordingly, fundamental confidence in financial institutions is a derived function of strategic confidence. Even the greed and incompetence of finance managers will have only a superficial and ephemeral impact on confidence in this sector if the strategic situation of society is sound. Certainly, these forces will have no impact on strategic confidence. Hence, if the strategic pursuit is viable, any independent financial misfortunes, such as those at the end of 2008, will be superficial and ephemeral. The correct policy conclusion, therefore, is that it is unnecessary, indeed a waste of time and public money, to attempt to bolster confidence in the financial sector by making grand statements about unlimited government guarantees concerning bank deposits, distributing large sums of taxpayers' money to failed financial institutions, and/or large-scale Keynesian pump-priming. In any case, central banks already possess the power of lender in the last resort, which is enough to protect depositors' funds without distorting markets. Also, investing public funds in failing institutions merely serves to distribute taxpayers' money to those who created the problem in the first place. It is fairer and less distorting to directly assist those borrowers/lenders who have suffered, through no fault of their own, at the hands of the unscrupulous. Current economic policy is a hugely costly trial-and-error procedure owing to the deficiencies of orthodox economics.

On the Role of Inflation

Inflation is widely viewed as a pernicious influence in the economy, at least until the spectre of deflation raises its head. The truth is that there are two broad types of inflation: "good" or strategic inflation; and "bad" or nonstrategic inflation. As shown in the next section—where I discuss the "growth-inflation curve"[5] that I first published in 1997—strategic inflation is the interface between a changing strategic demand and the supply response.

Strategic inflation, which provides the necessary signals and pressures to elicit the appropriate supply response to changes in strategic demand, is the inevitable outcome of a successfully unfolding dynamic strategy. It reflects the challenges that the unfolding dynamic strategy poses for the host society. Suppressing strategic inflation through the misconceived policy of inflation targeting distorts the strategic demand-response mechanism and applies the brakes to the strategic pursuit. When inflation targeting is pursued thoroughly and relentlessly for a longish (a decade or so) period of time, economic growth grinds to a standstill. Further, this policy is totally unnecessary as no viable strategic economy has ever experienced runaway or hyperinflation, as I show in Snooks (1993a, 1994a, 1996, 1997, 1998b) . Hyperinflation is the outcome of a failed strategic society, such as the Weimar Republic in the 1920s (owing to massive war reparations) and Zimbabwe in the 2000s (owing to political mismanagement). This is borne out by my studies of the growth-inflation curve.

Why has the policy of inflation targeting been pursued so relentlessly since the early 1990s, particularly as it has no theoretical or empirical justification? It would appear that most orthodox economists and policy makers have an irrational fear of inflation, even though no viable strategic society has ever experienced hyper-inflation. It is part of the age-old existential anxiety that humans experience in the face of change. The focus on equilibrium in orthodox economics is part of the ancient desire for balance and order that was discussed in chapter 8 on the ideology of the strategic *logos.*

The Western World has been pursuing the policy of inflation targeting for the past generation, despite the absence of a dynamic theory that can justify it. Although there are political difficulties preventing this pursuit being both thorough and relentless—the widely accepted inflation target has gradually risen from zero in the early 1990s to around 2 to 3 % pa today, without any change in the underlying theoretical argument—Western governments have been determined to constrain inflation. For the past two decades I have been warning that this will cause economic problems in the longer term by distorting the core dynamic mechanism of the strategic *logos.*[6] And those economic problems did eventually emerge. As argued above, while the problems experienced during the period from 2007 to 2009 were caused by strategic exhaustion in the USA, they were aggravated by inflation targeting throughout the West. Amongst the great powers, only China, which did not embrace inflation-targeting, escaped the downturn misleadingly known as the GFC. If we wish to experience sustained growth and prosperity and avoid periodic stagnation in the future, it will be essential to abandon the misconceived, theory-free policy of inflation-targeting.

Yet we do need to keep a watchful eye on nonstrategic or "bad" inflation. This is the inflation that arises from exogenous shocks (such as the sudden increase in oil prices in the 1970s), from inappropriate monetary (excessive reductions in interest rates or excessive increases in funds for lending) and fiscal (unnecessary pump-priming) policies, and from the action of monopolists.

Curiously, the existing orthodox position is to suppress good (strategic) inflation through inflation targeting, and to promote bad (nonstrategic) inflation through inappropriate monetary and fiscal policies. Clearly governments and central banks need to abandon the compulsion to intervene in complex dynamic processes if they insist on employing an orthodox economics devoid of dynamic theory.

On "Regulating Capitalism"

The combination of fear of the future, compulsion to intervene in matters we don't understand, and misplaced hubris in our ability to do so is generating a dangerous situation. Many social scientists, including those with training in orthodox economics, believe that modern capitalism is running out of control. These are the "naive institutionalists", who have political influence with the new interventionist "social democrats" such as Barack Obama and his fellow travellers in the USA and Kevin Rudd and his successors in Australia. They also believe their knowledge of human institutions gives them special insights into reshaping modern capitalism, despite having no understanding of the dynamics of human society or of the strategic *logos*. This can be done, they claim, by establishing a range of behavioural rules, which will redirect decision makers throughout capitalism. It has not occurred to them that human civilisation has managed without the presence of reforming institutionalists for the past 11,000 years, with even modern society flourishing unaided for the past couple of centuries. The truth is that the only danger human society faces is from interventionists determined to bend it to their will. The dangerous impact of determined and powerful "experts" can be seen in the case of the USSR, a tightly regulated system that collapsed after merely seventy years under the influence of the "metaphysical (non-empirical) interventionists".

But interventionists, uninformed about the dynamics of human society, fail not only in the big things but even in the little things, such as the various attempts in the last quarter of 2008 to "fix" the GFC. Governments around the world, who are advised by doctrinaire "experts", attempted to rescue their financial institutions by injections of large quantities of tax-payers' money, and by giving grandiose guarantees of unlimited protection to bank deposits. The large-scale injection of taxpayers' funds into failing financial institutions around the world has helped to distort the dynamic mechanisms of these countries. It has also led to the partial nationalisation of financial institutions, which is unlikely to increase either their efficiency or ethics. And it has unfairly distributed taxpayers' funds to excessively greedy and incompetent finance managers. It would have been better from this standpoint to allow the business of failing institutions to be taken up by more progressive corporations, as normally occurs, and to directly assist innocent consumers. There is a great deal of political grandstanding underlying these actions, which have been undertaken by ambitious but uninformed individuals—the new interventionists"[7]— attempting either to project their image on to the world stage or compensate for their feelings of inadequacies. What they should have done, was to invest in reviving the dynamic strategies of affected countries by providing the basic infrastructure for new technological change.

More worrying is the growing threat of the truly massive intervention that will be required to comprehensively implement climate-change mitigation programs of the type being demanded by the IPCC. Such programs, as discussed in the final chapter, will require the development of centrally determined mitigation economies throughout the world. Rather than being the "saviours of capitalism" these politicians are really the "new global crisis makers", as they will distort the dynamic mechanism and even derail the strategic *logos.*

A NEW REALIST DYNAMICS FOR THE MODERN WORLD

While the dynamic-strategy theory has been discussed in a more general way in the context of all living systems in chapter 4—the "engine of life"—in this chapter it is reformulated in a more specific way to make it applicable to modern advanced economies and to current economic policy. Some repetition, which will be kept to a strict minimum, is unavoidable. To understand the patterns of societal dynamics—including recessions, depressions, and financial crises— for today's advanced economies, we require a new dynamic model. The old models, unlike the dynamic patterns, tell a story only of selective comparative statics. The dynamic-strategy model, which has been developed in a long series of books,[8] is outlined by focusing on its central features: the driving force; the dynamic mechanism; strategic demand and strategic confidence; the strategic demand-response mechanism; and strategic leadership in the strategic *logos.*

The Driving Force

The endogenous driving force in the strategic *logos* is the competitive struggle of "materialist man" to survive and prosper. This is the major outcome of our biologically determined motivation, or "strategic desire", that has been shaped by genetic change over almost 4,000 million years (myrs). In the dynamic-strategy model, as in life, ideas are an effective way of achieving our desires, but they do so in a passive way. In the longrun, as we will see, effective ideas respond to "strategic demand". Two major implications emerge from this reality: altruism is not a prime determinant of human behaviour; and the decision-making process is not dominated by neoclassical rationality. The origin, evolution, and nature of strategic desire and human nature have been explored in considerable depth in my earlier book *The Selfcreating Mind* (2006).

If ideas do not drive society, but merely facilitate the desires of its members, we need to replace the neoclassical rationality model of decision-making with a realist model. Through the inductive method it is possible to derive such a model, which I have called the "strategic-imitation model".[9] In reality, decision-making is based on the need to economise on nature's scarcest resource—intelligence. Rather than collect vast quantities of information on a large range of alternatives for processing through a mental model of the way the world works, the great majority of decision-makers—the "strategic followers"—merely imitate those innovative people ("strategic pioneers") and projects that are conspicuously successful. The only information they require is that necessary to answer the key questions: Who and what is materially successful and why? Hence, the basic information required by decision-makers is the relatively inexpensive "imitative information", not the prohibitively expensive benefit-cost information. Even the leading decision-makers—the strategic pioneers—do not employ rationalist techniques when seeking new ways of exploiting strategic opportunities. Rather than exhaustively seeking out the best investment projects, they *believe* their investment projects are best. It is the market that adjudicates.

The Dynamic Mechanism

The endogenous driving force of strategic desire is a self-starting and self-sustaining force that drives a dynamic mechanism, which has at its centre the "strategic pursuit"—the pursuit of a dominant dynamic strategy. It is through the strategic pursuit that the objective of survival and prosperity is achieved. This dynamic strategy begins as an individual or family activity which, if successful, is adopted by wider social groups, at first local, then regional, and, finally, national. This takes place through the mechanism of strategic imitation, whereby successful pioneering initiatives are imitated by a growing number of individuals and groups. In this way, a successful dynamic strategy becomes the focus of political policies controlled by ruling strategists, or "strategic leaders". The role of "strategic leadership" is discussed below.

The choice of dynamic strategy—from the four possibilities of family-multiplication (procreation *and* migration), conquest, commerce, and technological change—depends on the underlying economic conditions, such as factor endowments and the nature of external competition. It is a choice made by strategists who invest time and resources in alternative dynamic strategies. The important point to realise is that investment in these various strategies is undertaken for the same objective—survival and prosperity—and involves a broadly similar process, which is the strategic pursuit. In each case the outcome of strategic success is economic growth. (Orthodox economists hold the mistaken view that economic growth can only be achieved through technological change.) The main difference is that investment in family-multiplication, conquest, and commerce is undertaken in order to achieve economic growth by gaining control of new *external* resources, while technological change is used to achieve economic growth by effecting greater efficiency in the use of existing *internal* resources. As far as the strategist is concerned—in contrast to the orthodox economist—there is nothing special about technological change. After all, Roman economic growth over a period of 1,000 years was generated knowingly through the systematic pursuit of conquest, not technological change. Roman innovation was focused on military machinery and civil engineering. Technological change, like the other three dynamic strategies, is just an instrument in the more general strategic pursuit. Similarly, within the context of a particular dynamic strategy, strategists attempt to gain a competitive advantage through the adoption of new substrategies that, where successful, generate new "technological styles".

As individuals and governments seek to exploit their physical and societal environments, setting in train a mass movement orchestrated through strategic imitation, the dominant dynamic strategy unfolds. Unfolds in the sense that its material opportunities are progressively exploited and, finally, exhausted. And it is this unfolding dynamic strategy (or substrategy) that shapes the expectations of decision-makers. The eventual exhaustion of a dynamic strategy is the outcome of the "law of diminishing *strategic* returns", whereby the revenue and costs of *strategies* rather than factors of production are finally equated.[10] The resulting "rise and fall" of dynamic strategies and substrategies traces out a distinctive wave-like pathway, which provides the dynamic form for this model discussed below. This supersedes the arbitrary dynamic forms— the equilibrium growth path and the bifurcated pathways—adopted by **supply-side** neoclassical, evolutionary, and complexity growth theorists. A meaningful dynamic form cannot be deduced logically from supply-side assumptions about society. It is an existential concept, not an optimising concept.

Strategic Demand and Strategic Confidence

The unfolding dynamic strategy, driven by the competitive energy of strategic desire ("materialist man"), plays a central role in the dynamic-strategy model. Not only does it provide the model with a realistic dynamic form, but it gives rise to two new concepts in economics—"strategic confidence" and "strategic demand". These concepts explain not only the dynamics of long-run investment and saving that are left hanging in orthodox comparative-static macroeconomics, but also how "dynamic order" (usually called spontaneous order) is generated. It is the exploration of the **demand side** of dynamics that makes the dynamic-strategy theory unique in a world of supply-side theories, not only in economics and the other social sciences, but also in biology and physics (Snooks 2008a).

"Strategic confidence", which rises and falls with the dominant dynamic strategy and its various substrategies, explains the changing investment climate in the strategic *logos*. It provides, for example, a dynamic explanation for Keynes' "state of long-term expectation". Accordingly it plays a central role in determining the willingness of strategists to invest, because of its influence on the longrun expected rate of return, and in the creation of dynamic order (through encouraging cooperation and an orderly institutional structure). Confidence and expectations rise as the dynamic strategy unfolds, and they decline, stagnate, and may even collapse as it is progressively exhausted. Strategic confidence also binds society together.

"Strategic demand" also waxes and wanes with the dominant dynamic strategy or substrategy. It comprises the effective demand exercised by decision-makers for a wide range of physical, intellectual, and institutional inputs required in the strategic pursuit. In exploiting expanding strategic opportunities, entrepreneurs need to invest in new infrastructure; to purchase intermediate goods and services; to employ labour skills; to acquire, renovate, or construct the necessary buildings, machinery, and equipment; to engage professional expertise; and to develop new facilitating social rules and organisations. Strategic demand, therefore, is the central active principle in our **demand-side** model. Naturally the supply responses—of population change, capital formation, technological change, and institutional transformation—which are influenced by changes in relative prices, will contribute to the way in which strategic opportunities are exploited; but they do so passively. This concept turns Say's Law—which was accepted explicitly by the classical economists and implicitly by neoclassical economists—on its head. In the strategic *logos*, dynamic demand creates its own supply.

The Strategic Demand-Supply Response

With the dynamic-strategy model we can shift focus from comparative-static macroeconomics to longrun dynamics by considering the interaction between strategic demand and the response of the supply-side variables. It is this interaction that causes the dynamic strategy to unfold and, hence, gives rise to the dynamic form of our model, and to the dynamic role played by *strategic* inflation in facilitating the supply response.

"Strategic inflation" is the widespread increase in prices resulting from the pressure of strategic demand on resources, commodities, and ideas. With the introduction of a new dynamic strategy/substrategy, the resulting expansion of strategic demand will lead to an increase in prices of key inputs, but will not generate strategic inflation until the new strategy exerts widespread influence throughout a given society. Economic growth of a traditional and unadventurous (that is, "nonstrategic") kind that occurs within the context of known and available resources (such as in Australia during the first decade of the twenty-first century), may not lead to much inflation at all. But this nonstrategic growth will not last for long. "Nonstrategic inflation", on the other hand, is the increase of prices resulting from errors in monetary policy and the action of monopolies in either factor or commodity markets at home and abroad.

Herein reside the major differences between strategic theory and orthodox theory. In neoclassical economics the supply side is, by default, treated as the active force in society (supply creates its own demand), which has no place for strategic inflation; while in Keynesian economics the supply-side variables are merely assumed to be given, and "effective demand" is a comparative-static, national-accounting concept. By contrast, in the dynamic-strategy model, strategic demand provides the active force to which the supply-side variables respond according to their supply costs. Strategic inflation, which provides the incentive system in this strategic demand-response mechanism, is a stable, non-accelerating function of economic growth. This theoretical relationship can be (and has been) estimated in the form of the "growth-inflation curve" over all timeframes—including the very long-run (past 1,000 years), the long-run (past 100 years), and short-run (1960s–1990s). These growth-inflation curves, which are estimated and discussed in my 1998 book *Longrun Dynamics*[11], were inspired by my study of the relationship between prices, GDP, and GDP per capita for England over the millennial period of 1000 to 2000 AD (see Figure 7.1 above).

Figure 11.1. The Very Long-Run Growth-Inflation Curve, Britain, 1370–1994

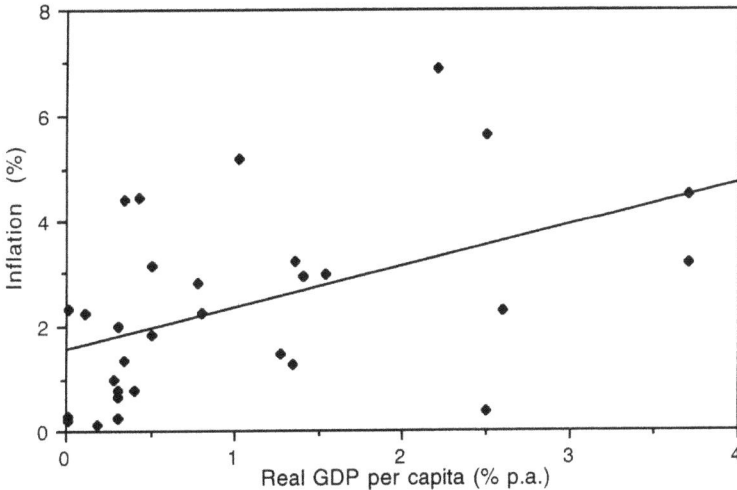

Note: Only positive values used.
Source: Snooks 1998b: 152.

Figure 11.2. The Long-Run Growth-Inflation Curve, Britain, 1870–1994

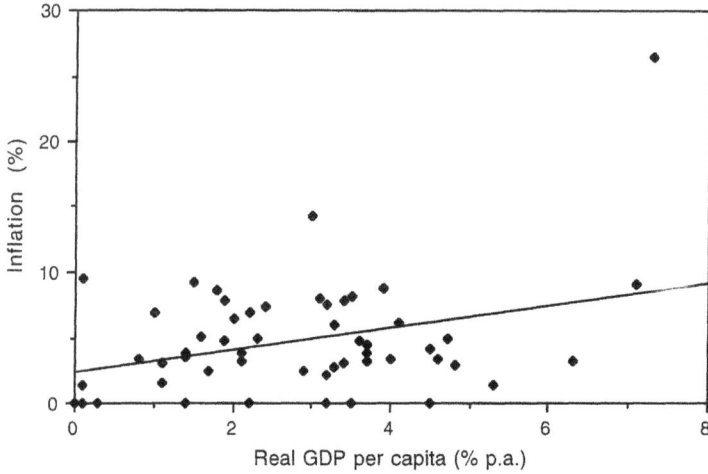

Source: Snooks 1998b: 154.

Figure 11.3. The Short-Run Growth-Inflation Curve, OECD Countries, Weighted Averages for 1950–70 and 1983–94

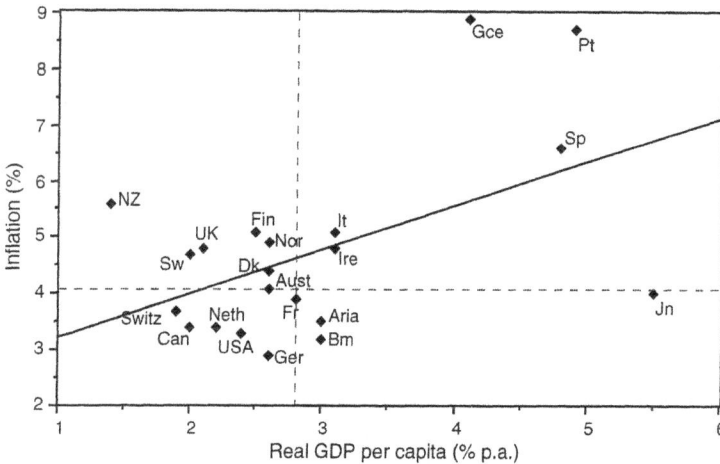

Source: Snooks 1998b: 155.

Figures 11.1 to 11.3 present the very long-run, long-run, and short-run growth-inflation curves that I first estimated in 1996. As can be seen, over all three timeframes, economic growth is highly correlated with strategic inflation. In other words, sustained economic growth is facilitated by strategic inflation. Further, as these estimated results suggest, and as the dynamic-strategy model explains, inflation targeting, where this constrains strategic inflation (as it invariably does), acts as a brake on the unfolding dynamic strategy. To eliminate strategic inflation in the longrun is to eliminate economic growth. This important dynamic relationship continues to be overlooked by a discipline preoccupied with equilibrium. As the old folk song aptly asks: "when will they ever learn; when will they ever learn?"

Population, labour supply, capital formation, and technological and institutional ideas all respond to the unfolding dynamic strategy. Changes in these supply-side variables, both in terms of composition and growth rates, are a function of changing strategic opportunities. These variables expand and become more complex as the dominant dynamic strategy is exploited; and they stagnate, decline, and lose purpose as the dynamic strategy is progressively exhausted and marginal *strategic* returns decline. Rapidly rising and falling prices form the catalyst for these dynamic developments. Naturally, supply-side costs play a role in shaping the strategic response, but this is a passive rather than an active role. Difficulties of supply are met by substitution of other resources and/or by innovation. In this way the supply-side variables are treated endogenously in the dynamic-strategy model. To repeat, *dynamic demand creates its own supply.*

The key relationship between the "strategic outcome" of survival and prosperity and the "strategic instruments" by which it is achieved—the supply response—is described by a relatively new concept, which I first introduced in my book *Global Transition* (1999) on the theory of economic development, called the "strategy function". While this function is formally established in the next chapter (12), it is briefly introduced here, as it is relevant to "leading" as well as "following" countries. As shown in Figure 12.1 (next chapter), the strategy function, which consists of a series of non-intersecting curves, shows how strategic instruments—natural resources, technology, institutions, organisations, strategic ideas, and strategic leadership—can be substituted one for the others to maintain the level of a given strategic outcome. This substitution of strategic instruments is facilitated by the changing relative prices (which feed into strategic inflation) in response to strategic demand as the dynamic strategy unfolds.

The Role of Strategic Leadership

Strategic leadership, which is also a response to strategic demand, is essential to the survival and prosperity of human society. It was the primary reason for the emergence of government at the dawn of civilisation and for its extension and maintenance ever since. Basically it involves facilitating the objectives of society's dynamic strategists by coordinating their efforts, directly through government directives and incentives, and indirectly through cultural institutions such as religion, ideology, and the arts. In particular the strategic state provides basic infrastructure required by the unfolding dynamic strategy that is beyond the risk threshold and financial resources of individuals and corporations; it negotiates political and commercial deals with other societies; it protects the dynamic strategy at home and abroad; it encourages the emergence of new strategies during recessions/depressions; and it provides basic facilities for education, training, and research required to nourish the long-term health of the prevailing dynamic strategy, whether it be conquest, commerce, or technological change. This is a proactive rather than a passive role, and it is undertaken by the representatives of the strategists for the benefit of the strategists.[12] But at the same time, it is not a response to the fantasies of the "metaphysical interventionists"—such as radical climate mitigationists—which will merely subvert the strategic pursuit and lead to serious economic problems or even societal collapse (as in the USSR).

It is important to realise that the strategists do not necessarily encompass the entire population of a society. They include only those individuals who invest in the dominant dynamic strategy, either in physical or human-capital terms. The proportion of the population that can be classified as being among the strategists has varied throughout human history, not in a linear but in a circular way.[13] In Palaeolithic (hunter-gatherer) society, almost 100 percent of adult members were actively involved in the family-multiplication strategy (for example, Aboriginal Australia). Hence, family and tribal leaders had to take into consideration the aspirations of all adults. By contrast, in "neolithic" (agricultural) societies, only a small proportion of the population was actively engaged in the strategic pursuit, while the great majority were nonstrategists, being effectively deprived of their liberty by the ruling elite. The proportion of strategists in the population ranged from less than 1 percent in conquest societies (for example, Anglo-Norman England) to about one-quarter in commerce societies (ancient Greece or medieval Venice). Only in advanced technological societies has the strategist/population ratio once more approached that of hunter/gatherer societies. It is these strategists that leaders of successful societies in the past have attempted to facilitate.

The modern world, however, appears to have lost sight of the strategic leadership that underpinned the emergence of great civilisations in the past. Instead of seeing themselves as facilitators of their society's long-run dynamic strategy and its driving strategists, contemporary governments have instead intervened in this core material process in a piecemeal and short-run manner in response to vocal minorities seen as electoral threats. As a result of this modern approach, long-run strategic interests have been disrupted in favour of short-run trendy ideas. This is particularly problematical concerning the highly distorting policies of inflation-targeting and climate mitigation. In political circles, in contrast to the business world, ideas are increasingly triumphing over desires.

The rediscovery of the lost art of strategic leadership is the greatest challenge facing potential new leaders throughout the world. And the greatest challenge facing human society this century will be to negotiate the rapidly approaching exhaustion of the industrial technological paradigm and its replacement with the forthcoming Solar Revolution (chapter 13). A failure of strategic leadership in the face of ideological attack from antistrategists could derail this critical transition with disastrous consequences. It is to be hoped that a new generation of leaders throughout the world will be more strategically aware than their immediate forebears. An understanding of my dynamic-strategy theory would help.

A Realist Dynamic Form

The supply-side approach of orthodox economics has had a characteristic impact on the dynamic form and the explanation of its growth models. The contribution that a demand-side approach might make to both has not even been considered. The argument here is that the dynamic form of a realist growth model is the outcome of the real-world interaction between strategic demand and the supply response. This section provides a brief outline of a realist dynamic form.

In neoclassical growth models, the steady state (a concept adopted from classical thermodynamics), or equilibrium growth path, is an attempt to provide not only a structure for the growth process but also an objective for a growing society. It is a dynamic centre of gravity towards which an economy is supposed to automatically converge. The equilibrium pathway for the Solow-Swan model, for example, is determined by the nature of the neoclassical production function. These models assume that the growth path is smooth and that the growth rate, which is determined exogenously, is constant over time. This picture can be varied, but only by making a number of arbitrary assumptions. John Hicks as well as Luigi Pasinetti and Robert Solow, for example, make the point that for each state of technology there will be a different equilibrium growth path, and that a society will move, or "traverse", to a new pathway with each discrete change in technology.[14] Apart from making the point that convergence is likely to involve a series of pathways rather than a single pathway, little is added to the Solow-Swan model. Any attempt to map these changes in pathways and growth rates would be pointless in the absence of real-world information, because Hicks and others do not provide models to suggest how these "traverses" would take place. It is the substance of the dynamic form, not its appearance, that we are chiefly interested in. And, as suggested earlier, the substance of neoclassical growth models is entirely artificial. As I argued in *Longrun Dynamics* (1998b), the new wave in growth theory of the mid 1990s, despite the enthusiasm of its participants, would soon dash itself on the barren rocks of deductivism. And it did.

A realistic dynamic form can only be derived by observing the way societies grow over the long run. This, of course, is only one aspect of the larger objective of inductively deriving a realist dynamic theory from historical analysis—from a remembrance of things past. We need to explain the underlying dynamic process as well as the dynamic pathway. To do so we need to draw the distinction between a "time path" on the one hand and a "dynamic pathway" on the other.

A time path is merely the statistical profile of an unexplained variable over time, whereas a dynamic pathway—what I call the "strategic pathway"—is the embodiment of an explained dynamic process. The basic theory is outlined above, and a brief sense of the strategic pathway is provided here.

A dominant dynamic strategy unfolds not in response to teleological forces but to the actions of individuals attempting to survive and prosper in a competitive world. In order to exploit strategic opportunities, individuals and their governments invest in the necessary infrastructure, plant and machinery, techniques, institutions, and organisations. And as the dynamic strategy unfolds, the living standards—the measure of strategic success—of the participants rise. This unfolding process continues until the strategic opportunities have been exhausted—the outcome of the law of diminishing *strategic* returns[15]—at the stage when marginal strategic returns and costs have been equated. It is important to realise that dynamic diminishing returns operate not on resources but on strategies. Also this dynamic law encompasses and transforms the static classical law of diminishing returns based on the misleading assumption of a fixed supply of land (or natural resources) in the long run; and it resolves the difficulty inherent in the neoclassical version of diminishing returns, which views all resources as being in fixed supply in the short run.[16]

The generalised strategic pathway consists of a series of economic waves carrying society to higher levels of complexity and prosperity. It can represent the very long run (which can be defined as 1,000 years or more), the long run (say 200 years), and the short run (from a half-century to a decade). There are significant differences between this realist strategic pathway and the steady state. The most obvious of these is the wave-like pattern of the strategic pathway in contrast to the smooth equilibrium path of the neoclassical model. This difference leads the neoclassically trained economist to think in terms of continuous and steady economic growth, while the economic stratologist thinks of growth at all levels as occurring in a fluctuating manner. In the very long run these waves are of *about* 300 years in duration (see Figure 7.1 in chapter 7), in the long run they are *about* 40 to 60 years, and in the short run they are *about* 5 to 15 years, and are the outcomes of the systematic exploitation and exhaustion of dynamic strategies, substrategies and strategic projects. The reason I refer to these somewhat regular fluctuations (distorted by existential external shocks, including weather, physical forces, and war) as "waves" rather than "cycles" is that each surge of economic activity is associated with a discrete strategy, that is worked out over a period of time. A further economic surge requires the adoption and exploitation of a new dynamic strategy. There is nothing automatic about this strategic renewal, which is why the interval between waves at the long-run and very long-run levels is a time of considerable concern. Examples include the USA between the mid-1920s and the mid-1940s and, more recently, Japan from the 1980s to the 2010s. These intervals should be thought of as "interregnums" rather than "troughs" (which implies an automatic cyclical momentum), as there is no guarantee that a new dynamic strategy will emerge before the beleaguered society begins to descend into chaos. This highlights the importance of pursuing strategic policy rather than counter-cyclical (or Keynesian) policy.

Speculation and Financial "Crisis"

Speculation is an outcome of the gambling instinct in mankind. The urge to make a quick dollar is overwhelming. This can be seen on the stock exchange as well as the race track. While the stock exchange provides an important function in the strategic pursuit by mobilising investment funds in both the national and international communities, the urge to speculate has turned the stock market into a casino. When an economy is pursuing a successful dynamic strategy, speculation attracts only a modest amount of attention. Some people, who are susceptible to an irresistible urge to become wealthy at any cost, are not particular about how riches are generated provided (presumably) the activity is legal. The proceeds from gambling on the stock exchange are just as good as those from more productive strategic activities—or so they convince themselves. The determining factor is the rate of return on their funds. Hence, while the real economy is booming, and the strategic rates of return are high, the majority of investors will place their funds in productive strategic activities, owing to the lower degree of risk. But as the dynamic strategy or substrategy increasingly approaches exhaustion, a growing number of investors will transfer their funds from productive to speculative activities in an attempt to maintain the high rates of return on their capital. By the time the dominant strategy/substrategy has been completely exhausted, the majority of "investors" will have become speculators.

From this point, the "economic casino" gains a momentum of its own, and prices of stocks and shares are driven up to unsustainable levels in a fever of speculative excitement fuelled by excessive funds. This can rapidly spread from the economic casino at the national level to that at the global level. These excesses may also infect financial institutions, which shift their lending activities from sound productive activities to unsound and unproductive activities (such as sub-prime lending in the USA during the first decade of the twenty-first century). Clearly this can only continue for a limited time. Once a sufficient number of speculators involved in this process finally realise that prices cannot continue to go up forever, and begin selling paper assets in sizable quantities, the game is up. Gamblers in the casino begin panic selling and the prices of stocks and shares fall as rapidly as they rose. This is what happened on Wall Street in 1929, in the global casino in 1987, and happened again in 2008. The real economy is rarely badly affected by fallout from a casino crash. In fact, it actually frees up funds for productive investment in the newly emerging dynamic strategy/substrategy. Any real downturn is an outcome of underlying strategic problems (such as substrategy exhaustion). It is essential to recognise that the stock exchange is not "the economy"—a widespread misconception—and the financial sector is only a supply-side instrument in the strategic pursuit. This is often forgotten because, while the stock exchange and the financial sector have a concrete physical presence, the dynamic mechanism is invisible to all but a few.

A MORE SCIENTIFIC POLICY-MAKING

Late in 2008 many economists were talking about the prospects of an "unprecedented" global recession or even depression as severe as that in the early 1930s; financial journalists with their usual purple prose were writing about a "global meltdown"; and national politicians, like king Canute, were making grand, if empty, gestures to hold back the incoming tide of disaster. We have heard it all before and we will hear it all again, at least until a serious attempt is made to understand the dynamics of human society. When this occurs even orthodox economists will be able to distinguish between recessions, depressions, and financial crises, and understand what causes them—the exhaustion of dynamic strategies and their substrategies. What this will mean is that we will be able to replace the existing trial-and-error method of policy making with a more scientific approach. What is required in a downturn is targeted government investment in the infrastructure of the future—the infrastructure of "knowledge"—rather than wasteful and ephemeral Keynesian pump priming.

As recessions (even depressions) and financial crises will continue to occur regularly in the future owing to material progress taking the form of waves of strategic activity, a rational strategic approach by governments will save the taxpayer a great deal of pain. Inefficient policy-making is always measured in terms of income forgone.

Chapter 12

The *Logos* at Large — Global Strategic Transition

Global transition is generated by the logos, not the "expert".

Economic development is one of the most important but least understood issues in the world today. It commands our attention because of the vast chasm in living standards between peoples of the most and least developed nations. Since the Second World War, considerable effort has been devoted to this issue by intellectuals, public agencies at the national and global levels, and private consultants. While the global development process has expanded steadily, particularly in South and East Asia, there are still large areas of the World, namely sub-Saharan Africa, that have been bypassed. Many observers, therefore, have become pessimistic about the future of the poorest nations. But, as we shall see, the lesser developed countries are being drawn steadily into the global strategic core through the dynamic mechanism of "global strategic transition"—the operation of the *logos* at large.

ECONOMIC DEVELOPMENT REDEFINED

While there is every reason to be pessimistic about the contribution of the "development industry" to resolving the problems of the poorest nations, there is no reason at all to doubt that the problem will be resolved. Both issues revolve around the dynamic-strategy project's discovery of the real nature of the global dynamic process. The reason that traditional development economics is widely regarded as having failed to meet the expectations of its pioneering practitioners[1] is that it has been unable to construct a general model of global economic development. Only when such a model became available—in *The Dynamic Society* (Snooks 1996) and *Longrun Dynamics* (Snooks 1998b)—could it be seen that the economic development of individual countries is part of a global dynamic process that is both systematic and continuing. Development economics may have missed its mark, but economic development is still on course. Global transition is generated by the *logos,* not the "expert". It is the purpose of this book to demonstrate the truth of these propositions by constructing and applying a general dynamic model of the development process that I have called the "global strategic transition" (GST). I will begin by suggesting how the GST model requires the redefinition of economic development.

It was my intention in *Global Transition* (1999) to redefine the objectives and nature of what we have come to know as "development economics". The objective should be not to focus on development policy to "reduce poverty" or to "close the income gap", but rather to understand the process by which societies are drawn into the prevailing technological paradigm and to formulate policy principles that will remove the barriers threatening to derail this global dynamic process. As the reduction in poverty is an outcome and not an objective of the GST, it cannot be achieved before the transition process has taken place. This new focus here on *processes* rather than *outcomes* involves a major reorientation in development economics.

The Traditional Approach to Economic Development

The existing paradigm of economic development has arisen not from an understanding of the global dynamic process but from a desire to eliminate the observed income gap between the most and least developed nations. In other words, the problem of economic development is generally viewed as an outcome rather than a process.[2] It will come as no surprise, therefore, that the traditional resolution of this problem is framed in static rather than dynamic terms.

The traditional focus

In pursuing its objective, the "development industry" has changed its focus over the past sixty years or so. The pioneering development economists and development agencies equated economic development with a growth in real GDP per capita, whereas many today see it in terms of "poverty reduction", "equity", "basic needs", and "human development". While this change may appear to be quite subtle, it has important policy implications. As H.W. Singer says: "we are all agreed—at least theoretically—to attribute more importance to reduction of poverty than to mere growth of GNP".[3] And Paul Streeten asserts that "the evolution from economic growth, via employment, jobs and justice, redistribution with growth to basic needs and human development represents a genuine evolution of thinking and is not a comedy of errors, a lurching from one slogan to the next".[4]

The reasons for this change of focus are that sustained economic growth in many lesser-developed countries has been difficult to achieve and, even when it has occurred, poverty reduction through greater equity and human development has not emerged.[5] But, only those with a naive and shortrun view of the relationship between economic and political change would expect it to. The dynamic-strategy model developed in chapter 11 shows that greater equity emerges only after a country's unfolding dynamic strategy draws a sizeable proportion of the population into its economic and, later, political processes. This requires the passage of some three or four generations. It cannot be achieved overnight.

Whatever the perception of the income gap between the most and least developed nations, there is little disagreement about the way it can be eliminated. Economic development, it is argued by development economists, is the outcome of appropriate international and national development policies—of intervention by intellectuals and bureaucrats. Hans Singer, for example, claims that "the development process has been shaped by interaction between global and domestic policies, although their relative importance has varied among developing countries".[6] Even neoliberals see an important role for international organisations such as the IMF and the World Bank in shaping national policy in the poorest nations. The irony, of course, is that, by forcing non-interventionist policies on national governments, these international organisations have become massively interventionist. I will argue that these policy initiatives are actually employed as substitutes for an appropriate understanding of the global dynamic process.

The failure to develop a model of global dynamics is reflected in the absence of both analytical content in and consensus about the basic terminology of economic development. This constantly changing terminology merely distinguishes between those societies that have passed through a process of economic development and those that have not. It does not reflect the changing nature of that dynamic process. A sample of this changing terminology includes: advanced/backward countries; developed/undeveloped countries; developed (DCs)/less-developed countries (LDCs); industrialised (ICs)/newly industrialising (NICs) countries; countries of the centre/periphery; North/South countries; high-/low-income countries; and First-World/Third-World countries. As will be discussed later, the development of a global dynamic model requires the adoption of an entirely new and, for the first time, *analytical* terminology.

Orthodox and radical models

In the absence of a workable model of global change, the development industry has fallen back on one of a number of tangential or partial approaches to the issue of economic development. These approaches, which are discussed in more detail in my book *Global Transition* (1999)[7], include those of the productionists, the poverty-trap theorists, the institutionalists, and the global-polarisation theorists.

The only comprehensive body of theory available to development economists is classical and neoclassical growth theory. There are, however, two major problems in employing this theory in development economics. The first is that it was constructed to analyse, in a highly abstract way, the growth of First-World economies. Hence it abstracts from those institutional and political issues that are central to the process of economic development. But as serious as this limitation may be, it is the least of the problems facing orthodox growth theory in a development context. The second, and fundamentally critical, deficiency is its restricted perspective. Growth theory not only lacks global perspective, it also concentrates on the system of production rather than the dynamic core of individual societies. In effect, mainstream economics treats human society as a giant factory dominated by the machine rather than a social organisation dedicated to the strategic pursuit, as it is in reality. Because economic growth is treated by the "productionists" as the outcome of a production processes rather than of a strategic pursuit, neoclassical growth models fail to encompass the dynamic core of society. In other words, *"endogenous" growth models endogenise the wrong variables.*

The widespread dissatisfaction generated by orthodox growth models unable to explain the persistence of underdevelopment has stimulated development economists to construct their own theories. The main theoretical explanation for the apparent persistence of underdevelopment concerns the low-level equilibrium, or poverty, trap. Escape from this trap was considered by these theorists to be impossible if left to the self-interest of entrepreneurs working independently. Only through a government-sponsored "big push" that would generate simultaneous development over a wide front could it be achieved. While these theories address the condition of underdevelopment, they do not model the growth process. They provide no basis for a general theory of global economic development and they focus on the system of production rather than the strategic pursuit. They are merely speculative partial theories and, as such, are of limited use in policy formulation.

A third group of development economists have attempted to explain the persistence of underdevelopment in terms of the failure of institutions in the Third World to evolve efficiently. This is due, the institutionalists claim, to adverse initial conditions inherited from an earlier era of colonisation together with path-dependent evolutionary processes. Only a major government initiative to remove, reshape, and replace old and inefficient institutions can eliminate this source of underdevelopment. While this approach takes into account institutional issues neglected by orthodox growth theory, it does so by asserting the dominance of evolutionary rules over more fundamental economic processes. The new institutionalism, however, shares the productionist vision of human society, merely extending the costs-of-production concept to include transaction costs.

The final group of development economists consists of what I have called the global-polarisation theorists. They include the "structuralists" and the "dependency theorists". While both are committed to the idea that society is a system of production, they do view economic development as a global process. Underdevelopment is seen as a direct outcome of the expansion and growth of the advanced industrial nations rather than of Third-World problems. The structuralists see the economic problems of the less-industrialised "periphery" as a direct, if unintentional, outcome of the expansion of the industrialised "centre", operating through the terms of trade. The solution for the periphery is to minimise contact with the centre through import-substitution industrialisation (ISI). Marxist-inspired dependency theorists, on the other hand, view global polarisation as the result of a more deliberate exploitative relationship that can be terminated only through a change in global power relationships. Neither explanation of global change is comprehensive or persuasive.

Development policies advocated by intellectuals and imposed by international organisations such as the IMF and the World Bank have reflected these changing fashions in the orthodox consensus. They have also reflected the changing success stories in the development "game": whatever country is currently successful is the "model" that all Third-World countries are to follow. From the 1940s to the 1960s, development economists under the influence of Keynesian ideas emphasised the roles of investment, government intervention, and planning.[8] This was the era of the "big push" with its focus on industrialisation, particularly in the form of heavy industry and engineering. It was to be achieved by tariff-inspired import replacement and by extracting the necessary surplus from a largely traditional agriculture. The Marxists advocated a similar approach, albeit through different political forms.

While a small group of dissenting neoclassical economists were active at this time,[9] it was not until the 1970s that neoliberalism began to emerge as the new orthodox consensus. Owing to the neoclassical resurgence, there was a shift of development policy from government planning and protection to freely operating markets and unrestricted trade, which was adopted from the early 1980s by the Thatcher government in the UK and the Reagan administration in the USA. This, in turn, led to the structural adjustment policies of the IMF and the World Bank during the 1980s aimed at reducing the debt burden accumulated by Third-World countries over the preceding three or four decades. The neoclassical structural adjustment policies have been described as follows:

> It holds that one can temporarily deflate, arrest growth, reduce government expenditures, reduce expenditures on physical and human investments and so on, while at the same time gathering strength for a new and, it is hoped, more sustainable period of growth and development.[10]

It is a faith misplaced. This "development" policy, which has no underlying dynamic theory, was merely transplanted from the First World where, as I argue in *Longrun Dynamics* (1998),[11] it has been undercutting longrun economic viability. In the Third World the timing, suddenness, and insensitivity of this new policy merely exacerbated the increasing difficulties that most countries, particularly in Africa and Latin America, were experiencing in maintaining the dynamic process throughout the 1980s and early 1990s.

By the second decade of the twenty-first century, the bold development experiment begun more than seventy years ago can hardly be regarded as successful. Despite a massive input of intellectual and financial resources the global development problem appears to many to be as intractable as ever. Large areas of the Third World, particularly in sub-Saharan Africa and Latin America, have performed poorly in growth terms since the early 1970s. Some of the difficulties experienced must be regarded as an outcome of inappropriate interventions by the development industry, which raised expectations about what could be achieved in the short-term and led to the waste of scarce resources on a massive scale, and which provided inappropriate neoliberal advice in times of crisis. The argument in this book is that these policy problems could have been avoided if a realist general theory of global economic development had emerged earlier in the twentieth century. Such a theory would have provided a realistic understanding of the global dynamic process together with the dangers of large-scale interventions of both the Keynesian and neoliberal kind.

The Global Strategic Transition—A New Approach

In *Longrun Dynamics* I argue that real-world dynamic processes can be understood only by abandoning neoclassical growth models, which are based on an inappropriate body of static microeconomic theory, and instead by employing an inductive approach. This is just as true for the Third World as it is for the First World. By taking an inductive approach in *Longrun Dynamics* it was possible to construct the dynamic-strategy model of economic change that was successfully employed to analyse First World economies and to generate more appropriate policy principles. With further theoretical development, the same model can be employed to analyse the economies of the Third World. The dynamic-strategy theory developed in chapter 4 contains a model of the global mechanism of economic development—a mechanism that I call the global strategic transition (GST). That model will be teased out here.

THE GLOBAL STRATEGIC TRANSITION MODEL

The "global strategic transition" **(GST)** is the process by which an increasing number of societies are drawn into the vortex of dynamic interaction between the world's most economically advanced nations. It is generated by the global unfolding of the prevailing technological paradigm. This unfolding process is neither inevitable nor smooth, a reality reflected in the fluctuating fortunes of the world economy throughout the history of civilisation. The twentieth century, for example, has witnessed the Great Depression of the 1930s, the "golden age" of the 1950s and 1960s, and slower, more uneven growth during the century's last twenty-five years punctuated by strategic crises such as those in East Asia at the close of the twentieth century; while the twenty-first century experienced its first global recession in 2008/09. As the dynamics of the "global strategic core" has waxed and waned, so has the economic development of the rest of the world. The attempt to model the GST in this chapter is based on my dynamic-strategy theory presented in chapters 4 and 11.

The Dynamics of Global Strategic Transition

As shown earlier, there have been four technological paradigms in human history—the pre-palaeolithic (scavenging), palaeolithic (hunting), neolithic (agriculture), and modern (industrial). In each historical era the technological revolution began in a narrowly defined region—a dynamic hot spot—and subsequently spread to the rest of the known world. The Palaeolithic Revolution, which emerged in East Africa about 1.6 million years ago, took about 1.2 million years to spread around the globe; the Neolithic Revolution (Old World), which first appeared in the Jordan Valley about 11,000 years ago, took only 3,000 years to extend to the rest of the known world;[12] and the Industrial Revolution, which began in Britain about 200 years ago, is still spreading around the globe but should approach (if not achieve) completion by the middle decades of the twenty-first century (Snooks 1996: ch. 12). The current laggards, however, are likely to be left stranded by the rapid emergence and progression of the forthcoming Solar Revolution. Clearly the GST is accelerating with the emergence of each new technological paradigm.

In order to understand the manner in which a technological paradigm unfolds, is exhausted, and leads on to a new paradigm shift, we need to model this global dynamic process. This can be achieved by adapting my dynamic-strategy theory for individual societies. The global-strategic-transition model is the dynamic-strategy model writ large. It consists of an endogenous driving force; the pursuit of dynamic strategies as part of a strategic struggle between various "strategic countries" (SCs)—including USA, EU, Japan, South Korea, Canada, Australia, NZ—on the one hand and between "emerging strategic countries" (ESCs)—including China, India, South America—and "nonstrategic countries" (NSCs)—including Afghanistan, Iraq, Bangladesh, sub-Saharan Africa—on the other; and a transition mechanism involving an interaction between strategic demand and strategic response. The outcomes of this dynamic process include a growing number of NSCs drawn into the global paradigm, increasing living standards of both SCs and NSCs, more equal distribution of income throughout the world, and a growing democratisation of the world's sociopolitical institutions—outcomes that have been achieved despite rather than because of intervention by the development industry.

The driving force and the strategic struggle

The motive force operating within and between societies is the same. It is the attempt by private individuals and their political representatives to survive and prosper in a world characterised by scarce resources. These circumstances have led to intense competition between individual societies as well as between individuals within societies. A measure of this intensity is the record of regular warfare that has occurred throughout the world even since the Industrial Revolution, that effectively made the conquest strategy obsolete as a means for achieving economic growth.[13] It is this intense competition that has led to the global "strategic struggle" for the material high ground.

To achieve their objectives, individuals and their strategic leaders adopt and pursue dynamic strategies that comprise families of substrategies. This is discussed in greater detail in chapters 3 and 4. It is essential to realise that the key to the dynamics of human society is this "strategic pursuit" rather than the way in which the resulting dynamic impulse is transformed into a larger per capita surplus. While the "surplus-generating medium" of our own era is the system of industrial production, in the neolithic era it was either the system of war or the system of commerce, and in the palaeolithic era it was the family system. As we shall see, traditional economics focuses on the system of industrial production rather than the strategic pursuit. Accordingly I call their practitioners the "productionists" and contrast them with the "stratologists".

Since the Industrial Revolution, the dominant dynamic strategy has been technological change, although some small societies—city-states like Singapore and the former Hong Kong—have been able to grow rich by handling the products of the technological strategy. These small commerce societies depend heavily on the new technologies, and will never develop into nation-states or mega-states as have the technological strategists. Indeed, as we have seen in the case of Hong Kong, they are vulnerable to takeover by the technological mega-states. The strategic struggle for global dominance, therefore, involves competition between rival technological substrategists or between rivals employing the same substrategy.

The industrial technological paradigm has been unfolding now for over two centuries since the beginning of the Industrial Revolution. It is a dynamic process that has been driven by competition between a growing number of new entrants, and which has passed through a number of distinct substrategies. The pioneering technological substrategy was pursued by Britain between the 1780s and the 1830s in order to maintain its global supremacy following the exhaustion by the 1750s of its highly successful commerce strategy that had generated a global empire. This first-generation substrategy was based on the innovations of practical men and was undertaken through the establishment of small-scale enterprises that focused on a range of basic commodities produced in one or two factories under common ownership. These enterprises began as small partnerships and family firms that gradually gave way to larger public companies. Individual initiatives were transformed into social objectives through the process of "strategic imitation" whereby successful pioneers are imitated by growing numbers of followers.[14] This type of development was well suited to the nation-state that had emerged in the pre-modern period in response to the older strategies of conquest and commerce.

The second technological substrategy was initiated by other nation-states in Western Europe between the 1830s and the 1870s. Earlier experimentation with industrialisation on the Continent had been disrupted by a continued fascination with conquest, particularly by France. But with the failure of conquest, Western Europe as a whole turned its attention to the technological strategy. In order to compete with Britain in the continual struggle to survive and prosper, France and Germany—and later Japan in the East—used tariff protection to imitate the British strategy and to build new capital-intensive industries in engineering and chemicals. These new industries relied to a greater extent than before on scientific ideas and institutional finance. While the enterprises in this second technological phase were more extensive and operated through a wider network of larger factories (except in France), they were able to develop within the existing nation-state, or in the newly emerging nation-states of Italy (1861) and Germany (1871). As competition grew more intense between these nation-states during the second half of the nineteenth century, they embarked on a process of empire-building in order to defend their technological strategies from each other. It was an extension of the balance of power concept from Europe to the rest of the world. The important point is that these nineteenth-century empires were not economically essential to the operation of the technological strategy, in contrast to the empires of the seventeenth and eighteenth centuries that were an integral element of the commerce strategy. It is for this reason that the European empires were dismantled during the mid-twentieth century, a time when the technological strategy could be defended by the mega-states using the threat of nuclear weapons.[15]

The third technological substrategy began in North America in the 1870s and flourished during the following century. It had its origins in the determination of American industrialists to drive the Europeans from the large US domestic market and, later, to make inroads into the world market. The USA was able to do so by employing existing technological ideas on a scale that no other nation in the late nineteenth century could emulate, rather than by developing a radically different technology. Herein resided the comparative advantage of the world's first mega-state. By large-scale investment in mass-production and mass-distribution techniques, the USA was able to exploit its giant domestic market by supplying goods at prices the Europeans were unable to match. The method was to employ a high degree of specialisation through assembly-line techniques in order to produce standardised products that could be distributed in bulk. Once the domestic market had been saturated by the mid-1920s, American entrepreneurs turned their attention—following a hiatus usually called the Great Depression—to world markets. After the Second World War this strategy was highly successful. It was a success based on the earlier development of mega-corporations—which could only emerge within a mega-state—producing an extensive range of commodities and services. When they established branches in overseas markets these mega-corporations became known as multinational or transnational corporations. They are, in effect, agents of the technological strategies of the mega-states, and they play an important role in the GST.

The fourth technological substrategy was developed by innovative nation-states in an attempt to undermine the post–Second World War dominance of the American mega-state. It is particularly interesting that those who were most successful in this new strategic thrust were the nation-states that had failed in the attempt to meet growing American hegemony by developing mega-states of their own through conquest in both Europe and Asia. In the 1960s, the reconstructed Japanese and German nations discovered that they could effectively compete against the USA both in its domestic and overseas markets by fully embracing the new microelectronic technology. If they were unable to transform themselves into mega-states at the expense of their neighbours, perhaps they could economically undermine the foundations of the American mega-state. Through more efficient production and organisation, Japan and Germany were able to offer consumers greater variety and choice, even though this meant shorter production runs (only one-quarter of that of the USA in the case of car production). They were able to combine old mass-production methods with the new microelectronic technology to make customised consumer products of a higher quality. These more desirable commodities included cars, household appliances, ceramics, textiles, consumer durables, computer software, as well as food and drink. Consumers, tired of standardised products, responded to this greater choice with considerable enthusiasm. The shift of consumers away from standardised products eventually forced American businessmen in the 1980s to compete with these new dynamic strategists on their own ground.

Finally, we come to the fifth technological substrategy, which is currently driving human society in the twenty-first century. With the conclusion of the Second World War, it became clear to the nation-states of Western Europe, on both the winning and losing sides, that none of them by standing alone could command the economic resources required to successfully compete, either economically or militarily, with America. It also became clear during the 1950s that, in the future, the USSR would become a mega-state to rival the USA. This ideological and strategic conflict, however, proved to be short-lived, as the antistrategic society of the USSR was unable to grow as rapidly as the strategic society of the USA. (I had predicted this in my university lectures on Comparative Economic Systems at the Flinders University of South Australia during the early and mid-1980s, using an early version of the dynamic-strategy theory.)

Mega-status, therefore, would be important for Western Europe not only to defend the technological strategy that they had given to the world but also to engage in economic bargaining on a global scale, to exercise strategic control over a large market, and to effectively control a massive resource base. The future would be determined by economic giants employing a microelectronic/biotechnological program. Here lies the real driving force behind that remarkable attempt to fashion Europe into a mega-state—remarkable because these constituent societies have been engaged in a ferocious struggle against each other for more than a millennium. And we can expect the USA and the EU to be joined in their mega-club by China, Russia, and possibly others as the twenty-first century unfolds.[16]

The mechanism of global strategic transition

The energy for the strategic transition is generated by this eternal strategic struggle between the peoples of different societies. It powers the unfolding of the industrial technological paradigm that is gradually drawing a growing number of societies into its vortex. This vortex, or "global strategic core", consists of a growing number of highly competitive and interacting strategic countries (SCs). The way in which this unfolding process occurs is through the mechanism of global strategic transition.

Box 12.1 The development impact of displaced persons

A relatively new aspect of the interaction between SCs and NSCs, is the massive increase in numbers of displaced individuals and families seeking resettlement in the developed world. In 2014 the number of people displaced by war, conflict or persecution—in countries such as the Congo, Iraq, Nigeria, South Sudan, Syria, and the Ukraine—reached nearly 60 million, which is a new record level (UNHCR Report 2015). Most of these people want to return to their homes and rebuild their communities, but there is a growing proportion seeking asylum in the West, both officially and, increasingly, unofficially. The problem has reached such a magnitude that the developed world is unable or unwilling to absorb the numbers knocking on their doors. Clearly, this forced displacement of such large numbers of people is not only causing massive social problems, it is also impacting negatively on the long-run GST mechanism, which in turn will further reduce living standards of the poorest people in the World in the future. It is imperative, therefore, that steps be taken to reduce the impact of these regional wars, conflicts and persecutions in order to re-establish an orderly process of global economic development. As shown in chapters 3 and 4, conquest in the modern era is neither economic nor sustainable in the longer term. Regional war lords need to be convinced that they will benefit more from participation in the GST than in destructive military activity; and governments in SCs need to understand that it is in their interests to accelerate investment in NSCs. If this cannot be achieved fairly quickly, the developed world may feel forced to take punitive action against not only war lords and but also unofficial asylum seekers, which would only compound both the social and economic problem. The only long-term solution to the problems of the Third world is to remove barriers to the effective operation of the GST—of the operation of the *logos* at large.

Central to the transition mechanism is "global strategic demand". This is the demand generated by the global unfolding of the technological paradigm. While most of this demand is met by SCs in the strategic core, some of it influences nonstrategic countries (NSCs) in the strategic fringe. This takes place through international trade and direct investment by SCs in NSCs to exploit lower labour costs. What attracts SCs to NSCs is the latter's stocks of relatively unused natural resources, cheap labour, and their potential supplies of raw materials and foods. The NSCs most able to respond to changes in global strategic demand are those drawn most quickly into the global strategic transition (GST). The NSCs respond to strategic demand by providing the labour skills required, making available their natural resources, and exporting primary and, even, manufactured products. And to do this they are required to change the nature of their institutions and organisations. The dynamic-strategy model, therefore, provides a new theory of international trade as well as a new theory of global economic development.

Of course, it is the SCs with their much greater economic and military power that gain most from the GST in the shortrun, but it can be turned to the account of emerging strategic countries (ESCs) and NSCs in the longer term. To generate this interaction, the SCs supply capital, technology, and institutions, and nonstrategic countries use these strategic inputs to construct their new "dependent-technological strategy". This is achieved through a process of "global strategic imitation". As the GST takes place, the living standards of nonstrategic countries rise, thereby providing markets for capital and intermediate goods from the SCs. In other words, the NSCs, on entering into the GST, pass through their own "national strategic transition" (NST). This has been the case with China, South Korea, and India in recent decades.

The global strategic demand–response mechanism is orchestrated by rising prices for natural resources, labour, and output in ESCs as it is in SCs. These rising prices provide the incentives for the ESC response. We can expect, what I call in *Longrun Dynamics* (1998b), "strategic inflation" in ESCs to be considerably higher than in SCs owing to the greater incentives required to induce the strategic response. This is due to the widespread existence of nonstrategic institutions and habits. We can also expect that strategic inflation will be more difficult to recognise in ESCs because the greater political instability in these countries leads to larger errors in policy, particularly concerning the money supply, and generates higher levels of "nonstrategic inflation". Nevertheless, as shown in my book *Global Transition* (1999),[17] where growth–inflation curves for nonstrategic countries have been estimated, the initial inflation rate— which is greater than that in SCs by a factor of three or four—is statistically significant. Because NSCs have not entered into the GST, they experience no strategic inflation, only nonstrategic inflation—no "good" inflation, only "bad" inflation..

THE NEW STRATEGY FUNCTION

In order to understand the "strategic response" to the demand of the *logos*, in both developed and underdeveloped economies, we need a new vision concerning the objectives of human society and its macroeconomic relationships. New visions are reflected in new metaphors. The neoclassical metaphor for modern society is the factory dominated by the machine. Orthodox economists see society as an organisation that maximises its economic output from a given set of inputs and state of technology. They see society working out its objectives within the context of the aggregate production function. This, I argue, constitutes a distorted vision of reality. Human society is not a factory but a "strategic organisation", and social dynamics is not a production process but a strategic pursuit. Accordingly we need to replace the neoclassical production function in our dynamic models with—what in *Global Transition* (1999) I called—the "strategy function".

What is the Strategy Function?

The "strategy function" describes the relationship between the "strategic outcome" of survival and prosperity and the "strategic instruments" by which it is achieved. While this is a static concept, it is determined by the unfolding dynamic strategy. It provides a number of snapshots at different point in time. Clearly it involves a more complex macroeconomic relationship than envisaged by orthodox economists. On the one hand, the strategic outcome, which is measured by real GDP per capita (or, better, real Gross Community Income—market plus household income—per household), is considered as an indicator not of "wellbeing" but of "economic resilience"—the ability to survive and prosper. It is economic resilience that is the central objective in the *logos*. Strategic instruments, on the other hand, include the familiar natural resources of capital stock (both physical and human), population, and technological ideas; together with the unfamiliar strategic institutions and organisations, strategic leadership, and strategic ideas. The strategy function can be expressed formally as:

$$O = f(N, K, R, A, E, So, Sl, Si)$$

where O is strategic outcome proxied by GDP (or GCI), N is population, K is capital stock, R is natural resources, A is technology, E is economies of scale, So is strategic institutions and organisations, Sl is strategic leadership, and Si is strategic ideas.

A new purpose and a new way

The strategy function is based on a new vision of mankind's social objective. As suggested above, neoclassical thinking is restricted by the need to see everything in terms of physical production. According to this outlook, the social objective is associated with the technological relationship between aggregate output and the aggregated factors of production including land, labour, and capital. Orthodox economists see human society essentially as a unit of production. It is a vision with a long history in the discipline of economics and it is a vision rejected in this book. Human society, I argue, is an organisation dedicated to the *creative* pursuit of strategic objectives. As such it embraces a set of novel strategic factors that require further consideration here and in subsequent studies.

Strategic ideas

The concept of strategic ideas is a novel idea. Essentially this concept concerns the ways in which the strategic instruments can be integrated in order to pursue the strategic objective of survival and prosperity. The accumulated flow of strategic ideas can be regarded as the state of "strategic knowledge", which defines the strategy function. Strategic ideas are not planned in advance, they arise in a pragmatic manner as individual strategists and their leaders attempt to exploit strategic opportunities in the face of competition and scarce physical and human resource endowments. They are, in other words, a response to changes in strategic demand. These strategic ideas operate at a number of levels, including that of the dynamic strategy and its various substrategies.

At the highest level, strategic ideas are responsible for defining and facilitating the major dynamic strategies of family multiplication, conquest, commerce, and technological change. They include ideas by individuals and their political leaders about how to exploit the prevailing physical and competitive environments by establishing and pursuing viable dynamic strategies. These are the ideas that facilitated Rome's pursuit from the sixth century BC of the conquest strategy in a highly competitive Mediterranean world; that facilitated the Venetian pursuit from the eleventh century of a commerce strategy; that facilitated Britain's pursuit of the technological strategy from the late eighteenth century: and that facilitate our passage through the twenty-first century. These strategic ideas changed with the demands of an unfolding dynamic strategy.

Each dynamic strategy, which is played out over three or more centuries, consists of a number of substrategies of shorter duration. The technological dynamic strategy, for example, has passed through five substrategies, each of which has involved different combinations of strategic instruments. As these technological substrategies have been outlined above, I will draw attention only to the different characteristics of each here. The pioneering technological substrategy pursued by Britain between the 1780s and 1830s was, as we have seen, based on the strategic ideas and innovations of practical men rather than systematic investment in research and development by large organisations and was undertaken through small-scale enterprises that focused on a limited range of basic commodities in one or two factories, which minimised the degree of capital investment. And these enterprises were based on small partnerships and family firms rather than large public companies. These developments did not just evolve, they were the outcome of the emergence of strategic ideas in response to strategic demand. This was part of the pioneering industrial strategy function. The state in its turn showed strategic leadership by dismantling restrictive mercantilist institutions, providing industrial strategists with new supporting institutions in the form of patent and company law, and by establishing military support and colonial administration for British interests overseas.

The second-generation substrategy was developed by other European countries between the 1830s and 1870s in order to compete with Britain. They, in effect, developed an alternative strategy function that reflected their different physical and competitive environment. Strategists in these countries employed the latest capital-intensive technology in heavy industry, engineering, and chemicals; they invested more heavily in science and research and development; they sought greater assistance from large financial organisations; and they operated through larger corporations that controlled wider networks of larger factories, thereby reaping economies of scale. All this was the outcome of new strategic ideas. Strategic state leadership was provided not only by establishing protective tariffs and infrastructure for the provision of human capital and scientific research, but also by extending the network of their overseas empires, particularly in Africa.

The third-generation substrategy was based on the scale of industrial activity, thereby producing an entirely different strategy function. It was the outcome of determined American industrialists in the late nineteenth century to drive out the Europeans from the world's first mega-market and, later, to make inroads into the global market. The USA was able to achieve this objective by employing existing technological ideas on a scale that no other nation in the late nineteenth century could emulate. This was a triumph for American strategic ideas. By large-scale investment in mass-production techniques, US strategists were able to exploit their large domestic market through the provision of goods and services at prices that Europe was unable to match. The key was the high degree of specialisation and division of labour that could be achieved using assembly-line production techniques pioneered by Henry Ford to produce standardised products that were delivered to customers through mass distribution methods and via new transportation (canals, railroads, and highways) and communication (telegraph and telephone) facilities.

Once the domestic market had been saturated in the 1920s, new strategic ideas were required as the US economy stagnated and descended into depression. Consequently America turned its attention to the global market, particularly during the 1950s and 1960s. This effective new substrategy employed systematic investment in R&D, mega-corporations with high degrees of vertical, horizontal, and geographical (including multinational) integration, together with institutionalised finance. Strategic state leadership was provided in the form of tariffs and subsidies, particularly in the earlier decades, public infrastructure for education and science, as well as military support for strategic interests overseas. America's success was the outcome of effective public and private strategic ideas rather than of technological ideas. It was an outcome of "strategic change" rather than technological change.

The fourth-generation substrategy was pursued by innovative societies to effectively undercut the seemingly impregnable global position of the USA after the Second World War. In the 1960s both Germany and Japan, who had failed in their earlier attempt to meet the American challenge through conquest, adopted the new microelectronic technology. This was a triumph for strategic ideas over sheer size—of finesse over force. They were able to seduce consumers away from standardised products by efficiently offering consumers greater variety and choice, even though this meant shorter production runs.

Yet while smaller societies with innovative strategic ideas will always be able to find a temporary niche in the global economy, the future—as I explain in *The Ephemeral Civilization* (1997)—lies with the mega-states.[18] Hence, the fifth substrategy involves emulating the US mega-state status. This is the real force driving the remarkable pace of the European Union over the past generation—remarkable because of the former 1500 years of intense competition between its member nations. And it is the force that will catapult China, India and a reconstructed Russia into that company as the twenty-first century unfolds. The mega-state will replace the nation-state. Yet even these mega strategy-functions will reflect the different combinations of strategic instruments that are the outcome of strategic demand operating on different physical and sociopolitical environments. This substrategy will propel the world towards the next technological paradigm shift—the Solar Revolution—unless, that is, it is derailed by the climate mitigationists.

Figure 12.1. The Strategy Function

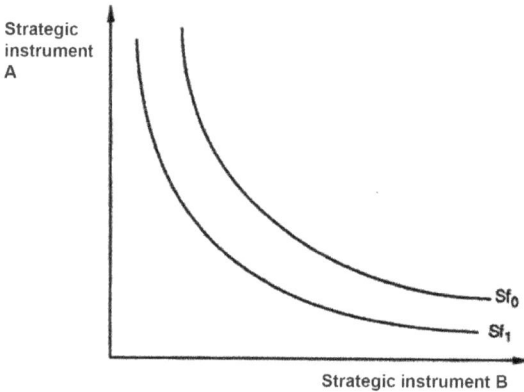

Strategic instrument A

Sf_0

Sf_1

Strategic instrument B

Source: Snooks 1999: 223.

Strategic substitution

The central point, therefore, is that societal objectives can be achieved using many different combinations of a wide selection of strategic instruments. As the above account suggests, the key instrument in this dynamic process is strategic ideas, which are responsible for coordinating the supply response to changes in strategic demand. "Strategic substitution"—or more correctly the substitution of strategic instruments—can be presented graphically in the limited case of two strategic instruments, A and B, in the two-dimensional Figure 12.1. Strategic instrument B can be substituted for strategic instrument A by moving along any given strategy function while maintaining the level of the strategic outcome. An increase in the level of strategic outcome is achieved by an inward shift of the strategy function from Sf_0 to Sf_1. This strategy function is driven towards the point of origin as the dynamic strategy unfolds and new strategic ideas are forthcoming in response to the resulting changes in strategic demand. An inward shift of the strategy function is an outcome of what I have called strategic change.

While this is a limited and static graphical representation, the strategy function does illustrate the essential substitutability of strategic instruments. This concept, as discussed in *Global Transition*[19], is important in any larger discussion of the responses of various strategic instruments to changes in strategic demand. In discussing the role of capital formation, for example, a frequent theoretical explanation provided for the persistence of underdevelopment is the low-level equilibrium trap, which is based on the idea that a barrier to economic development is provided by a "capital requirement" that persistently exceeds the quantity of aggregate saving. What our concept of strategic substitution— which could be examined in the usual marginal terms—suggests is that in an ESC with a low level of aggregate saving, it will be possible to substitute either other sources of funds, namely foreign, or, more interestingly, other strategic instruments for physical capital stock. A familiar form of technical substitution is of labour for capital, but it is also possible to employ strategic ideas to change the design of the existing strategy so that the 'capital requirement' is reduced to equality with aggregate saving. An obvious way of doing this is through the process of borrowing ideas, technological and otherwise, rather than investing in R&D infrastructure.[20] Hence, the low-level equilibrium trap model is an entirely artificial construct that is required in a discipline that has no sense of the strategic transition.

Outcomes of the global strategic transition

The modern global strategic transition, as we have seen, has been underway ever since the nation-states of Western Europe began in the early nineteenth century to imitate Britain's Industrial Revolution. It took a century for Western Europe and the US to overtake Britain. Southern Europe took even longer—not making significant inroads until after the Second World War. Clearly the GST takes time. Hence, it is not surprising that the income gap between the First and Third Worlds was not eliminated during the second half of the twentieth century. Yet there are positive signs particularly in East and Southern Asia, where relatively high rates of economic growth have been achieved since the 1960s. As is well known, the problem area is sub-Saharan Africa, but our model of global strategic transition suggests that it is only a matter of time until this region is drawn into the vortex of the strategic core—at least until the Solar Revolution begins in the middle decades of the twenty-first century, when all non-pioneering countries will fall far behind again. In the shorter term, the Solar Revolution will generate a few big winners and many losers. But in the longer term, a new GST will draw the losers into the new strategic core; provided they are not led by regional war lords, which would make them permanent losers. This prospect may change hearts and minds.

The main outcomes of the global strategic transition since the Second World War have been higher levels of real GDP per capita and changes in sociopolitical institutions required to adopt and pursue a dependent-technological strategy. These institutions include the rule of law, protection of private property, enforcement of contracts, a range of commercial rules, and a change in political systems and social customs. What it does not include are greater equity in the distribution of income, effective economic and political democracy, or "human development" in terms of universal education, health, and welfare.

To demand "human development" is laudable, but merely demonstrates a misunderstanding of the nature of the GST. Just as societies that are inducted into the unfolding technological paradigm gain greater global power, so individuals who are inducted into the ranks of the strategists gain greater political power through the process of national "strategic struggle". Elsewhere I have called this the "strategic transfer".[21] And with this power they are able to influence the distribution of income and the expenditure on education, health, and welfare. The proportion of strategists in NSCs and ESCs will increase steadily—just as it increased over the past in the present SCs—as the GST progresses. There is for any ESC a causal relationship between the stage reached in the GST, which is driven by the global strategic struggle, and the stage reached in the strategic transfer of political power, which is driven by the national strategic struggle. For intellectuals and bureaucrats to demand "human development" *prior* to the strategic transfer will merely endanger the dynamic process through the encouragement of antistrategic revolutions. Realism must replace idealism (often disguised paternalism) if the GST is to be optimised.

POLICY FOR THE GST

Development policy should be considered within the context of the dynamic-strategy model. This involves the recognition that economic development is a global process that is the outcome of the unfolding industrial technological paradigm driven by an interaction between (and within) the global strategic core and its fringe. Owing to this strategic interaction a growing number of nonstrategic countries (NSCs) gain entry into the global strategic transition and are transformed from NSCs to emerging strategic countries (ESCs) and, finally, to strategic countries (SCs). Economic development, in other words, is a self-generating and continuing, if not a continuous, process. It is not something that has to be created or forced by intellectuals, bureaucrats, and international organisations. Indeed, the GST has been no more successful since the emergence of the "development industry" (with its interventionist policies and global institutions) in the middle of the twentieth century than it was during the 200 years before its birth. The GST is a self-starting, self-sustaining dynamic process that is best left to its own devices, particularly as it is not recognised, let alone understood, by intellectuals or others associated with the development industry.

This is the old mystery of the "invisible hand" and "spontaneous order" with which Adam Smith and Friedrich Hayek were preoccupied, except that it concerns a dynamic rather than a static system. We can now identify this mysterious system as the strategic *logos,* and can model it using the dynamic-strategy theory, as undertaken in this book. The unavoidable and unalterable truth is that economic development is the unconscious outcome of the desires of mankind rather than the conscious outcome of its intellect. This is always difficult for academics and intellectuals to accept, owing to their misplaced intellectual pride. The best we can do in these circumstances, therefore, is to understand exactly what the dynamic process of the strategic *logos* involves, and to ensure that policy is used to remove obstacles (including wars and conflicts) in its path rather than to intervene blindly and unnecessarily, thereby diverting it from its path.

Policy Principles

The dynamic-strategy model provides both a new basis for analysis and, accordingly, a new set of policy principles relevant to economic development. In *Longrun Dynamics* (1998b), I reviewed the general principles underlying orthodox economic policy for developed countries. These principles are based on the static concepts of efficiency and market flexibility. Neoclassical economists would prefer to deal with the first of these—efficiency—in terms of a social welfare function that can be maximised subject to the usual economic constraints. As a unique social welfare function does not exist—see Arrow's Impossibility Theorem—neoclassical economists are thrown back on the concept of Pareto optimality, by which any change can only be regarded objectively as an improvement if it makes someone better off without anyone else becoming worse off. Although it was developed for shortrun analysis, Pareto optimality is also applied by orthodox economists to the longrun, mainly in support of notions of free trade and globalisation. The second orthodox policy principle of market flexibility is essential in neoclassical economics because it helps to prop up a supply-side theory. If supply is to create its own demand, the shape of the aggregate supply curve must be vertical, and this requires flexible markets. In turn this has led to the adoption of the concept of the natural rate of unemployment, or the "nonaccelerating inflation rate of unemployment" (NAIRU), that has caused the disruption of economic growth in the First and Third World's alike.

These artificial orthodox concepts, made necessary by a supply-side theory with no role for dynamic demand, have encouraged a policy stance that emphasises stability at the expense of dynamics. This has led to the use of what I call the policy rules of the four zeros—zero government deficits, zero government debt, zero inflation, and zero market imperfection. *It is as if neoliberals, frustrated that their models do not look like the real world, are attempting to make the real world look like their models.* And the attempt to do so in the Western world since the 1970s through anti-inflation and, hence, antigrowth policies has led to the deflation of "strategic confidence" and the undermining of longrun viability. Hence, the global downturn of 2008/09, while generated by strategic exhaustion (which in turn initiated a financial crisis) in the USA, was exacerbated by inflation targeting throughout the Western world. Only growth-focused countries, like China, which spurned inflation targeting, continued to grow rapidly throughout the GFC.

This discussion is relevant to the Third World because neoliberals have exercised considerable influence over international development organisations such as the IMF and the World Bank during the past few decades. This accounts for the structural adjustment programs that these international organisations have imposed on the Third World, and more recently (2015) Greece, whenever they required financial aid. These static, supply-side programs were an attempt to reshape the Third World in the image of neoclassical theory. Such policy is fatal to the longrun economic development of these countries, because it imposes stability at the expense of dynamics. It also leads to the disruption and delay of the GST.

The new strategic optimisation principle

What is urgently needed is a new key policy principle, together with policy rules, based on an appropriate general dynamic model. In *Longrun Dynamics* (1998b) I proposed the "strategic optimisation principle", which involves maximising the sustainable exploitation of strategic opportunities, and which is measured by real GDP per capita, not HDI. Based on the dynamic-strategy model, this policy principle is relevant to a dynamic rather than a static world. Hence, the "strategic test" replaces the Pareto efficiency test.

In a dynamic world, efficiency of production and distribution is secondary to strategic development. This has been the case with China over the past generation. The dynamic-strategy approach also demolishes the NAIRU rule of thumb by undermining the causal relationship between unemployment and inflation. Strategic inflation is, as shown in chapter 11, a central part of the strategic demand–response mechanism, while unemployment is a static outcome of the dynamic process at a particular point in time. They are not directly related in a causal sense and, hence, the Phillips curve has no meaningful existence in theory or reality. This is why the Phillips curve breaks down in periods of structural change, such as the stagflation of the 1970s. We should, therefore, think of a viable First-World economy as one in successful pursuit of its dynamic strategy, experiencing relatively rapid growth of *real* GDP per capita (say 2–3 per cent per annum), with low levels of unemployment (4 to 5 per cent), and moderate levels of strategic inflation (4 to 6 per cent).

While this new policy principle arose from the application of the dynamic-strategy model to the First World, it is just as relevant to the Third World. Just as relevant and even more crucial. All countries in the world are part of the same global strategic transition (GST) process. Accordingly, the appropriate test of performance for emerging strategic countries (ESCs) is just the same as that for strategic countries (SCs)—the strategic test of whether the exploitation of strategic opportunities is being maximised in a sustainable way. In the case of ESCs they should expect—as shown in *Global Transition*— to experience rates of economic growth and strategic inflation substantially higher than those in SCs.[22] ESCs have entered into the GST, but unless they maximise strategic exploitation they could well slip back into the nonstrategic countries (NSC) category. Certainly they will have little prospect of catching up to and joining the SCs. And the same is true for former antistrategic countries (FASCs), such as Russia and its old satellites, that are struggling to substitute strategic for antistrategic development programs. Neither group can afford the luxury of wasting resources either through speculation or through the pursuit of mistaken orthodox policies involving overinvestment in education, equity, or environmental programs. Even the strategic test for NSCs is but a variation on that for all other analytical categories. In this case it is not so much the maximisation of strategic opportunities, as maximising the growing signs of individual and group strategic (profit-seeking) activity as preparatory to entering into the GST.

The essential role of strategic leadership

How are Third-World countries to score well in terms of the strategic test? In *Longrun Dynamics* I suggested that SCs needed to ensure that static issues such as economic stability and external and internal balance should not be allowed to overwhelm the continuous exploitation of strategic opportunities.[23] I argued that governments should provide strategic leadership rather than just good economic housekeeping. Strategic leadership involves facilitating the objectives of society's strategists by actively promoting their cause. This includes investing in strategic infrastructure (research, educational, transport and communication facilities) where the social return is expected to exceed the private return; encouraging domestic innovation and facilitating technological transfer; spearheading the penetration of new markets by negotiating external trade and technological deals on behalf of the strategists; protecting the dynamic strategy at home and abroad; and operating proactively to secure control over external strategic resources or strategic locations. A government supplying strategic leadership, therefore, will respond to the demands of strategists (profit-seekers) rather than antistrategists (rent-seekers). And in difficult times strategic leadership will involve going beyond the Keynesian policy prescription of augmenting aggregate demand by detecting the strategic cause of downturn and assisting in the replacement of exhausted with new technological substrategies. It is essential to realise that "strategic distortion" created by disrupting the dynamic process is far worse than market distortion that may be created by this level of government intervention. Clearly strategic leadership requires a dynamic role for government denied in the Western world by neoclassical models.

Strategic leadership is just as central and even more crucial for the future of Third-World countries. It is essential that the governments of ESCs respond to the requirements of their strategists rather than to the demands of international organisations such as the IMF and the World Bank that are influenced by economic ideologues, or to the advice of "experts" in the wider development community. By providing strategic leadership, ESC governments will be following their own self-interest because their rent-seeking can be maximised only if economic growth is maximised. Their rule, however, will be limited. As a growing proportion of the population is drawn into the dynamic strategy, the strategists will assume greater political control, either gradually or following on from some sort of social and political upheaval, and will provide their own strategic leadership. It is possible that the old ruling elite may avoid being swept away if they also become strategists themselves by giving up rent-seeking for profit-seeking and by adopting more democratic political institutions. This may well happen with ruling elites in China, if they manage the sleight of hand from being "communist" autocrats to being "capitalist" barons. Whatever the pathway to strategic control, it is essential that ESC governments reject the debilitating neoliberal policies that have dominated the First World and its interventionist international organisations. To fail in this will be to substitute static management for strategic leadership and to experience stasis rather than dynamics. The same is true for former antistrategic countries (FASCs). It is important to realise, however, that the "new interventionism", currently prevailing in advanced societies, being based on nonstrategic principles—"social democracy", Keynesianism, and climate mitigationism—is not the answer.

But what about nonstrategic countries (NSCs)? In the absence of successful strategists in NSCs, the ruling elites focus on rent-seeking. They are not committed antistrategists of the Bolshevik kind, just opportunists that pursue the most remunerative pursuits. Only when a sizeable and growing proportion of the population turn to strategic pursuits will the ruling elite find it expedient to take account of the needs of the strategists. They do this because the taxing of strategists becomes the most rapidly growing source of their revenues. Until this time NSC governments do not provide any form of strategic leadership, nor will it be possible to induce them to do so. But from this time on, perceptive NSC leaders will become increasingly interested in removing obstacles to strategists pursuing their profit-seeking objectives. Even so, the ruling elite will view its relationship with the strategists as exploitive and they will regularly intervene to provide preferential treatment to favourites willing to provide extra gratuities and/or support. But gradually the ruling elite will become directly involved in strategic activities, granting themselves and their families substantial monopolies. Only when the strategists gain greater economic power will they challenge these corrupt practices and, eventually, insist that the ruling elite supply proper strategic leadership that is relatively free from corruption, cronyism, nepotism, and preferential treatment—leadership that is aimed at facilitating the objectives of the strategists. But, by this time, our NSC will have become an ESC. Strategic leadership has small beginnings in an NSC, but it expands as the society's technological substrategy unfolds.

When is democracy appropriate?

It is essential to realise that the changing political situation of NSCs is a response to an unfolding dynamic strategy. Hence, it is not appropriate for outsiders to suggest, as they regularly do, that the political system that has emerged in the most advanced SCs should be adopted by ESCs, FASCs, and even NSCs. There are some who naively argue that the adoption of democratic institutions will increase a country's rate of economic growth. This is based not on a general economic and political model of development but rather on simple correlations between the two variables in advanced societies. What is not understood is that both these economic and political results are independent outcomes of the modern dynamic process and are not causally related. In the early modern and pre-modern worlds—the greater part of human experience—it was possible to achieve high rates of economic growth with very undemocratic institutions. It all depends on the nature and success of the strategic pursuit. It is essential that political institutions be shaped by strategic demand rather than ideology, because the adoption of inappropriate institutions under external pressure either will be totally ineffective as the ruling elite employs its unequal power to reassert control or will be disruptive of the strategic transition.

Summing up

No attempt will be made to provide detailed policy prescriptions. While I have outlined clear policy principles for the Third World, these must be employed flexibly in different circumstances. There are no standard policy programs that should be followed by all countries in all circumstances. It is essential to resist the temptation to mindlessly follow the flavour of the month—for example, the so-called "Asian model" so popular in the 1980s and 1990s[24]—without investigating closely the relevance of such an approach. The central policy objective always is to respond to the society's strategists and to facilitate their objectives. In effect this means responding to changing strategic demand as the country's technological substrategy unfolds in the context of the developing GST. The essence of the strategic response is flexibility. Policies must not be perpetuated beyond their strategic effectiveness, as happened with import-replacement policies in Latin America. This can best be avoided by governments listening closely to their own strategists rather than to so-called "experts" either local or foreign.

The dynamic-strategy model enables us to draw a variety of detailed policy issues together by viewing them as "strategic instruments" that respond to changes in strategic demand. These strategic instruments include population, human capital, investment, technology, and institutions. The same is true of the supply-side sources of these strategic instruments, such as fertility, immigration, education and technical training, savings and foreign capital, together with knowledge and invention. In the light of the dynamic-strategy model we need to add strategic ideas/knowledge, strategic institutions, and strategic leadership.

Strategic leadership, in contrast to both the interventionist and neoliberal approaches, is based on a realistic analysis of the dynamic process. It does not impose an unrealistic production approach on an NSC, nor does it force an ESC to disrupt its own strategic demand–response mechanism. It accepts the reality of the strategic pursuit and it reinforces strategic confidence and facilitates the operation of the dynamic mechanism by assisting strategists to achieve their objectives. Strategic leadership requires limited intervention, and even then only to focus the efforts of the strategists and, thereby, facilitate the unfolding of the dynamic strategy. It should never be undertaken in support of rent-seeking, as it so often is. The success of appropriate strategic leadership will be seen reflected in rapid and sustained rates of economic growth.

THE WAY AHEAD

While the traditional approach is to seek intervention on the supply side, the dynamic-strategy approach is to argue that if we take care of strategic demand, the supply response will take care of itself. At best, the supply-side approach—emphasising the reduction of fertility through female education, growth through overinvestment in schooling, investment through promoting the saving rate, economic development through equity and democracy—will merely waste scarce resources and disrupt the development process. At worst it will derail it entirely.

The dynamic-strategy model shows that with the unfolding technological substrategy a Third-World country will experience changes in strategic demand that call forth a supply response articulated through strategic inflation. The essential requirement of policy-makers is that they recognise the true nature of this process and attempt merely to remove any stubborn institutional obstacles that might complicate or delay the response of these various strategic instruments. This includes the reduction, if not elimination, of "nonstrategic inflation" through a more sensible monetary policy. The greatest error they can possibly make is to employ stabilisation policies to eliminate strategic, rather than nonstrategic, inflation. By interfering with the core strategic demand–response mechanism of the *logos* in this way, the development process will be disrupted—and it will be derailed permanently if this disastrous neoliberal policy thrust is maintained indefinitely, as "experts" in the IMF are attempting to do. What the "experts"—those who "bark at what they cannot understand"—need to do is recognise the existence of the strategic *logos* and remove existing barriers to its effective operation, rather than undermine it through wrong-headed intervention. *There is an urgent need to get this right, because NSCs have only another half-century to join the "global strategic core" before the next technological paradigm shift leaves them struggling even further in the rear.* Now it's time to consider the imminent Solar Revolution.

Chapter 13
Choice of Futures for the *Logos*

"Experts" are the high priests of stagnation.

Some of the possible futures—both immediate and far reaching—facing mankind have been discussed briefly in the opening chapter of this book. Our final chapter focuses on the choice of futures to be made in the twenty-first century. As we shall see, the choices made will be critical, because human civilisation can either continue to develop exponentially as it has done over the past 6,000 years, or risk stagnation and collapse.

Two alternative futures for humanity are outlined in this chapter. The first involves the future that would be generated by the strategic *logos*, or dynamic life-system, left free to do what it does best—ensure the survival and prosperity of life forms in a hostile physical world. The second is that proposed by the "mitigation engineers", who are completely unaware of the presence or operation of the strategic *logos* either in the past or in the future: namely the introduction of a radical comprehensive climate-mitigation program that will distort, even derail, the global life-system, and inevitably delay, even completely prevent, the emergence of mankind's fourth technological paradigm shift. In effect this will involve a clash in the immediate future between the antistrategic mitigationists and the global strategists—a clash similar in nature to, but potentially much more destructive than, that between the antistrategists (USSR and Maoist China) and the strategists (the Western powers) during the Cold War. Whatever decision humanity makes in this respect, we should be aware of the likely consequences of our actions.

THE SOLAR REVOLUTION

First Sight of a New Dawn

When the dynamic-strategy theory was first published in *The Dynamic Society* (1996)—but actually worked out in the early 1990s—I made a number of predictions about the future technological development path for human society that is relevant to the climate-change debate. At the time there was a concern among the radical ecologists—who I called the "ecological engineers"—that population growth, which they wrongly viewed as an increasing function of economic growth, was irreparably damaging the natural environment and, thereby, leading to the inevitable collapse of human society. These doomsters included the "limits-to-growth" people (Meadows et al 1972; 1992) together with radical ecologists such as Paul Ehrlich (*The Population Explosion*, 1990) and David Suzuki (1990). They demanded that human society "immediately" attempt to live within its perceived physical limits by eliminating economic growth, which, they incorrectly claimed, was driving population growth and destroying the planet. If we failed to do this "immediately", human society would collapse sometime during the early part of the twenty-first century. These predictions were based, at best, on simple engineering models (with feedback effects) that extrapolate certain key variables into the future on the assumptions that appeared relevant to the ecological engineers at the time. This was an exercise in simple historicism.[1]

But their models were ideologically based, simplistic, and wrong. As the realist dynamic-strategy theory shows, population growth is a response, via strategic demand, to the type of dynamic strategy being pursued, not to economic growth *per se*. While earlier dynamic strategies of family multiplication, commerce, and conquest required population growth to feed the unfolding strategic process, the current dynamic strategy of technological change does not, because it is able to extract increasing services from a given supply of labour and resources. Hence, economic growth is even consistent with a decline in population. At heart, the historicist models of the "ecological engineers" have much in common with those used by climate-change scientists and orthodox economists today, who are the "mitigation engineers".

The Dynamic Society (1996) identified problems with both these models and the assumed relationship between variables like economic growth and population change. In particular, it was demonstrated that these models were not based on a realist general dynamic-strategy model and, as a consequence, could not foresee the forthcoming technological revolution that would enable human society to break through the alleged physical "limits to growth". As it turned out, global economic growth did not abate—in fact it increased owing to the rapid development achieved by China, India, and Southeast Asia, at a time of continued growth in the West. Despite this, the world was not overwhelmed by increases in population, and the dynamics of human society did not crash as the ecological engineers predicted. After the turn of the century, it became more widely recognised that there was no simple relationship between the growth of both living standards and population, just as had been shown theoretically and empirically in my books *The Dynamic Society* (1996), *The Ephemeral Civilization* (1997), and *Global Transition* (1999). But there still is widespread confusion about the real relationship between population and economic growth, owing to a general lack of understanding of the dynamic-strategy theory and the strategic *logos*.

Because their predictions of disaster failed to eventuate, and their theoretical models were irrelevant, the limits-to-growth groups (including the radical ecologists like Ehrlich and Suzuki) just melted away. They have been replaced, however, by the climate-change fraternity, who employ more sophisticated versions of the same historicist models. *It is a curious case of shape-shifting by radical ecologists.* Not surprisingly, these climate mitigation models are also unable to capture the dynamics of human society or predict the forthcoming technological paradigm shift. When pushed, the climate-change people also display the same anti-growth and anti-population sentiments, but, owing to the failure of their predecessors, they express these flawed ideas more carefully. I predict that the "mitigation engineers" will be no more successful than the "ecological engineers".

Here is what I said about the forthcoming technological revolution in *The Dynamic Society*[2]:

> In Chapter 9 it was shown that the distance between paradigm shifts and their duration has been declining in a geometric fashion. The time taken for the technological shifts to occur involved hundreds of thousands of years for the Paleolithic (c. 1.6 myrs ago), 4,000 years for the Neolithic (10,600 years ago), and 100 years for the Industrial (c. 1760) Revolutions. This suggests that the next paradigm shift could begin soon and could be completed in no more than a generation or so. The future revolution, as history has suggested, will release population from the present resources limit and, as a result, actually *reduce* environmental degradation. This is because it will no longer be necessary to push natural resources to their limits with an increasingly restricted technology, and because higher levels of real GDP per capita in the Third World will lead to a levelling-off of population, as has already occurred in developed nations ... The present concerns about overpopulation and environment degradation, therefore, will be overcome by the future technological paradigm shift ... But this is not to say that we should abandon attempts to protect the environment, just that we should not allow this remedial action to derail the Dynamic Society.

In the early 1990s, armed with the dynamic-strategy theory, it was clear to me that the industrial technological paradigm had already entered its exhaustion phase, and would be replaced in the middle decades of the twenty-first century by a new technological paradigm—just as the industrial paradigm had replaced the neolithic paradigm from the late eighteenth century (see Figure 3.5). The degradation of the environment that was of concern to the ecologists at the time was a sign of this. Their error was to read the evidence of paradigm exhaustion as signs of ecological and societal collapse, and this error was an outcome of the failure to develop a general dynamic theory of human society. As I said in *The Dynamic Society*,[3] the radical ecologists

> by persuading even a significant proportion of individuals and global organisations that the historically familiar signs of a technological paradigm approaching exhaustion are instead the signs of a world teetering on the edge of darkness ... may do considerable and unnecessary damage. Through costly and unnecessary government intervention at the national and global levels, they may contribute both to the weakening of Western civilisation ... and to the delay in any future technological paradigm shift.

The Solar Revolution Approches

Since the early 1990s, other evidence of an exhausting technological paradigm has emerged. This includes the rapidly diminishing reserves of fossil fuels—particularly petroleum—available at economic prices in the face of exponential industrial growth in China and India, and the growing costs of reducing the carbon emitted by their use in production, heating, and transport. In response to the potential energy-supply problems, industrialised countries are already positioning themselves strategically to secure oil supplies through war and the threat of war. These countries include the USA in the Middle East and Russia in Georgia. These wars are motivated by diminishing supplies of oil, not by "terrorism", "weapons of mass destruction", the existence of brutal dictators, or the rights of nationals in neighboring countries. The governments of these leading strategic societies deny this fundamental truth in order to make military intervention more palatable to their electorates. In *The Death of Zarathustra. Notes on Truth for the Risk-taker* (2011), I show how strategic leaders of democracies tell truth to their enemies and lies to their people.

Exhausting the energy sources of the Industrial Revolution

It is worth considering the situation regarding global oil and coal supplies in greater detail owing to the central role they play in providing energy in the industrial technological paradigm. The signs that the "golden age of oil" has passed have been accumulating for some time. In 1962 the global discovery of *new* oil fields peaked; in 1970 total oil production peaked in the USA (something the industry in the 1950s said could not happen), Venezuela and Libya; in the 1970s, 1980s and 1990s it peaked in Iran, Canada (conventional supplies), Romania, Indonesia, Egypt, India, Syria, Gabon, Malaysia, Argentina, Colombia, Ecuador and Great Britain; and in the early years of the twenty-first century these countries were joined by Norway, Oman, Mexico and Australia. Of the remaining oil producers, Kuwait, Saudi Arabia, and Iraq are expected to peak before 2020. While China and Canada (exploiting oil sands) are expanding production rapidly, they too are expected to peak during the 2020s.

Although the data are difficult to assess accurately, many observers believe that, even with unconventional sources currently being investigated, global oil production has either peaked or will peak sometime between 2010 and the 2020s.[4] Unsurprisingly, the situation is similar for the associated fuel of natural gas: world reserves (of which 42 percent are found in the Middle East and North Africa) are expected to peak around 2020 (Energy Watch Group, 2013). While, from time to time, new sources will be exploited using new technologies, this will merely result in fluctuations around a long-run downward trend in oil consumption, as reserves are progressively exhausted and relative costs of production rise. This phase of decline, will also be marked by periodic price wars between conventional and unconventional suppliers (as in 2015), but this will not alter the reality of paradigmatic exhaustion.

With the passing of global peak oil production and the exponential growth of world demand—driven particularly by the rapid industrialisation of China, India, and Southeast Asia—cheap oil will quickly become a thing of the past. Certainly by the middle decades of the twenty-first century, oil reserves will be unable to support civilisation as we know it (Hirsch 2005), *particularly if we become trapped in the current industrial technological paradigm.*

What of coal, that other energy mainstay of the industrial paradigm? The situation with coal is less clear owing to the poor quality of the data. It is generally thought, however, that published data concerning "reserves" and "resources" are considerably biased on the high side. Over the past couple of decades regional estimates of both reserves and resources have been downgraded quite dramatically in some instances. Only estimates of "proved" recoverable reserves can be used when evaluating global coal supplies. Of these total global reserves, some 81 percent are found in just six countries (in descending order): USA, Russia, China, India, Australia, and South Africa.[5] It is thought that coal production will continue to increase up to 2020, will then plateau, peak around 2025 at a level 30 percent higher than current levels, and then begin an inevitable decline.[6] This is regarded as a "best case" scenario. Of course, the ability of the coal industry to supply an exponentially growing demand for energy will be complicated by the interventions of the mitigation engineers. As with oil, it is highly doubtful that coal will be in a position to support civilisation as we know it if we are locked into the old industrial technological paradigm.

Those who are more optimistic about the supplies of oil, natural gas, and coal usually make the mistake of underestimating the demand for these resources, which will grow at a rapid exponential rate over the next generation, as China, India and the rest of Asia continues to develop rapidly in an effort to catch up with the West in terms of wealth and living standards. It is often not realised how large is the gap in living standards between the Asian giants and the West. Rapid rates of growth, which are relatively easily achieved when employing the dynamic strategy of imitation, are often confused with levels of achievement. A few basic statistics from the IMF and World Bank should dispel this confusion. In terms of GDP per capita (at purchasing power parity), China, India, and Indonesia in 2014 were still only 23 percent, 10 percent, and 19 percent respectively of that in the USA. In other words, China, India, and Indonesia will need to increase their GDP per capita by multiples of 4, 9, and 5 respectively to catch up with the standard enjoyed by the USA today. Of course, as the USA will continue to grow during the rapprochement process, these catch-up factors will need to be even larger! This "catch-up" will require a **massive** increase in absolute levels of GDP, particularly as the populations of China, India, and Indonesia are still growing significantly. To be able to catch up to the USA's 2014 level of living standards, China's GDP would need to increase from 10.4 to 74.4 trillion US dollars, India's from 2.1 to 68.4 trillion US dollars, and Indonesia's from 0.9 to 14.0 trillion US dollars (even if we assume, totally unrealistically, that their populations remain stable during the process)—increases by multiples of 7.4, 32.6, and 15.5 respectively! *The combined estimated GDP of China, India and Indonesia (only three ESCs attempting to industrialise) once they had caught up with the US as it is today, would be* **twice as large as the 2014 level of total world GDP!** This huge task will be even greater in proportion to the increase in populations in these countries during the catch-up phase. And it will be compounded by the growing industrialisation of other ESCs around the world.

This simple statistical exercise demonstrates that a proportionately **massive** increase in the consumption of fossil fuels (at least twice as great as that consumed by the entire world in 2014, *ceteris paribus*) will be required to facilitate the "catch-up" of the Asian giants. It is highly improbable that this absolute increase in GDP could be achieved using fossil fuels alone, or even supplemented with **existing** alternative energy sources (wind, solar panels, nuclear). In my opinion, this Asian "catch-up" would only be possible once the Solar Revolution—a new technological paradigm shift—is underway. And if this new technological paradigm shift occurs in the West and not the East (which will not have exhausted its old industrial technological paradigm before the next economic revolution), as it probably will, the Asian giants will be suddenly reduced to dwarf status, and will have to rejoin the catch-up process at the beginning once more—as they were forced to do when the Industrial Revolution began in the late eighteenth century. The history of non-Western countries could be a story about the myth of Sisyphus.

We have also begun to see land being diverted from the production of timber and food to the planting of biofuel crops. This is an echo of the situation in Western Europe during the mid-eighteenth century, when land for human food crops was being diverted to growing oats to feed the rapidly increasing number of horses, which were the main source of motive power for transport, agriculture, and even manufacturing. In addition, as timber and wood were major sources of construction, machinery manufacture, heat, and thermal power, the rapid growth of European societies was effectively eliminating accessible forests and increasing the cost of employing this essential resource in the pre-industrial era. Only the occurrence of the Industrial Revolution removed this pressure on the natural environment, reduced costs of production, and raised standards of living.

So it will be in the first half of the twenty-first century. As the industrial technological paradigm is progressively exhausted, costs of fossil fuels will continue to rise, long-run economic growth and living standards will stagnate and even begin to decline by the middle decades of this century. In turn this situation will generate the incentives—indeed the imperative if we hope to survive and prosper—to introduce an entirely new technological paradigm. This will not be a gradual development, but will involve a quantum leap for human society, most likely taking place within the generation following the middle of the twenty-first century. While the earlier Paleolithic, Neolithic, and Modern (Industrial) Revolutions also involved quantum leaps, the magnitude and rate and at which this has been occurring along the global technological development path is increasing exponentially (as measured by my "logological constant"). These remarkable great steps in human material progress are illustrated in Figure 3.5 and discussed in detail in chapters 3 and 4.

A radical new technology

The new technological paradigm will completely transcend any of the low-carbon technologies that are currently in operation or even on the drawing board, as these "alternative" technologies—wind and wave power and solar panels—are all part of the old industrial technological paradigm. The situation will be similar to the way the technology of the Industrial Revolution completely transcended the "alternative" technologies of wind and water mills—alternative to the use of animal and human power—of the existing neolithic paradigm.

What will this new technological paradigm involve? Nothing that we can currently detail very precisely. Here is what I said about the forthcoming technological paradigm shift back in the early 1990s.

> What will the fourth technological paradigm bring? To answer this question would be like attempting in 1750 to say what would unfold from the Industrial Revolution. While there were signs to be read in the mid-eighteenth century, such as the growing use of fossil fuels, there was no way to tell where it would all end. Yet we can speculate sensibly about a central feature of all economic revolutions— the source of energy. The first revolution saw the extension of human energy with the use of more efficient tools; the second revolution saw the partial substitution of animal, water and wind energy for human energy; and the third revolution saw the substitution of thermal energy based upon fossil fuels for both human and animal energy. It appears highly likely that the fourth revolution will involve the substitution of solar energy for fossil-fuel energy. This will resolve, for all practical purposes, the problem that increasing entropy … might ultimately pose for the dynamics of human society. From the fourth revolution, physical constraints upon growth will be limited only by the flow of solar energy.[7]

As discussed in chapters 3 and 4, I called this fourth technological paradigm shift the "Solar Revolution". And throughout my work, the term "Solar Revolution" has been employed only in reference to the fourth technological paradigm shift, not (as some have mistakenly done recently) to the low carbon technologies that have emerged from the old industrial technological paradigm.

What form will the technology of the Solar Revolution take? This is a very difficult question to answer, because the details of technological progress are impossible to predict. While it has been possible to model the process of technological paradigm shifts over the past 2 myrs and into the immediate future by using the dynamic-strategy theory, we cannot model the technical expression of these paradigm shifts, because of both the essentially trial-and-error nature of the process of innovation, and the shaping influence of unpredictable relative factor prices. The difficulty today is the same as that in the mid-eighteenth century had someone attempted to scientifically predict the flow of technology during the nineteenth and twentieth centuries. Nevertheless, in order to give some concrete expression to the concept of a Solar Revolution, a few broad brush-strokes are required. What I have in mind is a technology that will enable energy to be derived directly and continuously from the Sun, rather than through a sporadic (owing to night and bad weather) and hence highly inefficient, Earth-based solar panel technology. This will involve a complex system of energy-collecting-and-relaying satellites revolving around the Sun. It is similar to what has been called a "Dyson swarm".[8] Beyond this, we are very much in the dark.

Birthplace of the Solar Revolution?

Another key question is: Where will the Solar Revolution take place? In *The Dynamic Society* (1996) I argued that technological revolutions have occurred in "funnels of transformation", which can be thought of as geographically or economically constrained regions at the centre of an exhausting technological paradigm.[9] These regions are characterised by heightened competition, higher population interaction, greater pressure on natural resources, and greater exchange of ideas. These funnels of transformation—these regions in the vanguard of technological revolution—have included the Rift Valley of eastern Africa for the hunting revolution; the Fertile Crescent (Old World) and the Mesoamerican isthmus (New World) for the agricultural revolution; and the western edge of Europe—the interface with the stimulating outside world—for the Industrial Revolution.

What of the forthcoming Solar Revolution? The dynamic-strategy theory suggests that the future technological revolution will take place where the strategic pursuit is most advanced and least restricted by a command mitigation system; where pressure on natural resources is most intense; where investment in the infrastructure of deep scientific research and innovation is highest; and where economic growth is based on an internally generated dynamic process (as opposed to an externally dependent process). It will take place at the very centre of the "global strategic core" identified in chapter 12—possibly North America, which will become the new "funnel of transformation".

The initial losers, even in the developed world, will be those countries that intervene most in the operation of their strategic *logos*; that adopt a command mitigation economy; that fail to realise the current pressure on natural resources is a function of the approaching technological revolution; that do not regard deep scientific research (rather than superficial research into second-best technologies) as their top investment priority; that rely on external forces to drive their economies; and that take the advice of metaphysical economists (neoclassical) and scientists (climate mitigationists) seriously. Complacent developed countries (such as Australia), while currently affluent, fall into the loser category, because they are flirting with climate mitigation policies and are refusing to adopt progressive technological strategies.[10]

Hot spots of mitigation interventionism in these complacent developed countries—these potential paradigm-shift losers—can be seen emerging in regions with less involvement in the real world. One such hot spot is Canberra the Australian national capital in which I have lived for about 30 years. The economic activity of Canberra is less dependent upon real-world production requiring large amounts of energy and capital inputs, and more on the provision of education and government services requiring less energy-intensive processes. And its population (388,000 people at the end of 2014) has a higher average standard of living, and is more exposed to superficial forms of tertiary education (rather than profound forms of training in analytical thinking), which predisposes Canberrans to idealist rather than realist solutions, despite the rising costs of living that accompany second-best technologies. These dangerous hot spots of mitigation interventionism are currently pioneering forms of economic and social control that will spread out through their host nations. If steps are not taken to prevent it.

The few winners in the Solar Revolution race, therefore, will streak ahead of the crowd—just as Britain did in the early nineteenth century—and the many losers will accelerate backwards in a relative sense—just as China did during the course of the nineteenth century. Because governments rely on advice from those who have no understanding of the strategic logos*, this inevitable outcome will only be generally recognised after the rapid onset of the Solar Revolution.*

Derailing the Solar Revolution?

The Solar Revolution will not only transform human society, it will make the "need" for climate-mitigation policies totally redundant. But this will only occur if we refrain from the massive intervention being proposed by climate-change scientists and interventionist economists such as Nicholas Stern, as discussed below. Massive mitigation like that advocated in the *Stern Review* will distort the strategic *logos* at both the national and global levels; will lock in the old paradigm's low-carbon technologies; will keep us captive to an exhausted technological paradigm that is no longer capable of generating economic growth; and will provide regional strongmen with highly tempting incentives to pursue the only alterative dynamic strategy to outlawed technological change—the strategy of conquest.[11] This sequence of outcomes, which would follow directly from a rigid adherence to a thorough program of climate mitigation, would generate massive dynamic costs that Stern and other climate-change economists have completely overlooked in their comparative-static framework of analysis.

ORTHODOX ECONOMICS FAILS TO FORESEE THE SOLAR REVOLUTION

It is a mystery to many commentators that economists have become advisors to governments concerning climate mitigation, when it was natural scientists who conjured up the spectre of man-made global warming and climate change. The explanation is somewhat ironical. By claiming that climate change is man-made, natural scientists have immediately disqualified themselves from any further involvement in the debate, as they have no expertise in the study of human society, which is essential if we are to understand how human society is going to mitigate this problem of its own making. In effect, natural scientists have shot themselves in their collective foot. Unfortunately, orthodox economics is also lacking in the appropriate expertise.

Orthodox economists are completely confident that their theory of capitalist production is more than capable of handling all societal issues. But they are completely mistaken. I will argue that the ability of neoclassical economics to analyse reality is severely limited. Because this metaphysical discipline has failed to develop a realist general dynamic theory, it is unable to predict future structural change. Instead, orthodox economists employ simplistic historicist models to extrapolate recent trends into the distant future. This is remarkably ironical given their collective disdain for historical analysis. But, owing to the seemingly sophisticated mathematical techniques employed by orthodox economists, government policymakers have been blinded to this fatal flaw. It is a technical sleight of hand. For this reason, governments throughout the world are on the verge of committing their citizens to a hugely costly program of intervention that will cause global society to grind to a halt. "Experts" are the high priests of stagnation.

Why Isn't Economics up to the Task?

Neoclassical economics emerged from the so-called "marginal revolution" of the 1870s, which was pioneered by W.S. Jevons (1835–1882) in England, Carl Menger (1840–1921) in Austria, and Léon Walras (1834–1910) in Lausanne. This mathematically based "theory of value" or "theory of the firm", which was elegantly summarised by Alfred Marshall (1842–1924), is concerned with **small** (or marginal) changes in markets in the **short-term** within a comparative **static** (rather than a dynamic) framework. The theory of the firm, which is preoccupied with conditions of equilibrium (rather than the disequilibrium of dynamics), reflects the nineteenth-century influence of classical thermodynamics. This mechanical physics-like approach to human society displaced the earlier, more organic science of classical economics—pioneered by the French Physiocrats and Adam Smith (1723–1790) in the eighteenth century, and Karl Marx (1818–1883) in the nineteenth century—which focused on longer-run dynamic processes underlying the transformation of human society. These issues are discussed in greater detail in my book *Economics without Time* (1993). Since the late nineteenth century, orthodox economics has been largely concerned with everyday economic issues examined within a short-run, static framework. As the Cambridge Post-Keynesian economist Joan Robinson famously said, neoclassical economics is trivially concerned with "the price of a cup of tea".

The theoretical tools that orthodox economists bring to the (tea) table when discussing climate change—anything but a trivial or static issue—include: cost–benefit analysis, price theory, the shadowy theory of external diseconomies (somewhat loosely called "externalities"), and market failure. These somewhat meager tools of microeconomics are expected to handle the big macro issues of the dynamics of human society and its interaction with climate change throughout the next century or so. This is like turning up to the gunfight at OK Corral with a Swiss Army knife—a very effective tool for small jobs but completely outgunned in the world of realist dynamics.

It is hardly surprising that neoclassical economics has failed to develop a realist theory of dynamics. It's misnamed "growth theory" is not growth theory at all, as it focuses merely on convergence to equilibrium in the tradition of classical thermodynamics mentioned above. Economics failed to follow the lead of physics in the twentieth century when a reformulated thermodynamics shifted its focus to far-from-equilibrium conditions. As neoclassical growth theory has little to say about real-world dynamics, it is not even invoked by climate-change economists (or, as shown in chapter 12, development economists).

To his credit, Nicholas Stern, the guru of mitigation economics, is aware of some of the deficiencies in neoclassical economics. As a development economist he certainly should be. He tells us, for example, that:

> Standard externality and cost-benefit approaches have their usefulness for analysing climate change, but, as they are methods focused on evaluating marginal changes, and generally abstract from dynamics and risk, they can only be starting points for further work ...[for simple historicism]

> Standard treatments of discounting are valuable for analysing marginal projects but are inappropriate for non-marginal comparisons of [development] paths; the approach to discounting must meet the challenge of assessing and comparing paths that have very different trajectories and involve very long-term and large inter-generational impacts.[12]

But, as an orthodox economist, Stern's dilemma is that he has no other theoretical instruments to substitute for these static, short-term, marginal concepts. So, despite his qualifications, Stern is forced to resort to these inadequate theoretical instruments anyway, and hope we didn't notice the sleight of hand. But, by employing totally inappropriate tools of analysis, Stern and the rest of his tribe have contributed to *"the great climate-mitigation delusion"*. As the mitigation engineers have failed to understand the dynamics of human society, or even the existence of the strategic *logos*, they are unable to analyse the future either of human society or the planet. It is like placing a teashop proprietor in charge of the future of humanity.

Unfortunately most orthodox economists are just not aware of the full extent of the limitations of their profession. Why? Because these theoretically trained economists rarely encounter big issues in the real world; and, if they do, they skate across the deficiencies of their methods with heroic boldness. Whenever **static** costs exceed **static** benefits, which is often the case with big real-world issues, orthodox economists usually suggest that the participants must be economically irrational, or driven by non-material motivations.

The Persistent Failure of Economics to Explain Reality

The deficiencies of neoclassical economics are glaringly obvious when applied to big historical events, as has been done quite innocently by the so-called New Economic Historians—neoclassical economists who turned their attention to history, particularly in the USA, from the 1960s. A few examples—including US railroads, the American War of Independence, the US Civil War, and the economic pay-off of the British empire—will help to illustrate my argument about the limited ability of economics when examining big, real-world issues of a dynamic nature. In order not to obscure our main argument, these historical examples will be dealt with briefly. Interested readers may wish to consult my other books where they are developed in more detail.

In the celebrated case of the economic role of US railroads, the historical economist Robert Fogel (1964) employed neoclassical theory to measure the **static** costs and benefits of American investment in transport technology. He estimated the "social saving" from railroad investment to have been only about 4 percent of GNP in 1890 (which was much less than other economic activities) and concluded, therefore, that railroads played only a limited role in American economic development. According to Fogel—later jointly (with Douglass North) awarded the Nobel Prize in Economics for his promotion of neoclassical theory in history—railroads were not essential to American growth in the second half of the nineteenth century, and that their role could have been performed largely by existing river and canal systems. What his neoclassical analysis completely overlooks are the **dynamic** benefits of creating, in response to strategic demand, an integrated mega-market in the second half of the nineteenth century that was to facilitate the unfolding of the USA's technological strategy—an unfolding process that enabled the USA to achieve world economic dominance in the twentieth century. As I show in *The Ephemeral Civilization* (1997), railway construction was not economically marginal but rather was central to this strategic development.[13]

In the case of the American War of Independence, neoclassically inspired economic historians have attempted to measure the **static** costs and benefits to the American colonialists of British imperialism. To do this they have estimated the annual costs of "distortions of trade routes" resulting from the Navigation

Acts imposed by Britain between 1763 and 1775. Traditionally, these costs, which have been regarded as the main burden of empire, amounted to no more than 3 percent of gross colonial product. As such they would have been largely offset by benefits from being part of the British empire, which included British subsidies, bounties, and military protection. Others have argued that the costs of taxes and customs imposed by Britain after the war with France, together with the restrictions resulting from the 1763 Proclamation Line (defining the western boundary of the colonies) were not terribly onerous. The conclusion? That politics rather than economics explains the very costly and risky fight by the Americans for independence, when they had so little to gain economically. It was a long and costly war that was only won after French involvement. Yet why would the Americans risk so much for political ends? The real answer is that the neoclassical evaluation of the **static** costs of empire does not come close to approximating the **dynamic** costs. As we shall see in the next section, the same is true of the static costs of climate mitigation. The struggle for independence was a fight for control of very different dynamic strategies. The British were pursuing a global commerce strategy and wanted, as a maritime power, to confine American settlement to the eastern seaboard; whereas the colonialists were pursing the family-multiplication strategy and wanted, as a potential continental power, to expand westward. It was a clash of dynamic strategies, and the costs of being dominated by the British can be measured in terms of the huge potential gains that could be made by forging a mega-market across North America. To convert these potential costs into realised benefits was why the Americans were prepared to risk so much. There are, of course, lessons to be learnt here for the potential clash in the twenty-first century between the antistrategic mitigation engineers and the global strategists. It could become a clash of dynamic strategies on a far more massive scale than that of the War of Independence. And it would be far more costly.

When considering the **static** costs and benefits of the American Civil War (1861–1865), Robert Fogel (1989) is led by his neoclassical training to argue that as the cost of this internecine conflict—including the deaths of 600,000 men and the destruction of much infrastructure—outweighed the apparent benefits, the war must have been fought over the **moral** issue of slavery. This is a very odd conclusion, as my study of human history suggests that men in massive numbers do not surrender their lives for moral issues. And, in fact, when we take the dynamic benefits into account, as I did in *The Ephemeral Civilization*, it is clear that the US Civil War was a clash between two every different dynamic strategies.[14] The North was desperate to maintain the political integrity of the USA in order to develop a mega-market under tariff protection, which would drive its burgeoning technological strategy based on its industrial facilities in the north-east. In contrast, the South was equally desperate to achieve independence from the protectionist North in order to pursue its free-trade commerce strategy based on the export of plantation crops, particularly cotton, to Britain in exchange for cheap industrial products (much cheaper than could be purchased from the Yankees). The potential dynamic benefits to both camps arising from the success of their strategic goals were huge (and can be seen reflected in the different rates of growth of real GDP before and after the Civil War), and greatly in excess of the high costs of this long, drawn-out, and expensive war. The victory of the North led to the transformation of the USA into the world's largest and most prosperous society in the twentieth century, although at the cost of a depressed South. This global dominance would not have occurred in a politically and, hence, economically fragmented North America.

Finally, consider the economic basis for the British empire after 1885. Some have argued—as outlined in *The Ephemeral Civilization*—that after 1885, the return on investment in empire was significantly lower than that at home or abroad; that the real beneficiaries of empire were the colonials/dominionists; that those in the UK who benefited most were the aristocrats at the expense of the tax-paying middle classes; and that between 1870 and 1913, the **static** gains were only 1 to 6 percent of GNP, compared with 10 percent on railways.[15] Hence, the post-1885 empire is seen by neoclassically inspired historians as economically irrational and anachronistic. Once again, however, the **dynamic** benefits have been totally ignored. The major dynamic benefit of empire, which did in fact accrue to UK's tax-paying middle classes, was the role it played in *defending* and enhancing Britain's dynamic strategy of technological change, which generated high rates of continuous economic growth. Empire guaranteed Britain's post-1885 survival and security by preventing its European competitors starving it of natural resources and markets. I argue that empire was only abandoned when Britain found a more economical method of defending its technological strategy at home—the atomic bomb. As soon as the bomb was developed, Britain dismantled its empire and emerged richer than ever, something that no previous global empire had been able to achieve.

In all these historical case studies, the costs are easily measured in a static framework, but not so the most important benefits that are always dynamic in nature. As we will see in detail in the next section, the same is true when neoclassical economics is applied to climate change. As always, the dynamic benefits of the strategic pursuit are completely neglected. Also neoclassical economists fail to understand the mutual destruction that always arises from the clash of opposing dynamic strategies. The bottom line is that orthodox economics is a totally unsuitable discipline for dealing with the big dynamic issues in human society—particularly the big issue of climate change.

What About the Models Employed?

Because orthodox economics has failed to construct a general dynamic theory of human society, it is forced to fall back on naive historicist models when estimating the impact of either climate change or proposed mitigation policies.

There is a major irony here. Orthodox economists pride themselves on their superior deductive approach to constructing economic theory and are largely contemptuous of the work of historical economists who employ inductive techniques. While they continue to focus on problems of "the-price-of-a-cup-of-tea" variety—of short-term, static and marginal (trivial) issues—they can maintain their self-delusion. But when they take on long-term, dynamic, and non-marginal (important) issues they find themselves completely out of their depth. Of course, it usually takes someone else to point it out.

If neoclassical economists insist on exploring the big issues like climate change, their only option—like that of the IPCC—is to employ the historicist models that even historical economists reject as being simplistic and, therefore, dangerous. These historicist models involve extrapolating key economic variables into the future on the basis of a range of arbitrary assumptions. The technical sophistication of these models—which may seem impressive to the uninitiated—doesn't alter the fact that they fail to capture the dynamics of human society. They have, in other words, no way of taking into account any major structural changes that might occur as a result of the internal dynamics of human society. Ironically, only the inductively based theory of the historical economist is able to achieve this essential requirement.

The historicist models employed in the *Stern Review* are called "integrated assessment models" (or IAMs). These IAMs include a range of sectors, such as agriculture, forestry, fisheries, water systems, energy supplies, ecosystems, coastal zones and so on. Stern claims that: "IAMs simulate the process of human-induced climate change, from emissions of GHGs [greenhouse gases] to the socio-economic impacts of climate change".[16] The modeled chain of impacts—which also includes feedback effects—operates from population, technology, production and consumption to emissions to atmospheric concentrations to "radiative forcing" and global climate to regional climate and weather to direct impacts (crops, forests and ecosystems) to socioeconomic impacts.

The IAMs are employed to make calculations of impacts on climate, environment, and human society *for periods of up to 200 years into the future*. All without considering the probability of major structural change over this long period of time. Of course, if we go 200 years or so back into the past, we enter a very different (pre-industrial) world to that existing today. Imagine the impact that the structural change called the Industrial Revolution would have had on the credibility of any historicist models (using similarly unrealistic or ephemeral assumptions) that might have been estimated in the late eighteenth century for the following 200 years! It does not seem to have occurred to the neoclassical authors of these models that their projections will be just as wildly inaccurate. This problem is particularly acute because, as the "logological constant" discussed in chapter 3 shows, history is speeding up. Much more will happen in the next 200 years than has happened in the past 200 years.

What is the Economists' Story?

It is a simple story. Using the textbook theory of the firm, the *Stern Review* attempts to calculate the costs of "business as usual" pursued in the face of hypothetical climate change over the next two centuries, compared with the costs of "stabilising" climate change (by preventing any further increase in greenhouse gas concentrations) over the same time period. Of course, they employ estimates of emissions, concentrations, and temperature change generated by their unrealistic historicist IAMs. Stern summarises his simple analysis and calculations as follows:

> Using the results from formal economic models, the Review estimates that if we don't act, the overall costs and risk of climate change will be equivalent to losing at least 5% of global GDP each year now and forever. If a wider range of risks and impacts is taken into account, the estimates of damage could rise to 20% of GDP or more.
>
> In contrast, the costs of action—reducing greenhouse emissions to avoid the worst impacts of climate change—can be limited to around 1% of global GDP each year.[17]

On the basis of these simple calculations, the rational course of action, according to the orthodox economist seems clear: a climate-mitigation program will, in the long run, be less costly than "business as usual". The cost of mitigation is portrayed as being quite modest and manageable—merely 1% of GDP or $1 in every $100 we produce. A reasonable insurance policy? Actually it is not quite as reasonable as it looks, as it is about ten times the rate we would expect to pay on our house insurance, but I suppose a habitable planet is more important to us than our individual houses!

Actually, the scale of the intervention being proposed through climate mitigation can only be fully appreciated by looking at it in absolute terms. One percent of world GDP, which in 2007 (the base year for my calculations) amounted to $656.1 billion, is a very large figure—more than the USA spent on its military program (about $560 billion) each year at that time. And this would be required in each and every year forever. Another way of looking at this matter is to estimate the amount of cumulative investment and employment that would be required by 2050 in low-carbon technologies as part of this mitigation program. Stern tells us that the cumulative investment required will amount to US$13 trillion—that is 13 followed by twelve zeros!—and the number of workers required would be 25 million—more than the entire population of Australia. *Clearly, this is intervention on a massive scale.*[18] With this background sketched out, it is time to measure the dynamic costs of climate mitigation by employing my general dynamic theory.

DYNAMIC VERSUS STATIC COSTS OF CLIMATE MITIGATION

The Impact of Mitigation

The key argument in this chapter is that a determined global effort to impose a comprehensive climate-mitigation program on all nations would cause at least a significant delay in the emergence of the fourth technological paradigm shift— the real Solar Revolution. Why? Because, in effect, the strategic *logos* will be hijacked by the mitigation engineers. Instead of strategists responding *creatively*, as they always have done, to logosian strategic demand—see chapters 4 and 11—they will be forced to respond *mechanically* to a set of artificially imposed goals. Goals based on metaphysical values rather than existential realities. The mitigationists hope to achieve these antistrategic goals by imposing a large number of major government interventions in the form of a carbon tax/ trading system, together with a wide range of regulations, directives, incentives, financial manipulations, public preferences, propaganda (called "education") and persuasion (eventually coercion?) required to force the adoption of low-carbon technologies. The *Stern Review* is crystal clear on this matter. As suggested above, there will also be an attempt to manipulate consumer demand and behaviour as well as what is produced and how it is produced.

Owing to this web of centralised controls at both the national and international levels, the global community will be locked into a range of "alternative" (to fossil burning) technologies that are a **less economical** component of the old industrial technological paradigm—second-best technologies. As these low-carbon technologies become more efficient they will extend the dying agony of the old exhausting paradigm and, together with the mitigation command system firmly in place, will prevent the emergence of the new technological paradigm—the *real* Solar Revolution. By redirecting and constraining the global strategic *logos*, the Masters of Mitigation will also divert and derail the process of scientific development. The reason, as I show in *Dead God Rising*, is that science has no momentum of its own; it is a response to the changing logosian strategic demand.[19] In the absence of mitigation measures, however, the rapidly rising costs of the old fossil-fuel technologies, the rapid reduction in rates of return on capital invested in these technologies, and the stagnation in growth rates will cause a change in the global strategic *logos* and generate a powerful incentive to invest in an entirely new technological paradigm—just as happened in the late eighteenth and early nineteenth centuries in Western Europe as the old neolithic paradigm exhausted itself.

The mitigation engineers, if they can immediately press their plans into action, will cause the global economy to stagnate from the middle decades of the twenty-first century. In effect, the nirvana of neoclassical economics—global equilibrium—will be achieved. But not for long. What my fifty-year study of human society has shown is that societies within a competitive environment that do not continue to grow, either collapse or are taken over by more dynamic countries. As the mitigation economy is to be an experiment on a global scale, there will be an attempt to eliminate competition between countries, which may prolong the death throes of human civilisation at least until the end of the twenty-first century.

Mitigation and Revolution Scenarios

We are now in a position to consider two very different scenarios for the twenty-first century that have been generated by the dynamic-strategy theory, and to measure their dynamic costs and benefits. The alternative scenarios—which provide a choice of futures for the strategic *logos*—are those of "mitigation" and "revolution":

- *Mitigation scenario.* This is the scenario that would unfold if the climate-mitigation programs of the IPCC and the *Stern Review* were **fully** implemented over the reminder of the twenty-first century. The dynamic-strategy theory suggests that the Mitigation Scenario involves moderate world GDP (WGDP) growth (averaging out at 3.0% p.a.) until 2025, owing to the investment opportunities provided by the low-carbon technologies despite higher energy costs; slower growth (averaging 1.0% p.a.) between 2025 and 2050, owing to greater government intervention (and, hence, greater market distortion) imposed on the progressive exhaustion of the industrial technological paradigm; and virtual stagnation (averaging 0.5% p.a.) between 2050 and 2100, owing to the global mitigation economy being captured by an exhausted paradigm. Hence, growth of WGDP in the Mitigation Scenario slows dramatically once the investment opportunities provided by the low-carbon technologies have been fully exploited; and progressive stagnation is the outcome of being locked into the old exhausted industrial paradigm because of: (a) the shackles imposed by a command mitigation economy; (b) the distortion of the strategic *logos*; (c) the reduction of pressure driving the technological revolution owing to the premature reduction of greenhouse-gas concentrations; (d) the reduction of revolutionary pressure owing to the inevitable slow-down in the economic development of the lesser-developed world under the global mitigation command economy; and (e) the diversion and derailment of scientific progress owing to an artificially constrained *logos*. Remember, it is assumed that a full-on mitigation program—along the lines proposed by the IPCC and Stern—will be in place throughout the remainder of the twenty-first century.

- *Revolution scenario.* This scenario, as suggested by the dynamic-strategy theory, involves a modest, but declining, growth of WGDP (averaging out at 3.0% p.a.) until 2025, owing to the initial but increasing signs of paradigm exhaustion. This deceleration process is expected to continue more dramatically between 2025 and 2050 (averaging out at 1.5% p.a.). By the middle decades of the twenty-first century our model suggests that the old industrial paradigm will be completely exhausted. Around 2050—give or take a decade—the new technological paradigm, the Solar Revolution, kicks in and WGDP grows rapidly and exponentially owing to the sudden opening up of radically new strategic opportunities (averaging 5.0% p.a., which is a conservative rate similar to that achieved by the world economy between 1950 and 1973) until 2100,[20] and beyond. The rate of growth of WGDP under the new technological paradigm starts from a low base around 2050 (owing to its restriction to the pioneering societies), but grows exponentially thereafter, as it takes hold and spreads quickly around the globe.

Both the Mitigation Scenario and the Revolution Scenario generated by the dynamic-strategy theory are very different to the conventional growth scenarios suggested by the historicist and neoclassical general *equilibrium* (i.e. static) models, which have been modified to include assumptions about climate change by IPCC, Stern, Garnaut, and others. The conventional scenarios *considerably overestimate* the growth of the mitigation (or command) economy, as they completely overlook the lock-in effect of an exhausting/exhausted industrial technological paradigm (even one modified by low-carbon technologies); and they *massively underestimate* the growth of the non-mitigation (strategic or free enterprise) economy, because their models cannot capture the technological pathway or the technological paradigm shift. The *Garnaut Review* (2008) spells out its "assumptions" concerning the growth of WGDP: it over-optimistically expects WGDP to peak at 4% p.a. in the early 2020s; and even more optimistically expects it will fall no lower than 2.5% p.a. by 2075, and 2.0% by 2100. Like Stern and the IPCC, Garnaut does not recognise the progressive constraining influence of the old exhausting technological paradigm up to the about 2050, and a totally exhausted one thereafter.

Figure 13.1. World GDP Under Mitigation and Revolution Scenarios—2007 to 2100: (a) Geometric Curve

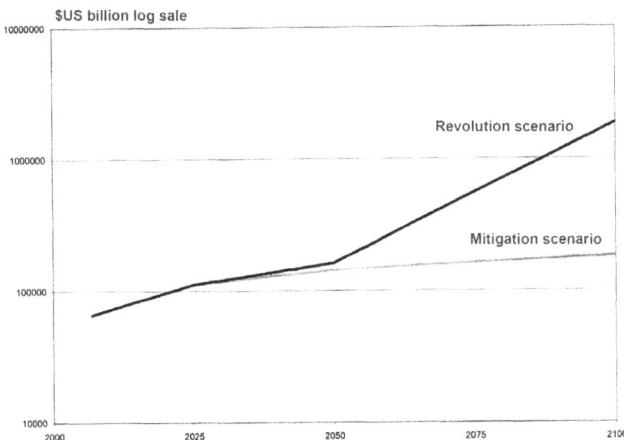

Source:
Snooks 2010a: 61
(author's estimations).

The outcomes of the Mitigation and Revolution Scenarios are summarised in Table 13.1 and Figure 13.1. In 2007, the world's GDP in US currency was $65,610 billion.[21] In the Mitigation Scenario, WGDP increased moderately to $111,599 billion in 2025; $142,941 billion in 2050; but only to $182,970 billion in 2100 (on the heroic assumption that civilisation had not yet collapsed under this command system instituted at the urging of the mitigation engineers). In contrast, the Revolution Scenario experiences a similar increase to $111,599 billion in 2025; a slightly better $161,726 billion in 2050; and then a very impressive $1,850,153 billion in 2100 as a result of the *real* Solar Revolution. Hence, WGDP in the Revolution Scenario is greater than that in the Mitigation Scenario in 2050 by a modest factor of 1.13 but in 2100 by a massive factor of 10.11.

Figure 13.1. World GDP Under Mitigation and Revolution Scenarios—2007 to 2100: (b) Arithmetic Curve

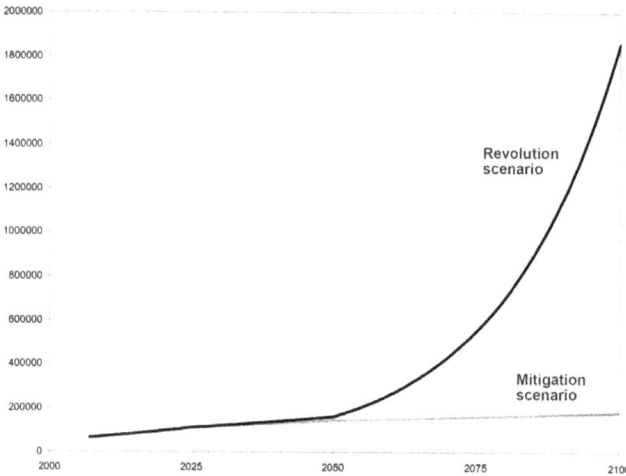

Source: Snooks 2010a: 62 (author's estimations).

Table 13.1 Projected Growth of World GDP (US$ billion), 2007–2100

	2007		2025		2050		2100
	WGDP	% p.a.	WGDP	% p.a.	WGDP	% p.a.	WGDP
Mitigation	65,610	3.0	111,599	1.0	142,941	0.5	182,970
Revolution	65,610	3.0	111,599	1.5	161,725	5.0	1,850,153

Note: These calculations abstract from price changes.
Source: See text

This then is the *real* cost—the **dynamic** rather than the **static** cost—of imposing a comprehensive climate-mitigation program on humanity. As shown in Table 13.2, rather than being a modest 1 percent of WGDP per annum, as argued by Stern and other climate-mitigation economists, *the real cost of a full-on mitigation program would be at least a worrying 12 percent by 2050, and a massive 90 percent by 2100.* And it would continue to increase into the twenty-second century as the global mitigation economy begins to disintegrate owing to antistrategic oppression and military conflict. So, what appears to be a modestly costly insurance policy in the **static virtual world** of neoclassical economics, is in the **real dynamic world** a total disaster from which we might never recover. Unless it is aborted before it gets this far. Even so, any delay in the emergence of a new technological paradigm will be very costly: each year we delay will cost between 12 and 90 percent of WGDP, depending at what point the command mitigation economy is dismantled. And, of course, it will take years to recover from the collapse of the mitigation economy, just as it has for Russia following the collapse of the USSR. While the human cost was tragically high in the USSR, this will be dwarfed by the imposition and collapse of the global mitigation economy in the twenty-first century.

Table 13.2 Costs of Climate Mitigation — Dynamic versus Static — 2025 to 2100

	Static costs (Stern) % of WGDP)	Dynamic costs (Snooks) (% of WGDP)
2025	1.0	0.0
2050	1.0	11.6
2100	1.0	90.1

Source: see text.

The choice of futures, therefore, is a critical one. By adopting the course of action proposed later in this chapter, and abandoning the comprehensive mitigation program proposed by the IPCC, Stern and the other mitigation engineers, *before it gets underway*, the world will save approximately US$27.7 quadrillion. This is an enormous sum of money—28 million, billion US dollars (or 28 followed by 15 zeros)—and is represented graphically by the triangular area between the two curves in Figure 13.1. In Figure 13.1a these curves are represented in geometric terms (showing rates of change), and in Figure 13.1b in arithmetic terms (showing absolute changes). *To put this in a context we can more readily understand: at the 2007 level of world GDP (WGDP) it would take us 422 years to pay for this mitigation cost.* Surely no rational person, organisation, or government would, in the light of these conservative estimates, be rash enough to want to impose a comprehensive mitigation program on the world. How likely are my predicted mitigation results? I rate these results as "very likely", owing to the proven explanatory and predictive outcomes of the realist dynamic-strategy theory in a wide range of disciplines in the social and natural sciences over almost three decades. Indeed, far more likely than current climate projections, which are based on simplistic historicist models that are unable to take structural change into account.

Figure 13.2. Carbon Dioxide Concentrations Under Mitigation and Revolution Scenarios—2007 to 2200.

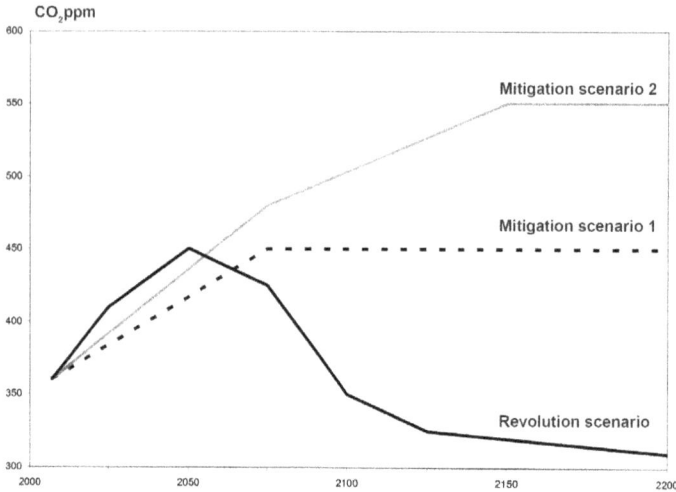

Source: Snooks 2010a: 64 (author's estimations).

In the face of a forthcoming technological revolution, a mitigation program would not only be incredibly costly, it would be totally unnecessary. The forthcoming technological paradigm shift will release pressure on the environment (just as an earlier paradigm shift did after 1780) and radically reduce greenhouse-gas emissions. Figure 13.2 shows schematically the changes in carbon dioxide concentrations in the atmosphere expected under both the Revolution and Mitigation Scenarios. Those readers who wish to opt for higher concentrations over the next century should think of the "mitigation" and the "revolution" curves in relative rather than absolute terms.

The mitigation scenarios for carbon dioxide concentrations are taken from IPCC reports. The "Mitigation 1" concentrations pathway is that expected if the full-on climate-mitigation program is undertaken seriously and immediately on a global scale. It shows CO_2 concentrations rising from present levels of about 350 ppm to about 450 ppm by 2075 and then stabilising at that level over the next century. The "Mitigation 2" concentrations pathway climbs at a higher rate until it reaches 550 ppm around 2150, and then levels off. Its higher levels are the result of delays in implementing the full mitigation program. Global temperatures are expected to be higher as a consequence of this tardiness.

Figure 13.2 also shows the expected concentrations pathway under the "Revolution Scenario" predicted by the dynamic-strategy model. Between 2000 and 2050, its levels are expected to be higher than those under mitigation, but, owing to the slow-down of growth, the rate of increase of concentrations between 2025 and 2050 will also slow down. But after 2050 when the real Solar Revolution kicks in, concentrations will begin to fall, slowly at first but then more rapidly. The present scientific consensus is that current carbon dioxide concentrations can only be reabsorbed into the carbon dioxide "sinks"—the deep oceans and the earth—slowly over the next couple of centuries.[22] Recently, some scientists have even controversially suggested that this process will take hundreds of thousands of years—that it "will last longer than Stonehenge, longer than time capsules, far longer than the age of human civilisation so far".[23] While the consensus viewpoint is a myopic, the controversial viewpoint is essentially defeatist. Fortunately, both viewpoints—*which implicitly assume that future technology (even over the next few hundred thousand years) will be limited to what can be achieved within the current industrial technological paradigm*—are fatally flawed owing to their failure to develop a realist general dynamic theory of society.

More realistically, the dynamic-strategy model suggests that technological breakthroughs (in response to strategic demand) will occur in the area of carbon dioxide absorption, particularly from 2075, as a spin off from the technological paradigm shift. My model further suggests that by 2200 carbon dioxide concentrations (around 300ppm) could approach levels that were experienced in the late eighteenth century (around 280ppm). Even by 2100 they could be in the vicinity of those experienced in the late twentieth century (around 350ppm), which compares more than favourably with the mitigation level of between 450–500ppm. Temperatures will, with a lag, also follow this rise in the first half of the twenty-first century, but will fall thereafter to levels that by 2100 will be comparable with those in the nineteenth century. Hence, the great irony is that by the end of the twenty-first century carbon dioxide concentrations and, hence, temperatures will be much higher under all versions of the climate-mitigation program than if we follow the dictates of the strategic *logos* as we have always done. *Climate mitigation will make the planet much warmer than if we merely allow the forthcoming technological revolution to take its course.*

Whatever course of action we take, major investment in adaptation programs will be required to minimise the impact of climate change already in the pipeline and as a result of rising greenhouse-gas concentrations to 2050. This will involve expenditures in repairing damage inflicted by more frequent and more severe storms; undertaking capital works to limit the damage from more regular flooding; to invest in greater water catchment, conservation and distribution; to repair drought devastated lands; to enable populations to shift to less flood-prone, drought-prone, fire-prone and storm-prone regions; and to invest in restorative technologies. Most of these expenditures would also have been required under the various mitigation regimes. We know this can be done because our strategic *logos*, which ensures our survival and prosperity, was shaped by large and abrupt climate-change events in the past—some 24 events in the past 100,000 years when temperatures increased by up to 10 degrees Celsius within a decade. Adapting to future climate change will be even more feasible in the future owing to the modern world's greater technical proficiency, and to boundless solar energy towards the end of the twenty-first century.

MITIGATION AS AN AGENT OF COLLAPSE

The range of mitigation outcomes summarised in Figure 13.1 is the most optimist version of what will happen in the twenty-first century if the world adopts the comprehensive program advocated by the mitigation engineers. As argued above, a full-on mitigation program will lock us into the old exhausted industrial paradigm from the middle decades of this century, and lead to economic stagnation from which we will be unable to escape. No antistrategic society, especially once it has stagnated, as it inevitably will, can last for long.

The USSR is an excellent example of a society hijacked by antistrategists, which totally lost its way. As the goals, directives and incentives were determined metaphysically (in response to philosophical ideas) rather than strategically (in response to the *logos* via strategic demand), the USSR lost all direction, became increasingly inefficient and unproductive and, within the space of just seven decades, collapsed. In the pre-industrial era when conquest was the dominant economic strategy, Russia and its satellites would have been invaded and taken over by other more viable European countries.

A similar fate awaits the global economy hijacked by the mitigation engineers. In a world dominated by antistrategic goals and incentives—a world in which the strategists are unable to respond to strategic demand generated by the *logos*—the only option for those wanting to survive and prosper will be for regional strongmen to defect from the climate-mitigation regime, and to pursue the only dynamic strategy available to them—war and conquest. This will bring them into conflict with the leaders of the global mitigation society, which will be backed up by multi-national military forces. In effect, the mitigation engineers will plunge us all back into the conditions that dominated the pre-Industrial Revolution era.

Why is this so? In a world where technological revolution and population increase are blocked by the Masters of Mitigation—the political leaders of the global mitigation society—the only way of generating economic expansion is through war and conquest. There are no other dynamic strategies that can be employed for this purpose. Needless to say, war and conquest is a zero-sum game, in which the victors gain at the expense of the vanquished. And in an era of nuclear weapons, it could even be an end game.

While a world that ends in Armageddon is an improbable outcome, it is not an impossible one. It will depend on how determined are the Masters of Mitigation to impose their metaphysical values on the strategic *logos* and whether they have been able to gain complete political control. It would probably take the emergence of a mitigation dictator to get this far. Improbable? Yes. Impossible?

No. Who in the late 1920s and early 1930s believed that the author of *Mein Kampf* would ever become dictator of Germany or that he would be able to bring continental Europe to its knees? Dictators emerge out of economic chaos and insecurity, and a full-on mitigation policy would certainly produce these conditions on a global scale. Even the ephemeral financial crisis of late 2008 and early 2009 has led to the re-emergence of the metaphysical interventionists.

At a recent (February 2009) World Economic Forum at Davos, the German chancellor Angela Merkel and the then British prime minister Gordon Brown advocated the establishment of a UN economic council modelled on the Security Council to "police" the global economy and to "enforce" new standards of finance on individual nations. In this model, the states represented on the council would become "the guardians of economic and social order"—similar, perhaps, to Plato's "guardians" who were designed to suppress the forces of desire (the driving force of human society) in his ideal Republic? Chancellor Merkel insisted that the world requires "clear-cut rules quite in contrast to an unfettered capitalism", which should be "enshrined in the form of a global economic order charter" (*Spiegel*: March 2009). This interventionist plan designed to create a "new economic order" was presented to the April 2009 G20 summit in London on the "financial crisis", and was supported by countries such as Australia (where then prime minister Rudd had already made a commitment to "social democratic" intervention in banking and financial markets in order to "save the system of open markets from self-destruction").[24] In July 2009, the German Chancellor, with the support of other "social democrats", urged the G8 meeting to adopt her "charter for a sustainable world economy". Of course, with the retreat of the threat of depression, the interventionists have toned down their threatening rhetoric. But, if large-scale global intervention could re-emerge at merely the *hint* of economic depression, imagine the reaction if climate change does cause substantial *actual* dislocation. This could well form the basis for a global command system.

Possibly more realistically, an unfolding Mitigation Scenario would lead to a growing realisation in saner societies that this policy was distorting the global dynamic system and leading the nations of the world into real and deep economic crisis. This might be sufficient to result in some nations defecting from the climate-mitigation cabal, possibly with the use of force. While this might not lead to collapse, it would certainly result in a much-delayed emergence of the real Solar Revolution—probably beyond 2100—which would cost humanity dearly (as suggested in Table 13.1). Climate mitigation or technological revolution? The choice is ours, and it will certainly be a critical choice.

WHAT'S TO BE DONE?

The world has arrived at a major crossroad. We are considering embarking on the greatest and most dangerous adventure in our entire history. And we are thinking of doing so on the flimsiest of information and knowledge. While the science of climate change is reputable and impressive, the message it has delivered is clear but concerning: we can only understand how climate will change in the future if we understand the dynamics of human society, owing to the influence of human activities on global warming. This is concerning because the traditional social sciences are unable to explain the dynamics of human society.

Without a realist general dynamic theory of human society the social sciences are unable to deal with the big issues of life, such as human-induced climate change. Consequently they have no idea how human society and human activity will unfold over the next century. Hence, the traditional experts cannot tell us how human-induced climate will change during this period. This is hardly a good basis from which to launch a comprehensive climate-mitigation program—a program that will entail massive government intervention in the global economy, including the distortion of the market mechanism and the employment of centrally determined directives and incentives, direct government involvement, the exercise of preferences for low-carbon technologies and producers, and the use of propaganda and persuasion to change consumer habits. Such a poorly researched and risky enterprise can only be regarded as totally reckless. It has become a matter of faith.

What's behind this Reckless Adventure?

Humans possess an inherent fear of the future, together with a compulsion to intervene in the world to ensure that it doesn't collapse. As I argue in chapter 8 (and in *Dead God Rising*), the early emergence and development of a belief in superhuman guardians was the outcome of this instinct to survive and prosper. It was recognition that, while we humans don't understand the strategic *logos* that ensures our survival and prosperity, we do understand that in the past this system has broken down many times. The ruins of earlier societies are all around us. So, if we don't understand how this life-system works and what is needed to sustain it, then we need to seek out those superhuman guardians who do. Every society in the history of our species has invested heavily, with both time and resources, in religions designed to gain the support of these special guardians or gods. Every society in the history of our species has looked to specialised professionals—the "priestly philosophers"—who claim to understand the ways of the guardians, gods, or forces of fate. In the past, these were the shamans, wisemen, and priests; today they are the climate scientists and orthodox economists. What these priestly philosophers have in common is their belief in metaphysical ideas based on a deductive methodology. As such, it contrasts with the realist ideas derived from empirical observation employed throughout this book. When it comes to the big issues facing the future of humanity, it is all a matter of faith not science, owing to the failure to develop a science of societal dynamics.

With the emergence of the dynamic strategy of technological change at the time of the Industrial Revolution, science rose to replace religion as a means not only of understanding our world but also of influencing it so as to maintain order and stability. We believe that, armed with science, we can dispense with the old gods. Investment in science—the social as well as the natural variety—is now considered a better way to ensure the stability of our world.

Unfortunately this is not so. Science is unable to provide a better understanding of the strategic *logos* today than religion was able to do in the past. Certainly science has provided us with considerable knowledge about the physical, natural, and human worlds, but it hasn't been able to show us how they work as dynamic systems. What it has provided, however, is greater confidence in ourselves. This is a double-edged sword. Once, we believed in the guidance of gods, now we believe in our own wisdom and abilities to reform the world. The **irony** is that our understanding of the strategic *logos* is, in orthodox hands, no better today than it has ever been; and the **danger** is that we believe the opposite.

We need only recall the confidence with which orthodox economists have entered the knowledge-free zone of climate mitigation to advise governments about launching the world on this reckless adventure. We have seen that economists are perfectly happy to employ their static, short-run, marginal theory, together with simplistic historicist models, to make judgments about the complex dynamics of human society. With a naive cheerfulness they tell us, in effect, that even if this great adventure fails it won't cost us much.

But as I've attempted to show above, orthodox experts are not in a position to estimate the costs of a mitigation program as they have no real idea of what it is that they are mitigating. How is it possible to estimate the costs of something when we don't know how it will unfold in the future? We desperately need a realist dynamic theory about the structural changes our society is currently undergoing and will continue to undergo in the future. Only then can we estimate the dynamic as opposed to static costs of climate mitigation. As I show above, the dynamic costs are massive.

The Inevitable Failure of Large-Scale Interventions

It is essential to consider how large-scale, if not global, interventions have turned out in the recent past. As mentioned earlier, the largest and most risky of interventions in the past was the establishment of the command system of the USSR. This experiment—which was massively expensive for the Russian people and their satellites in terms of time, resources, and lives—collapsed after a mere three generations. The reason for this collapse was that the Marxist interventionists, who devised this command economy, knew nothing about the dynamics of their strategic *logos*. As I explain in *The Ephemeral Civilization* (1997) they ignored it, abused it, and the Russian people and their neighbours paid the cost.

Another major series of metaphysical interventions can be seen in the economic and political manipulation of the lesser-developed world. In *Global Transition* (1999) I show that the "development industry" has little understanding of the real nature of the development process, which I call the "global transition"—a process by which the underdeveloped countries on the periphery are gradually drawn into the "strategic core" of interacting developed countries. This is also the process by which the development potential revealed by the last technological paradigm shift—the Industrial Revolution—is gradually and predictably achieved. This, in other words, is the predictable dynamic mechanism by which the old technological paradigm is exhausted and the new one emerges.

Not understanding this realist and predictable process, the development industry believes the material advancement of poorer countries can only occur through its interventions. The curious facts are that while the development industry has existed only for about half a century, societal material progress has been taking place along an exponential development path for the past two million years. During this time, as we have seen, there have been three global transitions and paradigm shifts. And between the Industrial Revolution (1780–1830) and the emergence of the development industry in the mid-twentieth century, a large number of countries passed through the development process without any "expert" advice. If anything, the development industry has slowed down the current process of global transition through its inappropriate and self-interested interventions. Interestingly, the development industry only emerged when European colonialism declined, suggesting that it is a way the developed world can exercise a degree of control over the less-developed world in a post-colonial era under the guise of altruism. Of course not all, or even a majority of, participants in the development industry have other than the best, if misguided, motives; the same cannot be said, however, for the rich countries financing this industry.

Further, there are many examples of interventions in Third-World countries by international organisations, such as the IMF and World Bank, which have been responsible for creating economic and social chaos. In *The Global Crisis Makers* (2000), I show that these international organisations have been employed by the developed world to impose their own inappropriate neoclassical economic policies—such as the deflationary and system-distorting policy of inflation targeting—on Third-World countries desperately seeking international aid. Also, through the WTO, these same countries are attempting to force neoclassical free-trade principles on poorer countries even though at a similar stage of economic development they employed tariff protection as a strategic instrument to assist their own economic transformation. These international organisations have made international aid and trade concessions conditional on the adoption of economic programs that undermine the dynamic life-systems of lesser-developed countries. More recently (2015), these international institutions have attempted to intervene in troubled developed societies such as Greece. While the viable part of the developed world is wealthy enough to pay the cost of neoliberal policies, lesser-developed countries are not, and, if they take these policies seriously, usually descend into economic chaos and war. This was the experience of countries such as Yugoslavia and Rwanda.

My point is that modern interventions in the world generally fail because the metaphysically influenced interventionists have no idea how the underlying strategic *logos* operates. The examples I've provided illustrate the considerable economic and social costs that flow from these ill-advised interventions. Interventions based on ideas and philosophies that have little contact with reality. Yet, as costly as these interventions have been, they are only a trial run for the massive global intervention being planned by the mitigation engineers. I have provided compelling theoretical and empirical reasons for believing that the global climate-mitigation program will fail spectacularly, will cost human society massively in terms of lost WGDP, and could, if pursued relentlessly, lead to the global collapse of civilisation as we know it. But the greatest failure of climate mitigation will reside in the fact that it will be to no avail, because greenhouse-gas emissions and concentrations under mitigationist policies will be much higher than if we just got on with the next technological revolution. That, however, is not the point of the interventionist agenda, which is all about power and control.

There *is* a Place for Positive Action

There is, of course, a role for human remedial action. What we can and must do is to come to a thorough understanding of the strategic *logos* that enables us to survive and prosper. Instead of studying human society in a short-term, static framework, we need to come to grips with the way our dynamic system works. The dynamic-strategy theory presented in chapters 4 and 11 is an essential start to this process. Once we understand the system, which has been driving human society for the past 2 myrs and life for the past 4,000 myrs, we will be in a position to optimise the progress of civilisation and the betterment of the natural world by removing obstacles to its effective operation. Obstacles that include inappropriate interventions—regarding societal goals, price systems, incentives, and technologies—formed by other-worldly ideas and philosophies.

It is essential to be sensitive to the requirements of the strategic *logos*, particularly to strategic demand. As we have seen, this is the demand generated by the unfolding dynamic strategy for a wide range of strategic inputs such as factors of production (land, labour and capital), institutions (societal rules), organisations (social networks), together with ideas of all types including those of a technological, cultural and strategic nature. In the process of this creative interaction between strategic demand and the agents of supply, appropriate goals of society—those ensuring survival and prosperity—will be established. Any barriers to the free working of this strategic demand-response mechanism—

such as inflation targeting, IMF-imposed deflation, market manipulation, or climate mitigation controls—should be removed. There is, however, one particularly important area where proactive policy will be beneficial, and that is government investment in the *general* infrastructure of science and technological change. We know from the dynamic-strategy theory that the future of humanity will depend upon the pursuit of the dynamic strategy of technological change; and we know that the next technological paradigm shift is imminent. The sooner the new technological revolution occurs, the lower will be the costs of climate change and environmental damage. What is required here is not gambling on any *particular* technological pathway, as that will be determined by individuals and companies responding to strategic demand, but investment in the generation of new knowledge through appropriate scientific, higher educational, and research facilities. Society must be able to respond quickly and effectively to the requirements of the new technological paradigm as it begins to emerge in the coming decades; and it will only be able to do so if it is committed to transforming itself into a knowledge economy. A doubling of the current levels of GDP devoted to these activities in the immediate future would be a good start.

While humans are good at responding to what has happened, we have great difficulty acting in anticipation of something we think might happen. We rarely understand the consequences of our interventions. This is how we have developed genetically as a species—by responding to strategic demand—as explained in chapter 9 on the selfcreating mind. Accordingly, investment in "adaptation" policies and programs, as well as remedial technologies, is a sensible way to go.

Under the Revolution Scenario outlined above—see Figure 13.2—the need for adaptation expenditures will be higher until 2050 than those suggested by the mitigation engineers, but thereafter the need for these policies will fall quite rapidly to 2075, by which time carbon dioxide concentrations will have returned to levels lower than today. Even by 2060 the need for remedial action under the Revolution Scenario will be less than that under even the most optimistic Mitigation Scenario (Mitigation I, Figure 13.2).

Although the Revolution Scenario will probably lead to higher carbon dioxide concentrations in the period before 2050, this may not be translated into higher temperatures. As discussed in my book *The Coming Eclipse,*[25] there are highly reputable scientists specialising in research on solar activity, who are convinced that solar activity and output will decline significantly over the next two decades, leading to modest reductions in global temperatures. If this does eventuate, it will fortuitously compensate for any temporary human-induced pressure on climate. And once solar activity increases again, say from the 2030s, we should be in a position technologically to reduce the adverse impacts of warmer temperatures on human society. These technological measures might, as some scientists have suggested, include a combination of space-mounted "sunshades", aerosol particles released into the atmosphere to reflect some of the inflowing sunlight, injection of sequestered carbon dioxide into the ground, and more. Of course, this all comes at a cost, but only a small fraction of the cost of the proposed climate-mitigation program. And it is a cost that we can easily monitor, as it is for *past* damage rather than a gamble on possible *future* damage. But this is not an argument in favour of relaxing our remedial vigilance, which must be conscientiously maintained.

There is an important issue here that should be recognised. The strategic *logos* is already correcting the impact we are having on climate by moving toward the next technological paradigm shift, and it is taking place unremarkably without any intervention on our part. As explained in chapter 5, the strategic *logos* of modern man developed to cope with the external impact of some twenty-four episodes of rapid climate change—of the order of 10 degrees C a decade—during the past 100,000 years. Accordingly, the *logos* has the ability to respond unaided to all external attacks of this nature. The "ark of the Sun" is an extremely robust life support system. Further, the impact of climate on the *logos* will hasten this normal corrective action, as the higher costs of doing business under global warming will be reflected in a stronger and more urgent strategic demand for technological transformation that will generate the *real* Solar Revolution.

The choices facing us in the opening decades of the twenty-first century are momentous. We can either attempt to understand our strategic *logos*—as our species has been trying unsuccessfully to do over the past few hundred thousand years—and commit ourselves to the imminent technological revolution, or we can leave our heads in the clouds and blindly place our faith in a metaphysically inspired and massively interventionist climate-mitigation program. If we choose the path advocated by the mitigation engineers, we will pay a very heavy economic and social price, from which we may find it difficult to recover. In ancient Egypt, those responsible for disrupting *maat*—or cosmic order—in this way faced the dreaded "second death". Let there be no doubt that today we face a critical choice of futures. But if we make the correct choice, the *logos* of mankind will flourish, and this "ark of the Sun" will continue its improbable voyage into the deep future of the Universe.

Epilogue

Solar Journey Challenged

Life first ventured on its solar journey some 4,000 myrs ago, followed by human society some 2 myrs ago. During that time, the societies and *logoi* of numerous life forms have emerged, flourished for a season, and then disappeared forever. Prior to the dominance of life by mankind, this ephemeral cycle passed through what might be thought of as a natural sequence of rise and fall, as individuals and their societies struggled for survival and prosperity but were ultimately overwhelmed once they exhausted their strategic capabilities. Since the emergence of civilisation together with its sophisticated ideologies, a new actor has appeared in this story: the "antistrategist".

The antistrategist, who challenges the viability of the solar journey, was made possible by the relatively recent emergence of that supreme strategic instrument, the conscious mind—referred to in my work as the "strategic brain". This emergence created a strategic dualism (not to be confused with the mystical concept of Cartesian duality) in life forms, a dualism consisting of the body driven by strategic desire, and the mind influenced by ideologies. In most instances, the mind operates as a strategic instrument facilitating the strategic desires of the body—"desires drive, ideas facilitate". This is why the brain emerged in life and developed in the manner that it has. But the mind, under the influence of various exotic ideologies, has the capacity to go its own way. In a disturbing number of cases, these ideologies undermine rather than support the prevailing dynamic strategy together with the *logos* that generated it. Whenever these antistrategists are highly determined, well organised and well-armed, they represent a very real danger to the prevailing *logos* and represent a challenge to the solar journey. As described in the Prologue, the ancient Egyptians were well aware that the forces of chaos (in the form of Apophis the chaos monster) were an ever-present danger.

Who are these antistrategists? They comprise two broad groups: terrorists, and radical interventionists. The first group needs little discussion as they have become a major threat to some lesser developed societies in the Middle East and a source of irritation to more advanced societies. There is nothing new in this. The Roman general Gnaeus Pompeius Magnus (known as Pompey), for example, was called upon by the Senate in 67 BC to clear the eastern Mediterranean of pirates, which had been seriously disrupting Rome's commercial activities. More recently, Middle Eastern groups, such as Al-Qaeda and ISIS, have pursued antistrategic military activities against strategic societies in the region and isolated acts of violence throughout the Western world. These antistrategic activities are confronted by the Western powers whenever the costs of these attacks become significant in the eyes of their electorates. Otherwise, containment is the preferred option. It is unlikely that this form of antistrategic activity will ever be more than an annoying irritation to wealthy strategic societies, but they are a serious challenge to the viability of lesser developed countries in the Middle East.

Of more concern is the second group of antistrategists, the radical interventionists. These antistrategists come from within rather than from without. They comprise individuals and organisations that reject the strategic aims of their own society and *logos*, in order to pursue antistrategic ideologies. These antistrategic ideologies, which are designed to undermine the existing strategic *logos*, include political philosophies such as Enlightenment ideas about the "brotherhood of man", Marxism, and radical ecological philosophies. These ideologies are based on a misunderstanding of reality and a failure to recognise the existence of the strategic *logos*. The "brotherhood of man", for example, is a seductive fiction, because individuals relate primarily to the strategic *logos* rather than to each other. As discussed in chapters 4 and 7, trust in society is not the outcome of human love for others, but rather of the success of the strategic pursuit. Trust, like other human qualities, rises and falls with the expansion and contraction of society's dominant dynamic strategy. Marx similarly based his theory of the fall of capitalism and the rise of communism on a set of false assumptions concerning human nature and the interaction between key variables in society (Snooks, 1998a: ch. 3). Not surprisingly, all attempts to usher in the idealist state of communism have, and will, fail. Finally, radical ecologists have also imposed a false vision on reality, in order to provide a comforting narrative about the need for human society to play a subservient role in the natural world—a false vision that, if imposed, will turn into a nightmare.

Usually, these ideologies are cynically employed by extreme activists to attract the attention of, and to manipulate, more moderate idealists. Examples include the French revolution through which radicals assumed political control and exercised a short-lived but brutal tyranny (in the name of the people) over France; the Russian revolution hijacked by the Bolsheviks, who suppressed the strategists and subverted the *logos* by instituting an oppressive command economy, in the name of Marxism; and the radical climate mitigationists who wish to cripple the strategic *logos* by substituting a command economy dedicated to creating stasis in order to "save" the natural world. As we have seen, the French and Russian revolutions ended badly. The antistrategists leading and participating in these power struggles destroyed the French and Russian economies of the time, and delayed the economic development of these societies for generations. If given the chance, the radical ecologists will do the same: they will disrupt the solar journey by derailing the Solar Revolution.

Antistrategists have always been, and will always provide, a challenge to the strategic *logoi* of human society. But the *logos*, which emerged as an entropy-defying, shock-deflecting life system, is particularly robust. It has seen off many challenges in the past and hopefully will continue to do so in the future. But this is a very costly procedure. If policy makers recognised and understood the strategic *logos*—through a familiarity with the ideas and theory in this book—these massive costs could be dramatically reduced. That is the challenge for human society in the future.

For the present, the "ark of the Sun" continues its uncertain voyage through time. On board are a variety of strategic and antistrategic actors, constantly changing places as they compete for prime positions in the solar barque. With the arrival of the Solar Revolution, the seating arrangements will change more dramatically, with the best positions going to those strategists who refuse to be diverted by the ideologically driven antistrategists, and who press on boldly in the face of paradigmatic exhaustion in an attempt to find radical new ways to harness the energy of the Sun. Those who are beguiled by fanciful antistrategic ideologies will be relegated to the back of the solar barque, and some may even disappear overboard to be devoured by the monster of chaos. If the "ark of the Sun" maintains a steady course, it will eventually travel through space as well as time, seeking out new suns as the old founding Sun eventually dies.

Notes

Preface

1. The Great Depression was the focus of my first research project, undertaken during 1966 and 1967 and published in 1974 as *Depression and Recovery* (Snooks 1974). Many of the themes explored in that study have been brought to fruition in *Ark of the Sun.* For example, the central focus in that early work was on the dynamics of cyclical activity, the role played by leading sectors, the way forces of expansion were exhausted and overtaken by forces of contraction, and finally how forces of expansion reasserted themselves. In the later "dynamic-strategy project" (1986 to 2015), these early ideas developed into a more general analysis of long-run economic dynamics, the role played by dynamic strategies, and how these strategies were exploited, exhausted, and replaced by new strategies: "In my beginning is my end ... In my end is my beginning".

2. The quantitative analysis of Domesday Book (1086) can be found in Snooks and McDonald (1986). This study emerged from my wider interest in Anglo-Saxon history—including learning Old English—which extended back to the late 1970s. While on study leave in London in 1979, I found it difficult to accept the long-standing conventional wisdom held by Anglo-Saxon scholars (J.H. Round, F.W. Maitland, H.C. Darby and their many contemporary followers) concerning economic relationships in medieval England. It was claimed that the key categories of taxation and manorial income in Domesday Book were "artificial". By "artificial", Domesday Book scholars meant that these outcomes were determined not by rough-and-ready considerations of rational governance, efficiency, productivity or profitability, but by the high-handed actions of powerful landowners and political leaders without regard to economic consequences.

    With the wealth of data in Domesday Book that could be used to test alternative hypotheses, this was a challenge too good to ignore; particularly as it has important implications for the dynamics of human society, which has always been my central long-term research interest. Between 1980 and 1982, I undertook preliminary research work to establish the Domesday Economy Project (joined by J. McDonald, at my invitation in October 1982, to strengthen the econometric analysis), which was financed by the ARC from 1983. As I had suspected from the beginning, a scientific study of the Domesday Book data showed the conventional wisdom to be completely wrong.

    The statistical analysis demonstrated conclusively that medieval society, just as much as modern society, was dominated by the desire to survive and prosper by employing natural and social resources as rationally and economically as possible. It was even possible to reconstruct the production system of Anglo-Norman England using modern production functions. This suggests that while the sophistication of technology between the medieval and modern worlds is vastly different, the economic way in which resources are used to pursue survival and prosperity is very similar.

    As my later research demonstrated, this economically rational outlook is the key necessary condition for the dynamics of human society. From the mid-1980s, my research work resumed its focus on developing a general dynamic theory to explain the progress and fluctuations of both human society and life. See Snooks (1993a; 1994a; 1994b; 1996).

3. On measuring English economic growth over the past millennium, see Snooks (1993a; 1994b).

4. On the materialism and growth of pre-modern societies, see Snooks (1997: chs 6–11).

5. The dynamic-strategy theory was developed in the following series of books—Snooks (1996; 1997; 1998b; 1999; 2003; 2006; 2010b).

6. For my critique of Darwin, see Snooks (2003: chs 2–4); and for that of neo-Darwinism, see Snooks (2003: chs 5–8).

7. My theory of the human mind and human nature can be found in Snooks (2006).

8. On strategic ideology and religion, see Snooks (2010b).

Chapter 1 Improbable Voyage

1. Lifeless equilibrium in the cosmos—Carroll (2008: 257).

2. Dark energy—Carroll (2008: 256-57).

3. Carroll (2008: 257).

4. The end of matter—Benford (2008: 276–77).

5. Nature of thermodynamics—Bais (2005: 47).

6. Carroll (2008: 261).

7. Very large numbers—Carroll (2008: 261).

8. Carroll (2008: 264–65).

9. Cosmic self-organisation—Hogan (1998: 136–39).

10. On the flawed concept of self-organisation, see Snooks (2007).

11. On the limits to the limits-to-growth argument, see Snooks (1996: ch. 13).

Chapter 2 Unfinished Odyssey

1. The pseudo-explanations of biometricians can be seen in Sepkoski (1978; 1979; 1984).

2. On Phillips and Sepkoski, see Cowan (2000: 80).

3. The poor fossil record—Benton (1985: 813).

4. Pattern of genetic diversity—Sepkoski (1978; 1979; 1984).

5. Genetic radiation of dinosaur, birds, mammals—Bakker (1986: ch. 9).

6. Emergence of protocells—Nutman *et al* (2000: 305) and Cowen (2000: 9).

7. Defining protocells—Cowen (2000: 12).

8. World's first energy crisis—Cowen (1990: 30).

9. "Oxygen holocaust"—Dure (1996: 44).

10. Ancient iron deficiency—Cowen (2000: 33–35).

11. Cowen (2000: 38). My emphasis.

12. Fossil evidence, emergence of eukaryote cells—Cowen (2000: 41); *Science* (1999: 981).

13. Spectacular burst of genetic innovation—Cowen (2000: 61).

14. Stromatolites become "quite rare"—Cowen (1990: 85).

15. Rhipidistians, aberrant and normal—Cowen (2000: 134, 135). My emphasis.

16. Siberian volcanic eruptions—Campbell *et al* (1992).

17. Emergence of protomammals—Bakker (1986: 410).

18. Downsizing of cynodonts—Cowen (2000: 250–51).

19. Titanic ecological battle—Bakker (1986: 416).

20. Origination rate—Benton (1985).

21. Archosaurs and warm-bloodedness—Ricqles (1974); Bakker (1986: 421–22).

22. Horde of new species—Bakker (1986: 422).

23. Other more direct evidence—Fisher *et al* (2000).

24. Puzzled paleontologists—Bakker (1986: 193). My emphasis.

25. Changing vegetation—Bakker (1986: ch. 9).

26. Bakker (1986: 425).

27. Death star—Raup and Sepkoski (1984; 1986).

28. Shift of habitat—Bakker (1986: 427).

29. Extinction causes—Bakker (1986: 431).

30. Collapse of species—Bakker (1986: 436–38).

31. Asteroid impacts—Alvarez *et al* (1980).

32. Volcanic eruptions—Rampino and Stothers (1988).

33. Regular return of "death star"—Raup and Sepkoski (1984; 1986).

34. Bakker (1986: 444).

35. The game of life and its players—Snooks (1996: chs 2 and 3).

36. The dynamics of life. In Snooks (2003: 179–80) I detail the problems with Bakker's hypothesis.

37. Rise and fall of marine dynasties—Bakker (1986: 429–30).

38. Darwin, *Origin*: ch. 11.

39. On *Stenonychosaurus*, see Russell (1969).

40. On the current missing-link debate, see Franzen *et al* (2009) and Wilford (2009); and on the parting of hominids and panids, see Easteal, Collet and Betty (1995).

41. The Australopithecines—Cullotta (1999: 572–73).

42. On the first humans, see Balter and Gibbons (2000: 948–50).

43. For a new (dynamic-strategy) interpretation of the nature of Neanderthal man and the reasons for his extinction in Europe, see Snooks (2008d).

44. Others have nominated *Equatorius africanus* as the first ape to occasionally leave the treetops, around 15 myrs BP—Zimmer (1999: 1335).

45. Geographical limitations of apeman—Reed (1997).

46. On changes in brain size, see Snooks (2006: ch. 8) and chapter 9 above.

47. Stone-age infant nutrition—Gibbons (1998: 1345–47).

48. Cooked tubers and large brains—Pennisi (1999: 2004).

49. Other supply-side theories, as in Crawford and Marsh (1989).

50. Strategic demand creates its own supply—Snooks (1998b; 1999; 2000) and chapter 11 above.

51. Evidence on A. *garhi* as scavenger—Cullotta (1999: 572–73).

52. Stone-age gender division of labor—Leaky and Lewin (1992) and Calder (1984: 140–41). On doubts about *habilis* being a direct ancestor of modern man, see Spoor et al (2007).

53. Problem-solving and languages—Eccles (1989: 95).

54. Wood and bone hunting weapons—Cowen (1990: 414).

55. Use of fire—Rowlett (1999: 741).

56. For a comparison of brain sizes of modern man and Neanderthal man, see Snooks (2008d).

57. On "peripheral isolates", see Mayr (1963) and Eldredge and Gould (1972).

58. On the "great wheel of civilisation", see Snooks (1996: ch. 12) and chapter 3 above.

Chapter 3 Patterns of the Past

1. The research underlying the "Snooks algorithm", which describes the exponential growth of life and human society over the past 3,800 myrs, can be found in Snooks (1996: 79–82, 92–95, 402–05). This book was completed by the end of 1993, but not published until 1996.

2. The geometric increase in biomass is discussed in Snooks (1996: 74–95) and Snooks (2003: chs 9 and 13).

3. Some seven years after my discovery of this algorithm, the Russian physicist A.D. Panov (2005) independently developed an algorithm with a very similar coefficient of acceleration—2.67±0.15 compared with my 3.0 (see Nazaretyan 2005a; 2005b). This combined research outcome is called the "Snooks-Panov vertical" in the literature.

4. The "Law of Cumulative Biological/Technological Change" was first presented in Snooks (2003: 287–88).

5. A discussion of the laws of both life and human society can be found in Snooks (1998a; 2003: ch. 5).

6. For an account of metabolic systems, see Bakker (1978: 137–40).

7. The detailed "finesse versus force" argument can be found in Snooks (2003: 182–95) and chapter 2.

Chapter 4 Engine of Life

1. A detailed discussion of the new concept of selfcreation—and its contrasting nature compared with self-organisation—can be found in Snooks (2003; 2007; 2008a).

2. Neo-Darwinist decision-making is discussed in Snooks (2003: chs 6 and 7), while rationalist decision-making is evaluated in Snooks (1997: chs 4 and 5).

3. For the development over time of my strategic-imitation decision model, see sequentially Snooks (1996; 1997; 1998b; 1999; 2003; 2006).

4. Early life forms could pursue a full range of dynamic strategies—see Snooks (2003: chs 9 and 12) and ch. 2 here.

5. For pioneering research on the use of special genes in simple life forms to direct, what I call, dynamic strategies, see Cairns et al (1988), Hall, (1988), and Foster (1999).

6. The confused "punctuated equilibria" concept was introduced by Eldredge and Gould (1972). I discuss it in detail in Snooks (2003: 71–78).

7. For the employment of "limited" genetic change in the development of biological weapons during a dynastic (e.g. dinosaur) conquest strategy, see Snooks (2003: ch. 9).

8. The role of strategic confidence in depression and recovery in history is discussed in Snooks (1997: 415–16), and in contemporary society in Snooks (1998b: 13–14, 256, 238–39, 163–64) and Snooks (2008e).

9. For a discussion of the strategic struggle between the protodynosaurs and the protomammals, see Snooks (2003: 169–73).

10. The struggle between the leaders of commerce and of industry for control of Britain's dynamic strategy in the first half of the nineteenth century is discussed in Snooks (1997: ch. 9).

11. The terminal struggle for control of Rome, once its conquest strategy was exhausted, is analysed in Snooks (1997: ch. 6).

12. For a discussion of coevolution and the "genetic leash" argument see Snooks (2003: ch. 8; 2006 242–47).

13. For an overview of the development of the concentric-spheres concept in my work, see Snooks (1994; 1997; 1998b; 1999; 2003; 2006).

14. The concept of "strategic exchange" was first suggested in Snooks (2007) and developed in Snooks (2008a).

Chapter 5 Strategic *Logos*—the Ark of the Sun

1. For a brief discussion of the "universal constants of nature"—including Newton's gravitational constant, Boltzmann's constant, Avogadro's constant, the velocity of light, Planck's constant, the electron charge, electron mass, proton mass, W-particle mass, cosmological constant — see Bais (2005). What scientists have overlooked is the "logological constant" discovered in Snooks (1996: 79–82, 92–95, 402–05) and discussed here in chapter 3.

2. For an evaluation of self-organisation and complexity theory see Snooks (2007; 2008a).

3. A discussion of the impact of the bubonic plague on the Hundred Year's War can be found in Snooks (1997: ch. 10).

4. Social physics and complexity theory are discussed from the dynamic-strategy theory standpoint in Snooks (2007, 2008a).

5. This survey of the efforts of various societies to understand the hidden system underlying their material fortunes—what I call the universal life-system or strategic *logos*—owes much to Roy Rappaport. It should be noted, however, that I didn't read (October 2005) his eccentric *Ritual and Religion* (2002) until after the typescript of my book on truth—in which the concept of the strategic *logos* was first developed in detail—had been completed (July 2004). The book on truth (*The Death of Zarathustra. Notes on Truth for the Risktaker*, 2011) was not published until after *Dead God Rising* had appeared (2010), owning to my desire to provide a more orderly sequence for my books in the "dynamic strategy" project.

6. The edition of Heraclitus consulted is by Brooks Haxton—see Heraclitus (2001).

7. The eccentric, but engaging, Roy Rapport (2002: ch. 11).

8. For the various names given to the mystery of mysteries in the ancient and premodern world, see Rapport (2002: 353–70), Grimal (1974: 190–93), Redford (2003: 189–91), and Spence (2004).

9. The laws of the strategic *logos*—or the laws of history and of life—are identified and discussed in Snooks (1998a; 2003: ch. 15) and chapter 6 here.

10. The concept of "strategic exchange" is introduced and discussed in Snooks (2007; 2008a); and it is contrasted with the flawed supply-side concept of "emergence".

11. Curiously, while physicists have been able to observe patterns in the cosmos and thereby construct physical laws, they have been unable to develop a general dynamic theory of the Universe that incorporates these laws together with the observable constants of nature. Instead they have focused on simple mathematical descriptions of all known laws at both the micro (quantum theory) and the macro (relativity theory) levels. Mathematics can limit as well as advance the development of science.

Chapter 6 Laws of the *Logos*

1. The dynamic-strategy theory is based on the systematic observation of both human society and life—see Snooks (1996; 1997; 2003).

2. Popper's attack on historicism is discussed and evaluated in Snooks (1998a: ch. 5).

3.   On Popper's use of historicist methodology—see Snooks (1998a: 147–50).

4.   Taming the "problem of induction"—see Snooks (1998a: ch. 7).

5.   For progress in the application of laws of the *logos* to economic and political change, see Snooks (1998b; 1999; 2000; 2008b; 2009a; 2010b).

Chapter 7 Citadel of the *Logos*—the Ephemeral Civilisation

1.   See North (1981; 1990; 1994) on the "new" institutionalism. Actually it is rather old fashioned.

2.   On mutual trust, see Casson (1991: 3).

3.   For a discussion of the flawed supply-side theory of "path dependence", see David (1993).

4.   North's (1990: 113–17) explanation of Spain's relative economic backwardness in the nineteenth century.

5.   On the changing nature of entertainment in Europe, see Snooks (1997: ch. 10).

Chapter 8 Ideology of the *Logos* — from Religion to Scientism

1.   Armstrong (2005: 4, 7).

2.   Hornung (1996: 17).

3.   For a discussion of, and theory about, the ephemerality of human society, see Snooks (1997).

4.   From the early Anglo-Saxon poem "The Wanderer", translated by S.A.J. Bradley (1982).

5.   Why is inflation-targeting irrational? See Snooks (1998b; 1999; 2000; 2008b; 2008c; 2008e).

6.   For a discussion of existential schizophrenia, see Snooks (1997: 1–2, 198, 520, etc.), Snooks (2006: 7, 164–67, 201–06, 234, 279) and chapter 10 here.

7.   The progression from existential schizophrenia to pathological schizophrenia—Snooks (2006: 202–207) and chapter 10 (esp. Table 10.1).

8.   Strategic frustration leading to social neurosis was introduced in Snooks (2006: 220–22) and developed in the religious context in Snooks (2010b: Chs 4 and 5).

9.   The discussion of the technological-paradigm-shift mechanism is based on Snooks (1996; 1997; 1998a; 2010b).

10. On the social costs of Egypt's great pyramid, see Snooks (2010b: ch. 3).

11. The Snooks-Panov algorithm is discussed in Nazaretyan (2005a; 2006b), Panov (2005), and Snooks (2005: 229–31).

12. For the first formal discussion of the future technological paradigm shift, see Snooks (1996: ch. 13). It is discussed in further detail—together with the implications for climate mitigation—in *The Coming Eclipse* (Snooks 2010a). Also see chapter 13 here.

13. On the future "Solar Revolution", see Snooks (1996: 429–30; 2003: 262–63) and Snooks (2010a) and chapter 13 here.

14. For a graphic account of the most important inventions of the ancient world, see Fagan (2004).

15. The technological strategy was not an economic option until the exhaustion of the neolithic technological paradigm in the mid-eighteenth century. This is why every ancient society returned to conquest once its commerce strategy had been exhausted.

16. For a discussion of the Greek "strategic sequence" and its societal impact, see Snooks (1997: ch. 8).

17. In this chapter, Greek science is of greater interest than Greek religion because it is the former rather than the latter that impacted on Western civilisation as the facilitator of the industrial technological paradigm shift.

18. For an outline of the outcomes of Egyptian science, see Fagan (2004).

19. The British Industrial Revolution is analysed in Snooks (1994b; 1997: ch. 10).

20. Shermer (2002). My emphasis.

21. The flawed nature of sociobiology is discussed in Snooks (2006: chs 7 and 8), and Chapter 4 above.

22. The limitations of social physics are outlined in Snooks (2007; 2008a).

23. On my discovery of the growth-inflation curve, see Snooks (1998: ch. 11); and for applications, see Snooks (1999; 2008b; 2008c; 2008e). The underlying idea first emerged in the early 1990s when examining long-run changes in price and real GDP data for England 1000–2000—see Snooks (1993a: 256–69)—and was first examined formally in ANU Economic History Working Paper No. 195 (July 1997), entitled "Strategic Demand and the Growth-Inflation Curve. New theoretical and Empirical Concepts". See: http://econrsss.anu.edu.au/~snooksweb/Articles/snooksWPEH195.pdf

    This paper (like all my other papers) can also be found on the "Graeme Snooks Researchgate" site.

24. The high priest of the cult of Gaia is James Lovelock (1990; 2006).

25. An enthusiastic advocate of "cosmotheology" is James Gardner (2003).

Chapter 9 Strategic Awareness of the Logos—the Selfcreating Mind

1. For a discussion of the deductive and inductive methods, see Snooks (1998a: Part I). More generally, it should be realised that selfcreation has no relationship with the fashionable, but limited, idea called "self-organisation"—the idea that order is the spontaneous outcome of a mechanical interaction between variables—that has arisen from complexity theory. Selfcreation is the outcome of highly motivated agents responding to their social environment rather than from the mechanical interaction of mindless particles obeying the laws of physics as in the theory of self-organisation. As will be seen, it is an endogenously determined demand-side theory, rather than an exogenously determined supply-side hypothesis.

2. On the dynamic strategies of organisms, see Snooks (2003: ch. 13).

3. The reasons for using biotransition rather than "evolution" are that the latter is indistinguishable from Darwinian natural selection and that it is carelessly used to refer to both systematic genetic change and the fluctuating fortunes of life (change in total biomass).

4. The surface area of the cortex has increased fourfold over the past 4 myrs. We know that the "ironed-out" cortex of modern humans—roughly equivalent to four sheets of typing paper—is four times the size of that of modern chimpanzees (Greenfield 1997: 15), and that a chimp's brain today is similar in size and complexity to that of our forebears about 4 myrs BP, when our lines of descent parted company.

5. The development of the strategic-imitation concept can be traced in Snooks (1996: 171, 182, 212–13, 394, 439) and Snooks (1997; 1998a; 2003).

6. The "Swiss-army knife" metaphor used by evolutionary psychiatrists is discussed by Tooby and Cosmides (1992) and Carruthers and Chamberlain (2000).

7. See MacLean (1990).

8. See Edelman and Tononi (2004).

9. On epigenetic rules and the structure of the brain, see Wilson (1998: 165).

10. Plasticity experiments on the brain are discussed by Greenfield (1997: 8).

11. The emergence of language is regarded conventionally as "mysterious"—Carter (2000: 228).

12. The historical development of language is discussed in Mithen (2000) and Dunbar (2000).

13. All quotations in this paragraph are from Chomsky (2002), namely pp. 11, 14, 16, 47, 57.

14. On the similarity between the models of Chomsky and the evolutionary psychiatrists, see Snooks (2006: ch.10).

15. Carter (2000: 228–9) discusses the historical emergence of both the language and visual-spatial regions of the brain.

16. For a new interpretation of Neanderthal language, see Snooks (2008c).

17. In most of my work I have explored the differences and conflict between deductive and inductive thinking. These methodological matters are central to the books I have published over the past couple of decades—see Snooks (1993; 1994; 1996; 1997; 1998a; 1998b; 1999; 2000; 2003; 2006; 2010b). I show that the so-called "problem of induction" is far less distorting than what I call the "problem of deduction", which arises from not being able to recognise and take into account the patterns of reality. Deduction is based on guesswork rather than real-world evidence.

In *The Selfcreating Mind* I associate induction with the pattern-recognition function of the ancient strategic brain, and deduction with the "tool-rule" abilities that have emerged more recently and only been formally developed since the arrival of civilisation. The deductive method forms the basis of robotic "thinking" and the inductive method of strategic thinking. Edelman and Tononi (2000: 212–18) also see the thinking processes of man and machine as being different—what they call "selectionism and logic"—but they do not relate it to the development of the strategic brain or strategic thinking.

The importance of pattern recognition in human activities is also recognised by those from a very different intellectual tradition. See the important work in "econophysics" by Roehner (2002) and Roehner and Syme (2002).

18. For the results from tests of rational ability, see Papineau (2000), Evans and Over (1996), and Stein (1996).

19. On the effects of damaged frontal lobes, see Greenfield (1997: 20).

20. The essential role of strategic leadership is argued in Snooks (2000), Snooks (2013b), and chapters 4 and 11 here.

21. The strategic struggle is discussed in detail in Snooks (1997: 8–12, 523–24, etc.), Snooks (2003: chs 9 and 10) and Snooks (2010b: 307–08, 367). Also see chapters 4, 7, and 11 above.

22. On "theory-of-mind", see Carruthers (2000: 266).

23. On the state of consciousness, see Carruthers and Chamberlain (2000), Block, Flanagan and Güzeldere (1997), Warner and Szubka (1994), and Humphrey (1993).

24. The failure and collapse of antistrategic societies like the USSR are discussed in Snooks (1997: ch. 12; 1999: ch. 5), and chapter 13 above.

25. Edelman and Tononi (2000: 103).

26. For the way strategic imitation operates at the individual and societal levels, see Snooks (1996; 1997; 1999; 2003; 2006; 2010b).

27. The interaction between strategists, nonstrategists, and antistrategists is discussed in Snooks (1997: ch. 1; 1998b: ch. 16; 2000: chs 4 & 6; 2003: 224–29) and chapter 7 here.

28. For a discussion of antistrategists in the world today, and in the Roman Empire, see Snooks (1997; 2000; 2010a).

29. "Strategic dualism" is a new concept introduced in *The Selfcreating Mind* (2006: part II).

30. The role of conquest in history is discussed in Snooks (1996: ch. 10; 1997: chs 6 and 7), and chapter 4 above.

31. The commerce wars are discussed in Snooks (1996: ch. 11; 1997: chs 8 and 9).

32. My concept of "existential schizophrenia" has its roots in Snooks (1996) and is formally discussed in Snooks (1997; 1998a; 2006; 2010b).

Chapter 10 Restoring Damaged Consciousness—A Strategic Psychology

1. This section relies heavily on the *Diagnostic and statistical Manual of mental disorders. Fourth Edition. Text Revision* (2000). This edition is usually referred to as *DSM-IV-TR*: I will merely call it *DSM* (2000) in these notes.

2. *DSM* (2000: 356).

3. Unscrupulous and sadistic managers sometimes deliberately induce depression in those staff members they wish to force out, hoping it will lead to their withdrawal from organised activities. They then use the fact of this withdrawal as a further weapon by accusing the hapless victim of not doing their duty. This sadistic behaviour is difficult to expose and eradicate as institutions tend to support their managers (potential abusers) rather than their workers (potential abused). From my experience, this is certainly the case in Australian universities today.

4. Stevens and Price (2000: 61), on the distressing nature of severe depression.

5. *DSM* (2000: 362).

6. On the incidence of social phobia, see *DSM* (2000: 453).

7. Ibid: 685.

8. For a more detailed discussion of strategy-challenging personality disorders, see Snooks (2006: 191–95).

9. *DSM* (2000: 704); Stevens and Price (2000: 86).

10. The concept of the antistrategist is developed in Snooks (1996; 1997; 1999; 2000). Also see chapter 7.

11. On suicide rates—which globally affect 10–13 per cent of people with schizophrenia— see Barbato (1997) and WHO (2000). It is estimated that over 40 per cent—60 per cent of males and 20 per cent of females—of schizophrenia sufferers attempt suicide at least once in their lives: see SANE (2000a).

12. *DSM* (2000: 692).

13. Stevens and Price (2000: 138).

14. Multiple personality disorder—rather than schizophrenia, as suggested by Edelman and Tononi (2000: 153–4)—could be the outcome of a division of the strategic core of consciousness into multiple sections.

15. Stevens and Price (2000: 141).

16. *DSM* (2000: 299).

17. Ibid: 309.

18. Ibid.

19. Ibid.

20. For a realist interpretation of "truth", see my recent book *The Death of Zarathustra. Notes on Truth for the Risk Taker* (2011).

21. *DSM*: 759. These defence mechanisms are included in *DSM*, "Appendix B".

22. Ibid: 807.

23. The concept of existential schizophrenia, originally based on historical observation, was developed in Snooks (1997; 1998a; 2006; 2010b).

24. For a detailed discussion of the basis of realistic decision-making, see Snooks (1996: 212–13; 1997: ch. 2; 1998a: 201–2; 1998b: 113–22; 1999: 194–8).

25. For a detailed discussion of the principles of a new strategic psychiatry, see Snooks (2006: ch. 12).

Chapter 11 Understanding the Modern *Logos*—Societal Dynamics

1. Keynes lacks a general dynamic theory—Snooks (1998b: ch. 4).

2. A new interpretation of the Great Depression—Snooks (1997: 384–90, especially 387–88).

3. Myths about the 1998 "global crisis"—Snooks (2000: 2–4).

4. Market economists falsely claim credit—Snooks (2000: 27-28).

5. Discovery of the growth-inflation curve—see note 8.23.

6. My predictions about the role of inflation targeting in generating economic recession—Snooks (1998b: 19–21, ch. 17; 2000: 114–23; 2000b: reprint preface; 2008b; 2008c).

7. The new interventionists—Snooks (2009a).

8. The dynamic-strategy theory has been developed in a long series of books–Snooks (1994a; 1996; 1997; 1998a; 1998b; 1999; 2000; 2003; 2006; 2010b).

9. For the development of the "strategic imitation" model, see Snooks (1996: 212–13; 1997: 36–46; 1998b: 113–22; 1999: 190–98; 2003: chs 2–3, 224–29; 2006: 207–09, 219–20).

10. The law of diminishing strategic returns–Snooks (1998a 202–03).

11. Estimation of growth-inflation curves—Snooks (1998b: 151–59).

12. Strategic leadership explained—Snooks (1997: 54–58; 2000: 57–111; 2003: 209, 321; 2006: 93–94, 209–21; 2013b).

13. The circular strategic development path—Snooks (1997: ch. 3).

14. Orthodox ideas on growth paths—Hicks (1965) and Pasinetti and Solow (1994: 359, 376).

15. Law of diminishing strategic returns—see chapter 6.

16. Classical and neoclassical concepts of diminishing returns evaluated—Snooks (1998b: 131–32).

Chapter 12 The *Logos* at Large—Global Strategic Transition

1. Wider perception about the shortcomings of orthodox development economics—Meier and Seers (1984).

2. For exceptions to the general view of economic development as an outcome rather than a process, see Arndt (1987), Clark (1940), and Maddison (1995b).

3. Singer and Roy (1993: 10).

4.   Streeton (1995: 17–18).

5.   Dutt (1992: 23–25.

6.   Singer and Roy (1993: 1).

7.   Orthodox and Radical models are discussed in detail in Snooks (1999: ch. 6).

8.   For the influence of Keynes in development economics, see Rosenstein-Rodan (1943), and Scitovsky (1954).

9.   Dissenting neoclassical economists include Viner (1953), Schultz (1964), Bauer (1971).

10. Singer and Roy (1993: 44).

11. For adverse effects of orthodox policy, see Snooks (1998b: ch. 17).

12. A detailed account of the great technological paradigm shifts can be found in Snooks (1996: ch. 12; 2010b: ch. 10); and an outline is provided in chapter 3 above.

13. Conquest is obsolete as a dynamic strategy in the modern world—see Snooks (1996: 307–14).

14. On strategic imitation, see note 11.9.

15. On nuclear weapons and the end of colonialism, see Snooks (1997a: 503–06).

16. On the emergence of mega states, see Snooks (1997: ch. 12).

17. On the growth-inflation curve in the Third World, see Snooks (1999: ch. 11).

18. The future lies with mega states—Snooks (1999: ch. 12).

19. The strategy function was first presented in Snooks (1999: Ch. 12). Further work in currently being undertaken on the Snooksian strategy function by Huw McKay, a former PhD student.

20. Snooks (1999: 341, note 12.1).

21. For the "strategic transfer", see Snooks (1997: see index).

22. Contrasting growth and inflation in ESCs and SCs, see Snooks (1999: ch. 11).

23. On strategic opportunities, see Snooks (1998b: 242).

24. *The Economist*, 20th December 1997: 15.

Chapter 13 Choice of Futures for the *Logos*

1.   On the simple engineering models employed by the limits-to-growth people, see Snooks (1996: 103–110).

2.   Introducing the idea of the imminent technological revolution, see Snooks (1996: 429).

3.   On radical ecologists, see Snooks (1996: 428–29).

4.   Source of global oil data—*Energy Bulletin* and *World Energy Council, 2015*.

5.   Major coal producers—*Coal Research 2007* and *World Energy Council, 2015*.

6. Future coal production—Zittel and Schindler (2007).

7. Snooks (1996: 430).

8. The "Dyson Swarm" is a variation on the less realistic concept by British theoretical physicist and mathematician Freeman Dyson (1923–) known as the "Dyson Shell" (or Dyson Sphere), which would ultimately completely surround the solar system, capturing all the Sun's energy and making our world invisible to any observers elsewhere in the galaxy.

9. The concept of "funnels of transformation" was introduced in Snooks (1996: 225–27, 434).

10. Will Australia be one of the many paradigm-shift losers? See Snooks (2009b).

11. Climate mitigation and technological "lock-in"—Snooks (2009b).

12. Stern (2007: 25).

13. On the dynamic role of US railroads, see Snooks (1997: 374–76).

14. On the real reasons for the US Civil War, see Snooks (1997: 378–84).

15. The conventional view of the benefits and costs of the British Empire are discussed in Snooks (1997: 299–300).

16. Stern (2007: 164).

17. Stern (2007: xv).

18. Stern (2007: 304) on amount of required mitigation investment in low-carbon technologies.

19. The development of science as a response to logosian demand—Snooks (2010: ch. 7).

20. World economic growth rates, 1950–1973, are from Maddison (2003: 260).

21. Estimate of world GDP in 2007 from *CIA World Factbook*.

22. On carbon dioxide "sinks", see Pittock (2006: 12–14).

23. Long delay in carbon absorption claimed unrealistically by Archer et al (2009).

24. On the Australian prime minister, Kevin Rudd's new interventionism, see Snooks (2009a).

25. The decline in solar activity over the next two decades predicted by Ken McCracken is discussed in Snooks (2009b: ch. 2).

Select References

This is a list of select references only. Over the course of the past few decades, the "dynamic-strategy project" has made reference to thousands of books and articles, which can be found listed in the dozen or so books I have published in this series. Only those books specifically mentioned in the text of *Ark of the Sun* are included here. The logosian maxims that head each chapter have been derived from the dynamic-strategy theory.

Alvarez, L. W., W. Alvarez, F. Asaro, and H. V. Michel (1980). "Extraterrestrial cause for the cretaceous–tertiary extinction." *Science* 208, no. 4448, (6 June): 1095–1108.

Archer, D. et al (2009), "Atmospheric lifetime of fossil-fuel carbon dioxide", *Annual Review of Earth and Planetary Sciences,* 37 (forthcoming, May).

Armstrong, K. (2005). *A Short History of Myth.* Edinburgh: Canongate.

Arndt, H.W. (1987), *Economic Development: The History of an Idea* (Chicago: University of Chicago Press).

Bais, S. (2005). *The Equations: Icons of Knowledge,* Cambridge, Massachusetts: Harvard University Press.

Bakker, R.T. (1978). "Dinosaur renaissance." Pp. 125–41 in *Evolution and the Fossil Record: Readings from Scientific American* (with introductions by Léo F. Laporte). San Francisco: W. H. Freeman and Company.

Bakker, R.T. (1986). *The Dinosaur Heresies: New Theories Unlocking the Mystery of the Dinosaurs and their Extinction.* New York: Morrow.

Balter, M., and A. Gibbons. (2000). "A glimpse of human's first journey out of Africa." *Science* 288, no. 5468 (12 May): 948–50

Bauer, P.T. (1971), *Dissent on Development* (London: Weidenfeld & Nicholson).

Benford, G. (2008). "The final dark." In D. Broderick (ed.), *Year Million. Science at the Far Edge of Knowledge,* New York: Atlas & Co.

Benton, M. J. (1985). "Mass extinction among non-marine tetrapods." *Nature* 316, no. 6031 (29 August): 811–14.

Block, N.J., Flanagan, O.J. and Güzeldere, G., eds (1997). *The Nature of Consciousness: Philosophical Debates.* Cambridge, MA: MIT Press.

Bradley, S.A.J. (1982). *Anglo-Saxon Poetry: An Anthology of Old English Poems in Prose Translation.* London: Dent.

Cairns, J., J. Overbaugh and S. Miller (1988). "The origin of mutants." *Nature* 335, no. 6186 (8 September): 142–5.

Calder, N. (1984). *Timescale: An Atlas of the Fourth Dimension.* London: Chatto & Windus, The Hogarth Press.

Campbell, I. H., G. K. Czamanske, V. A. Fedorenko, R. I. Hill, and V. Stepanov. (1992). "Synchronism of the Siberian traps and the permian–triassic boundary." *Science* 258, no. 5089 (11 December): 1760–2.

Carroll, S.M. (2008), "The rise and fall of time". In D. Broderick (ed.), *Year Million. Science at the Far Edge of Knowledge*, New York: Atlas & Co.

Carter, R. (2000). *Mapping the Mind.* (Consultant: C. Frith). London: Phoenix.

Casson, M. (1991), *The Economics of Business Culture: Game Theory, Transaction Costs and Economics.* Oxford: Clarendon Press; New York: Oxford University Press.

Chomsky, N. (2002). *On Nature and Language.* Englewood Cliffs: Prentice Hall.

CIA *World Factbook*, 2008.

Clark, C.G. (1940). *The Conditions of Economic Progress*, London: Macmillan.

Cowen, R. (1990). *History of Life.* Boston: Blackwell Scientific Publications.

Cowen, R. (2000). *History of Life.* 3rd ed. Malden, MA: Blackwell Science.

Cullotta, E. (1999). "A new human ancestor." *Science* 284, no. 5414 (23 April): 572–3.

Crawford, M., and D. Marsh (1989). *The Driving Force: Food in Evolution and the Future.* London: Mandarin.

Carruthers, P. (2000). "The evolution of consciousness." Pp. 254–75 in *Evolution and the human mind,* edited by P. Carruthers and A. Chamberlain. Cambridge: Cambridge University Press.

Carruthers, P. and Chamberlain, A. (2000). *Evolution and the Human Mind: Modularity, Language and Meta-Cognition.* Cambridge: Cambridge University Press.

Coal Research Committee (2007), *Coal: Research and Development to Support National Energy Policy.* Washington DC: National Academies Press.

Darwin, C. (1859). *On the Origin of Species by Means of Natural Selection; or, the Preservation of Favoured Races in the Struggle for Life.* 1st ed. London: John Murray.

David, P.A. (1993), 'Historical economics in the longrun: some implications of path-dependence', in G.D. Snooks, ed., *Historical Analysis in Economics.* London & New York, Routledge, pp. 29–40.

DSM (2000). *Diagnostic and Statistical Manual of Mental Disorders.* Fourth edition. Text revision. Washington: American Psychiatric Association.

Dunbar, R. (2000). "On the origin of the human mind." Pp. 238–53 in *Evolution and the Human Mind,* edited by P. Carruthers and A. Chamberlain. Cambridge: Cambridge University Press.

Dutt, A.K. (1992), 'Two issues in the state of development economics', in A.K. Dutt and K.P. Jameson, eds, *New Directions in Development Economics.* Aldershot, Hants, and Brookfield, Vt: E. Elgar, pp. 1–34.

Duve, C. de. (1996). "The birth of complex cells." *Scientific American* 274, no. 4 (April): 38–45.

Easteal, S., C. Collet, and D. Betty (1995). *The Mammalian Molecular Clock.* Austin and New York: R. G. Landes/Springer-Verlag.

Eccles, J. C. (1989). *The Evolution of the Brain: Creation of the Conscious Self.* London and New York: Routledge.

Edelman, G.M. and Tononi, G. (2000). *Consciousness: How Matter Becomes Imagination.* London: Penguin.

Eldredge, N., and S.J. Gould. (1972). "Punctuated equilibria: An alternative to phyletic gradualism." Pp. 82–115 in *Models of Paleobiology*, ed. T. J. M. Schopt. San Francisco: Freeman, Cooper.

Energy Bulletin (http://www.energybulletin.net)

Evans, J. and Over, D. (1996). *Rationality and Reasoning.* Hove: Psychology Press.

Fagan, B.M. (2004). *The Seventy Great Innovations of the Ancient World.* London: Thames & Hudson.

Fisher, P. E., D. A. Russel, M. K. Stoskopf, R. E. Barrick, M. Hammer, and A. A. Kuzmitz. (2000). "Cariovascular evidence for an intermediate or higher metabolic rate in an ornithischian dinosaur." *Science* 288, no. 5465 (21 April): 503–5.

Foster, P.L. (1998). "Adaptive mutation: Has the unicorn landed?" *Genetics* 148 (April): 1453–9.

Foster, P.L. (1999). "Mechanisms of stationary phase mutation: A decade of adaptive mutation." *Annual Review of Genetics* 33: 57–88.

Gardner, J.N. (2003). *Biocosm. The New Scientific Theory of Evolution: Intelligent Life is the Architect of the Universe.* Makawao, Maui, HI: Inner Ocean.

Garnaut, R. (2008). The Garnaut Climate Change Review. Draft report. (June). Canberra (www.garnautreview.org.au).

Gibbons, A. (1998). "Solving the brain's energy crisis." *Science* 280, no. 5368 (29 May): 1345–7.

Greenfield, S. (1997). *The Human Brain: A Guided Tour*. London: Weidenfeld & Nicholson.

Grimal, P. ed. (1974). *World Mythology*. London: Hamlyn.

Hall, B.G. (1988). "Adaptive evolution that requires multiple spontaneous mutations. I. Mutations involving an insertion sequence." *Genetics* 120 (December): 887–97.

Heraclitus (2001). *Fragments: The Collected Wisdom of Heraclitus*. Translated by Brooks Haxton. New York: Viking.

Hicks, J.R. (1965), *Capital and Growth*, Oxford: Clarendon Press.

Hornung, E. (1996). *Conceptions of God in Ancient Egypt. The One and the Many*. Translated by J. Baines. Ithaca, NY: Cornell University Press.

Humphrey, N. (1993). *A History of the Mind*. New York: Harper Perennial.

IPCC (2007). Fourth Assessment Report: Climate Change 2007. Geneva: IPCC. 4 vols: 1 *Synthesis report*; 2 *The physical science basis*; 3 *Impacts, adaptation and vulnerability; 4 Mitigation of climate change*

Leakey, R. E., and R. Lewin (1992). *Origins Reconsidered: In Search of What Makes Us Human*. London: Little Brown.

Lovelock, J. (1990). *The Ages of Gaia. A Biography of Our Living Earth*. Oxford: Oxford University Press.

Lovelock, J. (2006). *The Revenge of Gaia. Why the Earth is Fighting Back — And How We Can Still Save Humanity*. Camberwell, Victoria: Allen Lane.

MacLean, P.D. (1990). *The Triune Brain in Evolution: Role in Paleocerebral Functions*. New York: Plenum Press.

Maddison, A. (1995a), *Monitoring the World Economy, 1820–1992* (Paris: Development Centre of the Organisation for Economic Co-operation and Development).

Maddison, A. (1995b), *Explaining the Economic Performance of Nations: Essays in Time and Space* (Aldershot, Hants, and Brookfield, Vt: E. Elgar).

Maddison, A. (2003). *The World Economy: Historical Statistics*. Paris: OECD.

Meier, G.M., and D. Seers, eds (1984), *Pioneers in Development*. New York: Oxford University Press for the World Bank.

Mithen, S. (2000). "Mind, brain, and material culture: an archaeological perspective." Pp. 207–17 in *Evolution and the Human Mind,* edited by P. Carruthers and A. Chamberlain. Cambridge: Cambridge University Press.

Nazaretyan, A.P. (2005a.) "Snooks-Panov vertical." In Mazow, I.I. and Chumakov, A.N., eds, *The Global Studies Dictionary.* Moscow: Dialog Raduga Publications (Russian); and Amherst, New York: Prometheus Books (English).

Nazaretyan, A.P. (2005b). "Big (universal) History paradigm: Versions and approaches." *Social Evolution & History* 4: 61–86.

Newell, N.D. (1978). "Crisis in the history of life". Pp. 179–92 in *Evolution and the Fossil Record: Readings from* Scientific American. (Ed by L.F. Laporte.) San Francisco: W.H. Freeman.

North, D.C. (1981), *Structure and Change in Economic History.* New York: Norton.

North, D.C. (1990), *Institutions, Institutional Change, and Economic Performance.* Cambridge & New York: Cambridge University Press.

North, D.C. (1994), "Economic performance through time", *American Economic Review,* 84 (3), pp. 359–68.

Nutman, A. P., V. C. Bennett, C. R. L. Friend, and V. R. Mcgregor (2000). "The early archaean itsaq gneiss complex of southern West Greenland: The importance of field observations in interpreting age and isotopic constraints for early terrestrial evolution." *Geochimica et Cosmochimica Acta* 64, no. 17 (September): 3035–60.

Panov, A.D. (2005). "Scaling law of biological evolution and the hypothesis of the self-consistent galaxy origin of life". *Advances in Space Research* 36: 220–25.

Papineau, D. (2000). "The evolution of knowledge." Pp. 170–206 in *Evolution and the Human Mind,* edited by P. Carruthers and A. Chamberlain. Cambridge: Cambridge University Press.

Pasinetti, L.L. and R.M. Solow (1994), *Economic Growth and the Structure of Long-term Development.* Cambridge: Cambridge University Press.

Pennisi, E. 1999. "Did cooked tubers spur the evolution of big brains?" *Science* 283, no. 5410 (26 March): 2004–5.

Pittock, A.B. (2006). *Climate Change. Turning Up the Heat.* Melbourne: CSIRO Publishing.

Quirke, S. (2001). *The Cult of Ra. Sun-Worship in Ancient Egypt. New York:* Thames & Hudson.

Rampino, M. R., and R. B. Stothers (1988). "Flood basalt volcanism during the past 250 million years." *Science* 241, no. 4866 (5 August): 663–8.

Rappaport, R.A. (2002). *Ritual and Religion in the Making of Humanity.* Cambridge: Cambridge University Press.

Raup, D.M., and J.J. Sepkoski (1984). "Periodicity of extinctions in the geologic pPast." *Proceedings of the National Academy of Sciences of the United States of America* 81: 801–5.

Raup, D.M., and J.J. Sepkoski (1986). "Periodic extinction of families and genera." *Science* 231, no. 4740 (19 March): 833–6.

Reed, K. E. (1997). "Early Hominid Evolution and Ecological Change through the African Plio-Pleistocene." *Journal of Human Evolution* 32, no. 2/3 (March): 289–322.

Redford, D.B. (2003). *The Oxford Essential Guide to Egyptian Mythology*. New York: Berkley Books.

Ricqles, A. de. (1974). "Evolution of endothermy: Histological evidence." *Evolutionary Theory* 1: 51–80.

Roehner, B.M. (2002). *Patterns of Speculation. A Study in Observational Econophysics*. Cambridge: Cambridge University Press.

Roehner, B.M. and Syme, T. (2002) *Pattern and Repertoire in History*. Cambridge MA: Harvard University Press.

Rosenstein-Rodan, P.N. (1943), "Problems of industrialisation of eastern and south-eastern Europe", *Economic Journal*, 53, pp. 202–11

Rowlett, Ralph M. (1999). "Fire use." *Science* 284, no. 5415 (30 April): 741.

Russell, D.A. (1969). "A new specimen of *Stenonychosaurus* from the Oldman Formation (Cretaceous) of Alberta." *Canadian Journal of Earth Sciences* 6, no. 4, part 1 (August): 595–612.

Schultz, T.W. (1964), *Transforming Traditional Agriculture*. New Haven: Yale University Press.

Scitovsky, T. (1954), "Two concepts of external economies", *Journal of Political Economy*, 17, pp. 143–51.

Sepkoski Jr, J. J. (1978). "A kinetic model of phanerozoic taxonomic diversity, I: Analysis of marine orders." *Paleobiology* 4, no. 3: 223–51.

Sepkoski Jr. J.J (1979). "A kinetic model of phanerozoic taxonomic diversity, II: Early phanerozoic families and multiple equilibria." *Paleobiology* 5, no. 3: 222–51.

Sepkoski Jr. J.J. (1984). "A kinetic model of phanerozoic taxonomic diversity, III: Post-paleozoic families and mass extinctions." *Paleobiology* 10, no. 2: 246–67.

Shermer, M. (2002). "The shamans of scientism". *Scientific American* May 13th.

Singer, H.W., and S. Roy (1993), *Economic Progress and Prospects in the Third World: Lessons of Development Experience, 1945–1992 and Beyond.* Aldershot, Hants, and Brookfield, Vt: Edward Elgar.

Snooks, G.D. (1974), *Depression and Recovery in Western Australia, 1928/29— 1938/39. A Study in Cyclical and Structural Change.* Nedlands: UWA Press.

Snooks, G.D. (1993a). *Economics Without Time.* London: Macmillan

Snooks, G.D., ed. (1993b), *Historical Analysis in Economics.* London & New York: Routledge.

Snooks, G.D. (1994a), *Portrait of the Family within the Total Economy. A Study in Longrun Dynamics: Australia, 1788–1990.* Cambridge: Cambridge University Press.

Snooks, G.D., ed. (1994b), *Was the Industrial Revolution Necessary?* London & New York: Routledge.

Snooks, G.D. (1996). *The Dynamic Society.* London & New York: Routledge.

Snooks, G.D. (1997a). *The Ephemeral Civilization.* London & New York: Routledge.

Snooks, G.D. (1997b), "Strategic demand and the growth-inflation curve. New theoretical and empirical concepts". *Working papers in Economic History* (RSSS, ANU) no. 195 (July): 1–37.

Snooks, G.D. (1998a). *The Laws of History.* London & New York: Routledge.

Snooks, G.D. (1998b). *Longrun Dynamics: A General Economic and Political Theory.* London: Macmillan.

Snooks, G. D. (1999). *Global Transition. A general Theory of Economic Development.* London: Macmillan.

Snooks, G.D. (2000). *The Global Crisis Makers.* London: Macmillan.

Snooks, G.D. (2003). *The Collapse of Darwinism; or The Rise of a Realist Theory of Life.* Lanham, MD and Oxford: Lexington Books, Roman & Littlefield.

Snooks, G.D. (2005). "The origin of life on Earth: A new general dynamic theory", *Advances in Space Research,* 36: 226–234.

Snooks, G.D. (2006). *The Selfcreating Mind.* Lanham, MD and Oxford: University Press of America, Roman & Littlefield.

Snooks, G.D. (2007). "Self-organisation or selfcreation? From social physics to realist dynamics". *Social Evolution & History* 6 (March): 118–144.

Snooks, G.D. (2008a). "A general theory of complex living systems: Exploring the demand side of dynamics", *Complexity,* 13 (July/August): 12–20.

Snooks, G.D. (2008b). "Australia's long-run economic strategy, performance, and Policy: A new dynamic perspective", *Economic Papers* 27 (September): 208–32. http://econrsss.anu.edu.au/pdf/GDSC/WP002.pdf

Snooks, G.D. (2008c). "The irrational 'war on inflation': Why inflation targeting is both socially unacceptable and economically untenable", Global Dynamic Systems Centre (RSSS, ANU), *Working Papers,* No. 1 (March): 1–6. http://econrsss.anu.edu.au/pdf/GDSC/WP001.pdf

Snooks, G.D. (2008d). "The Neanderthal enigma: A new theoretical approach", Global Dynamic Systems Centre (RSSS, ANU), *Working Papers,* No. 5 (August): 1–42 http://econrsss.anu.edu.au/pdfGDSC/WP005.pdf

Snooks, G.D. (2008e). "Recession, depression, and financial crisis: Everything economists want to know but are afraid to ask", Global Dynamic Systems Centre (RSSS, ANU), *Working Papers,* No. 7 (October):1–17. http://econrsss.anu.edu.au/pdf/GDSC/WP007.pdf

Snooks, G.D. (2009a). "The new global crisis makers: Economic intervention and the loss of strategic leadership". Global Dynamic Systems Centre (RSSS, ANU), *Working Papers,* no. 9 (February). http://econrsss.anu.edu.au/pdf/GDSC/WP009.pdf

Snooks, G.D. (2010a). *The Coming Eclipse, or the Triumph of Climate Mitigation over Solar Revolution.* Canberra: IGDS Books.

Snooks, G.D. (2010b). *Dead God Rising. The Role of Religion and Science in the Universal Life-System.* Canberra: IGDS Books.

Snooks, G.D. (2011). *The Death of Zarathustra. Note on Truth for the Risk-Taker.* Canberra: IGDS Books.

Snooks, G.D. (2013a), "The Cosmos & the Logos (I)", Institute of Global Dynamic Systems (Canberra), *Working Papers*, no. 12, July 2013 (1st version, May 2009): 1–32.

Snooks, G.D. (2013b), "Rediscovering the Lost Art of Strategic Leadership", Institute of Global Dynamic Systems (Canberra), *Working Papers*, no. 11, July 2013: 1–10.

Snooks, G.D. (2015), "The Cosmos and the Logos (II): A Realist Theory of Life's Emergence, Evolution and Future", Ch. 8 in B. Rodrigue, L. Grinnin & A. Korotayev (eds), *From the Big Bang to Galactic Civilisation: A Big History Anthology. Volume I.* Delhi: Primus Books.

Snooks, G.D. and J. McDonald (1986), *Domesday economy. A new approach to Anglo-Norman history.* Oxford: Clarendon Press.

Spence, L. (2004). *Myths and Legends of the North American Indians.* London: CRW Publishing.

Stein, E. (1996). *Without Good Reason.* Oxford: Clarendon Press.

Stern, N. (2005). *Growth and Empowerment: Making Development Happen.* Cambridge, Mass: MIT Press.

Stern, N. (2007). *The Economics of Climate Change. The Stern Review.* Cambridge: Cambridge University Press.

Stevens, A. and Price, J. (2000). *Evolutionary Psychiatry: A New Beginning.* Second edition. London and New York: Routledge.

Streeten, P.P. (1995), *Thinking About Development.* Cambridge and New York: Cambridge University Press.

Tooby, J. and Cosmides, L. (1992). "The psychological foundations of culture." Pp. 19–136 in *The Adapted Mind: Evolutionary Psychology and the Generation of Culture,* edited by J. Barkow, L. Cosmides and J. Tooby. New York: Oxford University Press.

Viner, J. (1953), *International Trade and Economic Development: Lectures Delivered at the National University of Brazil.* Oxford: Clarendon Press.

Warner, R. and Szubka, T. (1994). *The Mind–Body Problem: A Guide to the Current Debate.* Cambridge Mass.: Blackwell.

Wilson, E.O. (1998). *Consilience: The Unity of Knowledge.* New York: Knopf.

Zimmer, C. (1999). "Kenyan skeleton shakes ape family tree." *Science* 285, no. 5432 (27 August): 1335, 1337.

Zittel, W. and J. Schindler (2007), "Crude oil: The supply outlook". A report to the Energy Watch Group (Germany). Ottobrunn Germany.

Ark of the Sun

About the Author

Graeme Donald Snooks is the Executive Director of the Institute of Global Dynamic Systems (IGDS) in Canberra. For twenty-one years between 1989 and 2010 he was the foundation Coghlan Research Professor in Economics & History in the Institute of Advanced Studies at the Australian National University. Some three decades ago he embarked on an ambitious research program to develop a realist dynamic theory of the changing fortunes of human society and life from their beginnings. This has given rise to the widely acclaimed dynamic-strategy theory (published in *Advances in Space Research,* and in *Complexity* the journal of the Santa Fe Institute), which Professor Snooks is employing to rethink all aspects of the life sciences. This is the first general dynamic theory in the history of human thought to employ an effective demand-side approach. The dynamic-strategy theory is unique in a world of unworkable supply-side theories.

The results of this research have been published in a number of well-received trilogies, including the global history trilogy (*The Dynamic Society, The Ephemeral Civilization,* and *The Laws of History*), the social dynamics trilogy (*Longrun Dynamics, Global Transition,* and *The Global Crisis Makers*), and the dynamics of life trilogy (*The Collapse of Darwinism, The Selfcreating Mind,* and *Dead God Rising*). More recently, Professor Snooks has published books on the role of truth in human society—*The Death of Zarathustra. Notes on Truth for thr Risk-taker*—and an overview of the entire research program—*Ark of the Sun. The Improbable Voyage of Life.* The core discovery of this research program is the universal life system, called the strategic *logos,* which was analysed for the first time in *Dead God Rising* and *The Death of Zarathustra,* and developed further in *Ark of the Sun.*

IGDS

About IGDS Books

IGDS Books is the imprint of the publishing activities of the Institute of Global Dynamic Systems in Canberra. It is the mission of **IGDS Books** to publish innovative work that pushes beyond the existing frontiers of knowledge—a challenge that major scholarly publishers have abandoned in this electronic era. As Executive Director of the Institute, Professor Graeme Snooks oversees the activities of **IGDS Books**.

For information about the Institute or **IGDS Books,** see the Institute's website, or contact Professor Snooks at **seouenaca@gmail.com**.

IGDS Books include:

G.D. Snooks, *THE COMING ECLIPSE—or The Triumph of Climate Mitigation Over Solar Revolution* (August 2010)

G.D. Snooks, *DEAD GOD RISING. Religion & Science in the Universal Life-System* (November 2010)

G.D. Snooks, *THE DEATH OF ZARATHUSTRA. Notes on Truth for the Risk-taker* (March 2011).

G.D. Snooks, *ARK OF THE SUN. The Improbable Voyage of Life* (November 2015).

For information about and orders for the Institute's publications—books and working papers—please contact the Institute Administrator at **institutegds@gmail.com**.

www.ingramcontent.com/pod-product-compliance
Lightning Source LLC
Chambersburg PA
CBHW062359090426
42740CB00010B/1340